# WRITING
## FANTASY *&* SCIENCE FICTION

# WRITING
## FANTASY & SCIENCE FICTION

## HOW TO CREATE OUT-OF-THIS-WORLD
## NOVELS AND SHORT STORIES

**Orson Scott Card, Philip Athans, Jay Lake,**

**and the Editors of Writer's Digest**

**WRITER'S**
**DIGEST**
**BOOKS**

www.writersdigest.com

Cincinnati, Ohio

For more resources for writers, visit www.writersdigest.com.

To receive a free weekly e-mail newsletter delivering tips and updates about writing and about Writer's Digest products, register directly at http://newsletters.fwpublications.com.

17 16 15 14 13 5 4 3 2 1

Distributed in Canada by Fraser Direct
100 Armstrong Avenue
Georgetown, Ontario, Canada L7G 5S4
Tel: (905) 877-4411

Distributed in the U.K. and Europe by F+W Media International
Brunel House, Newton Abbot, Devon, TQ12 4PU, England
Tel: (+44) 1626-323200, Fax: (+44) 1626-323319
E-mail: postmaster@davidandcharles.co.uk

Distributed in Australia by Capricorn Link
P.O. Box 704, Windsor, NSW 2756 Australia
Tel: (02) 4577-3555

Edited by James Duncan
Cover designed by Claudean Wheeler
Cover images by mirabella/Fotolia.com & Andriy Dykun/Fotolia.com
Interior designed by Grace Ring
Production coordinated by Debbie Thomas

# About the Authors

## Orson Scott Card

No one had ever won both the Hugo and the Nebula Award for best science fiction novel two years in a row—until 1987, when *Speaker for the Dead* won the same awards given to *Ender's Game*. But Orson Scott Card's experience is not limited to one genre or form of storytelling. A dozen of his plays have been produced in regional theatre; his historical novel, *Saints* (alias *Women of Destiny*), has been an underground hit for several years; and Card has written hundreds of audioplays and a dozen scripts for animated videoplays for the family market. He has also edited books, magazines, and anthologies. Along the way, Card earned a master's degree in literature and has an abiding love for Chaucer, Shakespeare, Boccaccio, and the Medieval Romance. He has taught writing courses at several universities and at such workshops as Antioch, Clarion, Clarion West, and the Cape Cod Writers Workshop. It is fair to say that Orson Scott Card has examined storytelling from every angle.

Born in Richland, Washington, Card grew up in California, Arizona, and Utah. He lived in Brazil for two years as an unpaid missionary for the Mormon Church and received degrees from Brigham Young University and the University of Utah.

## Philip Athans

Philip Athans is the founding partner of Athans & Associates Creative Consulting and the *New York Times* best-selling author of *Annihilation* and a dozen other fantasy and horror books, including *The Guide to Writing Fantasy & Science Fiction* and the recently released *The Haunting of Dragon's Cliff* and *Devils of the Endless Deep*. Born in Rochester, New York, he grew up in suburban Chicago, where he published the literary magazine *Alternative Fiction & Poetry*. His blog, Fantasy Author's Handbook, is updated every Tuesday, and you can follow him on Twitter (@PhilAthans). He makes his home in the foothills of the Washington Cascades, east of Seattle.

## Jay Lake

Jay Lake is the author of the Mainspring and Green series from Tor, as well as several independent press novels and numerous short stories. In 2013, his steampunk novella, "The Stars Do Not Lie," was nominated for the Nebula, Hugo, and Locus awards. He lives and writes in Portland, Oregon.

## Daniel A. Clark

Daniel A. Clark is a former English teacher who now works in information systems. He has published in *Studies in Popular Culture*, *The Journal of General Education*, and the *Masterplots* young adult literature supplement.

## Sherrilyn Kenyon

Sherrilyn Kenyon is a best-selling author of science fiction and fantasy novels and has won numerous awards. Her work includes the popular Dark-Hunter series, which includes *Fantasy Lover*, *Dance With the Devil*, and *Night Pleasures*.

## Allan Maurer

Allan Maurer has been published in *OMNI, Starlog, Twilight Zone, Fantastic Stories, Playboy, Modern Maturity*, and many other magazines. He was senior writer on *OMNI's Continuum* book (Little Brown, 1982) and the author of *Lasers, Lightwave of the Future* (Arco, 1982). His work for *OMNI's* "Antimatter" column was included in *OMNI's Book of the Bizarre* (OMNI Books, 1974). Maurer attended the 1974 Clarion Science Fiction and Fantasy Writer's Workshop, taught by such luminaries as Harlan Ellison, Kate Wilhelm, and Damon Knight. He has founded several regional magazines, including *Charlotte's Best Magazine* and *Beaufort (NC) Magazine*.

## P. Andrew Miller

P. Andrew Miller has published a number of fantasy stories in a variety of publications. His stories have appeared in *Sword & Sorceress* #13, *Dragon Magazine, Valkyrie, Odyssey*, and many others. He has been an attending author at the International Conference on the Fantastic in the Arts for the last five years.

Miller is also a member of the Science Fiction Writers of America. He lives and teaches in Cincinnati, Ohio.

------------------------------------------------------------------

## Michael J. Varhola

Michael J. Varhola is a freelance editor, writer, and publisher who lives and works in the Washington, D.C. area. As a journalist, he writes news and feature articles on many subjects, especially those involving world cultures, military history, and the Middle East. As a senior editor, he has helped found or run several publications, including *Living History* magazine, *Renaissance* magazine, *SKIRMISHER!* online gaming magazine, and *The Achiever*. He earned a bachelor's degree in journalism at the University of Maryland, College Park, with a minor in history. Varhola also studied European Culture at the American University of Paris in France.

## Renee Wright

Renee Wright is the former managing editor of *Charlotte's Best Magazine* in Charlotte, North Carolina. She was a founding editor of *Beaufort (SC) Magazine*. Wright published a long-running column in several Charlotte publications, covered the Caribbean for a travel book series, and art-edited a collector-coveted NASCAR season retrospective. She works frequently as a writer, editor, and researcher with Allan Maurer and researched his 1982 book on lasers. Wright is near completion of a master's degree in psychology and travels the United States in an RV with her daredevil mother.

# Table of Contents

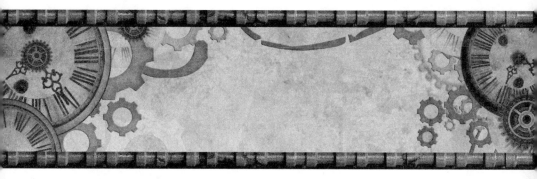

## PART 1

# How to Write Science Fiction and Fantasy

by Orson Scott Card

# Introduction

A writer never knows who's going to be reading his book, but I've made a few assumptions about you, anyway. I figure that you're probably not yet an established writer in the genre of speculative fiction, or you wouldn't feel a need to read a book on how to write it. Still, you have a genuine interest in writing science fiction and fantasy, not because you have some notion that it's somehow "easier" to make a buck in this field (if that's your delusion, give it up at once!), but rather because you believe that the kind of story you want to tell might be best received by the science fiction and fantasy audience.

I hope you're right, because in many ways, this is the best audience in the world to write for. They're open-minded and intelligent. They want to think as well as feel, understand as well as dream. Above all, they want to be led into places that no one has ever visited before. It's a privilege to tell stories to these readers, and an honor when they applaud the tales you tell.

What I can't do in a book this brief is tell you everything you need to know about writing fiction. What I *can* do is tell you everything I know about how to write speculative fiction *in particular*. I've written a whole book on characterization and point of view, so I hardly need to cover that same material here; nor will I attempt to teach you plotting or style, dialogue or marketing or copyright law or any of the other things that writers of *every* kind of fiction have to know something about. But I can attempt to tell you the things that *only* the writers of speculative fiction need to worry about: world creation, alien societies, the rules of magic, rigorous extrapolation of possible futures—tasks that don't come up in your average mystery or romance or literary tale.

To do that, I've divided this book into five chapters of varying length. Chapter one deals with the boundaries of speculative fiction; it's an essay on what science fiction and fantasy are, so you can get an idea of the range of possibilities and educate yourself with the literature that has gone before.

Chapter two, the longest, begins the practical, hands-on work of world creation, perhaps the most vital step in creating a good speculative story.

Chapter three deals with the structuring of a science fiction or fantasy tale—how you go about turning your world into a story, or making your story work well within its world.

With chapter four, we go through the actual writing process, dealing with the problems of exposition and language that only speculative fiction writers face.

The first part of chapter five deals with the practical business of selling science fiction and fantasy—though you'd better check the copyright date on this edition of the book before acting on my advice, since this is the section most likely to become outdated.

And also in chapter five, we get a little personal, and I offer you some advice on how to live successfully as a science fiction or fantasy writer. Not that I know how you should live your life—but I have made some really first-rate mistakes in my time, and have seen others make some doozies, too, and if by forewarning you I can forearm you, I think it's worth the effort.

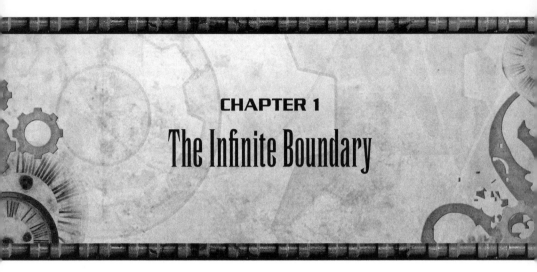

# CHAPTER 1

# The Infinite Boundary

It was 1975. I was twenty-four years old. The naïve ambitions of youth were beginning to be tempered by reality.

I had written a couple of dozen plays and more than half of them had been produced in college or community theatres—for a total remuneration of about $300. At that rate, I figured, I had only to write sixteen full-length plays a week to make $10,000 a year—hardly major money, even then. And I was fast, but not *that* fast.

Furthermore, the nonprofit theatre company I had started was tumbling toward bankruptcy with all its debts looming over me. My day job as an editor with a university press didn't pay me enough to live on, let alone pay what the company owed. The only thing I knew how to do that had any hope of bringing in extra money was writing—and it was plain that I'd have to find something else to write besides plays.

I had dabbled in science fiction for years, reading quite a bit of it, even trying my hand at a few stories. For a while in my late teens, I had even worked on a cycle of stories tracing the development of a family with peculiar psychic abilities as they worked out their genetic destiny on a colony planet. Now, with new enthusiasm—or was it desperation?—I dusted off the best of them, one that had once earned a nice note from an editor, and proceeded to rewrite it from beginning to end.

It was the tale of a wandering tinker who had a psionic gift that manifested itself in two ways: He could communicate with birds, and he could heal the sick. When he returned to his hometown, Worthing, a medievalish village deep in the Forest of Waters, he came into conflict with the villagers over their treatment of his birds; eventually he was blamed for an epidemic that carried off many villagers during a devastating winter storm, and they killed him.

In short, it was the sort of perky, cheerful little tale that I've been writing ever since.

As I rewrote "Tinker," I was delighted to see how terrible the earlier version had been. After all, if I could see, at twenty-four, how bad the story was that looked so brilliant to me at thirteen, it must mean I had learned something in the intervening years. So it was with high hopes that I typed the new draft, tucked it into an envelope, and mailed it away to *Analog* magazine.

Why *Analog?* Because in those days, it was the only science fiction magazine that was listed in *Writer's Market*. I had never actually read an issue of the magazine. Still, my story was science fiction, and *Analog* was a science fiction magazine. What could be more logical?

The story came back in due course, rejected. But there was something in the accompanying letter to encourage me. Ben Bova, then editor of *Analog*, told me that he liked the way I wrote and hoped to see more stories from me.

So why was he rejecting "Tinker"?

Because it wasn't science fiction. *"Analog* publishes only science fiction," said Ben, so of course a fantasy like "Tinker" simply wouldn't do.

I was outraged—at first. "Tinker" had psionic powers, a colony planet, a far future time period—if that wasn't science fiction, what was?

Until I looked again at the story the way Ben Bova must have seen it. He knew nothing about the other stories in the cycle. "Tinker" included no mention of its taking place on a world being colonized by human beings, and there was nothing alien about the landscape. It could have been an English village in about 950 A.D.

As for John Tinker's psionic powers, there was nothing in the story to suggest they weren't *magical* powers. There was nothing to suggest they *were*, either, of course—he chanted no spells, rubbed no talisman, prayed to no pagan deity.

But in the absence of other evidence, the landscape clearly marked "Tinker" as fantasy. It was all those trees in the Forest of Waters. A rustic setting always suggests fantasy; to suggest science fiction, you need sheet metal and plastic. You need *rivets*. The buildings in "Tinker" didn't even use *nails*!

I had discovered the first kind of boundary that marks the twin genres of fantasy and science fiction: the publishing category.

## BOUNDARY 1: A PUBLISHING CATEGORY

When fiction publishers send out books through the distributors and on to the bookstores, they have a few ways of influencing the way those books are displayed and handled. Naturally, every publisher would like to see all his novels displayed face out on the shelves, preferably in a section labeled "New and Brilliant." But in the real world, this is not going to happen. Instead, most novels will be crammed spine out into the store's precious shelf space, with only the alphabetical accident of the author's last name deciding where on the shelf the books will be placed.

Having to browse through a thousand spine-out volumes grouped by last names of authors he's never heard of would be quite inconvenient for the novel-buyer, of course. Fortunately, fiction publishers learned something from the nonfiction side of the business, which groups books by super-subjects, or categories. *How to Cross-Stitch* is grouped with *Plumbing Made Easy* under "How-to Books." Biographies are grouped by the last name of the *subject* rather than the *author*; history is roughly grouped by region and time period. New categories spring up as needed—in 1975, there was no bookstore section labeled "Computers."

Why not group fiction in a similar way? Micro-subjects wouldn't do—it wouldn't be practical to have sections called "Dog Stories," "Horse Stories," "Mid-life Crisis and Adultery," "Writers and Artists Struggling to Discover Themselves," "People in Past Eras Who Think and Talk Just Like Modern Americans," and "Reminiscences of Childhoods in Which Nothing Happened," even though these are all fairly popular themes for fiction.

But there *were* some broad categories that were quite useful, like "Science Fiction," "Fantasy," "Historicals," "Romances," "Mysteries," and "Westerns." Anything that didn't fit into those categories was lumped together under the heading "Fiction." Publishers could slap these labels on their books and know that the bookstore owners—who couldn't possibly be familiar with, let alone read, every work by every author—would know how to group these books within the store so readers could find them more easily.

For many years, the appetite of science fiction readers far outstripped the production of science fiction writers and publishers. About thirty to forty thousand readers were so hungry for another SF novel that they'd buy *anything*, however bad it might be, as long as it had a rocket on the cover. As a result, while science fiction never sold very much, it *did* sell a certain guaranteed minimum. You couldn't lose money publishing it, almost regardless of quality.

As a result, the publishing category was able to nurture many young, talented, but utterly inept writers as they served their apprenticeships and eventually learned how to write. Unlike the literary genre, where first novels often sell in the hundreds rather than the thousands, promising but clumsy SF writers could live on the advances and royalties from sales of forty thousand books. And a surprising number of us whose inept first novels exposed more of our weaknesses than our strengths eventually learned how to turn in work that had polish—and, sometimes, depth.

Those days have passed, however. The ceiling has come off the genre, with hardcovers by Herbert, McCaffrey, Asimov, Heinlein, Clarke, Crichton, Brooks, Gaiman, Martin, and Douglas Adams all having hit the best-seller lists since the 1970s. But the floor has also dropped out of the genre. As soon as there were big bucks to be made in science fiction and fantasy, publishers began to bring out more and more novels, until it was impossible for anyone to read half of them, let alone all. Instead of forty thousand readers buying one copy of everything, there were hundreds of thousands of readers buying copies of maybe half the books, and some books that almost nobody read.

The fantasy genre followed the same track with book publishing—only it was compressed into a much shorter time. With the word-of-mouth success of Tolkien's *Lord of the Rings* trilogy and *The Hobbit*, the fantasy genre was born in the late sixties. Only a few years later, Ballantine published Terry Brooks's *Sword of Shannara* and it hit the best-seller lists. At once fantasy was as big a business as science fiction was becoming.

The appetite for new writers in the field of speculative fiction (science fiction and fantasy) is still enormous. If you write competently and if your story has any spark of life, you will sell it. And, while you no longer have the guarantee that even your weakest early work will be read and remembered, that can also be a blessing: I'm currently glad that my first novel isn't trotted out and displayed wherever I go.

New writers are, if anything, even *more* welcome in the magazines. Here, too, the publishing categories matter. While the two most prestigious magazines, *Isaac Asimov's Science Fiction Magazine* (hereafter called *Asimov's*) and *The Magazine of Fantasy and Science Fiction* (*F&SF*), will occasionally publish rustic fantasies, all magazines *prefer* science fiction with rivets and plastic. And not because that is necessarily the editors' taste, but because that's what the majority of the magazine-buying audience wants most and rewards best, with sales, with favorable letters of comment, and with Nebula and Hugo awards. The other two major magazines, *OMNI* (which pays billions of dollars but buys only two stories an issue) and *Analog*, won't even consider rustic fantasy, though *OMNI* will occasionally buy a contemporary or urban fantasy—the kind of story where something magical is happening in a familiar high-tech environment.

All these magazines pride themselves on publishing stories from new writers. What doesn't get told quite as often is that they *survive* by discovering new writers. There's a cycle in science fiction that most writers follow. They break into the field by selling short stories and novelettes to the magazines until their names and styles become familiar to book editors. Then they sign a few book contracts, get some novels under their belts, and suddenly they don't have time for those $400 stories anymore. The magazines that nurtured them and gave them their starts watch as the novels flow and the short fiction trickles in. So the magazines are forced to search constantly for new talent.

This is even more true with the newer and smaller markets. *Aboriginal SF* and *Amazing Stories*—the newest and oldest magazines in the field—have much smaller impact on the field, in part because the strongest writers are generally selling to *OMNI, Asimov's,* and *F&SF*. But because of that, *Abo* and *Amazing* are that much more open to newcomers.

In practical terms, you'll have a better chance selling to the magazines if your story is (1) short and (2) science fiction rather than fantasy. My career followed that track; so did the careers of most other science fiction writers in the field. Only fantasy writers are virtually forced to begin selling at novel length because the market is so much smaller for fantasy.

## BOUNDARY 2:
## A COMMUNITY OF READERS AND WRITERS

It's important to remember that there was a time when every one of today's publishing categories was part of the mainstream of fiction. When *Gone With the Wind* was published it was simply a novel, not a "historical" or a "romance"—though it would almost certainly be categorized that way today. And back when H. G. Wells, Jules Verne, A. Merritt, H. Rider Haggard, and others were inventing the genre of science fiction, their novels were published and displayed right alongside contemporaries like James, Dreiser, Woolf, and Conrad.

Yet there was a clear difference even in the early 1900s between incipient science fiction, fantasy, and all the rest of literature. It was hard to put it into words then. H. G. Wells's *The Time Machine, The War of the Worlds,* and *The Invisible Man* were wildly different from each other, yet alike in the sense that they dealt with advances in science; hence he called these novels "scientific romances."

This surely made them similar to the works of Jules Verne, who also dealt with scientific advances in novels like *Twenty Thousand Leagues Under the Sea*. But Verne never seemed to see danger or a dark side in advancing technology, and in the long run, his novels were never so much about the science as about the sights and wonders to be found in strange and inaccessible places. *Twenty Thousand Leagues* wasn't *about* Nemo's submarine as much as it was about the marvelous sights to be seen from its portholes. *Journey to the Center of the Earth* was about survival in a strange, hostile environment, and included such delightful nonsense as the ruins of ancient Atlantis and dinosaurs that had survived deep in the bowels of the Earth.

Wells was much more serious and logical than Verne in his extrapolation of the possible results of scientific advances. And yet their stories sometimes had quite similar structures. For instance, while *Around the World in Eighty Days* dealt entirely with the sights and wonders of Verne's contemporary world, its ending absolutely hinges on knowledge of a scientific fact—that by traveling toward the east, the hero gained a day when he crossed the International Date Line. This is very much the same sort of structural game Wells played when he had the invaders from Mars in *The War of the Worlds* defeated by the common cold. Great events are changed by the most humble of facts—and yet when the reader reaches the surprise resolution, his faith in the order of the universe is restored. Humble little facts will save us in the end.

--------------------------------------------------------------------------------

A. Merritt's *The Face in the Abyss* and H. Rider Haggard's *She* had even less in common with Wells than Verne did. Both these novels have a traveler who finds himself in a land long forgotten by modern humans. In *She*, a magnificent woman has found a way to live forever, at the cost of the blood of her subjects; in *The Face in the Abyss*, lizard men descended from the dinosaurs keep a race of humans in thrall for their obscene sports and pleasures. There is more of magic than science in both of these books, yet there was a strong overlap of the readers who loved Wells, those who loved Verne, and those who loved Merritt and Haggard.

Indeed, when Hugo Gernsback founded the first magazine devoted entirely to science fiction, *Amazing Stories*, back in the late 1920s, he announced that he wanted to publish scientific romances like those of H. G. Wells; yet it is fair to say that, instead of the serious, rigorous scientific extrapolation found in Wells's work, Gernsback's magazine—and the others that soon imitated it—published stories that had far more of Verne's love of machines or of Merritt's and Haggard's romps into strange and dangerous places than of Wells's more serious treatment of science and the future. It wasn't until the mid-1930s, when John W. Campbell became editor of *Astounding* (now *Analog*), that Wellsian science fiction came to the fore in the American magazines.

Rigorous extrapolation, a gosh-wow love of gadgets, and mystical adventures in strange and mysterious places; every major stream in speculative fiction today can be traced back to authors who were writing before the publishing categories existed. From among the readers in the 1920s and 1930s who loved any or all of these authors arose the first generation of "science fiction writers," who knew themselves to be continuing on a trail that had been blazed by giants. Gernsback's publishing category of science fiction was a recognition of a community that already existed; once it was named, once it became self-conscious, that community blossomed and cast many seeds, giving rise to each new generation that repeats, revises, or reinvents the same literary tradition.

The boundaries that once were fluid now are much more firm, because the publishing category reinforces the identity of the community of readers and writers. Hilton felt no qualms about writing a lost-land novel, *Lost Horizon*; it troubled no one that it didn't belong in the same category as, say, his novel *Good-bye, Mr. Chips*. And so many readers responded to the book that the name of the lost land, Shangri-la, passed into the common language.

Today, though, an author who wrote a fantasy like *Lost Horizon* would immediately be placed into the fantasy category, and if he then wrote a *Good-bye, Mr. Chips*, American publishers would be at a loss as to where to place it. How could you call it fantasy? Yet if you publish it out of the fantasy category, the readers who liked the author's earlier books won't ever find it, and the readers who *do* browse the "Fiction" category won't ever have heard of this author and will probably pass the novel by. As a result, there will be enormous pressure on the author to write "more books like that Shangri-la book."

(Indeed, he will be pressed to write a whole series, which will be promoted as "The Shangri-la Trilogy" until a fourth book is published, then as "The Shangri-la Saga" until the author is dead. It happened to Frank Herbert with his Dune books, and despite her best efforts, it is happening to Anne McCaffrey with her dragon books. Only a few, like Marion Zimmer Bradley, manage to break out of such channels and take a sizeable audience with them.)

Yet my experience as a reader is that the category boundaries mean very little. There have been months, even years of my life when all I really wanted to read was science fiction; but I felt no shame or guilt, no enormous mental stretch when at other times I read historicals or mysteries, classics, poetry, or contemporary bestsellers. At present, my pleasure reading is history and biography, but that will certainly change again. And even at the height of a science fiction reading binge, nothing can stop me from devouring the latest John Hersey or William Goldman or Robert Parker novel.

The result is that today, while readers are very free, passing easily from one community to another, the publishing categories clamp down like a vise on the authors themselves. You must keep this in mind as you begin to publish. Do you wish to forever be known as a science fiction or fantasy writer?

Some writers whose careers have been largely based on science fiction writing have never been categorized that way. Kurt Vonnegut, for instance, stoutly resisted any claim that what he wrote was science fiction—though there is no definition of science fiction that does not include his novels within the genre *except* that the words *science fiction* have never been printed on his books.

John Hersey, as another example, has written such science fiction masterpieces as *White Lotus, The Child Buyer,* and *My Petition for More Space*; yet because he wrote other kinds of fiction first, he has never been locked into one category. ("Couldn't you, like, put some aliens into this book, Mr. Hersey?

I'm not sure your audience will know what to make of this historical set in China, of all places.")

Vonnegut and Hersey were never within the science fiction ghetto. A few rare writers like Bradbury and LeGuin have transcended the boundaries without compromising the elements of fantasy within their work. But most of us find that the better we do as speculative fiction writers, the *less* interested publishers are in our non-SF, non-fantasy writing.

## BOUNDARY 3: WHAT SF WRITERS WRITE IS SF

One surprising result of the ghettoizing of speculative fiction, however, is that writers have enormous freedom within its walls. It's as if, having once confined us within our cage, the keepers of the zoo of literature don't much care what we do as long as we stay behind bars.

What we've done is make the categories of science fiction and fantasy larger, freer, and more inclusive than any other genre of contemporary literature. We have room for everybody, and we are extraordinarily open to genuine experimentation.

Admittedly, *Asimov's* regularly receives letters that ask, "In what sense is this story by Kim Stanley Robinson or Karen Joy Fowler a science fiction or fantasy story? Why isn't it appearing in *The Atlantic* where it belongs?" Some readers complain; indeed, some fairly howl at what writers do under the rubric of SF and fantasy.

Yet the reason these stories don't appear in *The Atlantic* or *Harper's* or *The New Yorker* is that even though they aren't really science fiction or fantasy in the publishing-category sense or the community sense (there are neither rivets nor trees, neither science nor magic, and they certainly aren't what readers were consciously looking for), their stories are nevertheless strange, in ways that editors outside the field of SF and fantasy find quite threatening.

There is no particular reason why Karen Joy Fowler's "Tonto at 40" (published as "The Faithful Companion at 40" to avoid a lawsuit from the *Lone Ranger* people, who have no sense of fun) shouldn't have appeared in a literary magazine. But the story was too experimental for editors who are used to seeing only the "experiments" that follow the latest trend. Only within speculative fiction was there room for Fowler's work.

It has happened again and again, until it seems that there must be more room inside the ghetto walls than outside them. Even writers like Bruce Sterling and Lew Shiner, who have complained about the boneheadedness and unoriginality of most speculative fiction, discover that, despite the science fiction community's enormous appetite for stories with very bad thinking and worse writing, it remains the community most willing to sample something new.

Sample—not necessarily embrace. It is not experimental but traditional work that wins awards within in the field. What matters is that truly unfamiliar and untraditional work is published *at all*, first in the magazines, and, once the work has become somewhat familiar there, eventually in books.

In the long run, then, whatever is published within the field of science fiction and fantasy *is* science fiction and fantasy, and if it doesn't resemble what science fiction and fantasy were twenty years ago or even five years ago, some readers and writers will howl, but others will hear the new voice and see the new vision with delight.

Once, frustrated with the plethora of meaningless definitions of science fiction, Damon Knight said, "Science fiction is what I point at when I say science fiction." That may sound like a decision not to define the field at all—but it is, in fact, the only completely accurate definition.

The operative word in Damon Knight's definition is *I*. That is, if Damon Knight, a writer, critic, and editor of known credentials, says that a work is science fiction, then it is. When it comes to known science fiction writers, that power is almost absolute. Because I've been around long enough, if I write a book and decide to call it fantasy or science fiction, then it *is*; even if others argue with me, it will still be counted as part of my science fiction/fantasy oeuvre. If you doubt me, read Gene Wolfe's novel *Free Live Free*. He swears it's science fiction. There are even shreds of evidence within the novel that it might be so. That's enough for him, and so it is enough for us.

Editors and critics have the power to dub other people's work as well. If the editor at *Asimov's, F&SF, Analog, Aboriginal SF,* or *Omni* buys and publishes a story as fantasy or science fiction, then that writer's identity as an author of fantasy or science fiction is fairly launched.

Book publishers have similar authority. Patricia Geary was more than a little surprised to wake up one day and discover that her novels, including the brilliant *Strange Toys*, had been published by Bantam in the science fiction/

fantasy category. The thought that she was writing within a "category" never entered her mind. But she quickly learned that whether she sought the label or not, the speculative fiction audience was open to her stories in a way that her intended "literary" audience was not.

Like the stable in C. S. Lewis's last Narnia book, *The Last Battle*, the science fiction ghetto is much larger on the inside than it is on the outside. You think as you enter it that you'll be cramped and confined; but I can tell you that for many of you, it is only inside the SF community that you will find room enough to write all that you want to write and still find an audience for it.

Still, all this talk of freedom is pretty irrelevant to you. Why? Because unless you are already established as a science fiction or fantasy writer, you do *not* have the power to decide unilaterally that your work belongs in the category. You must persuade at least one editor that your novel or story is science fiction or fantasy—and with rare exceptions, editors have a finely discriminating eye.

While the marketing department at a publisher may think that a spaceship on the cover is enough to make a book SF, the editorial department knows better. Your story has to *feel* like science fiction or fantasy to the editor or it won't get published, and then you won't have access to the great freedom that speculative fiction writers get *after* they've become established.

So you need some sort of definition of speculative fiction that lets you know how to satisfy enough of the expectations of the genre so that editors will agree that your work belongs in the category. Let's take for granted at this point that your skills and innate genius make your stories publishable. You still need to make sure your story warrants being published as science fiction or fantasy.

The most complete definition will come to you only one way, and it isn't easy. You have to know everything ever published as speculative fiction or fantasy. Of course, you want to begin writing SF and fantasy *before* you die, so you know that you can't read every single book or story. You'll have to read a representative sample to get a feel for what has already been done in the field.

What makes this complicated is that the genres of science fiction and fantasy include not only what speculative fiction writers are writing now, but also everything they have ever written. This is because the entire history of speculative fiction as a self-conscious writing genre spans a single lifetime. Jack Williamson, for instance, was writing in the 1930s, when the adventure tradition of Merritt and Haggard and the gosh-wow science of Verne predominated. He wrote up until his death in 2006, producing work that is taken seriously by the most modern and sophisticated speculative fiction readers.

Fiction from every period of speculative fiction is still in print, not because it is required reading in college and high school English classes—thankfully it isn't—but because the community of speculative fiction readers keeps it alive.

Go into the SF/fantasy section of your bookstore and you'll find both recent works and early, seminal books by authors like Aldiss, Asimov, Bradbury, Clarke, Ellison, LeGuin, and Norton.

In the same section, you'll find books by late great writers like Alfred, Bester, James Blish, Edgar Rice Burroughs, Robert Heinlein, Robert Howard, E.E. "Doc" Smith, and J. R. R. Tolkien.

You'll also find writers like Larry Niven, Anne McCaffrey, Jack Chalker, C. J. Cherryh, David Drake, Octavia Butler, Roger Zelazny, Charles de Lint, William Gibson, Lisa Goldstein, James Patrick Kelly, Megan Lindholm, Pat Murphy, Pamela Sargent, and Bruce Sterling.

In fact, that's not a bad reading list, though it's far from complete. Even if you've already read quite a bit of science fiction, if any of those names sound unfamiliar to you then you need to do some homework. Pick several names from each group, buy a couple of inexpensive paperbacks by each author you choose, and read. You'll begin to get a sense of the breadth and depth of this field you're planning to write in. Some of the books you won't care for a bit. Some you'll admire. Some you'll love. Some will transform you.

Still, all that reading can take months. Though you'll have to do it eventually, you can start your education as a science fiction reader more modestly. Get a good overview of the field—I suggest David Hartwell's book *Age of Wonder: Exploring the World of Science Fiction* or James Gunn's *Alternate Worlds: The Illustrated History of Science Fiction.* Then get your hands on these great anthologies: *The Science Fiction Hall of Fame* (ed. Silverberg, Bova), *Dangerous Visions* and *Again, Dangerous Visions* (ed. Ellison), and *The Best of the Nebulas* (ed. Bova). Finally, subscribe to *Asimov's* and *F&SF* and read them from cover to cover every month; you should also sample *Analog, Aboriginal SF, OMNI,* and *Amazing Stories.*

*The Science Fiction Hall of Fame* is an anthology of the short stories, novelettes, and novellas voted by the Science Fiction Writers of America as the best ever published up to 1966, the year that the SFWA was organized. There is no better collection of classic short science fiction from the 1930s, 1940s, and 1950s.

*Dangerous Visions* and its sequel, *Again, Dangerous Visions*, were meant by editor Harlan Ellison to be anthologies of work considered too dangerous to appear in the magazines. However, before *Again, Dangerous Visions* came out, the magazines themselves had been transformed enough that the stories didn't seem so dangerous anymore. It doesn't matter—they are an excellent snapshot of most of the best writers producing innovative short fiction during the 1960s and early 1970s, most of whom are still major figures in the field today.

*The Best of the Nebulas* is an anthology of the Nebula-winning short stories, novelettes, and novellas published between 1966 and 1986 that were voted best by the members of the SFWA in the late 1980s.

And the current issues of the magazines will show you what is happening right this minute in the field of speculative fiction.

Read all this and you'll have a very good sense, not only of what science fiction (and to a lesser degree fantasy) has been and is becoming, but also of what sort of science fiction you are drawn to.

You may discover that your taste in science fiction is quite old-fashioned— that you don't like most of the stories in the Ellison anthologies, but love many in the *Hall of Fame*. No problem—those "old-fashioned" stories are still very much in demand, both in the magazines and at book length.

Or you may be interested only in the hottest, most innovative entries in the current issues of the magazines. Fine—there's always room for more.

Or you may realize that *nobody* is doing anything you really care for, and your fiction is going to stand the whole field on its ear. That, too, is perfectly acceptable—you don't have to imitate anybody; it's usually better if you don't. But, having read at least a sampling of stories from every era and tradition within the field, you'll at least know what has been done before: what clichés the audience will be weary of, what expectations the audience will bring to your tale, what you have to explain, and what you can take for granted.

One warning, though. If you try to read everything so as not to repeat an idea that has already been used, you'll go mad. And even then, after your brilliant, original story has been published, some helpful reader will point out that the exact same idea was used in an obscure story by Lloyd Biggle, Jr., or Edmund Hamilton or John W. Campbell or H. Beam Piper or … you get the picture.

You're reading all these stories to get a sense of how science fiction is done, not to become paranoid and decide that you can never come up with any new ideas as good as these. When I was reading Middle English romances for graduate class at Notre Dame, I realized that almost every one of these thirteenth-century stories would make a terrific science fiction novel if you just changed the sea to space and the boats to starships.

And most science fiction novels could easily be turned into fantasy by changing starships back into ocean-going vessels. Frank Herbert's *Dune* would fit right in with the best medieval romances, if planets became continents and the spice became the source of magical power instead of a drug necessary for space navigation. There is nothing new under the sun—or beyond it, either.

The novelty and freshness you'll bring to the field won't come from the new ideas you think up. Truly new ideas are rare, and usually turn out to be variations on old themes anyway. No, your freshness will come from the way you think, from the person you are; it will inevitably show up in your writing, provided you don't mask it with heavy-handed formulas or clichés.

If there's one thing you should learn from reading all these tales, it's that, unlike many other genres, speculative fiction is not bound to follow any particular formula. There *are* a few formulas, it's true, but most stories don't follow them—or else follow them only because what may seem to be a formula is really a mythic story that has shown up in every culture where stories have been told at all.

For science fiction and fantasy are the genres in which stories can hew closest to the archetypes and myths that readers in all times and places have hungered for. That's why writers in other genres often reach for *our* tools when they have a particularly powerful story to tell, as witness Mary Stewart's Merlin books, Mary Renault's novels of the ancient Hellenic world, E. L. Doctorow's slightly fractured history, and John Irving's talking-animal figures.

Writers of mythic stories don't use "formulas"; they just tell the stories they believe in and care about. Inevitably, archetypal themes will show up again and again. But they only work if you are not aware of them; the moment you consciously treat them as formulas, they lose the power to stir the blood of any but the most naïve readers.

-------------------------------------------------------------------------

# BOUNDARY 4: THE LITERATURE OF STRANGE

Having carefully explained to you that science fiction and fantasy are merely labels for (1) an arbitrary, viselike publishing category, (2) a fluid, evolving community of readers and writers, and (3) a ghetto in which you can do almost anything you like once you learn what others have already done, I will now essay a *real* definition of the terms.

This last boundary is the clearest—and probably the least accurate—definition of science fiction and fantasy:

1. All stories set in the future, because the future can't be known. This includes all stories speculating about future technologies, which is, for some people, the only thing that science fiction is good for. Ironically, many stories written in the 1940s and 1950s that were set in what was then the future—the 1960s, 1970s, and 1980s—are no longer "futuristic." Yet they aren't "false," either, because few science fiction writers pretend that they are writing what *will* happen. Rather we write what *might* happen. So those out-of-date futures, like that depicted in the novel *1984*, simply shift from the "future" category to:

2. All stories set in the historical past that contradict known facts of history. Within the field of science fiction, these are called "alternate world" stories. For instance, what if the Cuban Missile Crisis had led to nuclear war? What if Hitler had died in 1939? In the real world, of course, these events did not happen—so stories that take place in such false pasts are the purview of science fiction and fantasy.

3. All stories set on other worlds, because we've never gone there. Whether "future humans" take part in the story or not, if it isn't Earth, it belongs to fantasy and science fiction.

4. All stories supposedly set on Earth, but before recorded history and contradicting the known archaeological record—stories about visits from ancient aliens, or ancient civilizations that left no trace, or "lost kingdoms" surviving into modern times.

5. All stories that contradict some known or supposed law of nature. Obviously, fantasy that uses magic falls into this category, but so

does much science fiction: time travel stories, for instance, or invisible man stories.

In short, science fiction and fantasy stories are those that take place in worlds that have never existed or are not yet known.

The moment I offer this definition, however, I can think of many examples of stories that fit within these boundaries yet are not considered science fiction or fantasy by *anyone*. For instance, despite some romanticizing, Feliz Salten's wonderful novel *Bambi* is a brutally accurate account of the lives of deer. Yet because in his book the animals talk to each other, something that animals simply do not do, does *Bambi* become fantasy? Perhaps, after a fashion—but you'll never find it in the fantasy section of the bookstore; you'll never find it on any fantasy fan's list of his fifty favorite fantasy novels. It doesn't fall within the boundaries of the publishing category, the expectations of the community of readers and writers, or even the raw listing of what sf and fantasy writers have written.

What about *The Odyssey* and *The Illiad?* They contain magic and gods aplenty, and it's hard to imagine any contemporary reader claiming that they represent the way the world *really* was at the time of the Trojan War, yet they were composed for an audience that believed in these gods and these heroes. To taleteller and talehearer, they were poems about history and not fantasies at all; they were epic, not mythic, tales.

Indeed, there are many who would claim that my definition of speculative fiction clearly includes the Bible and *Paradise Lost*, though there are many other people today who would be outraged to hear of either being classified as fantasy.

And what do we make of Jean Auel's prehistoric romances? They certainly contradict an archaeologist's vision of the past, yet they are presented as if they correspond to reality. And what about genre-bending books like Janelle Taylor's *Moondust and Madness* or Jacqueline Susann's posthumously published first novel, *Yargo?* Both have spaceships and visitors from other planets, but everything else about them clearly identifies them as pure romance novels, with no hint of any knowledge or understanding of the science fiction tradition. They fit my definition—but anyone familiar with what science fiction and fantasy *really* are would repudiate them at once.

And what about horror novels? Many of the works of Stephen King are clearly fantasies—some are even science fiction—and both King and his audience would be quick to say so. Yet many other works in the horror genre don't contradict known reality in any way; they fit in the genre because they include perfectly believable events that are so gruesome or revolting that the audience reacts in fear or disgust.

Still, despite its inadequacies, my definition has its uses. For one thing, while it includes many works that really don't belong in the genre, it doesn't exclude any works that *do*. That is, your story may fit my definition and still not be SF or fantasy, but you can be sure that if your story *doesn't* fit my definition it definitely *isn't* within the genre.

Even works by established SF and fantasy writers that are included within the genre mainly out of courtesy (or force-fitting by publishers) make *some* bows, however desultory, toward fitting this definition. They at least offer the *possibility* that the story violates known reality at some point.

More important is the fact that by this definition, speculative fiction is defined *by its milieu*. The world in which the story takes place *is* the genre boundary line. If a story doesn't take the reader into an otherwise unknowable place, it isn't speculative fiction.

One of the primary appeals of all fiction is that it takes the reader into unfamiliar places. But *how* unfamiliar is it? Like chimps in the savannas of Africa, the human audience for fiction is both afraid of and attracted to strangeness. The chimp, confronted with a stranger who is not openly attacking, will retreat to a safe distance and keep watch. Gradually, if the stranger is doing something interesting, the chimp will be attracted. Curiosity overcomes fear. Or if the stranger's actions seem threatening, the chimp will flee, call for help, or try to frighten the stranger away, as fear overcomes curiosity.

Human beings also exhibit this love-fear attitude toward strangeness—for instance, we see the fear in racism, the curiosity in the way people slow down to rubberneck as they drive past an accident on the freeway. Our attitude toward strangeness is also a key element in the way we choose the stories we believe in and care about. If a tale we're reading or watching on the screen is too familiar, it becomes boring; we know the end from the beginning and switch off the set or set the book aside. Yet if it is too unfamiliar, we reject the story as unbelievable or incomprehensible. We demand *some* strangeness, but not too much.

Fortunately, no two people want exactly the same mix of strangeness and familiarity. Some are content to read the same stories over and over again, with only a few cosmetic details changed—or so it appears to those of us who don't enjoy gothics or bodice-rippers or teen romances or literary novels about writers who can't write or painters who can't paint. Others are forever searching for something new or different, so they can no longer recognize the verities contained in old familiar stories—or so it seems to those of us who don't enjoy literary experiments like those of Faulkner, Joyce, or Robbe-Grillet.

Speculative fiction by definition is geared toward an audience that wants strangeness, an audience that wants to spend time in worlds that absolutely are *not* like the observable world around them.

This is not to say that all science fiction and fantasy stories are fresh ventures into the unknown. Many readers, having once discovered a strange world that they enjoy, want to return to that same world again and again, until they're more familiar with that imaginary place than they are with the real-world town they live in. Many speculative fiction readers who came to the genre in their teens, when they hungered for strangeness and surprise and wonder, continue to read in the genre well into middle age, when they long for the repetitive or familiar—and such readers find no shortage of SF and fantasy that will deliver the right dose of nostalgia.

Yet even the most hackneyed, shopworn science fiction or fantasy tale will feel startling and fresh to a naïve reader who doesn't know the milieu is just like the one used in a thousand other stories. For the intrinsic difference between speculative and real-world fiction is that speculative fiction must take place in an unknowable world. At some point, every science fiction and fantasy story must challenge the reader's experience and learning. That's much of the reason why the genre is so open to the experimentation and innovation that other genres reject—strangeness is our bread and butter. Spread it thick or slice it thin, it's still our staff of life.

## BOUNDARY 5:
## BETWEEN SCIENCE FICTION AND FANTASY

There's one more boundary that will matter to you—the boundary between science fiction and fantasy. That's the boundary that I ran into when I tried to sell "Tinker" to *Analog*.

---

I have found these quarrels to be almost as sad as they are funny—like bitter arguments between small children in the same family. Don't touch me. You hit me first. I hate you. You stink. The fact is that what crowds out good science fiction is bad science fiction; science fiction improves when it borrows the best techniques of fantasy, and fantasy improves when it borrows appropriate techniques from science fiction. I suppose all the arguing does no harm—but it doesn't enlighten us much, either.

Most of us who write speculative fiction turn with equal ease from fantasy to science fiction and back again. I've written both, and have found my fantasy stories to be no easier to write, no less rigorous than my science fiction; nor have I found my science fiction to need any less sense of mythic undertone or any less passionate action than my fantasy stories.

Why, then, do you even need to think about the differences? First, because fantasy and science fiction are separate publishing categories. Most book publishers who offer both kinds of speculative fiction have separate imprints for fantasy and science fiction—or at least put one term or the other on the spine. Some even maintain a separate editorial staff for each genre. And the magazines are keenly aware of the difference between science fiction and fantasy, either because they don't publish fantasy or because they have to maintain the proper balance between them in order to hold their audience.

Yet in most bookstores, fantasy and science fiction are lumped together in the same group of shelves, alphabetized by author with no attempt to separate one from the other. And they're right to do so. Those few misguided bookstores that try to have separate science fiction and fantasy sections find that most authors who have books in one section also have books in the other. This can be very confusing to would-be buyers.

"Where's the latest Xanth novel?" asks the fifteenth kid today. "I found Piers Anthony's books in the sci-fi section, but you don't have *any* Xanth books there."

"That's because the Xanth books are *fantasy*," says the patient bookstore clerk. "They're in the *fantasy* section."

"Well that's stupid," says the kid. "Why don't you have his books *together*?"

And the kid is right. It *is* stupid. Science fiction and fantasy are one literary community; while there are many who read or write just one, there are many more who read and write both, and it's foolish to divide them in the store. After all, SF and fantasy have a largely author-driven market. While there are certainly some readers who buy SF or fantasy like Harlequin romances, picking up anything with a spaceship or an elf on the cover, there are many others who search for favorite authors and buy only their works, only rarely branching out to sample books written by writers unknown to them. These readers expect to find all of an author's books together on the shelves. They don't want "a science fiction novel" or "a fantasy"—they want the latest Asimov or Edding, Benford or Donaldson, Niven-and-Pournelle or Hickman-and-Weis.

But there is a time when the division between science fiction and fantasy really matters—and that's when you're writing the story.

Here's a good, simple, semi-accurate rule of thumb: If the story is set in a universe that follows the same rules as ours, it's science fiction. If it's set in a universe that doesn't follow our rules, it's fantasy.

Or in other words, science fiction is about what *could* be but isn't; fantasy is about what *couldn't* be.

In the main, this boundary works pretty well. As rational people, we know that magic doesn't work and superstitions are meaningless. So if magic works in your story, if superstitions come true, if there are impossible beasts like fire-breathing dragons or winged horses, if djinns come out of bottles or mumbled curses cause disease, then you're writing fantasy.

You must inform your reader as quickly as possible after the beginning of your story whether it's going to be fantasy or science fiction. If it's science fiction, and you signal this to the reader, then you have saved yourself enormous amounts of effort, because your reader will assume that all the known laws of nature apply, except where the story indicates an exception.

With fantasy, however, *anything* is possible. And where anything can happen, who cares what actually occurs? I mean, if your hero can get into trouble and then wish his way out, so what? Why worry about him? Why *care?*

The truth is that *good* fantasies carefully limit the magic that's possible. In fact, the magic has to be defined, at least in the author's mind, as a whole new set of natural laws that *cannot* be violated during the course of the story. That is, if at the beginning of the story you have established that your hero can make only three wishes, you better not have him come up with a fourth wish to save his neck right at the end. That's cheating, and your reader will be quite correct to throw your book across the room and carefully avoid anything you ever write in the future.

All speculative fiction stories have to create a strange world and introduce the reader to it—but good fantasy must also establish a whole new set of natural laws, explain them right up front, and then faithfully abide by them throughout.

Having said all this, I must now point out that there are numerous exceptions. For instance, by this definition time travel stories in which the hero meets himself and stories that show spaceships traveling faster than light should all be classified as fantasy, because they violate known laws of nature—and yet both are definitely classified as science fiction, not fantasy.

Why? One explanation is that people were writing these stories as science fiction before the relevant laws of science were widely known, and so these tales remain science fiction under a sort of grandfather clause. Another explanation is that there was no commercial publishing category of fantasy until the 1960s, so a lot of fantasy came to live quite comfortably within the tent of science fiction and, when the fantasy publishing category came into existence, nobody bothered to move them from one category to the other. They were already conventional.

But to all these explanations I say "bunk." Time travel and faster-than-light (FTL) starships respect the *real* boundary between fantasy and science fiction: They have metal and plastic; they use heavy machinery, and so they're science fiction. If you have people do some magic, impossible thing by stroking a talisman or praying to a tree, it's fantasy; if they do the same thing by pressing a button or climbing inside a machine, it's science fiction.

So in a sense even science fiction stories have to define the "rules of magic" as they apply in the world of the tale, just as fantasies do. If FTL travel is possible in your science fiction universe, you have to establish that fact early on. If you want time travel, you must either make the story be *about* time travel or establish immediately that time travel is commonplace in the world of the story.

Still, the difference remains: If a story is perceived as fantasy, the reader must be told as soon as possible the "natural laws" that apply in this fantasy world, whereas if the story is perceived as science fiction, the reader will assume that the natural laws of *this* universe apply until he is told otherwise.

Note that this applies only to the beginning of the story. Your "fantasy" might end up with all seeming magic explained away as perfectly natural phenomena; your "science fiction story" might end up being a tale of witchcraft or vampirism in space. Indeed, this is exactly what Sheri Tepper did in her nine-volume *True Game* series. The story deals with people who spend their lives acting out an elaborate chesslike game, discovering and using innate magical abilities like shape-changing. Never mind that by the third volume you learn that these people are all descended from colonists who came to this planet from Earth. Don't be distracted by the conclusion, which explains in perfectly natural terms where all their seemingly magical powers come from. The story begins with a fantasy feel, so that Tepper has to unfold the laws of the universe very early in the first volume, the way a fantasy writer must.

On the other hand, David Zindell's brilliant science fiction novel *Neverness* ends up with almost as many gods and mythical, magical events as the *Illiad* and *Odyssey* combined. Yet because it begins with a science fiction feel, the reader assumes from the start that the laws of the known universe apply *with exceptions*. The book is correctly marketed as science fiction, and that's how it's received.

These are the boundaries of speculative fiction, and within that country, the boundary between science fiction and fantasy. There are high walls here and there, and high-voltage fences, and moats with alligators—but there's always a way over or under or around the obstacle. You must be aware of the boundaries; you must tread carefully whenever you get near one; but you are not their prisoner.

Indeed, you might think of the genre boundaries not as obstacles, but rather as dikes and levees that hold out the river or the sea. Wherever they are raised up, they allow you to cultivate new land; and when you need a new space to plant your story, just put up a new dike where you want it to be. If enough of us like your story, we'll accept your new boundary as the true one, and plant a few stories of our own in your newfound land. It's the best gift we can give each other. We're all of us harvesting crops in lands opened up by the pioneers in our field—Wells, Verne, Merritt, Haggard, Lovecraft, Shelley, Tolkien, and many others. But we're none of us confined to the territory they discovered. It's just the starting point.

How can we create the literature of the strange if we continue to stay in well-mapped lands?

# CHAPTER 2

# World Creation

Stories start working on you in a thousand different ways. I'm going to give you some personal examples, so you can see something of the process one writer goes through. The point is not that you should do it my way, but rather that there *is* no right way to come up with a story concept.

## 1. WHERE IDEAS COME FROM

I was sixteen, and my older brother's girlfriend (now his wife) had urged me to read Isaac Asimov's Foundation trilogy (*Foundation, Foundation and Empire,* and *Second Foundation*). It had been years since I last read science fiction regularly, but these books so enthralled me that I wanted not only to read more science fiction, but also to try writing it. At the time I supposed that to write a science fiction story you had to come up with a futuristic idea. My older brother, Bill, was in the army, having just returned from a tour of duty in Korea, and so military thoughts were on my mind.

One day as my father was driving me to school through the bottomlands of the Provo River in Utah, I began trying to imagine what kind of war games would be developed to train soldiers for combat in space. It would be useless to have land-based training games, since that wouldn't prepare you for three-dimensional fighting in the null-gravity environment of space. Even training in airplanes would be pointless, since there is still a definite horizontal orientation to flying in an atmosphere—straight up and straight down are very different from straight across!

So the only place where soldiers could train to think and move easily and naturally in space combat would be outside the gravity well of any planet. It couldn't be in open space—you'd lose too many trainees that way, drifting off in the midst of the game. So there had to be a huge enclosed room in a null-G environment, with variable gridworks and obstacles from game to game, so the trainees could simulate fighting among spaceships or the debris of battle.

I imagined that they would play with small handheld lasers, while wearing suits of body armor that would serve a double purpose—to protect them against damage from collisions during mock battles, and also to electronically record when someone scored a hit on your body. If you were hit in the leg, your leg would become immobile; if you were hit in the head or body, your whole suit would freeze. But you would remain present in the battle, drifting just like a corpse, serving as one more obstacle or bit of cover.

This was in 1968. I didn't get around to writing the story "Ender's Game" until 1975. That's because the battleroom wasn't a *story*, it was merely a setting—and not a complete milieu either, since the soldiers training there wouldn't be in the battleroom twenty-four hours a day. There had to be a whole universe built up around the battleroom, and I was too young and inexperienced to know the questions that had to be asked.

In 1975, I asked them. Who was the enemy they were training to fight? Other humans? No, aliens—and cliché aliens at that. Bug-eyed monsters. Our worst nightmares, only now they were here in real life. And who were the trainees? Not combat soldiers, I decided, but rather people being trained to pilot starships into battle. The point was not to learn hand-to-hand combat, but rather to learn how to move quickly and efficiently, how to plan, how to take and give orders, and above all how to think three-dimensionally.

And then I asked the question that made all the difference. I knew that, having gladly missed out on combat in Vietnam, I hadn't the experience to write about the lives of *men* in combat. But what if they weren't men at all? What if they were children? What if the starships they'd be piloting were actually billions of miles away, and the kids thought they were playing *games*?

Now I had a world: humans fighting off alien invaders, with children as the commanders of their fleet. There was still a lot of work to do, but it was a simple matter to come up with my main character, the young child whose genius in three-dimensional combat in the battleroom would make him the ideal choice to command the human fleet.

Notice, though, that I didn't have even the seed of a good science fiction story until after I had a clear idea of the world in which the story would take place.

The same thing is true of fantasy. Another personal example:

I like to draw maps. That's how I doodle when other people are talking, by drawing coastlines and then putting in mountains, rivers, cities, national boundaries. Then, if the map that results intrigues me, I begin to make up information—which nations speak the same language, what their history has been, which nations are prospering, which waning.

In 1976 I was cast in a musical comedy playing in Salt Lake City. We rehearsed in an old building downtown that was scheduled for demolition to make way for the new Crossroads Mall. In one corner of the rehearsal area there was a pile of junk—broken chairs, tilting shelves, stuff that was utterly useless. But amid the garbage I found a ream of onionskin paper of an odd size, larger than normal. I can't let paper like that go to waste! So I brought it home and saved it.

Now it's 1979. I'm living in a house in Sandy, Utah, working on the first draft of my novel *Saints*. I'm also on a radical diet losing about a billion pounds. My wife and son are down in Orem, Utah, living with her parents so they can take care of her and Geoffrey while she recovers from a miscarriage; I can't do it because I have a deadline to meet. So I'm hungry, tired, and lonely.

One night, exhausted from writing, I wander around the house and find that ream of outsize paper, saved all those years and never used. I grab a few sheets and head upstairs. The television goes on, I lie on the bed, lay a sheet of paper atop a notebook, and begin to doodle a map while I listen to the Channel 2 news and then the Carson show.

Only this time, I doodle a different kind of map. After all, this paper cries out for something special, and I'm tired of coastlines and continents. I trace a bend in a river, and instead of dots for cities, I begin drawing tiny squares and rectangles to represent buildings, with gaps marking the streets. Heavy lines denote the walls of a castle; more heavy lines show the city wall. And I put gates in the walls.

A few nights later, the map is finished. Now it's time for naming. I had put in a few religious sites; the gate that leads into the main temple area gets the name "God's Gate." The gate near the commercial area is names "Asses' Gate" because that's the beast of burden the merchants use. One riverside gate, leading to the main street through the city, is "King's Gate"; another near the animal stalls outside the city and leading directly to the Great Market, is "Grocers' Gate."

Then the idea occurs to me that maybe when you enter at a particular gate, you get a certain kind of pass that limits you to certain areas and activities in the city inside the wall. If you come in at one gate, you find a completely different kind of city from the one you find when you enter at another. Come in as a pilgrim through God's Gate, and you don't leave the temple area. Come in as a grocer, and you have the run of the market but can't go near the trading floors.

Knowing this, I crudely named the gate near the poor section of town, with hundreds of tiny houses, "Piss Gate," because people who entered there only had a three-day pass allowing them to attempt to find work; if they remained after three days, they were imprisoned or killed or sold into slavery. A hopeless, desperate way to enter the city.

But not the *most* hopeless way. For there was one gate that, in the process of drawing, I had accidently drawn with no gap between the two towers that guarded it. Even after slightly redrawing the towers, there was no gap between them. Unless I resorted to Liquid Paper, that entrance to the city was spoiled.

Except that I believe, when it comes to storytelling—and making up maps of imaginary lands *is* a kind of storytelling—that mistakes are often the beginning of the best ideas. After all, a mistake wasn't *planned*. It isn't likely to be cliché. All you have to do is think of a reason why the mistake isn't a mistake at all, and you might have something fresh and wonderful, something to stimulate a story you never thought of quite that way before. So I thought—what if this gate has been permanently closed off? I drew houses right across both faces of the gate. That explained why there was no gap between the towers.

Now, as I was naming all the gates, I had to wonder why this gate had been closed. And then I realized that this gate was closed because it had been the magical way into the city. A walled city spoke of medieval times; what could be more natural than to have this be the setting for a fantasy? The political powers in the city would naturally resent or fear the rival power of magicians;

the gate would have been closed years ago. Only it wasn't closed completely. You can still get through, if you can pay the right bribes, but you enter the city as a criminal, with no pass at all, and the city you find is a dark, dangerous, magical one where the rules of nature don't work the way they used to.

It happened that this closed gate was near a section of town where I had drawn a small shrine that, for reasons I cannot remember, I had already named "Hart's Hope." I decided that this magical gate had once been the *main* route into the city, back when the Hart was the god of this place, long before the god called God came to be worshipped in the temple in the southeast corner. So the worshippers of the old god, the Hart, would enter town through this gateway.

Did I have a story? By no means. I still didn't even have a world. I set the map aside.

Around that time, the TV news was full of stories about a couple in Layton, Utah, who had just given birth to twins conjoined at the top of their heads. It was a tricky operation to separate them, and the photos before they were separated were disturbingly alien. But, being a perverse sort of person, I tried to imagine what could be *worse*. Not more life-threatening—simply worse to *see*. Worse to live through.

I came up with the idea of two sisters who were born joined at the face. One sister was staring directly into her twin's face; after separation, her face would be a blank mask, with no eye, no real nose, and only a gap for a mouth. The other twin, though, was facing half away; after separation, while one eye was missing and one cheek was a ruin, her profile from the other side would look perfectly normal. Which sister suffered more, the one who would never see how hideous she was, would never look at others looking away from her? Or the one who, by turning her face just so, could catch a glimpse of how beautiful she and her sister *could* have been; and then by staring at herself full in the face in the mirror, could see just how hideously deformed she was?

I even tried writing a story about these sisters. The draft is lost, which is just as well—it was going nowhere.

Around that time I discovered the writings of Mary Renault. When I read her book *The King Must Die*, in which the ancient Greek women have a separate, older religion which secretly rivals the public religion of the men, I realized that there mustn't be merely two rival gods in the city I had drawn—the Hart and the god named God—there must be another tradition of worship. A women's religion, and the god would be the Sweet Sisters, those two women who were born joined at the face. One of them was permanently staring inward, contemplating the inner secrets of the universe, breathing only breath that her sister had already inhaled; while the other, seeing half in and half out, was able to see our world and communicate with her worshippers. However, at the time of my story—whatever it would be—the two sisters had been forcibly separated, thereby making it impossible for *either* to see into the mind of God. The one was blind, remembering only the sight of the infinite; the other, with her single eye, could remember only the mortal world that constantly impinged on her vision.

Who would have the power to separate these women? I thought at first that it must be the god named God, and that the Hart would eventually ally with them and rejoin them. But that would be a story about gods, and that wouldn't be interesting even to me. So instead I knew it had to be a mortal who had somehow gained enough power to tame not only the Sweet Sisters, but also the Hart and the god named God.

Did I have a story yet? No. I had a map of a fascinating city (fascinating to me, at least) and a trio—temporarily a quartet—of gods.

I began teaching a science fiction writing class at the University of Utah, and on the first day of class, when there were no stories to critique, I began a spur-of-the-moment exercise designed simply to show that science fiction and fantasy ideas are ridiculously easy to come up with. I asked questions; they improvised answers; and out of the answers, we made stories. To my surprise, the idea was not just a five-minute exercise—it became a fun, exciting session that took almost the whole period. I have since used the process in every class or workshop I've taught, and have put on a "Thousand Ideas in an Hour" session at almost every science fiction convention I've attended and every school I've visited. Not only is the process always entertaining, but also the results are always different and *always* workable as stories. To wit: At the very first session, I asked them to think of the "price of magic." In a fantasy, if magic has no limitations, the characters are omnipotent gods; anything can happen, and so there's no story. There have to be strict limits on magic. *Dungeons and Dragons* uses a seniority system that may work well for games, but for stories it is truly stupid: The longer you manage to stay alive, the more spells you know and the more power you have. I wanted my students to come up with better limitations, and I wanted them to think of it as a price to be paid for every bit of magical power that was used.

Many ideas came up in such sessions, but one that came up the first time, which really stuck in my mind, was that the cost of magic was blood. How would that work? You wouldn't prick your own finger to get power—that was too easy. It had to be enough blood from the creature that the creature's whole life was contained in it; you could only get the power as the creature bled to death. The *amount* of power depended on the creature whose blood you used.

You could kill a fly and get the power to keep the soup from boiling over. You could kill a rabbit and make an enemy sick or heal a child. You could kill a deer—a hart!—and have the power to be invisible for hours or days. And you could kill a man and get *real* power.

But my students were just as perverse as I was. Wouldn't you get even more power if you killed a child? After all, children have more life in them—they haven't used up so much of it. And what if you kill your *own* child? Wouldn't that give you even more power?

Yes, but what sort of person would ever do what it took to obtain such power? Ultimate power would be in the hands of monstrous people. People monstrous enough, perhaps, to separate the Sweet Sisters and imprison the Hart and the god named God.

I had the whole milieu at last. The city of Hart's Hope was being ruled by a mortal so cruel he killed his own child—no, *she* killed *her* own child—in order to gain so much power that she could bind the gods. And my hero would be the one who undid her power, not by killing another child, but by turning her own power against her. I wasn't sure how that would be done, and *wouldn't* be sure until near the end of the first draft, but I knew that my hero would have been raised up by the gods—who were not *completely* bound—to have an anti-magical power. He would be a magic sink, a person who could absorb and use magical power without ever having the ability to use that power himself. He was a negation of power.

There was much *more* development before I was ready to write my fantasy novel *Hart's Hope*, but I knew the world in which it took place and I knew who some of my main characters were. What lay ahead was some of the most fascinating work—fleshing out the characters, discovering their unpredictable relationships with each other and with the world around them, and, finally, working out the storyline—the interesting pathways of those characters through the world I had created.

Still, after all this planning, some of the best parts of the story came on the spur of the moment as I was writing the first draft. For instance, it never occurred to me until I found myself writing it that the god named "God" should be a feeble old man polishing woodwork in the palace of Queen Beauty; nor did any of my planning include the writing system in which words have different meanings when read forward and backward, or when interpreted as numbers. But such impromptu additions would not have been possible had I not laid down many strata of creation before I started that draft.

## The Ripening Idea

The first thing you should learn from these two examples is that no two stories are developed in exactly the same way. However, in my experience one thing is constant: Good stories don't come from trying to write a story the moment I think of the first idea. All but a handful of my stories have come from combining two completely unrelated ideas that have been following their own tracks through my imagination. And all the stories I was still proud of six months after writing them have come from ideas that ripened for many months—usually years—between the time I first thought of them and the time they were ready to put into a story.

"Great," you say. "I pick up this book, hoping to learn how to write speculative fiction, and now this guy's telling me that I have to wait months or years before writing stories about any new ideas I think of."

That's what I'm telling you: You'll probably have to wait months or years before writing *good* versions of story ideas you come up with *now*. But you probably already have hundreds of story ideas that have been ripening inside you for many years. For some writers, one of the best ways to help an idea ripen is to try writing a draft of it, seeing what comes up when you actually try to make it into a story. As long as you recognize that the draft you write immediately after thinking of the idea will almost certainly have to be thrown away and rewritten from the beginning, you'll be fine.

That immediate draft—or, if you are another kind of creator, the first outlines and sketches, maps and histories, jotted scenes and scraps of dialogue—is the writer's equivalent of what a composer does when he plinks out a new theme on the piano, just to hear it. He doesn't immediately score and orchestrate the theme—first he has to play it over and over, varying it, changing rhythms, pitches, key, imagining different voices and timbres playing the theme, imagining different harmonies and counter-melodies. By the time the composer actually starts to arrange and orchestrate the piece, the theme will have been transformed many times over. The first version is all but forgotten.

Some writers have to do all their inventing before they ever try to write out a narrative. Other writers have to try out the narrative immediately, then rework it over and over, letting new ideas come to them as they write each draft. I'm somewhere between the two extremes: I do a lot of outlining and planning before I write, until I feel the story is ripe—but then, as I write, all kinds of new ideas come to me and I freely explore each new avenue that feels as if it might lead somewhere fun. As a result my novels almost never have much to do with the outlines I submit to the publishers at contract time—but since the novels are always much *better* than the outlines, the publishers haven't complained yet.

## The Idea Net

The second thing you should learn from my examples is that ideas come from everywhere, provided that you're thinking about everything that happens to you as a potential story. I like to think that the difference between storytellers and nonstorytellers is that we storytellers, like fishermen, are constantly dragging an "idea net" along with us. Other people pass through their lives and never notice how many stories are going on all around them; we, however, think of everything as a potential story.

And the idea net consists of three questions: "Why?" "How?" and "What result?" The first question is really two: When you ask, "Why did John slap Mary across the face?" I can answer with either the first cause, "Because she slapped him," or the final cause, "In order to show her who was boss." Both might be true at the same time. The first cause is like dominoes: Domino B fell over because Domino A fell first and pushed it. The final cause deals with purpose, with *intent:* Someone performs an action *in order to* bring about some desired result.

Both causes are acting on characters in stories all the time, and you must know answers to both kinds of "why" before you understand your characters.

In fact, to write stories that are any good at all, you have to realize that there is never just one answer to *any* of these questions. Every event has more than one cause and more than one result. When John slapped Mary, not only did she act more timidly around him, but also she resented him and constantly worked to find ways to make him suffer for having hit her.

Furthermore, John himself never realized that he was the kind of man who slapped women. Even though he excused himself by telling himself that after all, she slapped him first, it still gnawed at him that he had hit her; he felt guilty and tried to make it up to her.

Even that is too easy. Consciously, John feels guilty. Unconsciously, he's rather proud of it. He had never hit anyone in his life until now, and at the moment he struck Mary, he felt a sense of raw power that he had never felt. It made him a bit more belligerent, made him strut a little in his dealings with others. In fact, the unconscious psychological payoff was strong enough that he will seek, without knowing it, excuses to slap and hit and push more people. Especially Mary.

And Mary's resentment and subtle rebellion are also not complicated enough to be a fair representative of reality. Perhaps it gradually dawns on her that John is becoming even *more* domineering—her only way out is to leave him. So she leaves, taking the children with her, and he, feeling completely unmanned by this, begins to follow her. He tells himself that he's trying to find her in order to make it up to her and help take care of the children; even if she doesn't want him back, he has a right to see his kids. But unconsciously, he's following her in order to beat her up again, maybe kill her—*then* she'll know who's boss.

Or perhaps Mary's unconscious reaction is completely different. Maybe she was raised by a strong father or mother who slapped the family around. Maybe she unconsciously wanted John to act out this physically domineering role, and it wasn't until she slapped him herself that he actually did what she wanted. So her subtle vengeances for his violence are rally provocations. She stays with him, unconsciously hoping to continue provoking him into violence so she can fear and admire him the way she feared and admired her battering parent. Her unconscious strategy is completely successful; John finds himself hitting her more and more often. But he can't bear to be the person she is turning him into—he leaves *her*.

Or maybe they stay together and raise another generation just like them.

Or maybe there are still *more* results—and more hidden causes and motives—that will change the shape of the story. I hope you see, though, that with every variation, every new layer of cause and effect, the characters—and the story—become richer, deeper, more complex, and potentially more truthful and insightful.

This is not limited to individual characters. Nothing is sillier than a story that has some great event in the world that provokes only *one* response from society at large. Never in the history of the world has any society been perfectly unanimous in its response to any event. Nor has any innovation been introduced into the world without unpredictable side effects. When the car was invented and popularized, no one could have imagined that it would lead to the drive-in movie and the drive-up bank, to freeways and double-trailer trucks, to pollution and the greenhouse effect and the political ramifications of OPEC, and to the gathering of wealth and military power by a handful of Islamic nations, giving them influence in the world far beyond what their population and other resources would warrant.

Yet in your stories, *you* must imagine all these things, not just because it will make the world of your story more complete, but also because the very completeness of the world will transform your story and make it far more truthful. As your characters move through a more complex world, they will have to respond with greater subtlety and flexibility; the constant surprises they run into will also surprise the reader—and you!

## 2. MAKE RULES FOR YOUR WORLD

So far, world creation sounds like a marvelous free-for-all, in which you come up with all kinds of ideas, ask "why" and "how" and "what result" a lot, and when there's a really big pile of good stuff, you sit down and write.

I wish it were that easy. But that big pile of neat ideas is just that—a pile, shapeless, chaotic. Before you can tell a meaningful story, you have to hone and sharpen your understanding of the world, and that begins with the fundamental rules, the natural laws.

Remember, because speculative fiction always differs from the knowable world, the reader is uncertain about what can and can't happen in the story *until* the writer has spelled out the rules. And you, as a writer, can't be certain of anything until *you* know the rules as well.

## Rules of Starflight

Take space travel, for instance. Why would a story need space travel at all?

One reason might be simply that you want a landscape completely different from Earth. Another might be that you want your story to take place in a developing society, a *frontier* that is so far away from settled places that your characters can't call for help and expect it to come anytime soon.

But let's say your reason is even more basic. Your story centers around an alien society that you have thoroughly developed. The aliens live in an environment that is pretty much Earthlike, so that either species can live in the other's habitat. But the aliens are strange enough that there's no way they could have evolved on Earth. So you have to put them on another planet.

Other planets in our solar system just won't do. Despite speculation in earlier years, the *Voyager II* photographs seem to confirm that not only is there no planet or moon remotely suitable for Earthlike life, there isn't much chance of any kind of life at *all*. So your aliens are going to have to inhabit a planet in another star system.

This poses no problem if there are no humans in your story. If the story takes place entirely within the alien society, with no human perspective at all, then space travel plays no role in your story. But this sort of story—aliens but no humans—is fairly rare in science fiction, and for good reason. The presence of humans in a story about aliens, even if the story is told from the alien point of view, gives the reader (who is quite likely to be human) a frame of reference, a way to contrast the aliens with the humans and see exactly how the aliens are different and how this affects their society.

But if you tell the story with no humans at all, then your point-of-view characters will have to be alien, and since they have never seen a human, they cannot realistically provide a contrast. They can't even *explain* anything, unless you resort to tactics like this: "Digger-of-Holes imagined for a moment what it would be like if his eyes were on the front of his head, with overlapping vision, like the tiny shrew on the branch in front of him. How could the creature see what was happening behind it? And how could its tiny brain make sense of two overlapping but different fields of view?" This is sensible enough, but how often do you think you can get away with this before the reader gets quite impatient with a supposedly alien character who keeps thinking about things pertaining to humans that he's never seen?

(Usually, of course, such things are handled even more ineptly—by having Digger-of-Holes imagine binocular vision *without* seeing a tree-shrew, for instance—or, worse yet, having an alien scientist give a brief lecture on the benefits of binocular vision. Such techniques get the facts across, all right—but at the cost of shattering the believability of the characters and forcing the reader to be aware of how the author is manipulating the story.)

In any event, your story happens to be one that requires the presence of human beings, so you don't face the problems of the aliens-only story. However, now you *do* face the problems of travel between star systems.

Why? Your story isn't *about* space travel! At the beginning the humans have already arrived on the alien planet (or, perhaps, the aliens have already arrived on Earth).

I assure you, though, that you *must* determine the rules of interstellar flight in your story's universe, and, at some point early in the story, you must let the reader know what those rules are. The reason for this will become clear as we go over the possible rules.

The problem of interstellar flight is two fold: the speed of light, and the ratio of fuel mass to fuel energy.

Let's take the speed of light first. According to Einstein's theory, lightspeed is the absolute ceiling on the speed of any motion in the universe. *Nothing* can go faster than light. Furthermore, anything that actually *goes* the speed of light *becomes* energy. So you can't get from one star system to another any faster than a bit more than one year per light-year of distance between them. To get from Earth to a star system thirty light-years away would take, say, thirty-one years. Your human characters, who were in their twenties when they left, are now in their fifties.

What are the strategies for getting around the lightspeed barrier?

### Hyperspace

Though this goes by many different names, the idea is as old as the 1940s at least, and there's really no reason to make up a new term, since if hyperspace is ever found to exist it will almost certainly be *called* hyperspace—the way when robots were finally created, they were *called* robots because science fiction writers had been calling artificial mechanical men by that name ever since Czech writer Karl Capek coined the term in his play *RUR* back in the 1930s. You can call it hyperspace—in fact, you probably *should* call it hyperspace, since most of your readers will be familiar with that term and will recognize it instantly.

Hyperspace is based on the idea that space, which seems three-dimensional to us, is really four-dimensional (or more!); and that in another dimension, *our* space is folded and curved so that locations that seem far apart to us are really quite close together, provided you can find a way to get out of our three-dimensional space, pass through hyper-dimensional space, and then come back out at the point you desire.

This passage through hyperspace is usually called "the jump," and there are many different rules associated with it. Isaac Asimov had a robot story in which the jump to hyperspace caused human beings to temporarily cease to exist, a sort of mini-death that drove a robot pilot mad trying to take humans through the jump.

Timothy Zahn's "Cascade Point" and other stories set in that same universe propose that at the moment of the jump, there is an infinite array of possible points of emergence, in most of which you die; but since it is only the jumps that you survive that you remember, you're never aware of the universes in which you are dead.

Other versions of hyperspace require that you have to be near a large star in order to make the jump, or that you *can't* be near a large gravity source or the jump gets distorted. In some stories, Heinlein allows an infinite number of possible jumps, with your emergence depending on the elaborately careful calculations of your velocity and trajectory leading to the jump. Others, like Frederik Pohl with his Heechee novels, have written stories allowing only a limited number of gateways through space, each leading consistently to its own destination—which, until all the gateways are mapped, might as easily be an inhabited world or the edge of a black hole.

And some versions of hyperspace don't even require a spaceship. They place "doorways" or "gates" or "tunnels" on or near a planet's surface, and if you simply walk though the right spot, going in the correct direction, you end up on—or near—the surface of another planet!

Another version of this, often used by Larry Niven, is that such doorways are not natural, but are machines that create passages through hyperspace.

And in one variation of this, hyperspace isn't used at all. You get into a device that looks a bit like an old-fashioned phone booth, which analyzes your body, breaks it down into its constituent parts, and then transmits an image of it at lightspeed to a booth on another planet (or elsewhere on Earth) that carefully reconstructs you. In either case, booths can only send you to other booths, so that somebody has to make the long journey to other planets at sub-lightspeed *first*, in order to assemble the booth that will allow others to follow them instantaneously.

The advantage of hyperspace in all its variations is that it allows relatively quick, cheap passage between worlds. How quick and how cheap is up to you. Think of it as being like voyages between the New World and the Old World. In 1550, the voyage was uncertain; some passengers and crew on every voyage died before they reached land, and some ships disappeared without a trace. By the mid-1800s, the voyage was much faster and death far less likely, though the trip was still miserable. In the age of steam, there were still wrecks and losses, but the voyage was cut down to a week or two. Today, it can take only a few hours. You can have starflight using hyperspace that functions at any one of these danger levels. It's as safe and fast as the Concorde—or it's as dangerous and slow and uncertain as a caravel navigating with a quadrant and an unreliable clock.

Why must you decide all these things, when your story begins after the voyage is over? First, because the characters who did the traveling—human or alien—have just finished the voyage, and their relationship with each other and their attitude toward this new world and toward authorities on the old one will be largely shaped by what the voyage back entails.

If another ship can't come for months, if the whole voyage was at risk of death and some *did* die, and if there's only a sixty-forty chance of getting back home alive, then the voyagers will be determined to survive on the new planet, and will be grimly aware that if they don't make things work, their lives may end. They also won't take faraway authorities on their home planet half so seriously.

But if they reached the planet by taking a six-hour flight, and traffic between this world and the home planet will be easy and frequent, they have much less at stake, and their attitude will be far more casual. Furthermore, homeworld authorities will be much more involved, and reinforcements or replacements will be easy to obtain.

Why must you establish clearly what the rules of space travel are? So that the reader understands why the characters are getting so upset—or why they're *not* getting terribly upset—when things go wrong. So that the reader knows just what's at stake.

And—not a trivial consideration—so that the experienced science fiction reader will recognize your proper use of a standard device and feel confident that the story is being written by somebody who knows how this is done. Even if you plan to be rebellious and *not* use standard devices, you still must address the same issues; the effect on the reader is still reassuring.

### Generation Ships

You've decided you don't want to use hyperspace, either because it strikes you as nonsense science or because you don't want all that coming and going on your new planet. Another alternative is to send a ship at sub-lightspeed and let the voyage take as long as it takes.

Without getting into the science of it (primarily because I don't understand it in any kind of detail myself), the problem with sub-light voyages is that they take a *long* time. And you have to carry all your fuel with you. The good news is that you can coast most of the way—there's little friction in space, and once you reach a certain speed, you should continue traveling at that speed in the same direction until something happens to turn you or slow you down. So most of the voyage needs no fuel at all.

The bad news is that your fuel is part of the mass that your fuel has to lift. There comes a point when the fuel to accelerate any more will add enough weight that you either can't lift it or can't design a sturdy enough ship to hold it. Furthermore, because it takes just as much fuel to slow you down at the end of your voyage so you don't just sail right on past your destination, you have to save exactly half your fuel for the slowdown, plus any fuel required for maneuvering into orbit. That means that the fuel must be able to accelerate more than twice its own mass. Worse yet, if there isn't any more fuel *at* your destination, you're either not coming home again or you're going to have to carry more than *four times* the fuel needed to accelerate you to your traveling speed.

So that you don't waste fuel trying to lift a huge ship out of the gravity well of a planet like Earth, such ships are usually assumed to have been built out in space and launched from a point as far as possible from the Sun. Thus, when

---

they arrive at the new world, they put their huge ship into orbit and use landing vehicles or launches or (nowadays) shuttles to get down to the planet's surface.

Using the technology I've just described, you'll be lucky to get to ten percent of lightspeed. That's pretty fast—about sixty-seven million miles an hour—but at that rate, it will take your ship more than *three hundred years* to get to a star system thirty light-years away. And that doesn't even allow for acceleration time!

That's why such ships are called "generation ships." Assuming that the ship is a completely self-contained environment, with plants to constantly refresh the atmosphere and grow food, a whole human society lives aboard the ship. People are born, grow old, and die, and the elements of their bodies are processed and returned to the ecosystem within the ship. This idea has been well-explored in many stories—particularly stories about ships where the people have forgotten their origin, forgotten even that the ship is a ship—but it has a lot of life left in it.

The problem with this (besides the fact that a completely self-contained ecosystem would be almost impossible to create) is that none of the people who reach the new world have any direct memories of their home planet. Their whole history for generations has been inside a ship—why would they even *want* to go out onto a planet's surface? The fact of living inside a ship for so long is so powerful that it almost takes over the story. If your story is *about* that, like Rebecca Brown Ore's brilliant debut story, "Projectile Weapons and Wild Alien Water," then that's fine—but if your story is about something else, a generation ship is hard to get over.

### Cryo-travel

Another alternative is to have the crew travel for all those years in a state of suspended animation—either frozen or otherwise kept viable until the ship itself, or a skeleton crew, wakens the sleepers at the voyage's end. This has the advantage of not requiring living space and supplies for so many people for so many years, and it still achieves the result of making frequent voyages between the new world and the home planet unthinkable—or at least impractical.

The drawback is that if suspended animation is possible at all in your future universe, then you have to let it be used for anything it's needed for. Characters who get sick or critically injured or even killed must be rushed back to the ship and popped into a suspended animation chamber until a cure or repair can be worked out. Also, there are bound to be people who try to abuse the system to prolong their lives beyond the normal span of years. You can't have a technology exist for one purpose and then ignore it for another—not unless you want to earn the scorn of your more critical and vocal readers.

A variation on cryo-travel is to send colony ships that contain no human beings at all, but rather frozen human embryos; when the ship's computer determines that the starship has reached a habitable planet, some of the embryos are revived and raised to adulthood by computers or robots inside the ship. They come to the new planet as virtually new creations, having known neither parents nor any human society except the one they form. Obviously, this is a one-way trip with no hope of later visits or help from the home planet, since no one on the home world will know *whether* the colony ship happened to find a habitable planet, let alone *where*.

### Ramdrives

Long before the personal computer culture taught us to use the term *RAM drive* for a virtual disk in volatile memory, science fiction readers were introduced to the ramscoop stardrive, or ramdrive, that solved part of the fuel problem. Instead of carrying fuel enough to handle all of a ship's acceleration, a ramship would use conventional fuel to get up to a certain speed, then deploy a huge network like a funnel in front of it to scoop up the loose matter that is everywhere in space. This matter would then be used as fuel so that acceleration could continue without having to carry all the fuel along.

There are theoretical problems—the efficient use of the loose interstellar "dust," some structure for the net that isn't so heavy that the matter it collects can't provide enough energy to accelerate it, the fact that at velocities far below lightspeed the interstellar dust stops being harmless dust and starts being extremely dangerous and explosive debris that seriously harms any ship traveling that fast. But the ramdrive is fun and semi-plausible, and it allows you to have a starship that isn't the size of your average asteroid.

### Time Dilation

Time dilation space travel is a sort of middle path. With this set of rules, your starship can travel at a speed so close to the speed of light (say, 99.999 percent of lightspeed) that, while you don't turn into pure energy, you get from point A to point B at *almost* the speed of light. Relativity theory suggests that time aboard an object traveling at that speed would be compressed, so that while an outside observer might think thirty years had passed, people on the ship would only have lived through a few hours or days or weeks.

This allows you to get people from world to world without generation ships or cryo-travel. The travelers who reach the new planet have clear memories of their home world. But they won't be particularly eager to get back because, while to them it has only been a few weeks since they left home, back there it has been thirty years. Anybody they left behind has aged a whole generation or died. And if they turned around and went back immediately, they would return home to find that someone who was twenty when they left is now eighty years old. For all intents and purposes, it's still a one-way voyage—but one that allows the travelers to arrive with their society intact, relatively unchanged by the voyage.

Still, the characters will have been cut off from anyone they knew and loved. This suggests that either the travelers will be going through some degree of grief or they will have had no close friends or family on their previous world; in either case, this will have a lot to do with how you characterized them.

And pretend not to know that to a ship traveling at such a high percentage of lightspeed, space dust would strike them like intense gamma radiation. Just say that they use a half-mile-thick layer of crushed asteroid as shielding, or that they have a force field that shields them from the radiation. Or don't say anything at all—time dilation stories are such a staple in science fiction that you really don't have to apologize for them anymore.

### The Ansible

I first ran across this variation on time dilation in the works of Ursula K. LeGuin, and found it one of the most useful devices in space travel. In essence, the ansible is a device that allows you to *communicate* instantaneously, regardless of distance. Thus travelers can go on one-way time dilation voyages, yet still report to and receive instructions from people on the home planet.

This is enormously convenient if you want to have a fairly unified interstellar society and yet don't want people hopping from planet to planet the way some people commute by air from Boston to New York. A space voyage remains an irrevocable decision, cutting you off from everyone you leave behind, yet the whole interstellar society can share literature, politics, news—anything can be transmitted by ansible. It's as if the Pilgrims could have communicated with England by radio, but still had to do all their traveling in small, dangerous, unhealthy wooden ships.

As science, of course, this is pure nonsense—yet it is so useful that many of us have used some variation on it. After all, we're not trying to predict the future, only to tell a story in a strange place!

### Warp Speed

I haven't even touched on the silliest of space travel rules—the one used in the *Star Trek* universe, where the speed of light is no more a barrier than the speed of sound, and you only have to persuade Scotty in the engine room to really step on the gas to get to four, eight, ten times the speed of light. This sort of stardrive shows such contempt for science that it's best to reserve it for light adventures or comic stories—or, of course, *Star Trek* novelizations.

In fact, unless you're actually writing a *Star Trek* novel (which means you must already have a contract with the publisher licensed by Paramount Pictures) or are deliberately trying to be funny, *never* refer to "warp speed" in your fiction. It's not only bad science, it also pegs you instantly as a writer who knows science fiction only through *Star Trek*. Beware of *anything* that makes non-Trekkie readers think of *Star Trek*. That's the equivalent of applying for a position as a physics professor with a résumé that lists your training as "Watched every episode of Mr. Wizard." You may actually know something, but it'll be hard to get anyone to take you seriously long enough to find out.

### What the Rules Can Do for You

All this attention to space travel, and your story doesn't have a single scene aboard a ship! Do you really have to go through all this?

Yes—in your head, or perhaps in your outline. Just enough time to make your decisions about the rules and then make sure your whole story doesn't violate them. But your *reader* doesn't have to go through all that with you. Once you've decided that you're using a difficult, dangerous hyperspace where the emergence points can shift by parsecs without warning, then all you have to do is drop some reference into the story—perhaps a single sentence, like this:

"It was a perfect flight, which is to say that they didn't emerge from the jump through hyperspace in the middle of a star or heading straight for an asteroid, and even though everybody puked for days after the jump, nobody died of it."

That's it. That's all. No more discussion about the mechanics of starflight. But your readers will understand why none of the travelers is eager to leave the planet, and why it'll be quite a while before another ship comes. And now, with the rules established, you're free to do things like have your viewpoint character think of someone else this way:

> Back at Moonbase, Annie had thought Booker looked pretty good, thought he might be worth getting to know a little better. But after the hyperjump she had had to clean up his vomit while he whimpered and cried in the corner. He didn't emerge from his hysteria till they were in orbit around Rainbird. Annie knew that Booker couldn't help it, that a lot of people reacted that way to the jump, but then, she couldn't help it, either, that it was impossible to respect him anymore after that.

Maybe this relationship will be important in your story; maybe it won't. But if you didn't *know* that people puke a lot after the hyperspace jump, if you hadn't worked out the rules in advance, then you couldn't have given Annie this memory and this aspect to her relationship with Booker. The rules you establish don't limit you; they open up possibilities.

Know the rules, and the rules will make you free.

## Time Travel

You have to go through the same process with time travel. Without going into the same detail, let me just list some of the possible variations on time travel.

1. If you go back in time, you can make any changes you want in the past and you'll continue to exist, because the very act of traveling in time takes you outside timestream and removes you from the effects of changes in history. (See Asimov's *The End of Eternity*.)

2. If you go back in time, you *can* make changes that destroy your own society—so time travel is a closely guarded secret, and those who travel in time are only the most skilled and trusted people. Perhaps they are sent to rescue great works of art that have been lost for centuries. Or perhaps, as in John Varley's classic "Air Raid" (published under the pseudonym Herb Boehm), these time travelers are rescuing people from airplanes that are about to crash or ships that are about to go down with no survivors, so they can force these healthy people

to colonize planets and save humanity from extinction in a hideously polluted future.

3. If you go back in time far enough, any changes you make won't have major effects in your own time, because history has a kind of inertia and tends to get itself back on track. So if you kill Napoleon as a baby, France still has an early nineteenth-century empire and a protracted war with England, and by 1900 everything is right back where it would have been.

4. If you go back in time, you are only *able* to make changes that have no long-term effects, since any universe in which you change your own future could not exist.

5. When you go back in time, you're invisible and unable to affect anything. But you can *watch*—so there's quite a tourist business.

6. Time travel consists of going back into the *mind* of somebody living in the past, seeing events through his eyes. He doesn't know you're there. (But, in Carter Scholz's brilliant short story "The Ninth Symphony of Ludwig von Beethoven and Other Lost Songs," the presence of time-traveling observers in Beethoven's mind drove him mad and eventually killed him, stopping him from writing his greatest works. The time travelers never realized what they were doing, however, because with history altered, they "knew" that Beethoven had never written any such symphonies after all.)

7. Time travel consists of going back into your *own* mind at an earlier stage in your life, able to observe but not to act. Or, in a variation, you *can* act, but then your youthful self will have no memory of what you did while your future self was in control. I used that one in a love story called "Clap Hands and Sing."

8. Time travel consists of observation only, like watching a hologram or a movie. You aren't actually there, and perhaps you aren't altogether sure that what you're seeing is the real past. Maybe it's never the same way twice! (I actually don't remember seeing a story about that—feel free to use that set of rules and see what develops.)

9. Your body remains inside the time-travel device, but a semi-real body is assembled for you in the past; your consciousness remains with that simulacrum until it dies or fades, whereupon you wake up and emerge from the machine. In a story called "Closing the Timelid," I had a group of thrillseekers using such a machine in order to go through repeated deaths by making their simulacra commit suicide.

Do you get the idea? Each one of these sets of rules opens up a whole new range of story possibilities—and trust me, there are hundreds of variations that nobody's tried yet, or that have many, many stories left in them.

## The Rules of Magic

In workshops and conferences over the past decade, I've seen groups of writers and readers come up with hundreds of ways that magic might work within a fantasy society. But the basic idea is only the beginning. With magic, you must be *very* clear about the rules. First, you don't want your readers to think that *anything* can happen. Second, the more carefully you work out the rules, the more you know about the limitations on magic, the more possibilities you open up in the story.

Let's take, as an example, one of the ideas that commonly crops up in the fantasy part of my thousand-idea sessions: The price of magic might be the loss of parts from the human body. It's simple, it's painful, and it's grotesque to imagine—sounds like a great idea to me. And there are as many variations here as there were with time travel. Here are several different ways you might turn this idea into a useful magic system:

1. When the magic user casts a spell, he loses bits off his own body, always starting with the extremities. He's never quite sure how much he's going to lose. Inevitably, however, missing fingers or hands or feet or limbs begin to be taken in society as a sign of great power—so that young people who wish to seem formidable pay to have fingers, and sometimes limbs, removed, with scars artfully arranged to look like those that magicians have. It's hard to tell who really has power and who only seems to. (Your story might be about somebody who refuses to mutilate himself; he's universally regarded as a powerless coward. Which, in fact, he is—until there comes a time when a spell is needed

to save his city, a spell so powerful that *only* a person with his entire body intact can cast it—and the spell will use up all his limbs at once. Does he do it? If so, why?)

2. The magic user must actually cut off a part of his own body, or have it cut off, casting the spell while the bone is being incised. The longer he endures the pain and the larger the section of his body being removed, the more power he obtains. A whole profession of Removers would spring up, people skilled at the excruciatingly slow removal of limbs, using drugs that, while they don't dull the pain, do allow the magician to remain lucid enough to perform the spell. (Here's a chance for an interesting twist on a science fiction staple: a future society devoted to "harmless" recreational drugs. Why not have a Remover who goes into the underground apothecary trade, selling the drugs to people who just want the heightened mental effects? What will the magicians do to him then?)

3. The magic user does not have to cut off his *own* body part; he can cut off somebody else's. Thus magicians keep herds of human beings—social rejects, mental defectives, and so on—to harvest their limbs for power. In most places this practice would be illegal, of course, so that their victims would be concealed or masqueraded as something else. (A good horror story using this magic system might be set in our contemporary world, as we discover people living among us who are secretly harvesting other people's limbs.)

4. The magic user can only obtain power when someone else *voluntarily* removes a body part. Thus magic is only rarely used, perhaps only at times of great need. If a private person wishes to have a spell done, he must provide not only permanent payment to the wizard, but also a part of his body. And at a time of great public need, the hero is not the wizard, but the volunteer who gives up part of his body so the spell can be cast to save the town. (How about a psychological study of a pair of lovers, one a magician, the other a voluntary donor, as we come to understand why the one is willing to give up his or her body parts for the other's use?)

5. When the magician casts a spell, *someone* loses part of his body, but he can't predict who. It has to be someone known to him, however, someone connected to him in some way. And, while wizards all know this dark secret of their craft, they have never told anyone, so that nobody realizes that what causes limbs to wither up and fall off is really not a disease, but rather the wizard up the street or off in the woods or up in the castle tower. (And here's the obvious variation: What if some common but nasty disease in our world is really the work of secret magicians? That's why certain diseases go in waves: Twenty years ago it was bleeding ulcers; now it's colon cancer. And the hero of our story is a wizard who is trying to stop the suffering he and others like him are causing.)

6. When a wizard casts a spell, body parts wither and fall off the person he loves the most. The love can't be faked; if he loves himself the most, it is himself who loses body parts. The greater the love, the greater the power—but also the greater the suffering of the wizard when he sees what has happened to the person he loves. This makes the most loving and compassionate people the ones with the most potential power—and yet they're the ones least likely to use it. (Here's a monstrous story idea: The child of loving parents who wakes up one morning without a limb and, seeing her devoted father getting paid, begins to suspect the connection between her maiming and his wealth.)

You get the idea. There are at least this many permutations possible with every source of magic I've ever heard of. And the stories you tell, the world you create, will in many ways be dependent on the decisions you make about the rules of magic.

## 3. INVENT THE PAST

Worlds don't spring up out of nothing. However things are now, they used to be another way, and somehow they got from there to here.

### Evolution

Whenever you invent an alien creature, you should invest a great deal of effort in determining *why*, in evolutionary terms, its unusual features would have developed. Not that you have to figure out the exact mechanism of evolution—we're still arguing about that in the real world!—but you do have to think about why the alien's unusual features would have survival value.

For instance, take some aliens that were developed in a thousand-ideas session at the World Science Fiction Convention in New Orleans in 1988. I always start the alien-building part of the session by asking, "How do these aliens differ from human beings?" I reject the obvious similes: "They're like cats." "They're like dogs." I insist on something truly strange.

This time someone said, "They don't communicate by speaking."

I immediately insisted that I didn't want to deal with telepathy. "Find another way they communicate."

There were many good suggestions, but one that worked especially well was the idea that they lived in water and communicated by passing memories directly, in chemical form, from one alien's body to another. In fact, the memory of a particular incident would replicate like the DNA of dividing cells, so that after they traded memories, each person would remember the incident as if it had happened to him.

Such a society would have no need of writing anything down, or of language at all—indeed, individual identity would be much less important to them than to us. And death would be almost meaningless. As long as you passed memories before you died, then everything you thought and experienced would continue to live on, so that even though *you* might cease to take part, everyone in the community would clearly remember having done everything you did!

Someone in the group objected that they would eventually overload, remembering everything that had ever happened to everybody who had ever lived. So we decided there had to be a mechanism for forgetting—but not irretrievably. We imagined that they would have developed a way of encoding memories in solid form, building them into structures, perhaps even large edifices composed entirely of memory; and there would be many aliens whose sole job was to remember where memories were stored—librarians, in other words.

But why would such an ability evolve? We decided that this alien species of underwater creatures was fairly weak-bodied and not too fast, with many large, quick predators that often killed them. The tribes that survived were those that learned to manipulate rocks and corals and build shelters, or those that learned to consciously reshape their bodies into other forms—or perhaps, those that learned to join their bodies together into large, intimidating shapes. Each tribe had a different strategy, but it could never be passed from tribe to tribe. Now, though, let's say that the subspecies that has learned to join their bodies into large forms also passes chemicals, quite accidently, from body to body while joined. And some of those chemicals are memories.

Now let's say that the rush of new memories is like a drug, a rapturous experience. Aliens begin to seek it frequently, not just waiting until they're threatened. (Perhaps the pleasure comes from the fact that the joining behavior was always triggered by fear and immediately followed by safety and relief.) There is no particular advantage to random joining of memories—these creatures aren't all *that* bright yet—except that young aliens whose parents conjoin with them and pass memories to them gain a competitive advantage over other youngsters who remain ignorant of their parents' memories.

The result is that memory-passing is strongly reinforced from generation to generation, and in true Lamarckian fashion, learned behaviors become part of the heritage of each succeeding generation. In addition, since this developed among the shape-formers, these underwater creatures would continue the habit of joining into strange shapes.

It was a terrific base for an alien society, with a lot of story possibilities. Then, only a week later, I found myself in Gaffney, South Carolina, talking with Jim Cameron about the novel version of his movie *The Abyss*. His script was brilliant, but an area he had neglected—and properly so—was the aliens. There wasn't time or means in the film to explain them. But in the book version that I was writing, they *had* to be explained.

So I wrote the exploratory chapter (which never showed up in the book) from the point of view of the individual creature who became the original alien colonizer of Earth. I found that everything we had come up with in that thousand-ideas session in New Orleans was wonderfully useful. It was an evolutionary skeleton on which I could hang all the strange behaviors of the aliens in the film.

In fact, those are probably the best aliens I've ever devised for any of my science fiction, and one of the reasons they were better than usual is because I had two unrelated idea sources: the idea session and the movie script, which provided all kinds of anomalous behavior that had to be explained. Out of the tension between the film script and the evolutionary path traced in that idea session there grew what seemed to me to be a truly complex, believable, and interesting alien society.

You may think that you want the aliens in your story to remain strange and mysterious, but I assure you that you won't accomplish this by skipping the step of developing their evolutionary history. If you don't know why they are what they are, why they do what they do, then the result in your story will be mere vagueness. But if you know exactly why they do what they do, you'll develop their behavior with far more precision and detail; you'll come up with many surprising twists and turns, with genuine strangeness. You'll lead your readers to the brink of understanding why the aliens do what they do; the mystery comes from the fact that the reader is never quite sure. But *you* are sure.

Read enough science fiction, and you can almost always tell the difference between the writer who has done the development and the writer who's faking it.

### History

Even when you're working entirely with human societies, a vital part of world creation is knowing the history of communities in the story. You can't just put a demagogic preacher in your town, leading a mob of self-righteous church people into a book-burning frenzy; the result is invariably caricature. Instead, take the time to figure out *why* these people are following the preacher, why they trust and believe him.

Don't settle for the cheap answer, either—"Because they're a bunch of dumb bigots" doesn't make for honest fiction. They may be acting like a mob in the climax of your story, but until that time they were all individuals, all different from each other, following that preacher for their own reasons.

Part of the reason is that he's charismatic. But what does "charisma" mean? Think of some specific events that must have happened. For instance, the reason Mick and Janna would follow Reverend Bucky Fay to hell and back is because when their baby was sick, he came into their home and looked into the baby's eyes and then cupped the baby's head in his hands and said, "I see you're only a few weeks gone from the presence of Jesus, and he sent you into this world to do great work. Satan has filled your body with disease, but you are such a magnificent glorious spirit that you have the power to fight it off within you—if you want to. But I can't ask you to heal yourself, no sir. You can sense all the evil in the world, and you're so good and pure that I don't blame you if you decide not to live here a moment longer. But I beg you to stay. We need you."

The baby died a few days later, but instead of blaming Bucky Fay for not healing the infant, Mick and Janna felt sure their baby was so good that it simply couldn't bear to live in this wicked world. They tell the story to others, and because they speak with such fervency and belief, others believe them, too. Half their identity is based on the fact that God once chose them to be parents of one of his most perfect children; if they ever doubted Bucky Fay's spiritual insights, it would be like desecrating their lost baby's grave.

Now, maybe you won't even use an incident like that in the story. But you *know* it, and because it's there in the history of that town, the people in that mob are no longer strangers to you, no longer puppets to make go through the actions you want them to perform. They've come alive, they have souls—and your story will be richer and more truthful because of it.

## Biography

You'll also know more about Reverend Bucky Fay, too. You'll have pieces of his biography. And when it comes to fiction, biography isn't just a matter of filling out a résumé—when was he born, how did he do in school, what did he get his degree in, is he married or single or divorced? What matters with fiction is *why*.

Why did Bucky Fay ever go into the ministry? Was he once a believer? When he does things like that scene with Mick and Janna's baby, does he believe, or half-believe, the things he's saying? Or does he think of these people as unbelievably dumb suckers? Or is he consumed with guilt? Or has he come to believe that he has the power to "see" things about other people, simply because everybody else believes what he says? Maybe this is how prophecy felt to Moses, he says to himself. Maybe he just kind of made stuff up, only whatever came to mind turned out to be true because God was in him.

The more you know about what has happened in a character's past *and why*, the more complex and interesting the world of your story will be. The people, societies, all will seem real.

## 4. LANGUAGE

How does each community within your story speak? If you have people from more than one nation, they might well speak different languages; if they're from different worlds, they certainly will.

Perhaps there's a lingua franca, a trading language like Pidgin in the Pacific, or Swahili in East Africa, or English in India, that few speak as their native tongue, but everyone speaks well enough to communicate with each other. Some writers go so far as to actually *create* the various languages—look at Tolkien's *The Lord of the Rings*—but you don't really need to do that.

In fact, you probably shouldn't. For one thing, you're likely to embarrass yourself. Not many of us are gifted and deeply educated linguists like Tolkien, whose fictional languages sound so real in part because they're all based, however loosely, on real human languages.

### New Words for New Meanings

Nothing is more tacky than to have a bunch of foreign-sounding words thrown into a story for no better reason than to have something that sounds foreign. James Blish called such needlessly coined words "shmeerps." If it looks like a rabbit and acts like a rabbit, calling it a *shmeerp* doesn't make it alien.

If *mugubasala* means "bread," then say *bread!* Only use the made-up stuff when it is used for a concept for which there *is* no English word. If your viewpoint character *thinks* that *mugubasala* is nothing but bread, then later discovers that it is prepared through a special process that releases a drug from the native grain, and that drug turns out to be the source of the telepathic power the natives are suspected of having, then you are fully justified in calling the bread *mugubasala*. It really *is* different, and deserves the added importance that a foreign name bestows.

In Portuguese there's a common idiomatic expression based on the verb *dar*, to give. You ask someone, "Será que dá p'ra entrar?" and he answers, "Não dá." A literal translation would be "Will it give to enter?" and the answer means "It doesn't give." But that conveys none of the sense. When you say "Does it give?" to do something, it means "Is it possible? Is it proper? Is it right? Will it be resisted? Is it safe?" Yet not one of these terms actually conveys the precise meaning. In fact, in English there *is* no word or expression that conveys the exact meaning.

---

Your invented languages *should* have concepts that just can't be translated, not so that you can toss in cool-sounding phrases like "Hlobet mesh nay beggessahn dohlerem," but rather so that you can develop—and the reader can understand—the cultural and intellectual differences between cultures.

But don't leave those phrases untranslated. The commonly accepted way to handle this is to repeat the foreign phrase in English immediately afterward—provided your viewpoint character understands the language.

"Eu só queria tomar cafezinho," I said. All I wanted was a little coffee.

Indeed, you never actually have to use the foreign language itself to convey the same effect. After all, presumably you're translating *all* the dialogue and narration of all your stories that aren't set in contemporary English-speaking society—so why arbitrarily choose a few words to leave untranslated, especially if the word isn't important to the story?

"God give me strength not to kill you for having seen my ugliness," he said to me.

I blinked once, then realized that he was speaking Samvoric and had given me the ritual greeting between equals. I hadn't heard Samvoric in a long time, but it still sounded more natural to me than Common Speech. "God forgive me for not blinding myself at once after having beheld your glory," I said.

Then we grinned and licked each other's cheeks. He tasted like sweat. On a cold day like this, that meant he'd either been drinking or working hard. Probably both.

There's not one made up word in the whole paragraph (except for the name of the language, of course), and yet you definitely get the idea that you're dealing with a foreign language—a whole foreign culture, in fact.

(If you *are* using a known foreign language, by the way, take the time and effort to get it right. Among your readers there will always be someone who speaks that language like a native. If you get it wrong, those readers lose faith in you—and rightly so. Wherever you *can* be truthful, you *should* be truthful; if your readers can see that you're acting by that credo, they'll trust you, and you'll deserve their trust. But if they catch you faking it, and doing it so carelessly that you can easily be caught, they'll figure that if the story wasn't worth much effort to you, it shouldn't be worth much to them, either. They may still like the story, but you have blunted the edge of their passion.)

## Can the Human Mouth Pronounce It?

Be careful, too, that the language you invent is pronounceable for your English-speaking readers. Words or names that are mere collections of odd letters, like *xxyqhhp* or *h'psps't* are doubly dumb, first because they constantly distract the reader and force him to withdraw from the story and think about the letters on the page, and second because even strange and difficult languages, when translated into the Roman alphabet, will follow Roman alphabetic conventions.

If you doubt it, look at how languages as diverse as Chinese, Navaho, Arabic, Greek, and Quechua are represented in Roman characters. They're meaningless to those who don't speak the language, and when you pronounce them as written, they won't sound much like a real language, either. But you *can* pronounce them, after a fashion. And therefore they don't distract you from the story, but rather help the world of the story seem more real and complete.

This especially applies to alien and foreign names. You want that name to be an instant label for the character or place—but you must remember that it can't be a merely *visual* label. Even though most of your readers don't move their lips, you must take into account the fact that many (if not most) readers have a strong oral component to their reading. In our minds, we're reading aloud, and if we run into a word or name that can't be pronounced, it stops us cold. The visual symbols—the letters—are continuously translated into the sounds of the spoken language in our minds. And for those of us who read that way, names like Ahxpsxqwt are perpetual stumbling blocks.

## Subsets of English

Most of the time, though, the made-up languages in your story will all be English. Or, rather, a subset of English.

Every community develops jargon—words that have meaning within the context of that community, but have no meaning, or different meanings, to outsiders. Anthony Burgess's *A Clockwork Orange* is an extreme example of this, as the reader is almost overwhelmed by the strange and at-first-incomprehensible slang of the street hoodlums. Yet so artfully designed is his future street slang that in fact you grasp the meanings of most expressions intuitively, and quickly learn the other from context. Within a few pages you think you've been speaking this slang all your life.

But Burgess is better than most of us—his invented slang is so effective because he actually understands the many mechanisms by which slang develops: circumlocution, euphemism, rhymes, irony, foreign borrowings, and many, many more. When he had his characters use the word *horror-show* for "really neat," he was, in part, following the same path that, years later, led to the use among American black youths of the word *bad* to mean "really neat."

You don't have to go to Burgess's extremes in order to use made-up languages effectively—indeed, you probably shouldn't. Invented languages are a lot more fun to make up than they are to wade through in a story. Most of the time, you'll use just a few terms to *imply* a jargon or slang or cant, just as you use only a few phrases to establish that two characters are speaking a known foreign language.

## 5. SCENERY

This is the part that most people think of when they talk about world creation: coming up with a star system and a planet and an alien landscape. You calculate the diameter and mass of the planet, its periods of rotation and revolution, its distance from the sun, its angle of inclination, any satellites it might have, the brightness of the sun, its age.

The result is a very precise set of measurements: the surface gravity; the surface temperature; whether or not there's an atmosphere and, if there is one, what it's made of and what the prevailing winds are like; the climate in various regions of the planet; its oceans and continents (if any); tides; and, finally, the likelihood of life and the kind of life it would have.

The result can range from fairly simple things—low-gravity planets with very tall trees and animals; fast-spinning planets with high winds and very short day-night cycles; planets that don't rotate at all, so that life is only possible in a very narrow band—to complex systems that give rise to a whole novel's worth of possibilities.

A couple of examples. Robert Forward's novel *Dragon's Egg* came from a very simple proposal: What kind of life might emerge on the surface of a neutron star? The result was one of the best pure-science novels ever written, in which the coming of an exploratory starship from Earth, first seen as a light in the sky, gives rise to the first stirrings of intelligence and curiosity among the rudimentary life forms on the neutron star's surface. Yet because the star spins so fast and time flows so swiftly for these flat, heavy creatures, by the time the human starship actually arrives, these aliens we inadvertently created have already developed spaceflight and have advanced past our primitive technological level.

Indeed, Forward is the epitome of the "hard" science fiction writer. Himself a physicist of some note, Forward's approach to fiction is almost entirely from the scientific angle. Though he's a fine storyteller, the story is always the servant of the scientific idea.

And for a large group of readers and writers of science fiction, this is the only correct approach to the field. Their preference is for the hard sciences: physics, chemistry, astronomy, geology. They consider zoology and botany to be rather suspect, and as for the "sciences" of sociology, psychology, anthropology, and archaeology, it is to laugh—to them, the social sciences are just subsets of history, an art more literary than evidentiary, speculative rather than measurable.

To hear some hard-SF people talk, you'd think they invented science fiction and all these writers of anthropological or literary or adventure SF are Johnny-come-latelies. Alas, it is not so—anthropological and literary and adventure SF all predate hard SF. But for a long time, starting with John W. Campbell's editorship of *Astounding* magazine, the hard stuff, the stories that took science very, very seriously, were the very best work being published in the field. The cutting edge.

Today the cutting edge has moved on—it always does—but more than any other kind of science fiction, hard SF has maintained a core of loyal supporters. *Analog* magazine, while no longer the leading publication when award time comes around, still has a larger circulation than any of the other fiction-only magazines, even though its stories fall into a very narrow subset of the field. Indeed, *Analog* seems to be the only magazine that regularly publishes formula stories, but the formulas work within the hard-SF tradition:

1. Independent thinker comes up with great idea; bureaucrats screw everything up; independent thinker straightens it all out and puts bureaucrats in their place. (This story appeals to scientists and their fans because it is a reversal of the pattern in the real world, in which scientists generally prosper according to their ability to attract grant money from

---

bureaucrats, a relationship that forces scientists, who see themselves as an intellectual elite, into subservience.)

2. Something strange is happening; independent thinker comes along and after many false hypotheses, finally discovers the surprising answer. (This formula is a reenactment of the scientific method, but endowed with far more drama than scientists ever experience in real life.)

3. A new machine/discovery is being tested; something goes wrong and it looks like everybody's going to die; then, after mighty efforts, either everybody dies (tragedy) or everybody lives (happy ending).

Under the editorship of Stanley Schmidt, this approach seems to be inexhaustible, and it is impossible to argue with *Analog's* circulation figures compared to the other SF-only magazines. However, while the hard-SF audience remains loyal, the rest of the field has passed on by. The only stories to rise out of *Analog* and attract attention in the field at large are the ones that either *don't* follow these formulas or transcend them.

What separates the best hard-SF writers from the run-of-the-mill ones is the fact that while the ordinary guys usually invent the scenery of their created world and maybe work up a good evolutionary track for the life forms there, they then resort to clichés for everything else. Characters, societies, events—all are taken straight out of everything else they've ever read. That's why formulas are resorted to so often.

That's why one of the most annoying things about *Analog* fiction—annoying to me, at least—is the way that most stories there show little knowledge of fundamental human systems. Writers who wouldn't dream of embarrassing themselves with a faulty calculation of atmospheric density don't even notice when their characters—whether scientists, government leaders, or gas station attendants; men or women; young or old—all talk and act and relate with other people like smart-mouth schoolboys.

The irony is that the prevalence of bad fiction in the hard-SF subgenre has led many to think that hard science fiction, by its nature, *must* be bad. Indeed, some of the great writers in the field, who first became famous during the heyday of Campbellian hard science fiction in the 1940s and 1950s, have suffered a bit of tainting by association with their supposed successors in hard SF in recent years.

What we should learn from the bad writing so common in hard-SF circles today is not that hard sf can't be written well—we have Asimov, Clarke, Niven and Clement, Sheffield and Forward to prove otherwise—but rather that there is a tremendous opportunity in the area of hard science fiction for talented, skilled storytellers who have also mastered enough of the hard sciences to speak to this audience. The audience does not insist on bad writing, merely on good science; if they are offered good science *and* good writing, they almost invariably provide such an author with a very long, secure, and well-paid career.

On the other hand, many of us who write "soft" (anthropological or socio-logical), literary, or adventure science fiction have made the mistake of shunning the precise sciences in our storytelling. Most of us skip the whole issue by setting all our stories on planets "very much like Earth" or on worlds that have already been fully invented by other writers. Just like the weakest of the hard-SF writers, we concentrate only on the things that interest us—social structures, elegant prose, or grand romantic adventures—and completely ignore what doesn't. To the extent that we who are now the mainstream of science fiction ignore the hard sciences in our world creation, we are as guilty of shallowness as the hard-SF writers who pay no heed to social systems, characters, and plots.

There are some writers who have done it all at once. Larry Niven, for instance, is known as one of the great hard-SF writers—but I, for one, am of the opinion that he is a leading writer in our field because he is one of the best and clearest *storytellers* we've ever had. He works in the hard sciences to create worlds and generate his ideas—but what makes him one of our great writers is the quality of the tales he tells within those worlds.

Perhaps the most notable recent example of fiction that does it all is Brian Aldiss's brilliant and ambitious Helliconia trilogy: *Helliconia Spring, Helliconia Summer,* and *Helliconia Winter.* Conceived and executed as a Great Work, the entire story takes place on a planet that orbits two binary stars. Not only is there a fairly normal annual cycle of seasons, but also there is a thousand-year cycle of super-seasons. As the planet draws near to the larger star, the overall climate becomes almost unbearably hot; as it recedes, warmed only by the smaller, cooler star, the planet becomes so cold that it almost completely freezes over. All life on the planet, including human life and society, has adapted to the millennial cycle.

---

As literary, anthropological, and romantic science fiction the trilogy is unexceptionable; it is also excellent hard science fiction. Most of this is due to Aldiss's genius and to his unflagging integrity as a storyteller; part, though, is surely due to the fact that he is British, not American, and Britain has largely escaped the ghettoizing process that has long afflicted American letters. Not only is science fiction itself not so firmly subdivided, nor SF so thoroughly split from fantasy, but also the whole speculative fiction field is viewed by the British literary mainstream as a legitimate area for a "real" writer to venture into. After all, it was Britain that produced H. G. Wells, Aldous Huxley, and George Orwell, honoring them as great British writers, not just as great British writers of science fiction. Thus Aldiss—like many other British writers—has remained immune to the insularity that so often makes American writers of speculative fiction use only a fraction of the tools available to storytellers.

So, if you have a bent toward hard science fiction, I urge you to broaden your scope and expect all your stories to be good fiction as well as good science. And even if you have little interest in hard science fiction, I urge you to broaden your scope and explore the possibilities that the hard sciences offer to the storyteller. And even if you know nothing about the hard sciences—even if you think you want only to write fantasy—I suggest that you get your first overview of the sciences by reading as much fiction by the great hard-SF writers of the 1940s, 1950s, and 1960s as you possibly can. You'll come out marvelously entertained—with a good survey of what the cutting edge of science was at the time each story was written.

I firmly believe that a good storyteller's education never ends, because to tell stories perfectly you have to know everything about everything. Naturally, none of us actually achieves such complete knowledge—but we should live as if we were trying to do so. You can't afford to close off any area of inquiry. Writing the same book, I recently called upon ideas I learned from reading Robert Caro's biography of Lyndon Johnson, *The Path to Power*; the detailed reference work on medieval village society, *The Lost Country Life*; Rafael Sabatini's romance *Captain Blood*; Clifford Geertz's *Interpretation of Cultures*; and Plato's *Symposium*. Who knows how much better my novel might have been had I only read a half dozen other books, or examined a dozen other subjects that I'm still hopelessly ignorant of?

In creating the strange milieu in which your story takes place, you must first understand as well as you possibly can the familiar milieu in which your own life is taking place. Until you have examined and comprehended the world around you, you can't possibly create a complex and believable imaginary world.

Indeed, one of the greatest values of speculative fiction is that creating a strange imaginary world is often the best way to help readers see the real world through fresh eyes and notice things that would otherwise remain unnoticed. Speculative fiction is not an escape from the real world, and writing it is not a way to have a literary career without having to research anything! Speculative fiction instead provides a lens through which to view the real world better than it could ever be seen with the natural eye.

In other words: You can't know too much.

# CHAPTER 3

# Story Construction

You have your world, so deep and rich that you can hardly wait to get started with the story itself. The trouble is that you don't know yet what's supposed to happen in the story. In fact, you don't even know whom the story's about.

Sometimes this isn't a problem—sometimes it's the character you think of first, and the world creation comes after. Sometimes you already know the whole story.

Or do you? The process of world creation should have changed many aspects of your main character, just as character development changes the world. At some point you began to wonder why your main character ever came to this place. (That's where many of the best ideas come from—sitting around wondering about why things are the way they are in your fictional world.) As you thought of answers to that question, you decided that she has a family, including a younger sister that she's always been jealous of, and the reason she first left her home world for this colony was to get away from her sister. Now her sister has arrived in the colony—as the administrator in charge of the very program your character works in!

Your basic story outline may well remain the same: Your main character, Jia, discovers that the desert scavengers on this planet, called scabs, are actually sentient (literally "sensible" or "feeling") creatures deserving protection. Yet at the same time, her team of xenobiologists has succeeded in developing a biobomb that will wipe out the scabs to save the colony's crops. Nothing in your world creation has caused you to change this basic story.

But now everything is complicated by the fact that it's Jia's younger sister, Wu Li, who will make the final decision about deploying the plague that will exterminate the scabs. The story is now pulling the reader along in two ways at once: The reader cares about saving an endangered people, the scabs; and the reader sympathizes with Jia's family problems, and how hard it will be for her to swallow her pride.

In your original idea, you figured that Jia's team leader was the kind of martinet who went by the book and refused to consider the idea that the scabs were sentient. It was time to deploy, so the team leader was going to deploy. This sort of stock villain is a serviceable device for moving a plot along, but there's nothing to interest the reader. Now that the team leader is Wu Li, if you stick with that original plan and make Wu Li act out the part of an unmitigated jerk, you're going to be short-circuiting your own creative process. Because Wu Li and Jia are sisters with a long history between them, your story can— *must*—be transformed.

For instance: Jia "knows" that Wu Li will never listen to her, because in all their lives together Wu Li has deliberately rejected everything Jia asked her to do. So instead of reporting her findings to Wu Li, Jia can only think to stop the biobomb by sabotaging the project. When Jia is caught, she triumphantly tells her sister that the scabs are now safe; whereupon her sister makes it clear that if she had only known the scabs were sentient, she would have halted the project immediately. In fact, Wu Li was already concerned that the scabs had not been adequately studied before the previous team leader had made the decision to develop a biobomb against them. If Jia had only talked to her, they could have worked together to meet the colony's need to save their crops without wiping out the scabs.

Now, though, Jia has gone off on her own and sabotaged the project, and despite her excellent motives, there's no way she can be trusted again. Her career is over—if Wu Li reports her. Jia, still rejoicing at the fact that Wu Li believes her about the scabs' sentience, assumes that Wu Li will smooth over the whole incident and they can work together from now on. But Wu Li, weeping bitterly, refuses—she is not going to sacrifice her own integrity, even to protect her sister. The incident will be reported accurately; Jia's career is over.

---

This sets you up for a powerful scene in which Jia, angry and bitter at what she sees as her sister's disloyalty to her, nevertheless goes out into the desert with Wu Li and shows her everything she's discovered, including introducing her to the one scab with whom she has established a kind of communication. She's doing it for the scabs' sake, she tells herself—but the readers understand that it is really a kind of reconciliation with her sister. Jia now realizes that she *can* trust Wu Li implicitly, that Wu Li's integrity is so great that she can be trusted to treat the scabs properly.

Perhaps you'll write the story so that Jia knows that the blame is her own, that if only she had trusted her sister before, her own career would not be over. Or perhaps you'll leave her blind to her own failings, so that even as she tells Wu Li all she knows, Jia hates her and will never forgive her. This is perhaps the most painful ending, because your readers will be torn, wishing Wu Li had been more merciful to her sister, but also understanding that Jia is wrong and the ultimate fault is with her.

But you must notice that the most powerful aspects of this story were not in your original idea. In that version the team leader was a cliché villain, the bureaucrat who won't listen to a new idea. In that version, the sabotage of the project was the end of the story. What good would all your world creation do if now you stick with that original story plan? Your reader would probably feel quite dissatisfied at the end; the alert ones would be wondering why you bothered to make the team leader her sister since it made no difference in the plot.

You have to be willing to change *anything* during the creation phase; only that way can you make the story be true to yourself. There's nothing sacred about your original idea—it was just a starting point. The final story may end up being completely different. In fact, in the story we've been talking about, you may even discover that Jia isn't really the main character anymore. It's Wu Li who has the most painful decision to make—whether to report her sister's sabotage and ruin her career, or save her sister but perhaps endanger other projects because of her sister's proven instability. So instead of telling the story from Jia's point of view, as you always planned, now you realize you must tell it from Wu Li's viewpoint.

The story is nothing like what you first thought it would be. But so what? It's *better*—richer, deeper, truer—than that original idea. The idea did its work: It got you thinking. After that, if you feel bound to stick to it no matter what, that idea becomes a ball and chain that you drag with you through the whole process. Stick with it and you'll get nowhere. Cut it loose and you can fly.

So whether you think you already know your story or have no idea what should happen in your newly created world, you can still benefit from going through the following steps in working up the structure of your tale.

## 1. WHOSE STORY IS THIS?

When you're deciding whom the story is about, remember that the "hero," the main character, and viewpoint character *don't* have to be the same person.

Most of us use the term *hero* as an informal synonym for "main character." But in our day we often have an antihero as our main character (or protagonist), and it's useful to keep a distinction in mind.

The *hero* is the character that the audience hopes will achieve his goals and desires—the character we're rooting for. There's a moral judgment involved here. We not only care what happens to him, we also *want him to win.*

But the hero isn't always the main character. Sometimes the most important character in a story, the one who makes everything happen, the one whose choices and struggles the story is *about*, is a slimeball, and we watch him in horrified fascination, hoping *somebody* will stop this guy. Sometimes we even sympathize with him, pitying him or even admiring some aspects of his character—but we still don't want him to achieve his goal.

The best example of this is M. J. Engh's masterpiece, *Arslan*, in which the title character is a conqueror whose atrocities at the beginning are only matched by his nihilistic plan for the world he now rules. He is a combination of Hitler and Genghis Khan. We want him to lose; yet we also understand and care about him, are fascinated by him, sometimes in awe of him. By the end of this novel—which I believe is one of the great works of literature in our time—we understand something about one of the great mysteries of modern life: why people loved and followed Hitler, Stalin, Mao, and others whose cruelty seemed boundless. In no way is Arslan the "hero," but he is definitely the main character of the book.

Yet at the beginning of the book you don't necessarily realize this, because the story is told from the point of view of the principal of the local high school. We are seeing events through his eyes as he witnesses Arslan's initial atrocities and then comes to know the conqueror as his enemy. The relationship between the principal and Arslan is very important throughout the story, and we have great sympathy toward the principal, but when, a third of the way through the book, the viewpoint shifts to another character, we are ready. The principal was our eyes and ears, and for a time he was the hero—the person we hoped would win—but he was never the person that the story was about.

By no means is it a rule, but it's often a good idea, when your main character is an antihero, to have secondary characters who can function as the focus of your readers' sympathy—in other words, heroes. They don't have to occupy center stage, but they often provide a clarifying moral center. However, if the point of your story is that there *are* no heroes, then this advice doesn't apply—assemble your cast of rakes and racketeers, sleazebags and slimeballs, wimps and wastrels, losers and liars, and have at it.

### The Main Character

In choosing the main character for your story, there are a couple of questions you need to consider:

### Who Hurts the Most?

In the world you have invented, who suffers the most? Chances are that it is among the characters who are in pain that you will find your main character, partly because your readers' sympathy will be drawn toward a suffering character, and partly because a character in pain is a character who wants things to change. He's likely to *act.* Of course, a character who suffers a lot and then dies won't be a productive main character unless your story is about his life after death. But your eye should be drawn toward pain. Stories about contented people are miserably dull.

### Who Has the Power and Freedom to Act?

Your eye should also be drawn toward movement. Characters who are powerless aren't likely to be doing anything terribly interesting. Your main character usually needs to be somebody active, somebody who can change things in the world, even if it's a struggle.

Remember that you look for people with both the power *and* the freedom to act. Too often—particularly in medieval fantasy—writers think their stories must be about rulers. Kings and queens, dukes and duchesses—they can be extravagantly powerful, yes, but too often they aren't free at all. If you understand the workings of power in human societies, you'll know that the greatest freedom to act in unpredictable ways is usually found away from the centers of power.

Let me give you an example: the television and movie series *Star Trek*. The original series creator wanted characters with the power to make decisions, and centered on the captain and the executive officer of a military starship. Unfortunately, however, as anyone who knows anything about the military will tell you, the commanders of ships and armies don't have many interesting adventures. They're almost always at headquarters, making the big decisions and sending out the orders to the people who do the physically dangerous work.

In other words, the lives of commanders (and kings) are generally above the most interesting action. The really neat stuff is going to be happening to the people on the cutting edge—frontline troops, scouts, the people who get beamed down to the planet's surface to find out what's going on. It would be insane for the commander of a ship or any of the highest officers to leave their posts and do common reconnaissance. In any real starfleet there would be teams of trained explorers, diplomats, and scientists ready to venture forth at the commander's orders. If *Star Trek* had been about one such team, the stories would have been inherently plausible—and there would have been room for tension between the ship's officers and the exploration teams, a rich vein of story possibilities that was virtually untapped.

Instead, *Star Trek* centered around the characters with the highest prestige who, in a realistic world, would have the least freedom. But since commanding officers who behaved like commanding officers would make boring television, the writers simply allowed these characters to go exploring, constantly leaving their duties on the starship as they merrily went about getting kidnapped, lost, beaten up, or whatever the plot of the week required. Any captain of a ship or commander of an army who behaved like Captain Kirk would be stripped of command for life. But the series would not have worked otherwise.

At this point you must be saying to yourself, "I should be so lucky as to make mistakes like *Star Trek*—I could use a few bestsellers." But the point I'm making is that *Star Trek* could not possibly have succeeded if the captain had actually behaved like a captain. Centering the series around a commanding officer was such a bad mistake that the show immediately corrected for the error by never, for one moment, having Kirk *behave* like a captain.

While a television show can get away with having a captain who acts like the leader of an exploratory team, the readers of prose science fiction have no tolerance for such nonsense. If your hero needs to act like a landing team leader or an industrial spy or a frontline grunt, then you'd better not make him an admiral or a general or a corporate CEO.

Novice writers continue to make this same mistake, choosing as the main character people who don't—or shouldn't—have enough freedom to be interesting. If the story is about a great war, they assume their hero must be the commanding general or the king, when in fact the story might be most powerfully told if the main character is a sergeant or a common soldier—someone who is making choices and then carrying out those choices *himself.* Or the main character might even be a civilian, whose life is transformed as the great events flow over and around him. Think of the movie *Shenandoah,* and then imagine what the story might have been if Jimmy Stewart had played the commander of an army corps. A character who is a loner or who leads a small group—a squad of soldiers, a single family—has so much more freedom to act than people in high office that it's far easier to tell stories about them.

Sometimes the main character *must* be the commander, of course. But don't just assume that to be the case. In fact, a good rule of thumb is to start with the assumption that your story is *not* about the king or president, the admiral or general, the CEO or the hospital administrator. Only move to the characters in positions of highest authority when you are forced to because the story can't be told any other way. And then be very sure that you understand how people in such positions make their decisions, how power actually works.

Think of the movie *Dirty Harry.* Whatever you may think of the moral message of the film, the author was aware of the fact that real policeman don't go around blowing people's brains out week after week. Yet that was precisely the cliché on television and in the movies in those days—cops who were, in essence, quick-draw gunfighters transposed from the dusty streets of Dodge City to the asphalt of New York or L.A. So the writer played with that cliché—he created a character who, precisely because he acted like a western sheriff, was always in trouble with his superiors.

Furthermore, just like the cliché cops on TV, his partners were constantly getting shot—but in *Dirty Harry* people actually noticed this and considered an assignment as Harry's partner to be a virtual death sentence. They *blamed* him and he actually had to live with the consequences of his decisions. Whatever else the filmmakers might have done wrong, they certainly did one thing right: They knew something about how a police department works and took that into account in developing their main character. Or at least they did it better than most other cop stories of that time.

Who is your story about? A person who has a strong reason to want the situation to change—and has both the power and freedom to set about trying to change it.

## The Protagonist

Who do we hope succeeds? Usually you'll want your audience's sympathy to be with your main character, if only because it's a lot harder for a writer to make an anti-hero work well in a story. But sometimes you can't get away from the fact that wherever the action is, the story must follow. If all the important and interesting choices are being made by the bad guy—especially if the climax depends on what the bad guy does—chances are he's the main character of your story whether you like it or not.

Take the *Star Wars* movie, *Return of the Jedi*. The first two movies had focused on Luke Skywalker, Princess Leia, and Han Solo—but it was clear that the story was *about* Luke Skywalker. As the movies became hits and penetrated American culture, however, a curious thing was happening. An extraordinary number of children seemed to admire the monstrous villain, Darth Vader. Why did they want to act out the part of this casual murderer?

I suspect it's because, no matter how busy the good guys were, everything they did was in reaction to Darth Vader. *He* was the one calling the shots. He was the one with the power and freedom to act—and, too, he was made somewhat sympathetic by the fact that his body had been ruined and he depended on a machine for survival.

Darth Vader was also the most mysterious—how did he become the way he is? Why did he turn to the dark side of the force? How did he become so powerful? This sense of mystery and awe is one of the things you must look for when searching for the main character of your story. The audience is drawn to the strange, the powerful, the inexplicable.

By the third movie, probably without any of the filmakers being aware of it, Darth Vader was the main character, even though Luke, Leia, and Han remained protagonists. Yes, they have neat adventures and discover things about each other (Don't kiss me Luke; you're my long-lost brother), but all of these events are just devices to get them ready for their confrontation with the one character whose choices actually matter: Darth Vader. It's no accident that the climax of *Return of the Jedi* is Darth Vader's choice to turn against the evil emperor and save the life of his son—his choice to reject the dark side of the force. Everything came down to Darth Vader's choice. He was the center of the film. It was *his* story. And yet we never, not once, hoped that he would win.

## The Viewpoint Character

Often—perhaps I should say *usually*—your main character will also be your viewpoint character. Since I've written a book that is in large measure about what a viewpoint character is *(Character and Viewpoint),* I'm not going to say much more here than this: The viewpoint character is the person through whose eyes we see action. If it's a first-person narrative, then the viewpoint character is the person telling the tale. If it's a third-person narrative, then the viewpoint character is the person that we follow most closely, seeing not only what he does, but also why; seeing not only what he sees, but knowing how he interprets it, what he thinks about it.

A quick example, from Octavia Butler's novel *Wild Seed* (Warner/Popular Library/Questar, 1980/1988, pp. 138–39):

> "Anyanwu would say you have on your leopard face now," Isaac commented.
>
> Doro shrugged. He knew what Anyanwu would say, and that she meant it when she compared him to one kind of animal or another. Once she had said such things out of fear or anger. Now she said them out of grim hatred. She had made herself the nearest thing he had to an enemy. She obeyed. She was civil. But she could hold a grudge as no one Doro had ever known.

The viewpoint character at this moment is Doro, and so we are shown not only what was said, but also what Doro thinks of it, how he interprets it.

The passage tells of a conversation between Isaac and Doro, but it is largely *about* a character who is not present, Anyanwu. Obviously, though, she is very important to the viewpoint character, Doro. In fact, she is the protagonist of the story, the person whose side we are on, the person that we hope will win. Doro, on the other hand, is like Arslan and Darth Vader, in that his choices are the cause of almost everything that happens in the story—and his choices are often dark and terrible, so that we hope the good characters overcome him. He is the main character, an antihero whom we only gradually come to understand.

*Wild Seed* is thus about the struggle between the main character, Doro, and the protagonist, Anyanwu. And Butler quite properly alternates between the two of them as her viewpoint character. There are chapters from Anyanwu's point of view, so that we can see how she interprets events, what she wants, and why; and there are chapters from Doro's point of view, so we can also see the world the way he sees it and get some idea of his purposes. The story could probably be told from just one of these viewpoints—but it would be much harder for us to understand and sympathize with the character whose viewpoint we never saw.

But there are times when you simply can't do this. In mysteries, for instance, where the point of the story is to discover who committed the murder, it is traditional to make the viewpoint character the detective's sidekick. Why? Because the detective usually knows the identity of the murderer a good while before the end of the book. If he were the viewpoint character—if we were inside his head—the suspense would bleed away far too soon. So Nero Wolfe's stories are told by Archie Goodwin and Sherlock Holmes's by Dr. Watson.

There's another strategy, however, and that is to make the detective not be the main character of the novel. This is the strategy Ross MacDonald and other "hard-boiled detective" authors use. The detective is the viewpoint character— we see everything through his eyes—but the story's focus is on the characters caught up in the events surrounding the murder. Theirs are the lives in turmoil; they are the people in pain. While the detective often gets emotionally involved, he is not the person whose life needs to be resolved. And the suspense now is moved, at least in part, away from the question of whodunit and toward the question of how these people are going to reestablish their lives. Thus we can find out a bit earlier in the story who the murderer was—and still be eager to read on and discover the whole outcome.

Yet even when the viewpoint character is not the main character of a novel, he is nevertheless a major character, if only because we get to know him so well. So he has to be well developed, and his personal dilemmas must also be resolved by the end of the story or the audience will, quite properly, feel cheated.

Who should your viewpoint character be? If it isn't the main character or the protagonist, your viewpoint character must be someone in a position to see—and usually take part in—the major events of the story. If you find that your viewpoint character is constantly finding out about the most important events as people tell him about it after the fact, you can be almost certain you have chosen the wrong viewpoint character.

Here are some guidelines for choosing a viewpoint character who isn't the main character.

1. The viewpoint character must be present at the main events.

2. The viewpoint character must be actively involved in those events, not always a chance witness.

3. The viewpoint character must have a personal stake in the outcome, even though the outcome depends on the main character's choices.

(Of course, like all rules, these can be broken. You can have a viewpoint character who is *never* there for the main events—if your story is at least partly about the fact that he is frustrated because he constantly misses the important moments. But this moves your story toward comedy, which is fine if comedy is what you're writing; and it focuses your story on the viewpoint character's absence and not the events themselves. Break the rules if you like—but make sure you understand the consequences and know how to turn them to your story's advantage.)

## 2. WHERE DOES THE STORY BEGIN AND END?

Once again we find ourselves needing to distinguish between some terms that are often used interchangeably.

The *myth* of the story, as opposed to the *text*, consists of what happens and why. The myth is usually very simple, but it also begins long before the beginning and goes on long after the end. This is because causal chains are infinite. For instance, the story of Oedipus is usually thought to begin when his parents, to save themselves from the prophecy that their son will kill his father and marry his mother, bind his ankles and abandon him to die.

But the causal chain actually begins long before. The parents did what they did because they lived in a culture that believed in prophecy and in which it was not thought a heinous crime to leave a monstrous child to die. And there are reasons why their society adopted these beliefs and attitudes, and reasons for those reasons. The causal chain also continues long after—as we know from the plays *Oedipus at Colonus* and *Antigone,* which are about the consequences of the events and choices made in the play *Oedipus Rex.*

So the myth of the story is actually a long network of cause and effect that begins long before the story and continues long afterward. You, however, must choose a point where the story begins and a point where it ends. You must decide the story's structure.

## The Beginning That Sets Up the End

Let's go back to Octavia Butler's *Wild Seed.* The story is about Doro, a character born thousands of years ago. He is immortal, not because his body cannot die, but because whenever his body is about to die—or at other times—his spirit or essence immediately and involuntarily jumps to the nearest living person, taking over their body completely. Thus the displaced spirit ceases to exist, while Doro lives on in his victim's former body.

Butler could have begun *Wild Seed* with the scene of Doro's first transition from one body to another—the time when he first realized that he could not die. It is indeed a powerful scene, because the person he killed, the first person whose body he took, was his own mother. Not understanding what happened, he looked down and saw his old body—his own body, lying there dead in "his" arms—and panicked. How had he suddenly become a woman? He screamed; his father, trying to calm and comfort the person he thought was his wife, touched him and Doro inadvertently jumped to *his* body. Without meaning to, Doro discovered his powers by killing his own parents. It took a long time before he came to terms with what he was and what he had done. Those events could have been a novel in their own right.

In fact, that's one reason why Butler was correct not to begin *Wild Seed* with that event. She does include an account of his first killing—but it comes on page 177 of a 179-page book. It is a flashback, a memory. Receiving that memory makes the audience revise its view of Doro, so that we reinterpret all that he has done from the beginning. Yet by coming when it does, that event doesn't take over the book. It is one more piece fitted into the whole.

If it had come at the beginning, the event is so strong, so powerful, that the audience would have expected the whole story to be about Doro's struggle to know and control himself. It would have made Anyanwu a fairly minor character and perhaps a bit contrived. "Oh, right," we would say. "Doro is a slimeball until the love of a good woman transforms him. How convenient that she happens along."

Butler wanted to tell the story of Doro's relationship with Anyanwu, a woman with extraordinary talents on her own—a shapechanger, a healer. Butler's story ends when Anyanwu and Doro reach a sort of accommodation with each other—when Doro is at last able to love and respect another human being instead of regarding them all as his tools and subjects, when Anyanwu is at last able to reconcile herself to a world that includes a monster like Doro—and reconcile herself to the fact that she understands and, in a way, loves him despite his monstrousness. The only way Butler could do that was to make Doro and Anyanwu equal in our eyes—and if we spend the first fifty pages of the novel watching Doro struggle with his powers several thousand years before Anyanwu is born, that balance between them would be almost impossible to achieve.

All that I've said, however, comes with hindsight. Perhaps Butler was aware of all this; perhaps she wasn't. I haven't asked her. What matters is that there *is* a way to determine where a story should begin and end.

Since the story will end with their accommodation with each other, the story must begin in such a way that the audience will expect that ending. That is, the beginning must make the audience ask questions that are answered by the story's ending, so that when they reach that ending they recognize that the story is over.

The beginning of a story creates tension in the audience, makes them feel a *need*. The ending of that story comes when that tension is eased, when that need is satisfied. So in determining your structure, it is essential for you to make sure your beginning creates the need that your ending will satisfy; or that your ending satisfies the need that your beginning created!

You'd be amazed how many stories fail precisely because the writer began one story and ended another. Or began the story long after it should have begun, or long before. Yet how can you know where your story should begin, or what the right ending is? Most writers learn to do this instinctively—or never do it at all. But there is a way to look at your own story, discover the possible structures, and choose among them.

## The MICE Quotient

All stories contain four elements that can determine structure: Milieu, Idea, Character, and Event. While each is present in every story, there is generally one that dominates the others.

Which one dominates? The one that the author cares about most. This is why the process of discovering the structure of a story is usually a process of self-discovery. Which aspect of the story matters most to you? That is the aspect that will give you your story's structure.

Let's take each element in turn and look at the structure that would be required if that is the dominant element in the story.

### The Milieu Story

The milieu is the world—the planet, the society, the weather, the family, all the elements that came up during the world creation phase. Every story has a milieu, but in some stories the milieu is the thing the storyteller cares about most. For instance, in *Gulliver's Travels*, Swift cared little about whether we came to care about Gulliver as a character. The whole point of the story was for the audience to see all the strange lands where Gulliver traveled and then compare the societies he found there with the society of England in Swift's own day—and the societies of all the tale's readers, in all times and places.

So it would have been absurd to begin by spending a lot of time on Gulliver's childhood and upbringing. The real story began the moment Gulliver got to the first of the book's strange lands, and it ended when he came home.

Milieu stories always follow that structure. An observer who will see things as we would see them gets to the strange place, sees all the things that are interesting, is transformed by what he sees, and then comes back a new man. Stephen Boyett's *Architect of Sleep* follows that structure, as a modern man passes through a cave in Florida and comes out in a world in which it is the raccoon and not the ape that gave rise to a sentient species. He is the only human in a world of brainy raccoons.

But it isn't only in science fiction and fantasy that this structure occurs. James Clavell's *Shogun,* for instance, follows exactly the same structure. It begins when his European hero is stranded in medieval Japan and ends when he leaves. He was transformed by his experiences in Japan, but he does not stay—he returns to "our" world. Other stories are told along the way—the story of the shogun, for instance—but however we care about those events, the closure we expect at the end of the story is the main character's departure from Japan.

Likewise, *The Wizard of Oz* doesn't end when Dorothy kills the Wicked Witch of the West. It ends when Dorothy leaves Oz and goes home to Kansas.

As you work with your story, if you realize that what you care about most is having a stranger explore and discover the world you've created, chances are that you'll want to follow the Milieu Story structure. Then your beginning point is obvious—when the stranger arrives—and the ending is just as plain—the story doesn't end until he leaves (or, in a variant, he finally decides not to leave, ending the question of going home).

And who is your viewpoint character? The stranger, of course. The milieu is seen through his eyes, since he will be surprised by and interested in the same strange and marvelous (and terrible) things that surprise and interest the audience.

### The Idea Story

"Ideas" in this sense are the new bits of information that are discovered in the process of the story by characters who did not previously know that information. Idea Stories are *about* the process of finding out that information. The structure here is very simple: The Idea Story begins by raising a question; it ends when the question is answered.

Most mystery stories follow this structure. The story begins when a murder takes place; the question we ask is, Who did it and why? The story ends when the identity and motive of the killer are revealed.

In the field of speculative fiction, a similar structure is quite common. The story begins with a question: Why did this beautiful ancient civilization on a faraway planet come to an end? Why are all these people gone, when they were once so wise and their achievements were so great? The answer, in Arthur C. Clarke's "The Star," is that their sun went nova, making life impossible in their star system. And, ironically, it was the explosion of their star that the wise men saw as the sign of the birth of Christ. The story is told from the point of view of a Christian who, like most of the audience at the time Clarke wrote the story, will believe that this must have been a deliberate act of God, to destroy a beautiful civilization for the sake of giving a sign to the magi.

Many other stories follow this pattern. A question is raised:

Who buried this monolith on the moon, and why did it give off a powerful radio signal when we uncovered it?

Why did this young man try to kill himself after his brother was drowned in a storm while they were boating together, and why is he so hostile to everyone now?

The story may take many twists and turns along the way, but it ends when the question is finally answered:

In *2001: A Space Odyssey*, we find out that the monolith was left for us to find, so that when we reached it the master race that created it would know we were ready to move on to the next stage in our evolution.

In *Ordinary People*, we find out that the main character tried to kill himself because he believes that his mother blames him for not dying in his brother's place; and he discovers that he has been lashing out at everyone around him because he can't express his anger at his brother for letting go of the hull of the boat—for dying.

When the mystery is resolved, whether by a detective, a scientist, or a psychiatrist, the main tension is resolved and the story is over. So Idea Stories begin as close to the point where the question is first raised and end as soon as possible after the question is answered.

You may notice that some mysteries don't reach the discovery of the body until many pages into the story. Aren't they following the Idea Story structure? In most cases they are, but they can bend the rule about starting with the question because the mystery tradition is now so well established that mystery readers take it for granted that someone will be killed; they're willing to wait a little while to find out who dies. Thus mystery writers have the freedom to spend quite a few pages establishing the character of the detective or setting up the society in which the murder will take place. But the audience is quite aware that a murder *will* take place, and soon becomes impatient if the writer takes too long getting to it.

------------------------------------------------------------------------

Outside the mystery genre, there is a good deal less leeway because the audience doesn't know that the story will be about the process of answering a question. If you begin the story by establishing character at great length and don't come to the main question until many pages into the tale, readers will expect the story to be about the character, and not about the question; if you then end the story where the mystery is solved but never resolve the character, they'll be quite frustrated. You must begin the story you intend to end—unless you *know* that the audience already knows what the story is about.

## The Character Story

All stories have characters, and in one sense stories are almost always "about" one or more characters. In most stories, though, the tale is not about the character's character; that is, the story is not about who the character is.

The Character Story is a story about the transformation of a character's role in the communities that matter most to him. The Indiana Jones movies are Event Stories, not Character Stories. The story is always about what Indiana Jones *does*, but never who he *is*. Jones has many problems and adventures, but at the end of the movie his role in society is exactly what it was before—part-time archaeology professor and full-time knight-errant.

By contrast, Carson McCuller's *Member of the Wedding* is about a young girl's longing to change her role in the only community she knows—her household, her family. She determines that she wants to belong to her brother and his new wife; "they are the we of me," she decides. In the effort to become part of their marriage she is thwarted—but in the process her role in the family and in the world at large *is* transformed, and at the end of the story she is not who she was. *Member of the Wedding* is a Character Story; the Indiana Jones movies are not.

It is a common misconception that all good stories must have full characterization. This is not quite true. All good Character Stories *must* have full characterization, because that's what they're about; and other kinds of stories *can* have full characterization, as long as the reader is not misled into expecting a Character Story when that is not what is going to be delivered. On the other hand, many excellent Milieu, Idea, and Event Stories spend very little effort on characterization beyond what is necessary to keep the story moving. The Indiana Jones stories don't require us to get more of Jones than his charm and his courage. In short, he is what he does in the story, and while it's delightful to meet his father and learn something of his background in *Indiana Jones and the Last Crusade*, the first two movies certainly did not leave us wishing for more characterization. That's not what they were about.

Having said that, I must also point out that to be taken seriously as a writer, and not just a writer of speculative fiction, you must be able to draw interesting and believable characters; and most stories are improved when the author is skillful at characterization. But only when the story is *about* the transformation of a character's role in his community do you have a true Character Story.

The structure of a Character Story is as simple as any of the others. The story begins at the moment when the main character becomes so unhappy, impatient, or angry in his present role that he begins the process of change; and it ends when the character either settles into a new role (happily or not) or gives up the struggle and remains in the old role (happily or not).

Just as mystery readers give authors a little leeway at the beginning to establish the detective and the situation out of which the murder arises, so also the readers of Character Stories will accept the narrative equivalent of an "establishing shot." After all, if we are to care whether the character succeeds in changing, we must understand what it is he's changing *from*.

But, with rare exceptions, you should still begin the story as close to the point at which the character begins to attempt to change as possible. Few things in fiction are more tedious than reading a Character Story that begins many years—and many pages—before the character actually attempts to change his life. The author may be doing a lovely job of showing us the character's past and letting us in on his thoughts and feelings, but we keep waiting for something to happen, asking, "Why am I reading this? *So what?*"

This is not because we want adventure—no car chase is required. All we need is a sense of direction, a sense that the character is in motion. I have read many a student story in which it's not until page 10—or 20, or 50—that we finally get a sentence like this: "That was the day when Albie decided he had had enough." By then it's too late—the attempt to change will usually seem too feeble for the long build-up that preceded it.

The character's attempt to change doesn't have to be a conscious decision; it can be an inadvertent move, an instinctive seizing of opportunity. The character can find himself wondering, "What did I do *that* for?"—or thinking, "Why didn't I do that *long* ago?"

Characters in the other kinds of story *can* change, too, though they don't have to. You can embed Character Stories as subplots within Milieu, Event, and Idea Stories, but in that case the characters' changes are not the climax of the whole work, not the signal to the reader that the story is over, that the tension of the tale is now released.

Even within a Character Story, the main character is not the only one who will change. Since a person's role in a community is defined by and defines his relationships with other people, a change in his own role will change theirs, too. Much of the plot in a Character Story rises out of the other characters' resistance to change. Often the climax will involve the final battle between characters in their war to establish incompatible identities. Think of *The Barretts of Wimpole Street*, in which Elizabeth Barrett's love for Robert Browning makes her become so dissatisfied with her role in her father's family that she decides to leave. But her father is unwilling to allow any such change in any of his children—it would require *him* to go through more self-redefinition than he is willing to bear. The story ends when Elizabeth cuts loose and leaves; we see that she has successfully transformed herself, and we also relish the forced transformation in her tyrannical father's life.

*The Barretts of Wimpole Street* absolutely follows the structure of a Character Story: No matter how many characters are in flux, the Character Story begins close to the point where the main character begins to attempt to change his role, and ends at the point where the struggle ends.

If the transformation of character is what you care about most in the story you want to tell, then identify which character's changes trigger all the other transformations. That's your main character, and your story begins when he just can't take it anymore.

### The Event Story

In the Event Story, something is wrong in the fabric of the universe; the world is out of order. In the ancient tradition of Romance (as opposed to the modern publishing category), this can include the appearance of a monster *(Beowulf)*, the "unnatural" murder of a king by his brother *(Hamlet)* or a guest by his host *(Macbeth)*, the breaking of an oath *(Havelock the Dane)*, the conquest of a Christian land by the infidel *(King Horn)*, the birth of a child portent who some believe ought not to have been born *(Dune)*, or the reappearance of a powerful ancient adversary who was thought to be dead *(The Lord of the Rings)*. In all cases, a previous order—a "golden age"—has been disrupted and the world is in flux, a dangerous place.

The Event Story ends at the point where a new order is established, or, more rarely, where the old order is restored, or, rarest of all, where the world descends into chaos as the forces of order are destroyed. The story begins, not at the point where the world becomes disordered, but rather at the point where the character whose actions are most crucial to establishing the new order becomes involved in the struggle. *Hamlet* doesn't begin with the murder of Hamlet's father; it begins much later, when the ghost appears to Hamlet and involves him in the struggle to remove the usurper and reestablish the proper order of the kingdom.

*Macbeth* is eccentric in that the main character is the source of the disorder rather than its opponent. Yet it doesn't begin with the murder of the king, either; it begins much *earlier*, when the witches first put the improper thought of becoming king into Macbeth's mind. And it ends when, after much struggle to reconcile himself with the chaos he brought into the world, Macbeth is killed, thus restoring a proper order.

Because the story concerns the restoration of the proper order of the universe, it's not surprising that Romance traditionally concerns itself with grand people—royalty, nobility, heroes, even demigods. But this is not necessary. Think of Megan Lindholm's superb fantasy *The Wizard of the Pigeons;* the hero is a wizard, yes, but he is also a Seattle streetperson living on garbage and the occasional handout. Lindholm draws the real Seattle street life very convincingly; yet her hero is no less concerned with the fact that an enemy has crept into his modest, orderly little "kingdom," sowing confusion and threatening destruction.

And the disorder in the world can be even more subtle, the character even less obviously heroic. Jane Austen's *Emma* concerns a woman who acted on bad advice and refused to marry the man who would have brought her happiness. This private decision is nevertheless a violation of the natural order of the universe in which Emma lives; she herself becomes then a disorderly force, sowing difficulties in the lives of others until at last she realizes she made a mistake and marries the man she should have married in the first place. The story begins at the point where Emma becomes involved in the disorder and ends where the order is restored.

Almost all fantasy and much—perhaps most—science fiction uses the Event Story structure. Nowhere is it better handled than in Tolkien's great trilogy. *The Lord of the Rings* begins when Frodo discovers that the ring Bilbo gave him is the key to the overthrow of Sauron, the great adversary of the world's order; it ends, not with the destruction of Sauron, but with the complete reestablishment of the new order—which includes the departure of Frodo and all other magical people from Middle-earth.

Notice that Tolkien does not begin with a prologue recounting all the history of Middle-earth up to the point where Gandalf tells Frodo what the ring is. He begins, instead, by establishing Frodo's domestic situation and then thrusting world events on him, explaining no more of the world than Frodo needs to know right at the beginning. We only learn of the rest of the foregoing events bit by bit, as the information is revealed to Frodo.

In other words, the viewpoint character, not the narrator, is our guide into the world situation. We start with the small part of the world that he knows and understands and see only as much of the disorder of the universe as he can see. It takes many days—and many pages—before Frodo stands before the council of Elrond, the whole situation having been explained to him, and says, "I will take the ring, though I do not know the way." By the time a lengthy explanation is given, we have already seen much of the disorder of the universe for ourselves—the Black Riders, the hoodlums in Bree, the barrow wights—and have met the true king, Aragorn, in his disguise as Strider. In other words, by the time we are given the full explanation of the world, we already care about the people involved in saving it.

Too many writers of Event Stories, especially epic fantasies, don't learn this lesson from Tolkien. Instead, they imagine that their poor reader won't be able to understand what's going on if they don't begin with a prologue showing the "world situation." Alas, these prologues *always* fail. Because we aren't emotionally involved with any characters, because we don't yet *care,* the prologues are meaningless. They are also usually confusing, as half-dozen names are thrown at us all at once. I have learned as a book reviewer, that it's usually best to skip the prologue entirely and begin with the story—as the author also should have done. I have never—not once—found that by skipping the prologue I missed some information I needed to have in order to read the story; and when I *have* read the prologue first, I have never—not once—found it interesting, helpful, or even understandable.

In other words, writers of Event Stories, *don't write prologues.* Homer didn't need to summarize the whole Trojan War for us; he began the *Iliad* with the particular, the private wrath of Achilles. Learn from Homer—and Tolkien, and all the other writers who have handled the Event Story well. Begin small, and only gradually expand our vision to include the whole world. If you don't let us know and care about the hero first, we won't be around for the saving of the world. There's plenty of time for us to learn the big picture.

### Deciding Which Is Which

How do you know which structure your story should follow? The fact is that most stories could be made to follow any of these structures. The most important thing is that you must end the story that you begin. If you promise a Character Story by the way you begin your tale, then your story can only achieve closure by having the main character end his attempt to change his role—not by solving a mystery! And if you promise an Idea Story by beginning with a vital question, you can't achieve closure by having a character find a new role in life.

Still, there is almost always a best structure for a particular story. You often can't find it until you've attempted a draft and find yourself bogged down only a few pages or chapters into it (often a pretty good sign that you're using the wrong structure, beginning at the wrong place). Chances are, that early exploratory draft will end up being thrown away—but not too soon! First, read it carefully, not to fix up the prose or correct minor story flaws, but rather to discover what you like best in it.

What did you spend the most time on? Were you fascinated with the main character's unhappy relationships with other people? Then you may need to structure it as a Character Story. Did you devote a lot of time to exploring the world, showing its wonders and oddities? Then perhaps you need to structure it as a Milieu Story, bringing in an outsider as the viewpoint character. Or is it the grand events, the disorder in the world that interests you? In that case, you need to identify who it is that will end up restoring good order to the world and begin with his or her first involvement in the struggle against disorder.

One thing, though, that you must beware of is the natural tendency of novice writers to automatically structure all their stories as Idea Stories. Judging from student and workshop stories over the years, both in and out of the field of speculative fiction, I believe that most stories that fail do so because the

---

writer, having thought up a neat idea for a story, then structured the story so that it leads up to the moment when that neat story idea is revealed.

This is fine, of course, when the story really is about the struggle of a character to find the answer to a question. But it's terrible when it's the readers, not the characters, who are doing the struggling. The mystery in these cases is not a single question: Who killed this man? Why does this large planet have such low gravity? Instead the questions are more basic: What's going on? Why am I reading this?

A student story I read recently consisted of a long monologue by a man giving directions to a small town, but as he spoke, he constantly digressed, telling of memories associated with certain landmarks along the way. Only near the very end did we discover that this monologue was a telephone conversation, that the man knew the person he was speaking to, and that they planned to meet. And the most important information of all was only implied in one of the last sentences: The person he was speaking to was his lover, coming for a rendezvous in his old hometown.

That sort of sudden surprise ending (Ah! *That's* what it all meant!) rarely works, and for this reason: Because the writer had to labor so hard to conceal what was actually going on in the story, he was unable to accomplish anything *except* concealment. The entire story consisted of withholding from the reader every speck of information that would have made the story interesting. If he had begun by telling us that the man was giving directions to his love, then he could have used that monologue to show us their relationship and how the man's life led up to betraying his wife with this other woman; he could have shown us the pain and guilt—not to mention the ecstatic anticipation of the tryst.

In other words, it could have been a Character Story, in which the man was struggling to change his role and, at the end, either succeeded or failed; it could have been an Event Story, in which either his marriage or his love affair was a bit of disorder in the universe that had to be resolved; it could even have been a Milieu Story, in which he took his lover exploring through the back-country world he grew up in. But by structuring it as a mystery, he left himself none of these possibilities. Indeed, he couldn't even write honestly. Because the author couldn't tell us that the man was talking to his lover, it was impossible to have the man even speak as men speak to their lovers—the monologue was impersonal, as if he were giving directions to strangers in a passing car. There could be no reference to shared memories between them; no expressions of emotion that might give things away.

So as you look at your bogged-down first draft, look to see how much of your effort is spent on withholding information, and then examine whether your reader has any reason to care about what's going on as long as that information is withheld. Most novice writers imagine that this is how suspense is created—by holding back key information from the reader. But that is not so. Suspense comes from having almost *all* the information—enough information that the audience is emotionally involved and cares very much about that tiny bit of information left unrevealed.

Usually the only information that you withhold is this: what is going to happen next. The climax of a story isn't created by suddenly discovering what's going on. The climax of the story is created by suddenly resolving issues that have been causing the audience a great deal of tension throughout the story. There's no tension without information.

If you find that all your stories are structured as Idea Stories in which the reader never knows what's going on until the end, then stop it. Forbid yourself to use that structure again until you have mastered one of the others. You *only* use the Idea Story structure when the *characters* are searching for the answers to questions. When the characters know the answers and only the audience is asking the questions, you are definitely using the wrong structure. Your story idea may be terrific—but your execution of the story is killing it.

What about plot—deciding which scenes to show, structuring those scenes, building from one minor climax to another? I told you from the first that I would concentrate on those aspects of writing that are peculiar only to speculative fiction. Plotting is handled no differently in SF than in any other genre. If you feel you need help in that area, I recommend Ansen Dibell's book *Plot*, a companion volume in the same series as my own *Character and Viewpoint*.

Most of the things we've talked about so far—world creation, structure—I usually work on extensively before ever writing a draft of a story or novel. There are many other writers—perhaps more—who can only develop these aspects of a story while writing narrative drafts, and that's fine, too. In fact, I continue creating my world and revising and clarifying my story's structure while writing drafts, so I know that much of the best invention only comes while you're actually telling the tale. Your order of working is entirely up to you—as long as you actually do all the work I've talked about in these chapters.

The unfortunate thing is that too many writers—though not very many writers actually making a career out of this—skip the entire process of invention and construction. Once they have the first glimmer of an idea they proceed immediately to writing a draft and spend all their effort on producing beautiful prose. Alas, they're wasting their time. As William Goldman had a character say in *Boys and Girls Together*, speaking of a play that was in rehearsal, "Wash garbage, it's still garbage." It doesn't matter how beautifully a story is performed if the story itself—what happens and why—is crippled with clichés or badly structured.

Still, after all your preparatory work, there comes a time when you have to produce the draft that counts. The world is well invented, the structure is solid. Now you have to get this story from your mind into the minds of your readers. And that's where your skill with stories must be matched by skill with communication. You've got to have the language; you've got to be able to *write*.

**CHAPTER 4**

# Writing Well

Good writing is good writing, no matter which genre you work in. But there are some areas of special concern to writers of speculative fiction. Don't be misled by the fact that this is the shortest section of the book. It is brief because the basic information is simple; but the technique itself is difficult and requires practice—particularly the handling of exposition—and you'll get the best results from the chapter if you reread it more than once, using the techniques shown here to analyze your own story drafts.

## 1. EXPOSITION

One area in which SF differs from all other genres is the handling of *exposition*—the orderly revelation of necessary information to the reader.

It may seem that in the last chapter I told you two bits of conflicting advice. First I warned you against using prologues with Event Stories and said you should only reveal information about the disorder in the world as it becomes available to the viewpoint character. Then I told you *not* to withhold information, but instead to let the readers know at least as much as the characters do about what's going on.

It's not a contradiction—but it *is* a balancing act. It's like watering a plant. Too little water and it dries up and dies; too much water and it rots and drowns. Information is to your audience as water is to a plant—it's the life of the story, and yet you have to keep it in balance. Too much raw information up front and the reader can't keep it all straight; too little information and the reader can't figure out what's happening. The result in either case is confusion, impatience, boredom. The audience quickly learns that you don't know how to tell a story, and you've lost them.

Instead, information must be trickled into a story, always just enough to know what's happening. If the audience must know a fact in order to understand what's going on, then you must either present the information at the moment, or make sure the information was available—and *memorable*—earlier in the text. In particular, if the viewpoint character knows a fact that gives a different meaning to an event, then the audience must also know that fact—though if the viewpoint character *doesn't* know, it's perfectly all right for the audience to share his ignorance.

This balance is especially difficult to achieve in science fiction and fantasy because our stories take place in worlds that differ from the known world. We not only have to introduce characters and immediate situations, we also have to let readers know how the rules of our universe differ from the normal rules, and show them the strangeness of the place in which the events occur.

In the early days of science fiction, when the genre was still being invented, key information was given in huge lumps, often by having one character explain things to another. This was often badly handled, as when one character explained things to another who already knew it:

> "As you know, Dr. Smith, the rebolitic manciplator causes the electrons of any given group of atoms to reverse their charge and become anti-electrons."
>
> "Yes, Dr. Whitley, and of course that will cause an immediate explosion unless the rebolitic manciplation is conducted inside an extremely powerful Boodley field."
>
> "And the only facility in Nova Scotia that is capable of maintaining a Boodley field of sufficient power is—"
>
> "That's right. Dr. Malifax's lab on his houseboat in the Bay of Fundy."

I hardly need to tell you that this is no longer regarded as a viable solution to the problem of exposition.

Exposition is even more complicated today because of the development of an extremely tight third-person-limited point of view, in which the only information given is what the viewpoint character sees and thinks, with no obvious intrusions on the part of the narrator. Most professional fiction today uses this viewpoint because of its great advantages. But the disadvantage is that you generally can't "notice" anything that the viewpoint character doesn't notice, or "think of" anything that the viewpoint character doesn't think of.

This is particularly challenging for speculative fiction writers. If your viewpoint character is a participant in the strange society you're trying to reveal to your audience, he wouldn't suddenly start noticing things he's taken for granted all his life.

So you have to reveal information very carefully, and usually by implication. The best way to tell you what I mean is to show you, by going through the opening paragraphs of Octavia Butler's novel *Wild Seed*. (I've chosen this book because nobody handles exposition better than Butler—and also because it's a terrific novel that you ought to read for the sheer pleasure of it.)

Let's start with the first sentence:

> Doro discovered the woman by accident when he went to see what was left of one of his seed villages.

You have just been given an astonishing amount of information—but it has been done in such a way that you probably aren't aware of how much you already know.

### Naming

First, we know the name of the viewpoint character: Doro. Later we'll learn that Doro has many names, but Butler gives us the name by which he thinks of himself—and whenever we're in Doro's viewpoint that's the only name used for him. Bad writers keep changing the name of their viewpoint character, thinking they're helping us by telling us more information: "The starship captain walked onto the bridge. Bob glanced over and saw the lights were blinking. 'What are you thinking of, Dilworth?' said the tall blond man." Is Bob the starship captain? Or is Bob Dilworth? And is it Bob or the starship captain who is the tall blond man? One tag per character, please, at least until we know them better. Above all, don't coyly begin with pronouns for the viewpoint character and make us wonder who "he" or "she" is—give us a name *first*, so we have a hook on which to hang all the information we learn about that character.

Second, we know that Doro will discover "the woman," and we assume that this discovery will be important to the story. Because Butler is a first-rate writer, that assumption is correct—she would never mislead us by putting a trivial character so portentously in the opening sentence. Yet she doesn't name the woman yet. In part this is because naming two characters immediately is often confusing. Too many names at once are hard to keep track of, and we aren't always sure which is the viewpoint character. Another reason for not naming "the woman," however, is because at this exact moment in the story— as Doro goes to see what is left of a village—he doesn't know her name. The narrator knows her name, of course, but at this moment Doro does not, and so it's right not to give that information to the reader.

### Abeyance

What else do we learn from these three sentences? Doro didn't intend to meet the woman. His purpose at the time was to see what was left of—what? A "seed village."

What in the world is a seed village?

We don't know what a seed village is. And Butler doesn't tell us—because Doro, who knows perfectly well what a seed village is, wouldn't stop and think about that information right now. But in due time we *will* find out what a seed village is. So we hold that question in abeyance. We have a hook with the label "seed village" over it; we trust that the author will let us know in due course what information should be hung on that hook.

This principle of abeyance is one of the protocols of reading speculative fiction that makes it difficult for some people who aren't familiar with the genre to grasp what's going on. Experienced SF readers recognize that they don't know what a seed village is, and that the author doesn't expect them to know. Instead, this is one of the differences, one of the things that is strange in this created world, and the author will in due course explain what the term means.

But the reader who is inexperienced in SF thinks that the author expects him to already know what a seed village is. He stops cold, trying to guess what the term means from its context. But he *can't* guess, because there isn't enough context yet. Instead of holding the information in abeyance like a small mystery, he is just as likely to think that either the writer is so clumsy that she doesn't know how to communicate well, or that this novel is so esoteric that its readers are expected to know uncommon terms that aren't even in the dictionary.

This is one of the real boundaries between SF and non-SF writing. Science fiction and fantasy writers handle exposition this way, by dropping in occasional terms as the viewpoint character thinks of them, and explaining them only later. The SF reader doesn't expect to receive a complete picture of the world all at once. Rather he builds up his own picture bit by bit from clues within the text.

## Implication

Butler is not being obscure; she is being *clear*. While "seed villages" goes unexplained, we *are* told that this is merely one of them, and that Doro thinks of more than one seed village as "his." Furthermore, "seed village" is not a wholly obscure term. We know what a village is; we know what *seed* means when it's used as an adjective. Seed potatoes, for instance, are small potatoes or parts of potatoes that are planted in the ground to grow into larger ones. By implication, Doro is somehow using villages as seed—or perhaps he has the villagers growing seeds for him. We aren't sure, but we do know that Doro is working on growing *something* and that he has more than one village involved in it.

This, again, is one of the protocols of reading SF. The reader is expected to extrapolate, to find the implied information contained in new words. The classic example is Robert Heinlein's phrase "The door dilated." No explanation of the technology; the character doesn't think, "Good heavens! A dilating door!" Instead, the reader is told not only that doors in this place dilate, irising open in all directions at once, but also that the character takes this fact for granted. The implication is that many—perhaps all—doors in this place dilate, and that they have been doing it for long enough that nobody pays attention to it anymore.

The SF writer is thus able to imply far more information than he actually states; the SF reader *will* pick up most or all of these implications. Indeed, this is one reason why you must be so rigorous about creating your worlds to quite a deep level of detail, because your readers will constantly be leaping past what you actually say to find the implications of what you're saying—and if you haven't thought things through to that level, they'll catch you being sloppy or silly or just plain wrong.

## Literalism

The protocols of abeyance and implication, which give you a great deal of power, also remove one of the tools that mainstream writers rely on most heavily: metaphor. Especially at the beginning of a speculative story, all strange statements are taken *literally.* "Seed village" isn't a metaphor, it's what the village actually is.

I think of a story by Tom Maddox that appeared some years ago in *OMNI.* In the first or second paragraph he had passengers taken from their airplane to the terminal on what he called a "reptile bus." I was teaching a SF literature course at the time, and my students were pretty evenly divided between those who had been reading SF for years and those who had never read it before that semester.

The majority of the experienced SF readers reported the same experience I had: At least for a moment, and often for quite a way into the story, we thought that Maddox wanted us to think that reptiles were somehow being used for airport transportation. We pictured a triceratops with a howdah perhaps, or an allosaur towing a rickshaw. It was an absurd sort of technology, and it would have strained credulity—but many SF stories use such bizarre ideas and make them work. Maddox might have been establishing a work in which bioengineers had created many new species of very useful but stupid dinosaurs.

Those who had never read SF, however, were untroubled by such distraction. They knew at once that "reptile bus" was a metaphor—that it was a regular gas-burning bus with several sections so it snaked across the tarmac in a reptile-like way.

This is one of the key differences between the SF audience and any other. When confronted with a strange juxtaposition of familiar words, both groups say, "What does the author mean by this?" But the SF audience expects the term to be literal, to have a real extension within the world of the story, while the mainstream audience expects the term to be metaphorical, to express an attitude toward or give a new understanding of something that is part of the known world.

When a SF writer says, "She took heavy mechanical steps toward the door," there is always the possibility that in fact her legs are machinery; the mainstream writer assumes this metaphorically expresses the manner of her walking, and would regard that word usage as a grotesque joke if she *did* have artificial legs.

This doesn't mean that you, as a SF writer, are forbidden to use metaphor. It *does* mean that early in a story, when the rules of your created world are not yet fully explained, you have to avoid metaphors that might be confusing to experienced SF readers. Later, when the rules are firmly set, your readers will know that terms that imply things that are not possible in your world should be taken metaphorically.

Do recall the difference between metaphor, simile, and analogy. Similes and analogies, which explicitly state that one thing is *like* another thing, are still available; it's only metaphors, which state that one thing *is* another thing, that are forbidden. "You could treat Howard Merkle like dirt and he'd still come fawning back to you, just like a whipped dog," a simile, is perfectly clear and usable in speculative fiction, whereas the metaphor "Howard Merkle was a dog, always eager to please no matter how you treated him" is problematic early in a speculative fiction story, because it *could* be taken literally.

Also, beware of analogies that remove the reader from the milieu of the story and remind him of the present time. "The aliens had facial structures like eyebrows, only arched in an exaggerated way, so they walked around looking like a McDonald's advertisement." This sentence would be fine in a near-future story about contact with aliens; McDonald's would presumably still be around. But the same sentence would be quite out of place if the story were set in a time and place so different from our own that the characters do *not* have McDonald's restaurants as part of their daily experience. In that case, such a sentence is clearly the writer talking to the contemporary American reader, not the narrator creating the experience of another time and place. And it's almost worse if you try to compensate for this dislocation by making it explicit: "The aliens' eyebrows arched like the logo of that ancient fast-food restaurant, McDonald's, which Pyotr had seen once in a history book about the twentieth century on Earth." This sort of thing throws the reader right out of the story. There's a natural impulse to compare something strange to something that will be familiar to the reader—but as a general rule you should use only similes and analogies that would also be available to the characters in the story, so that the entire experience of reading contributes to the illusion of being in the story's milieu.

### Piquing Our Interest

All this, and we're only one sentence into *Wild Seed?* Remember, though, that while it takes pages to explicate all the processes going on here, the sentence takes only a moment to read; most of these processes are quite unconscious, and while Butler certainly chose this sentence carefully, many of the things that are right about it are simply good habits that she instinctively follows—like immediately naming the viewpoint character and *not* naming a character whose name is unknown to the viewpoint character.

But you can also be certain that she thought carefully before choosing the term "seed village," to make sure that it was evocative and interesting. It is the mysteriousness of that term that first piques our interest, that makes us wonder, "Who is Doro? What is it he's trying to grow? In what sense is this village *his?*" Without that term, all we're left with is the much less intriguing mystery of who "the woman" is.

Mystery? Is *Wild Seed* an Idea Story? Not at all. These "mysteries" are very small, and no time at all is spent on them. Doro isn't wondering who the woman is or what a seed village is. He hasn't met this woman yet, so we know that when he does meet her, our questions will be answered; and he already knows what a seed village is, so we fully expect that we will soon be informed as well. These are transient mysteries, part of the exposition process, not the kind of story-driving mystery that can give shape to an entire novel.

It's important, especially at the beginning, that you reveal information that promises your reader an interesting story to come. Those promises must be honest ones that you intend to keep. Because Doro is set up as the kind of character who can somehow "own" villages, we see him as a bit larger than life—Butler definitely will deliver on this promise. And the concept of seed villages is absolutely central to the story; it isn't a trivial bit of strangeness to be tossed in and thrown away. In other words, Butler isn't just giving us random but interesting information to fool us into going on—she's giving us interesting information that is vital to the story.

## A Workshop in Exposition

Let's go on now with the entire opening paragraph of *Wild Seed*:

> Doro discovered the woman by accident when he went to see what was left of one of his seed villages. The village was a comfortable mud-walled place surrounded by grasslands and scattered trees. But Doro realized even before he reached it that its people were gone. Slavers had been to it before him. With their guns and their greed, they had undone in a few hours the work of a thousand years. Those villagers they had not herded away, they had slaughtered. Doro found human bones, hair, bits of desiccated flesh missed by scavengers. He stood over a very small skeleton—the bones of a child—and wondered where the

survivors had been taken. Which country or New World colony? How far would he have to travel to find the remnants of what had been a healthy, vigorous people?

What do we learn from this paragraph? First, the immediate situation is absolutely clear—we aren't wondering what's happening. Doro has come to one of his seed villages and finds all the people gone—either dead or taken off into slavery—and he now is thinking about going to find the survivors.

The immediate situation is powerful. The image of bones and hair and bits of flesh, the small skeleton of a murdered child—these arouse a sense of loss and outrage in us, even when we hear about such things happening to strangers. There are good guys and bad guys already being sorted out in our minds: The slavers are bad and the villagers are their innocent victims.

But this is still only part of what Butler is telling us in this paragraph. Many other things are hinted, things that we may not consciously pick up but which are nevertheless working on us unconsciously; they are the foundation on which we'll build the rest of the story and the rest of the world of this book.

For instance, we are getting a sense of the time frame of the story. The village is mud-walled, which suggests a pretechnological society—but the slavers have guns, a key piece of information that tells us that if the story takes place on Earth, it is set in fairly recent times. By the end of the paragraph, Butler's reference to New World colonies gives us the strong implication that the story is set on Earth during the era when there was a market for slaves in the New World; and that means that this village is almost certainly in Africa. ("New World" might also be taken literally, as another planet, but the feel of the story so far is low-tech, and so a spacefaring culture is not our first assumption.) All these inferences are confirmed by later information, so that readers who don't get all this from the first are not abandoned—but the fact remains that Butler has essentially set the time and place for us within the first paragraph and *without* stopping the action to tell us outright that we are in Africa in the slave-trading era.

Even more important is the information we're given about Doro. The fact that he regards a mud-walled village as "comfortable" tells us that he doesn't feel at all out of place in primitive settings and that he can feel at home in one of "his" villages.

Doro also knew that the people were gone *before* he reached the village. How did he know it? He might have observed that there was no one working in the

---

fields; he might have noticed it because there was none of the usual noise of the village. Butler doesn't tell us how he knows, though, so the possibility remains open that his knowledge is not based on the normal means of ascertaining such things. The reader may or may not notice it, but the implication is there.

We get Doro's attitude toward the slavers—he thinks of them as greedy—but then as Doro observes the village, as we are shown the bones and hair and bits of flesh, the child's skeleton, what surprises us is his lack of appropriate emotion. Standing over the skeleton, he doesn't wonder *who* the child was, doesn't grieve at all, doesn't even think with outrage of the inhumanity of the butcherous slavers. Instead he wonders where and how far the survivors have been taken. And his wondering is not sympathetic ("He imagined their terror as they were dragged away from the screams of their dying loved ones ... "), but wholly practical: "How far would he have to travel?" Even his memory of the people is the way a man remembers a valued but unloved animal: "A healthy, vigorous people." The phrase "his seed villages" begins to be clarified: Doro is the farmer, and the human beings themselves are his crop.

The next two paragraphs tell us that Doro is not unemotional—but confirms that his relationship with other people is indeed strange:

> Finally, he stumbled away from the ruins bitterly angry, not knowing or caring where he went. It was a matter of pride with him that he protected his own. Not the individuals, perhaps, but the groups. They gave him their loyalty, their obedience, and he protected them.
> He had failed.

It's his pride that is injured; he hates failing. His affections are not for individuals, but rather for groups. It was the village as a whole that he cared for, not the people. He really is just like a farmer, who would hardly notice the death of a few stalks of wheat but would be bitterly angry at the destruction of an entire field.

Yet in the strength of his emotions, he does stumble away, not knowing or caring where he goes. So while he doesn't relate to other people in a natural way and clearly regards them as being less than he, like a flock or a field, he *is* human himself, after a fashion. It is possible to understand at least some of his feelings. He is at once strange and familiar.

It is in the fourth paragraph that we are given the final bit of information about Doro that tells us exactly how strange he is:

> He wandered southwest toward the forest, leaving as he had arrived—alone, unarmed, without supplies, accepting the savanna and later the forest as easily as he accepted any terrain. He was killed several times—by disease, animals, by hostile people. This was a harsh land. Yet he continued to move southwest, unthinkingly veering away from the section of the coast where his ship awaited him. After a while, he realized it was no longer his anger at the loss of his seed village that drove him. It was something new—an impulse, a feeling, a kind of mental undertow pulling at him. He could have resisted it easily, but he did not. He felt there was something for him farther on, a little farther, just ahead. He trusted such feelings.

Notice how casually Butler lays the information that he is killed more than once. She doesn't make a big deal about it, because to Doro being killed isn't terribly important. But to us it is, and the very fact that Doro can be killed several times and still continue to move southwest tells us that he is very strange indeed. He looks down on human beings like crops or herds because he is, somehow, immortal, able to be killed and yet go on.

We know he owns a ship and that its crew expects to meet him at a prearranged place—this suggests what we will eventually discover is a network of servants and possessions that reaches all around the world.

We also know that he is sensitive to sources of information that normal people just don't have—he is drawn by a "mental undertow" and willingly goes along with it because he trusts such feelings. Obviously, he's had experiences like this before.

And because Butler is one of the best writers of SF during a time when there are many very good ones, this whole passage is imbued with emotions and we are carried along by language that flows and swirls with grace and power.

Two paragraphs later, after a line space (on a manuscript, you mark such spaces with an asterisk), she changes point of view. Now we're seeing what's going on through the eyes and mind of a woman named Anyanwu. Naturally, we assume that Anyanwu *is* that woman—and we are correct. A good writer like Butler would never confuse us by leading us to incorrect assumptions.

We soon realize that Anyanwu is, in her own way, as strange and remarkable as Doro. First, we know that she is capable of killing—she once killed several men who were stalking her with machetes—but that she regrets it and regards killing as a terrible thing to be avoided when possible.

She is aware of a lone intruder now, prowling the underbrush near her.

---

We immediately assume—again correctly—that this is Doro, though of course Butler can't say so because Anyanwu doesn't know him yet. Anyanwu is still "the woman" to Doro; Doro is still "the intruder" to Anyanwu.

We also learn that Anyanwu is a healer, and that "often she needed no medicines, but she kept that to herself"—so she, too, has some kind of transcendent power. Like Doro, she thinks of the people of her village as "her" people—but they are not just one village among many, and she doesn't just come to pay a visit now and then. She lives among them; she serves them by healing them and also by allowing them to spread stories about her healing powers, so they can profit when people from other villages come to her to be healed.

A reference to Anyanwu's long life and her "various youths" implies that she, like Doro, is somehow immortal—but unlike Doro, she fears death and tries to avoid it through vigilance. So they do not have the same powers and don't live by the same rules. Doro can be killed by men or animals or disease and yet go on living; Anyanwu lives a long time but must avoid murderers in order to do it. Anyanwu fears no poison because of her superior understanding of them, not because she can't die.

And yet all this information is conveyed within a tense scene in which Anyanwu is mentally tracking the intruder—Doro—and trying to determine whether she is going to have to kill him in order to defend herself.

At this point we are only three pages into Butler's novel, yet she has conveyed an enormous amount of information to us, all through the thoughts and actions of her two viewpoint characters. We have never, not for a moment, been aware of the exposition, because she never stopped the action to tell us.

Furthermore, she has not yet explained the whole situation; we don't yet know that the disorder in the world is Doro himself, a man who can't die, who has to kill whether he wants to or not. True to the Event Story structure, Butler has begun the story exactly where her protagonist, the person who will restore order to the world, gets involved in the struggle to solve the problem—the point where she meets Doro. The actual meeting is on the fourth page of the book; she is aware of him by the middle of the second page; and Butler refers to that meeting in the very first sentence of *Wild Seed*.

From the very beginning, Butler promises us a story she means to tell, and then delivers on every promise. From the start we know why we should read on, and as we read we effortlessly receive every bit of information we need to have in order to understand the whole story. Many writers handle SF exposition very well; almost all handle it with at least minimal competence. No one does it better than Butler; I urge you to pick up any of her books or stories. Read them once for pleasure; then study them to learn how it's done.

## 2. LANGUAGE

Some stories demand different kinds of writing; what's good for one story may not be good for another.

### Diction

In her essay "From Elfland to Poughkeepsie," Ursula K. LeGuin makes such a point with great eloquence: When fantasies are writing about people of high station living in heroic times, a more formal, elevated level of diction is called for. On the other hand, when you're creating low comedy, diction can range from the mock heroic to the coarse.

However, there is great danger in trying for elevated diction—primarily because it's so easy to overdo it or do it very badly. You have to read a lot of brilliantly written formal prose before you're able to handle it well—and there isn't much of it being written these days. LeGuin herself and Gene Wolfe are the two most reliable sources of that level of diction within the field of speculative fiction; outside it, you are best served by reading Jane Austen or, for a contemporary example, Judith Martin; when writing as "Miss Manners" she uses excellent formal diction, often with devastating irony.

Here is the same scene, three ways.

Sevora read the letter, showing no emotion as she did. Tyvell only realized something was wrong when the letter slipped from her fingers and she took a single hesitant step toward him. He caught her before she could fall to the floor.

He laid her gently on the thick fur before the hearth, then sent his dwarf to fetch the surgeon. Before help arrived, however, her eyes opened.

"The surgeon is coming," Tyvell said, gently holding her hand.

"Read the letter," she whispered. "Lebbech has destroyed me."

...

Sevora perused the missive, displaying none of the turmoil of her feelings on her impassive, stonelike face. Tyvell only became aware of the tumult within her when she let fall the curled parchment and staggered toward him. With the utmost hurry he caught her in his arms before her delicate frame could strike the floor.

Gently he laid her on the pliant bearskin before the merrily dancing flames of the hearth, then sent Crimond, his astonished and frantic dwarf, to fetch the cirurgeon. Before the diminutive servant's abbreviated stride could bring the desired aid, however, Sevora resumed consciousness and her eyes fluttered open.

"Fear not," said Tyvell, stroking the smooth white skin of her hand. "I have sent for the cirurgeon."

"I need him not," whispered Sevora. "How can I be holpen now by his herberies? Nay, even his knife shall not serve me in my present need. Under the hideous spells of Lebbech I now lie destroyed."

...

Sevora read the letter as best she could, moving her lips and stumbling now and then when there were too many letters in a word. Tyvell realized it was bad news when Sevora crumpled it up and stumbled toward him, her eyes rolling back in her head. Here he was minding his own business and now she had to fall on him in one of her damn faints.

He dragged her over by the fireplace and yelled for Crimond to go get the doctor because Sevora was out cold. The dwarf took off like a shot, but before he could get the old surgeon sobered up enough to come, Sevora had gotten tired of Tyvell patting her hand. She opened her eyes and glared at him.

"Look, I already sent for the doctor," he said. She always got so ticked off at him when he didn't take her faints seriously.

But it was the letter she was thinking about—it really was pretty bad. "Screw the doctor," she said. "Lebbech's got me cursed six ways from Tuesday. If we can't get these spells off me before the baby's born, I'm toast."

The first example is plainly meant to be taken seriously as a tale of highborn people caught up in heroic events. The second example, however, is trying too hard. There is no grace in a surfeit of adjectives, and high language doesn't consist of using twisted "poetic" syntax and needless archaisms like "holpen" and "cirurgeon." Indeed, elegance usually requires simplicity and clarity.

The third example is plainly meant to be comedy—but I have read many a story that was in dead earnest that was scarcely less funny in the choice of words. Modern slang is just as obnoxious in serious formal language as phony archaism; few solemn fantasists would use expressions like "I'm toast" or "six ways from Tuesday," but even more normal diction like the use of the terms *look* or *pretty bad* or even *bad news*—these would all be out of place in the first example.

If your characters are elevated, their language should be also; if they are common, then common language is appropriate. Furthermore, the language of the narrative should be a good match for the language in the dialogue; it was quite annoying, for instance, in a fantasy I read recently, set in Elizabethan England, to have the lowborn characters speak like highborn heroic Shakespearean characters—while the narrative was in fairly common modern English. The constant shifting only called attention to the language and distracted from the story.

If you want to see the levels of language clearly differentiated within a single work, the best teacher (as is so often the case) is Shakespeare. Look carefully at plays like *A Midsummer Night's Dream* and *The Taming of the Shrew*. In both there are "high" characters and "low" characters. The high characters speak in blank verse, with clean, elegant, figured diction. The low characters speak in unrhymed lines, with coarse humor and often with mangled English. Yet there is hilarious comedy in both levels of diction—and both levels of diction are extremely well written. Formal English isn't "good" while colloquial English is "bad"—good diction is the diction most appropriate to the scene at hand.

### Profanity and Vulgarity

There are no hard-and-fast rules of decorum anymore. You can pretty much use the language you want, though the magazines do have *some* limits. That doesn't mean that writers are "free" now, however. It only means that the burden of deciding what to do is thrown back on the writer.

What you must remember is that language has real effects on people. If you have a character who constantly uses foul language, that language will have an effect on the people around him. But if you actually put that language explicitly in your story, that bad language will have a similar effect on your audience. They will learn the fact that your character is a foul-mouthed boor, which is what you intend; but a substantial number of them will also be put off by your story to exactly the degree they would have been offended by the character, which may not be at all what you have in mind.

I would never change anything essential in order to pander to a particular

---

audience segment, but it would be just as absurd to include something non-essential when it would drive away an audience segment that might otherwise enjoy the story. It always comes down to what is or is not essential. Freedom of the press means that the decision is entirely up to you; it doesn't mean that you always have to decide in favor of being offensive.

However, if you decide against using vulgar or profane language, I urge you simply to leave out expletives entirely rather than replacing them with euphemisms. One well-known writer tried using the acronym *tanj* (there ain't no justice) exactly as the coarse Anglo-Saxon word for copulation is used. "Tanj off!" "Get your tanjin' hands off me!" It may have been a noble experiment, but as far as I could tell it proved that euphemisms are often worse than the crudities they replace, because they make both the story and the character seem pretty silly. Either use indecorous language or don't use it—don't try to simulate it because, unless you have more genius than I've ever heard of, it just won't work.

On the other hand, when you're creating an alien society, one of the best ways to suggest their values and culture is through your choice of which words are regarded as too indecorous to be used by decent people. In our culture, the words associated with coitus and elimination are too powerful to be spoken without care—and this tells you something about us. What about a culture in which the words for *eating* are regarded as indecent, while the words we are shocked by are easily used? A visitor from contemporary America might get into a lot of trouble moving through a culture where sex is as casual as blowing your nose, but where the idea of *owning* something, of keeping property that you withhold from general use, is as outrageous as pederasty. He's going to get his face slapped and not have the faintest idea why.

# PART 2

# The State of the Genre: Fantasy & Science Fiction in the 21st Century

## by Philip Athans

# THE STATE OF THE GENRE:
# Fantasy & Science Fiction in the 21st Century

## by Philip Athans

We are living in a true Golden Age of science fiction and fantasy.

Whether or not you agree, the figures don't lie. Even though (as of this writing) the science fiction genre is struggling a bit in the publishing world, it continues to be Hollywood's blockbuster genre of choice. Movies like *The Avengers*, *Prometheus* (the *Alien* prequel), and the *Transformers* franchise are generating hundreds of millions in revenue, as are science fiction games like *Halo 4*. Author Ed Greenwood, the creator of the Forgotten Realms world, has seen science fiction and fantasy drift into the popular culture until they've become "the very heart of mass-shared or experienced entertainment and unthinkingly accepted as such."

On the bookstore shelves, fantasy continues to sit atop the bestsellers lists with the other two "evergreen" genres: mystery and romance.

According to *USA Today*, twenty-two of the 150 best-selling books of the fifteen year period between 1993 and 2008 were science fiction or fantasy titles, including seven of the top ten, all of which feature a certain young man by the name of Harry. The list is a mix of old and new, with the Twilight saga and Christopher Paolini's *Eragon* and *Eldest* in the rankings along with George Orwell's *1984* and the J. R. R. Tolkien classic *The Hobbit*. That number would be higher, too, were one to count the children's picture books, some of the religious titles, and some of the more iffy "nonfiction" books like *The Secret* to that list.

But again, about 15 percent of the best-selling books of that fifteen year period are fantasy. That's a significant share of the overall publishing business, especially since the number-one spot belongs to a fantasy novel: *Harry Potter and the Sorcerer's Stone*.

J. K. Rowling, R. L. Stine, Dean Koontz, Stephen King, J. R. R. Tolkien, C. S. Lewis, Michael Crichton, Stephenie Meyer, Anne Rice, and Edgar Rice Burroughs all show up on the list of the best-selling authors of all time—a list that includes William Shakespeare and Agatha Christie, as well as authors who have written their share of fantasies, like Charles Dickens and Roald Dahl, and authors who walk a very fine line between "techno thriller" and science fiction, like Robin Cook and Dan Brown.

Clearly it's in the Young Adult section that fantasy has exploded onto the scene, and that's not just limited to Harry Potter. "The best selling of the best sellers in fantasy and SF aren't being published by the adult houses," says Stacy Whitman, publisher of Tu Books, an imprint of Lee & Low Books, Inc. "The biggest titles in children's and Young Adult fantasy sell in the hundreds of millions of copies, whereas *Game of Thrones* and The Wheel of Time series have sold in the low tens of millions."

Nina Hess, the author of the New York Times best-selling *A Practical Guide to Monsters* and a writing instructor of children's literature at the University of Washington, sees the mainstreaming of fantasy and the rise of genre in the young readers section as intrinsically linked. "It used to be the badge of teen nerddom to know the difference between Sauron and Saruman. Now, it seems if you haven't experienced *The Lord of the Rings* or Harry Potter or *Twilight* in film or fiction (or both), there's something wrong with you. Either it's cool now to be a nerd, or nerds are going to have to find a new genre."

This expansion of the audience has brought with it a much-needed democratization of the genres, which for decades had been nearly exclusively white male territory. The Tu Books imprint, for instance, focuses on racially diverse fantasy fiction for young readers, and a new generation of female authors, including mega-bestsellers J. K. Rowling and Stephenie Meyer, have breathed a new life into some older sword and sorcery and space opera tropes.

"When I was a teenager, I never got very interested in science fiction and fantasy as a reader because I consistently found it such 'guy fiction,' a genre where too few women were even real characters, let alone protagonists," says Laura Resnick, author of the popular Esther Diamond urban fantasy series. "Even as late as 1998, when my first fantasy novel was released, under 'Marketing Strategy,' in the publisher's printed promo materials for the novel, it said: 'The author is female in a traditionally male genre.' And that was *all* it said. That was the entire strategy thought up by the marketing mavens of a major science fiction and fantasy house: I was a *girl*!"

## HARRY POTTER & BEYOND: THE YOUNG READER FANTASY EXPLOSION

Fantasy, in particular, has always been a mainstay of children's literature. What is L. Frank Baum's classic *The Wonderful Wizard of Oz* (first published in 1900) if not fantasy? Most of the great classics of children's literature, from Aesop's Fables through *The Phantom Tollbooth,* are firmly rooted in fantasy, but then came a bespectacled young chap named Harry.

What was it about that first book, that character, and that author that started a renaissance in children's literature? Most of the fantasy archetypes infused into the Harry Potter world by author J. K. Rowling had been around for some time—centuries, even millennia, in some cases—but it was her particular blend of the familiar and the fresh that grabbed kids and adults alike.

Timing, and even a little luck, can go a long way. According to Stacy Whitman, Harry Potter "came at a time when the Internet was really taking off as a way to get things going viral. So the classic word-of-mouth in which a friend tells a friend about a great book was multiplied to the nth power." And what's come to be known as the "transmedia intellectual property" was here and ready for a character with such universal appeal. When Warner Brothers entered the scene, they took Harry Potter off the bookstore shelves and into movie theaters and theme parks—and every other licensing expression you can think of.

This remarkable success led a number of publishers to jump on the band-wagon, and the call went out far and wide: We need fantasy for young readers.

Authors across the spectrum stepped up, including first-time author Stephenie Meyer, whose new take on the old vampire myth, *Twilight*, met the aging (going from elementary school to middle school) Harry Potter audience with the perfect blend of fantasy, horror, and romance. *Twilight* also gave birth to a successful movie franchise and put the sleepy little town of Forks, Washington—a town the author had never visited—on the map.

Like most "bandwagons," what followed was a mix of success and failure, quality fiction and, well, knock-offs. But most of all, these two major franchises in particular, and a few others that followed, like *The Hunger Games*, gave birth to the Teen section in bookstores. But did they have a noticeable impact on the reading habits of kids?

By all accounts, kids are reading less, even post-Harry Potter and post-*Twilight*. According to a University of Maryland study cited in an article in the *Washington Post*, "Pleasure reading dropped 23% from 2003 to 2008, from 65 minutes a week to 50 minutes a week—with the greatest falloff for those ages 12 to 14."

The secret behind the success of the bigger Young Adult (YA) properties seems to be the growing number of adults who gravitate toward the YA/Teen section. Everyone has seen a grown woman voraciously pouring through *Twilight* on a bus or airplane—and she's not the only one.

The line between "adult" and "young adult" can be a very fine one indeed. For instance, Holly Black's best-selling novel *Tithe* deals with some surprisingly mature themes, which are wound through an urban fantasy fairy tale. But what tends to set these two categories apart is the age and attitude of the protagonists.

The hero, or more commonly heroine, of a YA fantasy tends to be a young adult or teenager. But contemporary teens not only know when they're being talked down to, they really don't like it. And for a generation of kids whose parents grew up with a very small handful of authors like Judy Blume, who started to understand that thinking and write about the real challenges that teens face, fiction—however rich in fantasy and/or science fiction tropes—has never been more relevant.

Authors still need to make some careful decisions about their audience. Teen books are pushing the limits of acceptable depictions of sexuality, and, like *Tithe*, don't shy away from the four-letter words that fly freely through the air of most middle school and high school cafeterias.

"On the gore front," said Nina Hess, "*The Hunger Games* really crosses the line for some people. Kids killing kids is shocking and repugnant to adults—and yet teens have loved this series. What makes that book succeed is how the author shows the main character reacting to the horror of the situation. As a writer, it's all a matter of how you show how it impacts the characters."

Young Adult and Young Reader fantasy and science fiction are very much still wide-open fields for aspiring authors, but it's always important to keep in mind that mega-successes like the Harry Potter series and *Twilight* are still quite rare. With a marketplace now well stocked with books ranging in quality from poor to extraordinary, there's no formula for a sure thing.

Stacy Whitman advises authors to "read what's out there. If you want to write YA, you need to read YA." This is especially true in terms of the emotional impact that Nina Hess mentioned or the peculiar point of view of a young protagonist, which can be difficult for adult authors to remember, let along successfully re-inhabit.

But read carefully. It's impossible to successfully surf the waves of popular trends—especially for someone outside the industry—so aspiring YA authors should take care in trying to write "the next *Twilight*" with a pen in one hand and a copy of *Twilight* in the other. By the time your book is written, edited, sold, and published, that trend will surely have given way to another, as was the case when *Twilight* gave way to *The Hunger Games*.

Author Laura Resnick voiced a similar warning: "When I was a young writer, various older, wiser, and quite successful writers all told me the same thing about trends, and it's a piece of advice which I have since then observed to be consistently true: By the time you identify a trend, it's always on the wane, so just write what you want to write, because consistently producing what you love to write and what you write best is the surest way to find your audience and build your sales."

Who knows what the next "hot property" will be, but chances are it will be as different as *Twilight* was from Harry Potter and *The Hunger Games* was from *Twilight*.

## DUNGEONS & DOLLARS: THE RISE OF THE MEDIA TIE-IN

It's possible that the first game tie-in novel was *Quag Keep* by legendary science fiction and fantasy author Andre Norton, which was specifically commissioned in 1978 by Gary Gygax as the first *Dungeons & Dragons* novel and published by DAW Books. The era of the successful game tie-in began in earnest with *Dragons of Autumn Twilight*, the first Dragonlance novel by Margaret Weis and Tracy Hickman, published in 1984 by TSR.

TSR, Inc. (short for Tactical Studies Rules) was founded in 1973 by Gary Gygax, co-creator of *Dungeons & Dragons*, the first role-playing game (RPG). *Dungeons & Dragons* was a unique twist on the table-top game, with most of the gameplay actually happening in the imaginations of the assembled players who were led by a "Dungeon Master" who took them on a journey through a shared storytelling experience.

It wasn't such a great leap for these story-based games, which were sold in book form, to eventually spawn novels based on the increasingly complex and richly realized fantasy settings created to support the game.

Since the release of *Dragons of Autumn Twilight*, which was based on the *Dungeons & Dragons* adventure *Dragons of Despair*, TSR went on to publish literally hundreds of titles. Dragonlance was not the only game setting for the *Dungeons & Dragons* game, and novels set in the Forgotten Realms world, Greyhawk, Birthright, and others soon followed. When TSR merged with Wizards of the Coast in 1997 (which itself became part of Hasbro in 2000), that output not only continued but increased until its book publishing enterprise was a multimillion-dollar business, launching the careers of some of the genre's biggest names, including the aforementioned Weis & Hickman, R. A. Salvatore, and even horror superstar Laurell K. Hamilton, who began her career with the Ravenloft novel *Death of a Darklord*.

What made the TSR novels something special was their open approach to the settings. The *Star Trek* novels that preceded TSR's book-publishing efforts, for instance, featured the further adventures of the familiar crew of the *Enterprise*. But the Forgotten Realms setting didn't have a "cast." Each author was free to create his own characters and send them on adventures in a shared world. Dragonlance's world of Krynn and the Forgotten Realms' continent of Faerûn were the same from book to book and shared the basic fantasy assumptions of the *Dungeons & Dragons* game (how magic worked, a bestiary of common monsters, and so on), but individual authors enjoyed (and still do enjoy) considerable latitude in populating their own stories with unique characters and situations.

Ed Greenwood created the Forgotten Realms world as a setting for his own fiction, and when he first discovered *Dungeons & Dragons*, he adapted his

---

world as the setting for his ongoing game. As a prolific and imaginative creative mind, Greenwood created a wealth of material for this ever-evolving world and eventually started contributing articles to TSR's own *Dragon Magazine*, introducing the *Dungeons & Dragons* fan community to the Forgotten Realms world in little snippets that got them hooked—so much so that TSR eventually bought the world from Greenwood. This may be the first time that a fantasy setting in and of itself was a salable commodity.

According to Greenwood, "The opportunity to 'belong' to an imaginary world in which ongoing life/stories never end, and there's no lone creator bottleneck/abrupt unfinished ending when the creator dies," is the heart of the appeal of shared-world fiction. "The shared nature of creation almost guarantees a variety of approaches and styles, providing something for everyone, from the dark and violent to the light and comical, and an ongoing experience of a pace and richness few lone creators can sustain."

Early successes with tie-in novels and novelizations based on *Star Wars*, *Star Trek*, *Doctor Who*, and other franchises aside, it was TSR that moved the tie-in into a new era of relevance because of the open nature of the settings themselves.

Game tie-ins, in particular, are developing as the video game revolution steps in front of "traditional" RPGs like *Dungeons & Dragons*, and most of the bigger video game franchises like World of Warcraft and Halo currently support active novel lines.

Robert E. Vardeman, author of more than a hundred science fiction, fantasy, and high-tech thriller novels, including his share of tie-ins, believes that "readers want to explore the characters and worlds more thoroughly, and different writers' imaginations roving wild there provide added depth. Many shared worlds are incredibly rich in detail. No single book or author can do justice to the possibilities."

But just as authors of Young Adult fiction are well served by reading Young Adult fiction, going into a shared world property "cold" is a recipe for disaster. Ed Greenwood recommends: "Ground yourself in the setting you want to write in. You may never 'know' it as thoroughly as an eagle-eyed fan, but you can capture the essence and feel of the world and so contribute to it in a way that 'feels right' to most fans."

Those fans can sniff out a "cookie cutter" tie-in from a thousand leagues, and as such the media tie-in has become something of an editor's medium. In the interest of full disclosure, I worked at TSR and Wizards of the Coast for fifteen years between 1995 and 2010 as an editor—and author—of *Dungeons & Dragons* and other tie-in novels. A huge part of that job—much more so than for a traditional editor—was spent tending to the care and maintenance of the various intellectual properties: the settings themselves. These are valuable properties. How much is *Star Wars* worth? Probably even more than the $4.05 billion Disney paid for the franchise in 2012. As such, the proper care and feeding of those properties is taken very seriously by the entities that own them, and authors are expected to treat them with the care they're due.

For an author who's willing to put in the work, the experience is closer to writing historical fiction in terms of the research necessary and the intractable nature of established "canon." But, like Weis & Hickman, Salvatore, and Hamilton, the dedication can pay off with a successful career—not only by beginning in tie-ins, but by coming back to them as well.

Noted science fiction author Greg Bear wrote the *Star Trek* novel *Corona* in 1984, then went on to one of the most successful careers in contemporary science fiction. In 2000, he wrote the *Star Wars* novel *Rogue Planet* and came back to the tie-in again in 2011 with the Halo novel *Cryptum*.

"Authors are fans, too," says Ed Greenwood, "and often leap at the chance to play in a sandbox they have loved for years, and do things with specific characters they've always wanted to do."

And Robert Vardeman agrees: "Writers can enjoy a tie-in world like any other reader. The difference is the 'what if?' trigger writers apply. A particular scene in an existing work can set a writer off on an incredible new adventure with fascinating characters. The more varied the world, the more likely a writer/fan will find a niche to explore—to want to explore."

## MEAN STREETS: THE URBAN FANTASY WAVE

The horror boom of the 1980s generated enormous sales and built careers for some of the most successful authors of all time, including Stephen King, Anne Rice, and Dean Koontz. But horror tends to wax and wane in popularity and is sometimes linked to the economy. The timeless Universal monster movies *Frankenstein* and *Dracula* were products of the Great Depression, and decades later, in the recession-era 1980s, we got Stephen King. Now, in the so-called Great Recession, horror has made another comeback.

Horror movies like the popular *Paranormal Activity* franchise are burning up the box office, but on the bookstore shelves, the Horror section has all but disappeared. The popular appetite that sold books by the millions in the 1980s flagged somewhat during and after the 1990s.

So what's changed?

What would have been called "horror" in the 1980s now tends to fall under the heading "urban fantasy."

In some cases there's really no difference between horror and urban fantasy—both are set in the contemporary or historical real world, and both involve the infiltration of some supernatural force or entity into the normal lives of the human characters. It may be fair to say that horror has always been a form of fantasy, but with the intention to scare its audience.

Urban fantasy may borrow heavily from horror archetypes, but there is a difference in the basic approach. In horror, the goal of the protagonist tends to be a simple one: survival. He or she has to escape the monsters, get out of the haunted house, or simply live through the night. But urban fantasy borrows the more active hero or heroine from fantasy and lets contemporary characters do battle with vampires, werewolves, zombies, or whatever.

Author Laura Resnick has found that humor is another key difference between horror and urban fantasy. And that, among other things, is a reason for its widening appeal. "I think urban fantasy has attracted a huge audience who thoroughly enjoy the notion of supernatural, paranormal, and magic adventure in the context of a world they can still identify with the world they know and live in," Resnick elaborates.

And it's this recognizable context that brings a wider readership into fantasy, what Resnick calls, "a mystical adventure that doesn't involve the reader having to learn a map, customs, and vocabulary for an imaginary fantasy world, and a great appeal in the experience of seeing the world they know through a magical lens, and where protagonists who dress in ordinary street clothes (rather than medieval costume) and who use cell phones (rather than swords) have exciting magical adventures."

This ready context has also helped bring in a new audience, including more women, both as readers and as authors. Critic and blogger John Ottinger notes that urban fantasy "was an outgrowth of the increasing popularity of Anne Rice that began in the 1990s and grew exponentially in the early millennium to include not just Stephenie Meyer but also Kat Richardson, Charlaine Harris, Kim Harrison, and Laurell K. Hamilton. Even those writers who began their careers writing paranormal stories, like Carrie Vaughn, have broadened their range and so are making an even greater, more visible impact on the genre— and for its betterment."

As with fantasy for young readers, urban fantasy has seen various trends come and go, with some hits that crossed over into other media. Charlaine Harris's Sookie Stackhouse novels, in which vampires reveal themselves to an uneasy human population and cause a certain amount of trouble for a certain psychic waitress in rural Louisiana, has been adapted for television by HBO as the series *True Blood*. Jim Butcher's successful Harry Dresden series also came to TV but didn't quite catch on. Original series like NBC's *Grimm* and Syfy's *Haven* are bringing new urban fantasies to the small screen, and movies like *Vamp U* and *The Sorcerer's Apprentice* are doing the same on the big screen.

But sometimes quality writing in a genre isn't able to make the leap, no matter how much talent or effort comes from the author. Laura Resnick wrote the proposal for her urban fantasy series in 1995 and spent over a decade try-ing to find a publisher for it. "So I was pounding on the gates well before the bandwagon ever showed up," she says, "and when it did finally show up, there wasn't a seat available for me! I only found the right publisher, DAW Books, after the trend had already risen, thrived, started to sag, and then suffered a tired and flabby market glut. So I write my urban fantasy series because I love it and wanted to write it for years, and DAW publishes it because they love it, too. Something you love writing and believe in still has legs long after a bandwagon has run out of gas."

## DIY: THE E-BOOK INDEPENDENTS

As of March 2013, two of the fifteen titles appearing at the top of the *New York Times* bestsellers list, which combines print and e-book sales, are self-published: *Fallen Too Far* by Abbi Gaines and *Wait for You* by J. Lynn. As of March 24, 2013, Lynn's title was the #2 book in the country. The other thirteen books are published by major houses, including Simon & Schuster and Penguin.

People who have spent a significant number of years working in the publishing business will find the appearance of two self-published books on the coveted *New York Times* bestsellers list as something more than a minor shock. It's fair to say that this is unprecedented in the history of American publishing, at least since the turn of the twentieth century.

What does this mean? How did this impossible thing happen? And what does it mean for the future?

The e-book came to us slowly, with different incompatible formats quietly—almost silently—duking it out for supremacy over the fraction of 1 percent of the overall publishing business they occupied for years. Then 2012 ended with a Pew Internet & American Life Project survey showing that 23 percent of Americans read e-books (up from 16 percent), while the percentage of adults who read paper books fell from 72 percent to 67 percent. This transposition is not showing any signs of stopping.

Despite arguments over whether someone would prefer reading paper books over e-books, the economics behind the so-called "e-book Revolution" are undeniable. Most of what we know as the traditional publishing business was developed during the Great Depression and was slanted to heavily favor retailers in an effort to keep thousands of independent bookstores open.

A lot has changed in the intervening decades, but all along, the idea of self-publishing, usually written off as "vanity publishing," was a minor blip on the bigger radar screen of the publishing business. Authors who attempted it had to put their own money on the line, paying to print and distribute their own books without the help of the sales forces and connections of the major publishers. Just finding a bookstore to carry any of your books was nearly impossible, and like the rest of the business, self-published authors were selling on consignment.

When Amazon began its open beta of Kindle Direct Publishing toward the end of 2007, a whole new avenue was available to independent publishers. The e-book provided a way to publish your book without any up-front cost at all. The number of available titles quickly exploded, and the Internet, the publishing business, and even the mainstream business press started to buzz: *Is this the end of publishing as we know it?*

"New York publishers are not going to go away," answers author Mel Odom, who publishes both with traditional publishing houses and on his own in the indie e-book sphere. "They are going to transform, reshape, and rededicate themselves. New York publishers have been shown that they are not the only game in town these days, but a lot of readers have also learned that a good editor is every bit as important as a good writer."

At this point, anyone with basic computer skills and a manuscript can publish an e-book via services like Kindle Direct, Smashwords, Barnes & Noble's PubIt!, and many others. But the question remains: Just because you can, does that mean you should?

According to R. T. Kaelin, who made a splash in the indie publishing world with his epic fantasy *Progeny*, "The very thing that makes indie publishing so wonderful also happens to be the albatross hanging around its neck. The ease of e-book publishing paired with the ability to do POD (print on demand) has made it so that anyone can put a book out. The problem with that? Well ... anyone can put a book out.

"The wringer books used to be put through—a long line of agents, editors, copyeditors, etc.—can now be circumnavigated by anyone with a keyboard and the desire to throw some words on the screen. There is a plethora of poorly conceived, written, and executed work in the indie market now. More noise than signal. Some are doing it right—hiring editors, designers, copyeditors— and that material is good. Most are not, and that material is ... not so good."

And now that the e-book has fully infiltrated the smartphone and tablet market via free apps for Kindle, Nook, and many other formats, and all of the big publishers have hopped on the e-publishing bandwagon, there's no shortage of e-books available. What any author needs to keep in mind when considering self-publishing is that once you make that decision, you're now not only an author, but a publisher, too, and you're going to need to learn to do what publishers do. Shipping off a manuscript to a printer is only the smallest part of that.

"The connections the traditional industry has with trade journals, popular reviewers, and the like gives their books and authors a massive advantage," R. T. Kaelin said. "Indie publishers and authors must fight for every review, often personally contacting anyone with a blog who might want to read and write up something on their published work."

It may be tempting to see the ease of entry into self-publishing and hear the whispered voice say, "If you build it, they will come." But that's simply not the case.

---

And many authors with established careers, like J. A. Konrath and Mike Resnick, are taking on their own e-book publishing, cutting publishers out entirely. But again, heed R. T. Kaelin's warning: "Many authors from traditional publishing make the case that self-publishing is the way to go, that they can make more on their own without the publisher taking a big cut. And they are right. They can. They have name recognition, a brand, credentials, and a fan base on which to draw. For the unknown author entering the industry via the indie world, they have none of that."

Still, self-publishing presents several advantages and can serve as a way for a new writer to kick start a career. Having started in the indie world, Kaelin himself has recently signed with a well-known agent, and major publishers are looking to the indie world in search of the next generation of bestsellers.

There are also creative advantages that are worth considering, including, as Mel Odom has found, "the ability to write whatever you want at whatever length you wish. A new writer with nothing to lose or a professional writer who is making a comfortable living and can still turn out a few personal projects should definitely put out some independent books. Pursuing a digital career allows a professional writer to return to his or her roots, to write fearlessly for the sheer love of the craft about whatever idea has claimed his or her imagination. Indie publishing means that any story at any size has every chance of meeting with success."

Traditional publishers almost never publish works shorter than 50,000 words, and most science fiction and fantasy novels tend to be in the 90,000 word range. Publishing a 30,000-word novella would cost almost as much as a 90,000-word novel, forcing the publisher to fix the same cover price to a noticeably shorter book. But in the e-book world, length has become rather more plastic. As soon as a reader alters the size of the text on his or her screen, page count goes right out the window. Likewise, most of the e-book resellers are happy to sell books for as little as $0.99 or even allow author/publishers to give them away for free. That means an author can now sell a 30,000-word e-book for $2.99, and it makes sense to all involved. It's a third of the length, and a third of the price.

"Writers who pursue independent publishing exercise a whole lot of freedoms that have been MIA for a good long while," Odom continued. "Indie writers are getting to write whatever they want to write at whatever length they wish to. There's an awful lot of freedom in that. I have noticed over the last year that many of the New York publishers are now opening up digital arms, working with authors to prepare great e-books at different lengths and in some very interesting and open genres."

## MESSAGES FROM CYBERSPACE: ENTER THE BLOGOSPHERE

Before Amazon made creating your own e-books easy and free, the blogosphere did the same for magazines—after a fashion. For zero cost, anyone can publish anything on the Internet, and science fiction and fantasy fans jumped on this trend early. An explosion of fan sites and review sites started early and has not let up. And like the plethora of e-books out there, blogs and fan sites range in quality, from extremely professional to those doomed to obscurity.

Blog followers don't just want content, they want *quality* content. If you're posting book reviews, you'll need to have something of real value to say. Saying "this book sucks," or "this book is awesome," doesn't cut it.

John Ottinger III, the editor of GraspingfortheWind.com, whose reviews, articles, and interviews have appeared in *Publishers Weekly*, *Electric Velocipede*, *Strange Horizons*, *Black Gate*, and at Tor.com, as well as other venues in print and online, has this advice: "If you set out as a reviewer seeking to write critiques in a way no one else ever has, then you will fail. However, if you simply write your thoughts cogently and supported by the text, your authority and clarity will shine through. Readers of reviews, I believe, are looking for another reader, a reviewer, to be honest with them about likes and dislikes with clearly stated reasons why. Do this honestly, with no hedging, and your voice will be clear and authoritative."

Blogs and fan sites share another trait we've discussed in terms of writing in a specific genre or subgenre: You have to know what you're talking about.

John DeNardo, managing editor of SF Signal, a group blog devoted to speculative fiction in all of its forms, is "first and foremost a fan. Sharing that love of genre has been my motivation for starting SF Signal and continues to be my motivation today."

Historically, mainstream review sources like major newspapers and national magazines have shown a general ambivalence toward science fiction and fantasy. Many—and it may even be fair to say most—critics tend to dismiss genre fiction out of hand. So where do science fiction and fantasy fans go to find out about the next great book? In the past, there were review columns in magazines like *Analog*, and *Locus* has long been the genre's journal of record, but there have always been more books published every month than these scattering of critics could effectively read and critique.

The Internet comes to the rescue.

"In one sense I am nothing more than a fan with a bully pulpit," says John Ottinger, "but in another I am engaging with the aether of literature, touching the soul of books and their writers. I analyze, critique, engage with fiction so that others like me will find those books best suited to their tastes, because, after all, the thing readers most often like to see in fiction is themselves or the people they would like to be or become. If my criticism can lead a reader to such a book, then I have achieved my goal."

Launching a blog is easy, but finding an audience is much more difficult, and anyone looking to go that route should take John Ottinger's advice to heart. John DeNardo agrees: "Like any giver of opinions, to establish a foothold, one's views need to be consistently well-formed and well-communicated. It's not easy by any means, but with that formula and a bit of perseverance, the cream rises to the top."

The best blogs go beyond simply posting reviews and start to build communities of like-minded individuals. From the very early days of sci-fi fandom, fans gathered together at conventions and traded cheap, mimeographed "fanzines." With the instant availability and global nature of the Internet, these communities have migrated into cyberspace. And smart publishers and authors alike are keeping a close eye, if not actively joining in and interacting, with those communities.

"No doubt, the professional community is more aware of the size and voice of the fan community and has taken that into account in marketing and writing," says John Ottinger. "We have all become one giant focus group for the professionals in our community. But it is also true that any SF&F professional is a fan at heart. There is no distinction (other than that of remuneration) between a fan and a professional these days, and that is due in large part to the growth of the blogosphere. The distinctions (which were always rather arbitrary) have blurred beyond recognition, and this, I think, is positive change."

Ottinger went on to point out that "for all the glitz and glamour of various media campaigns, the truth is, it is your neighbor, your fellow church member, that guy at work with a crush on you, or your geeky roommate who is going to hook long-time and new readers of SF&F onto a new writer. Bloggers are that neighbor, geeky roommate, or potential lover. The big publishing houses now know this and so actively court bloggers as the word-of-mouth experts."

For more than one writer, the blogosphere has been a way to "break in" to the publishing business and explore opportunities for their own writing, but as John DeNardo points out, this is hardly a sure thing: "Some will say that maintaining a blog is time taken away from 'real' writing (whatever that is). Others say that blogging exercises writing skills, helps you build an audience, and helps you network with others in the industry."

Much more common are authors who have "broken in": published a few short stories or a novel, then use a regular blog to help spread the word and both create and nurture a fan community of their own.

"For some reason I do not yet clearly understand," John Ottinger muses, "we readers like to feel connected to the authors of our favorite books, as if they were people we *know*. And in a sense, we do, as no author can write a work without putting something of themselves into it, but by no means does reading a work make us the author's best friend or even really tell us about an author. A blog or website regularly updated with news, writing advice, opinions, memoirs, or the like helps readers feel more connected. Having this habit from the very start of opening yourself (within reason) to your readership engenders that intimacy and can gain you popularity that could potentially lead to fiction sales."

## FROM THE EDGE: THE NEW LITERATI

The history of the science fiction genre, as opposed to fantasy, has always been one of "Great Upheavals." From its wildly controversial beginnings with the 1818 publication of Mary Shelley's *Frankenstein* through the dueling Industrial Age adventures of Jules Verne and H. G. Wells, science fiction ended up, by the 1950s, as a pulp medium, dominated by the so-called "potboiler" space operas. Though there are some outstanding stories in that mix, the plot-oriented stories of ray guns, rocket ships, and bug-eyed monsters were easy prey for dismissing critics and for more forward-thinking authors.

The 1960s counter-culture brought us a science fiction renaissance thanks to authors like Harlan Ellison and Philip K. Dick. The accepted SF tropes were thrown off, and critics started having to invent new terms like "speculative fiction" or "slipstream" to come to grips with stories like Ellison's "'Repent, Harlequin!' said the Ticktockman," or Dick's *The Man in the High Castle*. And Frank Herbert (*Dune*) and Robert A. Heinlein (*Stranger in a Strange Land*) brought politics back to science fiction, lacking since Orwell's *1984*.

Then the 1970s came. In the post-Apollo era, a sort of malaise set in again until the 1984 publication of *Neuromancer* by William Gibson, which brought to life the "cyberpunk" subgenre and made science fiction cool again.

Most of us are still waiting for the next Great Upheaval in science fiction, and the lack of a clear game-changer may account for the general malaise in science fiction publishing.

Fantasy, on the other hand, has never really been about Great Upheavals. Trends in fantasy tend to come and go much more slowly, and fantasy authors, editors, and readers alike exhibit a sort of conservatism that's hard to ignore. This isn't conservatism in a Tea Party/FOX News sense of the word, but a set of expectations for the content and delivery of fantasy fiction.

Critic and blogger John Ottinger points out that "this genre of Tolkienesque fiction ruled the bestseller lists. It was this era that gave rise to or increased popularity for George R. R. Martin, Robert Jordan, Terry Brooks, Terry Goodkind, David Eddings, Robin Hobb, Margaret Weis, Lois McMaster Bujold, Mercedes Lackey, and a slew of others. Perhaps it was the end of the Cold War, perhaps something else, but readers were looking for the triumph of good over evil in a clearly defined sense."

It's fair to say that, conceptually, fantasy's Great Upheaval was the publication of *The Fellowship of the Ring* in 1954, and most of us have been drawing from that well ever since. But Ottinger is quick to note that "the backlash against such clear definitions has given rise or increased popularity to fantasists like Glen Cook, Joe Abercrombie, Richard Morgan, and Mark Lawrence, who eschew clear heroes and villains and opt instead for amoral actors in an amoral world. But even this backlash would not be needed without its predecessor. These epic fantasies are often the standard by which, fairly or unfairly, all other fantasy subgenres are judged."

--------------------------------------------------------------------------------

But even beyond the edgier side of traditional fantasy, or a hoped-for sword and sorcery renaissance, there are other authors who are working to test the limits of the fantasy genre not only in the approach to the relationship between heroes and villains, but in the art of the written word. Notable "literary fantasy" authors like Jeff VanderMeer, Catherynne M. Valente, Hal Duncan, and J. M. McDermott keep one eye on the archetypes of the genre and another on their own artistry, leaving that good vs. evil, third-person past-tense, three-act, medieval European genre conservatism behind entirely.

It's worth considering that with a clearer distinction between fantasy for adults and fantasy for children—now segregated in bookstores between the SF/Fantasy section and the Teen/YA section—authors now have the freedom to explore stories for younger readers, and other authors are taking advantage of that split in the opposite direction, leaving the kids to Harry Potter and asking Mom and Dad to join them in the sexually-charged dream world of *Palimpsest* (Catherynne M. Valente) or the urban spiritual decay of *When We Were Executioners* (J. M. McDermott).

Whatever the reason, McDermott doesn't see himself as a culture warrior doing battle against traditional epic fantasy. "I'm not interested in fighting anyone," he said. "And it's not about being obtuse for the sake of being different, but about being committed to a voice or vision. We get the genre we deserve. We make decisions on what the genre will be based on what is purchased. When you purchase something, you promote it. What is purchased the most will become the genre's center, even if it isn't really read, because editorial decisions will be wrapped around the sales figures. So, if you want things to be better or just different than they are, write those books and sell them."

## ONWARD AND UPWARD

The science fiction and fantasy genres have made great strides in the past twenty years or so, fueled as much by the computer as anything else. This one invention is responsible for the startlingly realistic computer-generated imagery that made *The Lord of the Rings*, *The Avengers*, *Avatar*, and the current generation of Hollywood blockbusters something for everyone, not just the B-movie cultists. It was the Internet that democratized the book review and brought discoverability to what would have otherwise been obscure mid-list releases, while at the same time building robust and engaging fan communities. It was the computer that gave us the e-book, independent/self-published and otherwise, which has also led to the re-publication of some older genre titles that otherwise would have fallen into total obscurity. It was the Internet that spread the word on Harry Potter and *Twilight*, building a whole new category, and at least temporarily saving an ailing publishing business. And then there are the video games like *Halo* and *Skyrim*—immersive science fiction and fantasy experiences giving birth to expansive new transmedia properties.

So then, what's next?

It's easy to look around now and feel as though we live in a science fiction world already. Every day we hear of advances in science and technology: astronomers finding planets around distant stars, the first hints of a possible cure for HIV, cloning, self-driving cars ... and at the same time, e-books are replacing the traditional bound, printed book that has been the default format for centuries. Will the e-book be around for centuries, then?

Technology is moving so fast now that the only sure bet is that nothing will be around for centuries, and there's basically no way to predict what will replace it. The world of 2113 will be even less recognizable to us than the world of 2013 would be to someone brought forward in time from 1913.

But what always has and always will remain is the human imagination.

Homer wrote *The Odyssey* some three thousand years ago—a fantasy if there ever was one. And people from every culture across the globe have been telling tall tales for at least that long—certainly much longer than that. It's what we do—we're a creative species.

Fantasy works on a very primal level. Our brains are hardwired for allegory, analogy, and metaphor. We communicate ideas through fable and story and have continued to do so regardless of technological or social advances. The fantasy and science fiction genres have grown in the past few decades to include women and a wide spectrum of ethnicities, cultures, and religious and political viewpoints. We all have stories to tell, and we'll always be looking for fresh, creative, fanciful ways to tell them.

And even as scientific and technological advances accelerate toward the so-called "singularity," there will always be something we can't quite do, and like Leonardo da Vinci sketching something that looks a bit like a helicopter five hundred years before a real one ever flew, today's science fiction authors are imagining the faster-than-light engines and artificial intelligences of some centuries hence. And there's no reason to believe that the nano-enhanced immortals of the Intergalactic Age won't still be looking forward to a time when someone will invent something that ... what?

And that's what science fiction and fantasy do. They ask, "What if?"

Where would we be if no one ever asked that?

# PART 3

# The World of Steampunk

## by Jay Lake

# The World of Steampunk

## by Jay Lake

Personally, I think Victorian fantasies are going to be the next big thing, as long as we can come up with a fitting collective term for Powers, Blaylock, and myself. Something based on the appropriate technology of the era; like 'steam-punks', perhaps.

—K. W. Jeter, *Locus* magazine, April, 1987

More than a decade passed between author K. W. Jeter coining the term "steampunk" in 1987 and the emergence of the speculative fiction subgenre as a strengthening trend with readers and publishers. Nowadays, the gear-encrusted guns, corsets, airships, tiny hats, and matching parasols grace the covers of adventures and romances alike. These visual cues signal "steampunk ahead!" Reading and writing this subgenre can be a lot of fun, but the enjoyment of steampunk's frivolity and trappings should not be taken to imply that this is all good times and games.

Steampunk is speculative fiction usually set in the Victorian and Edwardian eras, or in a pseudo-Victorian setting reflecting the visuals and values of those eras. The subgenre adopts a nostalgic, retrofuturistic view of the technology of the times and frequently takes the form of a high-stakes adventure tale. Stories in a steampunk world may explore societal conflicts and divisions, such as classism, imperialism, and chauvinism, or they may look backwards at the nineteenth century and its steam-based technologies with a displaced longing.

Like writers of alternative histories, steampunk writers twist the past, using that tension between the historical and the imaginary to ask what might have happened if steam and other nineteenth-century technologies were taken a few steps further or a few steps sideways. This produces a rich set of rococo images that has greatly captured the imaginations of writers, artists, filmmakers, game designers, musicians, performance artists, costumers, and fans over the past two decades.

While no specific elements of steampunk are absolutely essential, there is a generally understood group of features, at least some of which should be included for a work to be recognizable as steampunk. The dominant element that indicates steampunk is a real or imagined version of the technology of the nineteenth century. This specifically includes devices driven by steam power or counterweighted clockwork with its tightly wound springs. This technology is often used anachronistically and in excess of historical achievements.

Equally significant elements of steampunk include Victorian-era class and economic structures, implicit or explicit social critique, a Great-Game style of international politics, British imperialism or American westward expansion, an adventure-oriented plotline, and an emphasis on the empowerment of individuals in the face of industrial standardization and the advance of modern bureaucratic government. Some stories may also feature magic or paranormal or mythical creatures such as ghosts, vampires, and zombies. Others rely on fictional chemicals or substances, such as aether, to drive the technology. As a result, steampunk straddles some of the dividing lines between fantasy and science fiction as it looks to the reimagined past with nostalgia.

This "future that never was" is perhaps the heart of steampunk. The idealized intersection of accessible technology, the power of an individual creator, and the wide-eyed optimism that represented the best of the Victorian world is where the steampunk novel or story abides. And this is where the fun comes in: when the great machines in the back of your creative writer's mind start to hiss and clank and lurch into motion amid the brass-glinting shadows of a blood moon.

Steampunk is closely related to the long-established subgenre of alternate history. However, steampunk often sidesteps the careful research and meticulous accuracy found in the best of alternate history, such as *For Want of a Nail* by Robert Sobel (1973) or the works of Harry Turtledove, in favor of a looser association of elements driven by their entertainment value. It's as if alternate history decided to let its freak flag fly.

Steampunk is also often compared with cyberpunk, an association that comes as much from the similarity of names. "Steampunk" is a bit misleading. K. W. Jeter almost certainly had his tongue firmly planted in his cheek when he wrote his now infamous 1987 letter to *Locus* magazine. His use of the suffix "punk" was trading off the prominence of cyberpunk at that time, while referring back to work by himself, James Blaylock, and Tim Powers, which embodied the antiestablishment sensibilities of both cyberpunk and the original punk movement. But the suffix "-punk" has come to mean "genre" or "movement," at least in the SF field, diluting its original impact.

Cyberpunk embodied biting contemporary social critique that was very self-consciously woven into its narratives. Steampunk, on the other hand, is a subgenre defined by and dominated by its surface style and uses the structures and tropes of alternate history to frame plot and setting. The social critique is certainly present, either directly or by implication, but it's not a defining characteristic of steampunk, and it doesn't have the contemporary immediacy of cyberpunk's cynical worldview.

While the original cyberpunks really did have some roots in the musical and cultural punk movements, not to mention quite literally a political manifesto of their own, the original steampunks played with style rather than the deep substance that the cyberpunks embraced. Many of today's steampunks are carrying on that stylistic tradition to pen both serious and lighter stories.

In other words, steampunk is not so much a deeply-rooted literary movement but more of a stylistic trend—a flavor, or a skin.

This is not a negative observation. Quite the opposite. While some steampunk work can have deep and abiding critical substance, such as Philip Pullman's *His Dark Materials* trilogy, with its deep examination of the religious impulse, it is stylistic strength that gives steampunk adaptability and staying power. The subgenre's ability to evolve over time is one of its greatest assets. What started out as a grace note in the ongoing symphony of fantasy and science fiction has blossomed in dozens of different directions. These offshoots range from a significant influence in film and gaming to an entire genre of music, costuming extravaganzas, and a significant role in the Maker movement. Since it never had a box to fit inside in the first place, steampunk has succeeded, much like its namesake *steam*, in expanding to fill a number of cultural spaces.

With all fiction, you must never lose sight of the fact that your goal is to tell a good story. This is especially true of steampunk. At its heart, the genre is adventure fiction in the tradition of Victorian-era *Boy's Own* books—ripping good yarns filled with tales of derring-do and high adventure, packed with cool toys, and voyaging to interesting places.

The primary appeal of steampunk is that it is fun. Without a sense of humor and a willingness to play, you will struggle to write compelling steampunk stories. Intriguing technology and killer style counts for a lot with steampunk aficionados, but making your reader want to stand up and cheer for your characters counts for everything.

> Steampunk is what happens when goths discover brown.
> —Jess Nevins, as quoted by Cherie Priest (2010)

## ORIGINS AND GROWTH OF STEAMPUNK

While Jeter coined the term "steampunk" in the late twentieth century, the roots of the subgenre are far deeper and older. Seminal works in the speculative fiction canon date back to a time when the retrofuturism that characterizes steampunk today was simply futurism, with no "retro" expressed or implied. Novels and stories written by Jules Verne, H. G. Wells, and Rudyard Kipling are the forefathers of steampunk. Their stories are ur-steampunk as they anticipate a future, rather than look backwards, to revise the past. Their contemporary speculation has evolved into our technological nostalgia.

Reading these classics will ground you in the common vision that forms the bones of modern steampunk. Many of our concepts and clichés alike were coined a century or more in the past by these writers whose works are still remembered.

It can also be interesting to compare the well-known classics with stories from that same era that have become obscure over time. *The Log of the Flying Fish: A Story of Aerial and Submarine Peril and Adventure* by Harry Collingwood, written in 1887 and now seldom read, is a good example. Very much a story of its time, *The Log of the Flying Fish* tells the tale of well-funded gentleman explorers in their experimental amphibious airship who travel to the ends of the Earth in search of treasure, glory, and adventure. This short novel encapsulates much that is true of both the Victorian era in general and steampunk in particular: wincingly offensive in some ways because of its classism, racism, and imperialism, while also utterly charming in others.

Two other largely lost examples are *The Last American: A Fragment from The Journal of Khan-li, Prince of Dimph-Yoo-Chur and Admiral in the Persian Navy* by John Ames Mitchell (1889) and *The Wonderful Electric Elephant* by Frances Trego Montgomery (1904). These stories inform the thoughtful reader about the unselfconscious internal perspective of the times, giving you another view of the roots of steampunk.

By the second half of the twentieth century, Mervyn Peake was anticipating steampunk with his Titus Groan series (1946-1959), best known for *Gormenghast* (1950), which features a post-Victorian noble house in sharp decline, the remains of their ambitions still buoyed by a combination of what might be steampunk and what might be magic. Likewise Keith Roberts with *Pavane* (1968), an alternate history of a very steam-powered twentieth-century Britain, as well as Michael Moorcock's *The Warlord of the Air* (1971) and *The Land Leviathan* (1974), which narrate Edwardian military adventurism through the lens of what we would now call steampunk technology.

Film and television progressed similarly. Fritz Lang's *Metropolis* (1927) is often cited as a very early steampunk influence, largely for the production design and art direction. The CBS television series *The Wild Wild West* (1965–1969) combined adventure plots with steam-powered Gatling guns and endless Mission Impossible-style nineteenth-century gadgetry. Later movies, including David Lynch's *Dune* (1984) and Terry Gilliam's *Brazil* (1985), while not working within the explicitly proto-steampunk plots of The Wild Wild West, explored the visual elements of steampunk, including costuming, set design, and alternative technology.

All of these works carry significant elements we can now recognize as steampunk. This includes (for most of them) the layering of nostalgia and retrofuturism that is absent from earlier works that were written in and of the times we now view as the re-imagined past.

The self-conscious application of the term "steampunk" comes into play with the works of James Blaylock, K. W. Jeter, and Tim Powers. Their work was swiftly followed by such now-classics as *The Difference Engine* by William Gibson and Bruce Sterling (1990), an alternate history based on the premise that mechanical engineer Charles Babbage's analytical machine worked, and Paul Di Filippo's *Steampunk Trilogy* (1995), which uses the stylistic elements of steampunk in a cockeyed exploration of life in Great Britain and New England a century ago.

The beginning of the twenty-first century saw important new work in this mold, including China Miéville's *Perdido Street Station* (2000), which melded a steampunk sensibility into urban fiction in a subgenre called the New Weird. At about the same time, the beginning of the *Mortal Engines* quartet by Philip Reeve (2001) was published, portraying a grim future of roaming mechanical cities parasitically consuming the ravaged landscapes of the world. At that point, the genre began to explode. Works from Gail Carriger, Cherie Priest, and Stephen Hunt, along with many others, filled bookshelves and e-readers across the fandom of science fiction and fantasy.

This growth also drove an expansion of steampunk into a number of other areas. This includes unabashed secondary world fantasy, such as Perdido Street Station, which sidestepped the alternate history roots of steampunk in favor of exploring realms of the imagination. Future history in the tradition of Asimov and Heinlein emerged, for example, Stephen Hunt's *The Court of the Air* books (2009), about a far future England, as well as the twenty-second-century Mark Twain analog *Julian Comstock* by Robert Charles Wilson (2010). Dark alternate history strayed into Cherie Priest's *Boneshaker* (2009), which leveraged steampunk's connections with American westward expansion, and military fiction such S. M. Stirling's *The Peshawar Lancers* (2001).

There is also a strong body of steampunk short fiction. An excellent overview of this can be found in the anthology series edited by Ann and Jeff VanderMeer, including *Steampunk* (2008) and *Steampunk II: Steampunk Reloaded* (2010). There is also the more introspective consideration of *The Steampunk Bible* edited by Jeff VanderMeer and S. J. Chambers (2011).

Beyond that, steampunk began colonizing other genres and subgenres, including fantasy, romance, mystery, Web comics, and comic books—those last being famously exemplified by the gaslamp fantasy of Phil and Kaja Foglio, beginning with *Girl Genius* (2001), where clockwork often features prominently in place of the more usual steam power.

At its heart, steampunk has a powerful appeal to readers' sense of fun, and this broad expansion into other genres is further evidence that steampunk is as much a stylistic trope as a deep-rooted literary movement. The river burst its banks, and flooded out the neighbors.

That same diversity continues to be on display in steampunk's explosive growth outside books and stories. Art, music, costuming, gaming, and the Maker movement—the visual language and cultural messaging arising from steampunk's literary wellspring has seized a very wide audience across many areas. Look to work from the League of S.T.E.A.M., Abney Park, Steam Powered Giraffe, Thomas Willeford, Geoff Falksen, Austin Sirkin, Jess Nevins, and many more for inspiration beyond stories that you can fold back into your own writing.

In short, from its origins as the mainstream of science fiction well over a century ago, steampunk has alternately gone underground, gone punk, then once more gone back into science fiction's mainstream. Understanding some of that history and using it as a touchstone can be incredibly helpful to newer writers interested in diving in. The water's fine, the pool is fun, and some of the swimmers have been in here a long time.

> Few witnesses agree, and fewer still were granted a glimpse of the Incredible Bone-Shaking Drill Engine. Its course took it under the earth and down hills, gouging up the land beneath the luxurious homes of wealthy mariners and shipping magnates, under the muddy flats where sat the sprawling sawmill, and down along the corridors, cellars, and storage rooms of general stores, ladies' notions shops, apothecaries, and yes ... the banks.
> —Cherie Priest, *Boneshaker* (2009)

## ESSENTIAL ELEMENTS OF STEAMPUNK

So how do you bring this miracle of creation to pass? By exploiting the essential elements of steampunk, of course. Understand them and make them your own.

Any genre or subgenre has its tropes, its well-understood conflicts and story elements, its stock characters, and bog-standard plots. These are the signifiers by which works in that genre or subgenre identify themselves to fans and critics. In other words, they are what noted science fiction editor and critic Gardner Dozois calls "the furniture of science fiction"—the passwords, if you will, into the realms behind the doors of those fields.

As always, the best way to develop a vocabulary of the essential "furniture" of steampunk is to go back to the classics as well as the newer novels and stories that have shaped the subgenre. Whether you choose to read steampunk in its earliest contemporary form (in the original Klingon, so to speak), pursue the mid-century sources, or follow the modern movement from its 1980s origins forward—read it. Read it a lot. Dive in, get the flavor. See where the fun is. Roll around inside the stories. See what kinds of plots people use as skeletons to hang the story on, how the characters behave in those worlds.

Steampunk is more than cogwheels and tiny hats. Be conscious of the types of adventures, the classic protagonists, the variety of social, cultural, economic, and technological details that can drive a story, motivate characters, and flesh out a world.

Let's explore the elements and archetypes that you will use or react to in your own writing.

## STEAMPUNK PLOTS

Because steampunk can be interpreted as a skin or a style rather than a deep genre of its own, a wide range of plot structures and devices are available to you, the writer. This is how steampunk can embrace the diversity discussed earlier while still holding on to its clanking heart. Hence the emergence of steampunk romances such as Meljean Brook's *The Iron Duke* (2010), steampunk Westerns such as Felix Gilman's *The Rise of Ransom City* (2012), and steampunk mysteries such as *The Affinity Bridge* by George Mann (2008).

Much of steampunk literature falls into the category of a hero's journey. That can take the form of an adventure quest, the struggle of a benighted or outcast individual to find their way back into or around society. But a steampunk plot also can focus on outsider conflict, for which the Victorian class structure and political environment offers very fertile ground. Even where steampunk concerns itself with the powerful, you will find conspiracy plots akin to thrillers, wheels within wheels driving action and shaping changes for the protagonists and secondary characters alike.

Likewise, the old classics work well, such as divergence between two main characters' goals. This is usually the case in steampunk romances.

Steampunk plots do not tend toward validation of social norms with a focus on restoration of order. This reflects the subgenre's roots in science fiction, where disruptive or nonnormative plots and story outcomes are stereotypical. When steampunk moves into romance, detective, or fantasy fiction, those genres' drive toward the restoration of order as a character motivator is automatically in conflict with steampunk's disruptive, outsider nature. Within those genres, a character's inability to restore the desired order drives them to dramatic change. For example, *Tarnished* by Karina Cooper (2012), part of the St. Croix Chronicles, features a main character who is an opium addict and an heiress, and acts as a detective of sorts in Victorian England because her allowance doesn't cover her addiction. Steampunk romances, detective stories, and fantasies follow science fiction into disruptive plot arcs, which often bring about profound changes not only in the characters but in the world surrounding them.

You can find pointers to this kind of plotting not only in the works of fiction in the steampunk canon, but also in nonfiction covering the era. Mike Jay's *The Air Loom Gang* (2004), for example, is as strange a story of murder, mind control, and disruptive technology as you'll find. Yet is it also a true-to-life tale from the late eighteenth century, when the Industrial Revolution was just stirring and Queen Victoria was not even conceived.

The main thing to keep in mind when plotting a steampunk story is that a sense of fun, often bordering on sheer, wall-eyed weirdness, is one of your best keys to the subgenre. Steampunk was born to be an over-the-top form. The characters might be wry, understated persons of mordant wit and significant accomplishment, but if you give them a story which carries the reader along in a flood of action analogous to the classic cyberpunk "eyeball kick", you will fulfill the promise of steampunk.

Have fun with your story or novel, and make the reader have fun with the characters to be found within it.

## STEAMPUNK CHARACTERS

Speaking of characters, what sorts inhabit steampunk worlds? All types, really, with an emphasis on the economy, culture, and technology of the times. To name a few of the archetypes, there are the scientist, explorer, commoner/

laborer, polymath/Renaissance man or woman, genius mechanic, airship captain or navigator, fallen gentry, orphan, gifted teacher, trusted lady's maid or butler and other servants, con-artist, and social reformer/labor organizer.

The most obvious, perhaps, is the scientist-as-hero, such as Langdon St. Ives in James P. Blaylock's novel *Lord Kelvin's Machine* (1992). One of the key elements driving steampunk is the nostalgia for a technology that was accessible to any competent, educated pair of hands with the right tools and a suitable workshop. This is reflected in the rakish steampunk cast to the Maker movement, for example, and likewise the fanciful props of fabricators and performance artists like Thomas Willeford and the League of S.T.E.A.M.

Closely related to the scientist-as-hero is the polymath. The Victorian era is often seen as the last period in history where a well-educated man or woman really could have a grasp on most of the body of human knowledge. In Gail Carriger's Parasol Protectorate series, Madame LeFoux, a supporting character, is well versed in history, science, and several languages and can manufacture ornithopters, tanks, and cunning devices, such as weapons concealed within parasols.

In real life, the deep specialization required in modern science and engineering and academic disciplines was already coalescing in the nineteenth century, but the trope of the all-knowing (if not all-wise) polymath is still viable within the steampunk framework. That close view of everything appeals to modern technophilic readers immersed in geek culture and our world of constantly evolving gadgetry, goods, and services.

Keep in mind that you as the writer do not need to keep your sights focused on society's elites. Another steampunk character archetype is the navvy—someone from the working class, perhaps one of the laborers who worked so hard on the construction of the glorious brass-riveted airships steaming their way through your narrative skies. Consider the intersection between the fallen nobility and the aspiring commoner, a dynamic that Scott Westerfeld leverages in his novel *Leviathan*. Westerfeld's main character, Deryn Sharp, is both a commoner and a girl disguised as a boy to join the British Air Service. Her brilliance as a midshipman brings her into contact with the upper-class scientist and others.

Look to that pairing of extremes and the accompanying comparison of classes in transition to provide significant character motivation and plot drivers.

---

The social and economic pyramid of the Victorian world was built on the backs of the industrial peasantry, those shovelers of coal and workers of metal and builders and craftsmen who made possible all the magic machinery.

In this same vein, useful contrasts can be drawn between the polymath or scientist-as-hero at one end of that scale and the laboring class at the other. No one builds a great, steam-powered, iron-walled fortress without hundreds of minions laboring at their behest. Those minions can have fascinating stories, too.

The Victorian era also saw the emergence of the general staff model within the military and similar middle management structures in the corporate and economic world. There you will find further fertile ground from which to draw characters—those indispensable men-in-the-middle (or women, depending on how you build your world) who know how everything is supposed to work but struggle under the burden of ill-informed and strangely-motivated decisions from on high. If you're going to write about the military, do some research on how the various armies and navies filled their ranks and how they were supported. This will help you understand why someone would join, how a soldier became an officer, and the impact of social class on military decisions and orders.

Another steampunk favorite is the Victorian archetype of the explorer. In this last era before air travel, much of the world was not yet mapped in detail. This gives writers the freedom to create characters who search for lost cities in the desert, find uncharted islands in the deep ocean, and discover glittering caverns carved with the faces of ancient, eldritch gods. There are plenty of hair-raising narratives of real life exploration you can research to help prime the pump of your imagination.

Be aware that many of the archetypal steampunk characters fit into or drive various critiques of steampunk discussed later in this chapter. Without intending to, you can invoke racist, classist, sexist, and imperialist stereotypes and plot elements. Whether or not you want to write steampunk as social critique—remember, your primary purpose is to entertain—it is very helpful to keep these pitfalls firmly in mind. Own them in your work, and make your story transcend those concerns, and you will have the potential to reach an even wider audience.

Another place to look for steampunk character types is among the roster of workaday occupations in Victorian times. Even if you stay within the bounds of Anglo-American culture, the list is nearly endless. It can range from the very obvious to the very strange, including almoners and aurifabers as well as zitherers and zoographers, and everything in between. See a website entitled *Victorian Occupations: Job Titles in the 19th Century* for a good summary of hundreds of occupations.

A final consideration when contemplating steampunk character types is to reflect on what genre underpins your steampunk story. Assuming you accept the notion that steampunk is a skin or a stylistic wrapper, what lies beneath? Is your story a western, a bodice-ripping romance, an occult horror story, or an espionage thriller? Each of those genres and subgenres comes with its own furniture, its own stock cast of archetypes and stereotypes. Look for intersections between your core dynamic and the flash of steampunk. That's where characters will arise in your writing who can be well fleshed, fully formed, and attractive to your readers.

## STEAMPUNK SETTINGS

As the saying goes, a story starts out with a character with a problem in a setting. If plots are the problems and characters themselves, then the setting is the stage on which they act out their desires, hatch their fiendish plans, and meet their just (or unjust) desserts. Steampunk, with its obsession with the rococo excesses of Gilded Age technology, design, and style, provides fertile ground for glorious settings on which to play out your stories.

The classic default is some version of Victorian London, suitably modified to support the fantastic or science fictional elements of your story. The economic and political heart of the globe in late-nineteenth-century London offers an infinitely diverse urban geography, the cutting edge technology of the times, and the seat of the British Empire with all the pomp and politics that implies.

However, London and the British Empire have become something of a cliché. If you're going to play there, do it well. Authors Gail Carriger and Karina Cooper embossed their own and very different stamps on London. Or look beyond the British capital to other parts of the world. The American West, especially in the post-Civil War era, has been fertile ground for steampunk. The lingering trace of the old magical world, the fading ghosts of Native American culture, the half-healed social wounds of the War Between the States, and the vastly varied terrain of North America all intersect to provide a rich breeding ground for setting. Through setting, they can also drive story.

If you want to escape Eurocentrism, go to China and a culture where technology already was flourishing when the ancestors of the Victorians still wore uncured animal skins and hunted with sticks. Or classic African settings such as Zimbabwe, the Kingdoms of Dahomey and Ife, or Timbuktu at the height of its power as the center of Islamic learning. Likewise the New World, where pre-Columbian cultures of great sophistication flourished along the rivercourses, coastlines, and high mountain valleys of two continents.

Some focused reading and research into the history of the world and of non-Western cultures in particular will provide many choices for fascinating settings and backgrounds that carry the rich texture of reality while also providing the novelty that so many readers crave. But setting does not refer just to story fodder on a national or continental scale. You must also conceive your setting by considering details on a human scale. What kind of workshop does your coppersmith labor in? Is your fallen lord's ruined manor supported by sheep farming or fields of barley and rye? What was the prevailing architecture of British colonial homes in Ceylon or South Africa or Singapore in the era of your story? What kind of hammock did Royal Navy sailors use, that your airmen in Her Majesty's sky trawlers might sling between the stanchions supporting their vessel's looming gas bag?

The Victorian era is the first period of history for which we have contemporary photo references, along with copious engravings and illustrations, to show us what the world actually looked like to the people who inhabited it at the time. Artists of earlier eras, dependent on patronage, often idealized their subjects and their surroundings. By the second half of the nineteenth century, images in both photography and art were becoming ubiquitous enough that the mundane, as well as the terrible, were recorded.

Use those images and the world they represent to build your own. Go beyond Hollywood and the works of other writers to see what those settings were really like and what they meant to the people who lived and worked there. Then your fiction will feel real. In creating that feeling of reality, you will capture the reader.

## STEAMPUNK TECHNOLOGIES

In some ways, technology is the Achilles heel of steampunk. Much of the subgenre relies on rubber science deployed to cover a multitude of impossibilities around the power-to-weight ratios and materials strengths involved in using steam for real-life applications. There are some very good engineering reasons that no one ever successfully built a steam-powered airship. Even as far back as Collingwood's 1887 *The Log of the Flying Fish* this issue was obvious. The author goes to some trouble in his story to make his hero's airship work with a newly-invented, ultralight, very strong material which serves as both the gas bag and the fuel. (Think carefully about that for a minute...) Collingwood buries his handwavium layers deep behind artifice and narrative contrivance.

It's a truism in speculative fiction that you get one impossible thing for free. In science fiction, this might be FTL or strong AI—or both, if you combine them into one trope as the Federation's starships do within the *Star Trek* continuity. In fantasy, this can be the magic sword the farm boy finds in the rafters of his grandfather's hut. In steampunk, readers will give you a free pass for the technological improbabilities that infuse much of the work within the subgenre. Everything that follows that first impossible thing will have to be justified in your text.

A number of technological signifiers help mark a narrative as steampunk. The airship is a notorious symbol of the genre—one I've been quite guilty of heavily exploiting in my own work—and it serves a number of symbolic purposes. Airships float above the Earth, detached from mundane terrestrial concerns, providing the escape of travel with the romance of a bygone era and offering sheer, old-fashioned coolness.

A number of other technologies come into play as well. Steam power plants. Cunning clockwork mechanisms. Gatling guns and Congreve rockets and early generations of repeating rifles. Famously, real-life incarnations of Charles Babbage's difference engine, perhaps programmed by students of mathematician Countess Ada Lovelace, who in reality was the world's first hacker. Railroad locomotives and landwalkers and steam-powered elephants. All the arts and crafts of the first generations of modern metallurgy, of sound refining and production techniques, straddling the intersection between the old guild and crafts model of production and the inevitable march of standardized manufacturing and economies of scale.

Invented technology should fit the type of story a writer is telling. For example, mechanical ladybugs attack the protagonist in one installment of Carriger's witty Parasol Protectorate series. In Cherie Priest's darker *Boneshaker*, protagonist Zeke Wilkes must face the consequences of his father's Incredible Bone-Shaking Drill Engine.

Much as with questions of setting, questions of technology are a basic part of steampunk's view of the world. The common plots, the archetypical characters, the times and places the stories take place in—these are all informed by the technologies of both the real Victorian era and the imagined Victorian era of our steampunk dreams.

Research Isambard Kingdom Brunel and the *Great Eastern* to learn how big these people thought. As with setting and characters, dig into the real history and you will see all kinds of bizarre ideas that were proposed and even attempted in this time when a well-funded entrepreneur or a lone, dedicated genius still could seriously contemplate taking the world head-on.

## PULLING IT ALL INTO TROPES

Much of what is discussed in this chapter can be thought of as the tropes of the subgenre—the furniture of steampunk. These tropes are the signifiers by which we know our work and our work knows us. None of them is required—not airships, not Victorian London, not the scientist-as-hero, none of them—but some combination of them is essential to signal your narrative's intention to be a part of this particular stream of storytelling.

Think of these tropes as the holistic integration of the elements already reviewed. Taken as a loose and clanking whole, those parts assemble into story elements and then into fully formed narratives that participate in the ongoing conversation that is steampunk. Indeed, this is how any genre or subgenre evolves, advancing itself through an iterative process of dialogue and reaction. Any genre is a sort of literary call-and-response that can be as fresh as this month's issue of your favorite magazine while simultaneously as old as storytelling itself.

Whatever its deeper meanings might be, steampunk is first and foremost a

---

style. An understanding of the real history of the Victorian era, combined with awareness of modern critique of the attitudes embodied in that era's legacy, will ground you to build that style in your own work. Following the through-line of steampunk plots, characters, settings, and technology will create the stage for your stories and set mechanisms of wondrous device marching across that stage in quickstep.

Learn this, internalize this, make it your own, and your steampunk will shine, clank, and hiss with the best of them.

## VARIATIONS AND NEW DIRECTIONS

The subgenre has spawned a number of collateral threads in fiction—or per-haps more accurately in some cases, merged with them. Clockpunk, for exam-ple, which can be found in Roger Zelazny's *Jack of Shadows* (1971), expands into the steampunk world with books like my own *Mainspring* (2007). Other threads include dieselpunk, which is steampunk stories pushed into the post World War I era, when diesel and petrol power had thoroughly overtaken the early promise of steam in all but the heaviest-duty applications.

Likewise, through backformation, the speculative fiction field has seen the emergence of alternatives such as sandalpunk—Bronze Age adventure fiction—and sailpunk—naval stories from the eighteenth and nineteenth centuries.

The spirit of playfulness which already inhabits the idea of steampunk in all its manifold forms certainly applies to the future of the subgenre as well. We cannot dwell forever in Victoria's house. Speculative fiction is like rock and roll: Once a movement is born, it never really dies. The threads become layered into the tapestry of the whole as one more tradition, one more stream of sound and color.

Right now, in the mid 2010s, steampunk is a major thread which even in its contemporary form stretches back over a quarter century. That thread will stay bright and vibrant for many years to come. At the same time, some of these newer variations will gain traction, perhaps blossom into major threads of their own, much as steampunk paranormal already has, and steampunk romance is in the process of doing now.

The opportunity this represents for a newer writer with commercial aspi-rations should be obvious. The playground of steampunk is still wide open and available for all sorts of innovation. The flow of new extensions to that playground remains strong. You can write strong, classic steampunk adventure stories. Sort of like playing four-bar rock and roll—satisfying work with a steady market, and a heck of a lot of fun. Or you can experiment, explore new vistas, and use the current forms of the field as a touchstone to advance your own career and hopefully bring a whole world of readers, writers, and critics with you.

This subgenre offers many uncharted waters and wide-open skies. Grab your goggles, board the airship of your imagination, and go forth to build a retrofuture distinctively your own.

> Away down the Ulundi River's long, lush valley the dirigible floated, freshly loaded with tin and tea, cocoa and hemp, the region's produce. Leopold's guns posed it not the slightest danger; they were gone. The flight to the lowland ports would be as uneventful as her voyage here. This was 1914. The tyrant had been vanquished for almost ten years.
> —Nisi Shawl, "The Return of Cherie" (2011)

## CRITICAL REACTIONS TO STEAMPUNK

As with any prominent entertainment vehicle, steampunk has provoked a wide range of response from literary critics and observers of speculative fiction. A frequent critique of steampunk is that it glorifies and valorizes the Victorian era without acknowledging or making amends for the notorious problems of that time. This view can be loosely divided into three related areas: racism, classism, and imperialism.

For many writers and observers of the steampunk movement, this is a touchy subject. The racist critique is perhaps the most difficult of all because of its powerful resonances in contemporary society. For all of our widely touted values of acceptance and inclusiveness, speculative fiction fandom and writerdom alike tend heavily white. This offers an automatic barrier to entry for persons of color that is almost always invisible to others not subject to such issues.

Combine that ever-present touchpoint with the egregious embedded racism of an upper-class view of Victorianism and you begin to see the problem. People of color were marginalized both at the time and in later histories of the time. African-American writer and fan Doselle Young calls this "cotton gin punk" (in conversation with Nisi Shawl). This makes it very easy for even the most well-meaning writer to frame a story that echoes the racism of the era without ever intending to do so.

This is by no means a call for political correctness or didactic multiracial-ism. Instead, I am strongly suggesting that writers maintain an awareness of the complex and difficult social issues inherent in the milieu of steampunk. You can incorporate that awareness into the stories you wish to tell in whatever way fits your narrative and your goals. Just don't write in ignorance.

While steampunk does not have a deeply embedded ethos of social criticism as cyberpunk did, nonetheless, some authors are using the subgenre to take these issues head on. Writer and critic Nisi Shawl, who is African-American, addresses racism and imperialism in her story "The Return of Cherie" (2011). Shawl writes of a Congo at the turn of the twentieth century where the hideous and genocidal misrule of King Leopold II of Belgium has been overturned, ending what in real life was one of the most tragic human rights disasters in recorded history. In place of Leopold's exploitative rule stands a cluster of independent fictional kingdoms that deploy a clever combination of indigenous technology and resources. Shawl's narrative is peppered with classic steampunk elements, such as airships and Great-Game politics, but with a distinctly African twist.

Shawl is writing from the perspective of a person of color (the contem-porary context of her work) about the aftermath and recovery from one of the worst racial injustices in history (the textual content of her work) while maintaining the attitude and sense of adventure that keeps the label of steampunk firmly affixed to her work. This is social criticism-by-example rather than social criticism-by-lecture. If anything, Shawl's work is the oppo-site of political correctness and a terrific demonstration of how to fold a cultural and social consciousness into a work of entertainment.

When writing steampunk, classism is also an easy trap to fall into. While we as modern readers and writers tend to be correctly embarrassed—and even horrified—at the Victorians' view of ethnicity and race, we often glorify their view of class. Witness the popularity of television shows such as *Downton Abbey* in the mid 2010s. Let's face it—to Americans especially, there is some-thing very glamorous about blue blood nobility. On our own turf here in the United States, we often see robber baron capitalism as romantic and fascinat-ing, for all that it was built on the suffering of millions, encompassing child labor, unregulated pollution, and half a hundred other horrors.

Steampunk definitely goes there. In some cases, steampunk protagonists are from the underclass. In other cases, they may be born of higher station but fall, or are pushed, to the belowdecks portion of society where the black gangs labor to ceaselessly shovel coal into the fiery furnaces that power the worlds of our imaginations.

Scott Westerfeld's *Leviathan* (2009) combines both these archetypes in the dual protagonists of Deryn Sharp, a commoner girl who serves as a British airman in an alternate WWI, and Prince Aleksandar of Hapsburg, a fallen scion of a noble house who is on the run. Westerfeld's project isn't analogous to Shawl's—he's not embarking on an explicit critique of classism in steampunk—but he is using the elements of classism to drive his adventure story with a self-conscious awareness of the real-life roots from which he is drawing.

More generally speaking, the nobility and great houses of Victorian England, as well as their Edwardian successors, were like icebergs—the glittering façade above the surface is supported by a much larger and more complex mass hidden from view. For every intemperate second son or consumption-raddled heiress, there are platoons of servants, farmers, and soldiers laboring to keep those at the top of the hierarchy in their effortless style.

Again, tell the story you are drawn to tell, but don't lose sight of how nineteenth-century societies really functioned. The girl who brings the tea and the boy straining to push the lawn roller are just as much a part of the tale as the princess of industry on her clockwork carriage. Likewise the paper boy, the factory hand, and the urban beggar.

Imperialism is inextricably linked with Victorian practices of race and class. Contemporary Americans often don't tend to recognize themselves as living in an imperial era, but many people around the world see imperialism as alive and well. To a significant degree, the trappings of imperialism are almost inescapable in this literary form. Much as with the trappings of industrial capitalism, they are bred in steampunk's bones. That doesn't mean people can't or won't write explicitly anti-imperialist steampunk. Shawl is one of the writers doing so. To a milder degree Westerfeld does as well. Both authors offer alternatives to imperialism and respectfully explore issues associated with empire building. Likewise, literary and academic critiques have covered this ground. See Paul Jessup's online article "The Future of Steampunk" (2010), where he quantifies the problem of imperialism and darker tendencies in the subgenre.

Writers who remain conscious of the imperialist roots of Victorian and pseudo-Victorian societies as stereotypically celebrated in steampunk literature and art can make better choices and potentially pen a better rounded and more fulfilling tale.

The imperialist critique is perhaps less culturally sensitive than the racist and classist critiques, but it's no less important. Taken together, these three elements represent a fractured pedestal of the steampunk edifice. Not a weakness, per se, but veins to be mined to expand the richness of your narratives and the depths of your world-building.

A handful of editors and writers are tackling the issues of classism, racism, and imperialism head on, including the independent Hades Publishing anthology *Shanghai Steam* (2012), which offers a Chinese view of the steampunk world. Likewise, the blog *Beyond Victoriana* explores the multicultural possibilities of steampunk, offering insights into other cultures and modalities for the aspiring steampunk writer to explore.

Your story probably shouldn't indulge in a didactic critique—that would make for poor steampunk reading, not to mention lousy story-telling in general. But you should be aware of the potentially controversial underpinnings in a buckets-of-fun subgenre that's supposed to be spewing brass bolts and dark, satanic smokes as it lurches across the page.

A somewhat less controversial critique of steampunk concerns the inherent nostalgia built into the subgenre. This is close to the German concept of longing for a place you have never been—*Sehnsucht*—than to the true nostalgia for childhood or a home long since left behind.

Science fiction is by definition a forward-looking genre, almost always concerned with the future, yet steampunk, one of the hottest subgenres in the field, has its feet firmly planted in an often idealized version of the past that doesn't correspond well to the realities of the Industrial Revolution and the Gilded Age. We fantasize about what once was, then project forward, remaking the past to suit our current obsessions with technology, social change, and the true nature of progress in society.

All of these critical concerns should fall away in the face of your creative vision. Save these issues for when you are revising and then marketing your story, and possibly first conceiving of it. When actually writing a story, the rivets should gleam and the boilers should shriek and the madwoman with her hands clenched bloodlessly tight on the levers of power should have a laugh

---

that could call down the north wind and sing up the morning sun.

The lack of a political ambition corresponding to the earnest *Kulturkampf* of the cyberpunks has kept much of literary steampunk from recognizing its own roots and deeper meanings. In surfing the roiling surface of technological and social nostalgia, the steampunk movement has preserved much of its innocence. Willfully so, some critiques argue when talking about the imperialism, classism, and racism inherent in the Victorian social template.

Another aspect of steampunk to keep in mind when approaching the subgenre as a writer is how it lines up with the established parallelism of fantasy and science fiction. Steampunk, in point of fact, straddles some of the key dividing lines between the two genres.

For example, science fiction's demand for technological consistency, even within the bounds of so-called "rubber science," is routinely glossed over with steampunk technology. Steampunk often violates the power-to-weight ratios governing steam efficiency, at least in the context of the metallurgy and materials science available to Victorian-era inventors and craftspeople. Fantasy's classical requirement for a moral axis in the narrative is often lost in the situations and plots that drive many steampunk stories. To put it in simpler terms, authors often mix zeppelins and angels, or steam engines and zombies, and very few people complain.

You may want to consider the implications for marketing your story or novel when deciding whether to adhere to or violate conventions of science fiction and fantasy. While the old advice of never writing to market is sound and solid for very good reasons, keeping in mind what your market will bear is still a good idea for the author, especially when practicing the craft of revision.

Speaking in terms of marketing steampunk fiction, there's an interesting dispute emerging now in the 2010s. As with any evolving movement in art, music, or literature, there is an old guard interested in the original vision and newer people creating new directions under the same label and tradition.

Simply put, the question being asked is, "What is steampunk?" Underneath that question is another one: "Who gets to decide what steampunk is?" This pertains both to steampunk culture at large as well as to a literary framework.

Author, academic, and critic Jess Nevins describes this as steampunk becoming "the battleground for an intense semantic and philosophical war, albeit one whose combatants have little time for or interest in their opponents.

The combatants are the prescriptivists [...] and the descriptivists."

Put simply, the prescriptivists are those following along the tradition of K. W. Jeter's intentions in his 1987 coinage of the term "steampunk," meaning Victorian alternate history with fantastic or science fictional elements. The descriptivists are following the "I can't define it, but I know it when I see it" test (originally proposed in a different context by former U.S. Supreme Court Justice Potter Stewart). This is a dispute about authenticity, an argument between early adopters and those who came along after the light and heat and noise became more prominent.

From the point of view of an emerging writer, the nice thing about steampunk is precisely what bothers Nevins in his critical perspective. It's escaped both Jeter's original tongue-in-cheek coinage as well as the critical consensus that emerged in the 1990s and 2000s to become a marketing term in its own right—a highly successful marketing term that can help brand you and your work on the bookshelf, in the e-book world, and in the reader's mind.

For writers new to steampunk, this means you have the freedom to make steampunk whatever you want it to be. Repurpose and redefine the elements of steampunk to suit your personal vision. Own the narrative, make it yours, and strive to make it better than it was before. All fiction is layered upon the generations of work that came before it.

Still, just as understanding of the historical roots and context of steampunk is important to the emerging author, so is an understanding of the critical response to steampunk. You are certainly not required to hew to any of these critical concerns, but it's smart for you to be aware of them and understand the sorts of reactions your work might well draw.

Write a good story first. That's the beginning and the end of writing success, in any genre. But once you've written your steampunk story, know where you stand. Then you'll know what you've written and how to pitch your book and market your story. That will win you readers. Which is the real win.

# RECOMMENDED STEAMPUNK READING

Following is a list of works referenced in this chapter, along with some additional material, which should give you ample resources for both education and inspiration about the world of steampunk. The world of steampunk is, of course, much bigger and more complex than can ever be contained in this or any list, but this is a decent place for you to start.

## Novels

*20,000 Leagues Under the Sea*, Jules Verne, Pierre-Jules Hetzel, 1870

*The Affinity Bridge*, George Mann, Snowbooks, 2008

*Boneshaker*, Cherie Priest, Tor Books, 2009

*The Court of the Air*, Stephen Hunt, Voyager Books, 2007

*The Difference Engine*, William Gibson and Bruce Sterling, Victor Gollancz Ltd., 1990

*The Etched City*, K.J. Bishop, Prime Books, 2003

*For Want of a Nail*, Robert Sobel, Macmillan, 1973

*The Golden Compass* (first published as *Northern Lights*), Philip Pullman, Scholastic Point, 1995

*Titus Groan*, Mervyn Peake, Eyre & Spottiswoode, 1946

*The Iron Duke*, Meljean Brook, Berkley Trade, 2010

*Jack of Shadows*, Roger Zelazny, Walker and Company, 1971

*Julian Comstock*, Robert Charles Wilson, Tor Books, 2009

*The Land Leviathan*, Michael Moorcock, Quartet, 1974

*Leviathan*, Scott Westerfeld, Simon Pulse, 2009

*Lord Kelvin's Machine*, James P. Blaylock, Arkham House, 1992

*Mainspring*, Jay Lake, Tor Books, 2007

*Mortal Engines*, Philip Reeve, Scholastic, 2001

*The Rise of Ransom City*, Felix Gilman, Tor Books, 2012

*Pavane*, Keith Roberts, Rupert Hart-Davis, 1968

*The Peshawar Lancers*, S.M. Stirling, Roc, 2002

*Perdido Street Station*, China Miéville, Del Rey, 2003

*Soulless*, Gail Carriger, Orbit, 2009

*Tarnished*, Karina Cooper, Avon, 2012

*The Time Machine*, H.G. Wells, William Heinemann, 1895

*Warlord of the Air*, Michael Moorcock, Ace Books, 1971

*The Wonderful Electric Elephant*, Frances Trego Montgomery, he Saalfield Publishing Co., 1903

## Anthologies, Short Fiction, and Miscellaneous

*Beneath Ceaseless Skies*, www.beneath-ceaseless-skies.com

*Boilerplate*, Paul Guinan and Anina Bennett, Abrams Image, 2009

*Girl Genius*, Phil and Kaja Foglio, Airship Entertainment, 2001; www.girl geniusonline.com

*The Last American: A Fragment from The Journal of Khan-li, Prince of Dimph-Yoo-Chur and Admiral in the Persian Navy*, John Ames Mitchell, Frederick A. Stokes & Brother, 1889

*The Log of the Flying Fish: A Story of Aerial and Submarine Peril and Adventure*, Harry Collingwood, Blackie and Son, Ltd., 1887

"With the Night Mail", Rudyard Kipling, *McClure's Magazine*, November, 1905

*Shanghai Steam*, ed. Ace Jordyn, Calvin D. Jim and Renee Bennett, EDGE Publishing, 2012

*SteamPowered II: More Lesbian Steampunk Stories*, ed. JoSelle Vanderhooft, Torquere Press, 2011

*Steampunk*, ed. Ann and Jeff Vandermeer, Tachyon Publications, 2008

*Steampunk II: Steampunk Reloaded*, ed. Ann and Jeff VanderMeer, Tachyon Publications, 2010

## Television, Movies, and Media

*Abney Park*, www.abneypark.com

*Brazil*, dir. Terry Gilliam, Universal Studios, 1985

*Dune*, dir. David Lynch, Dino De Laurentiis Corporation/Universal Pictures, 1984

*The League of S.T.E.A.M.*, leagueofsteam.com

*Metropolis*, dir. Fritz Lang, UFA, 1927

*Steam Powered Giraffe*, www.steampoweredgiraffe.com

*The Wild Wild West*, dir. Irving J. Moore and others, CBS Television, 1965–1969

## Nonfiction and Criticism

*The Air Loom Gang*, Mike Jay, Four Walls Eight Windows, 2004 (reissued as

The Influencing Machine)

"Like Sculpting With Smog: Defining Steampunk", Jess Nevins, SF Studies

*Locus* magazine, Oakland, CA, www.locusmag.com

*The Steampunk Bible*, ed. Jeff VanderMeer and S.J. Chambers, Abrams Image, 2011

## Online Resources

Beyond Victoriana, beyondvictoriana.com

G.D. Falkesen, www.gdfalksen.com

"The Future of Steampunk" by Paul Jessup, Booktionary, booktionary.blogspot.com/2010/10/future-of-steampunk-by-paul-jessup.html

Evelyn Kriete, www.jaborwhalky.net

Jess Nevins, jessnevins.com/blog

Austin Sirkin, austinsirkin.tumblr.com

"Stupid Things We Say" by Nishi Shawl, Tor.com, www.tor.com/blogs/2010/10/stupid-things-we-say

What is Steampunk?, www.steampunk.com/what-is-steampunk

Thomas Willeford, www.steam.netmagicllc.com

Victorian Occupations: Job Titles in the 19th Century, www.census1891.com/occupations.htm

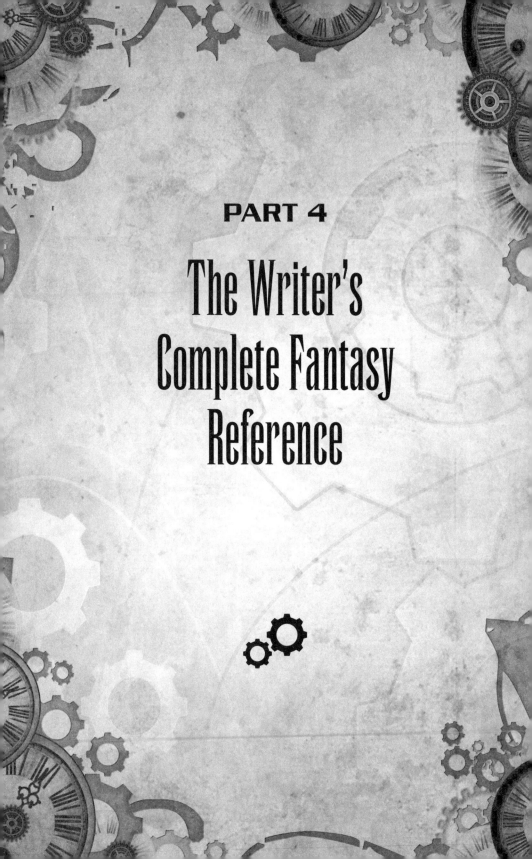

# PART 4

# The Writer's Complete Fantasy Reference

# CHAPTER 1
# Traditional Fantasy Cultures

## by Michael J. Varhola

At the heart of most traditional fantasy milieux is a culture derived from that of the European Middle Ages, in large part the medieval societies of what are now Great Britain, France, and Germany. This culture is a synthesis of both the Roman culture that dominated western Europe for some five centuries and of the Germanic culture that eventually overran and absorbed it.

Three major institutions formed the basis of medieval society and dictated how most people lived. These were feudalism, manorialism, and Christianity.

## FEUDALISM

**FEUDALISM** was a pyramidal system of contractual relationships in which lords granted lands to their retainers in exchange for oaths of loyalty and military service. Feudalism was most prevalent in France, Germany, England, Sicily, northern Spain, and the Crusader states, and its specifics varied from region to region. The vast majority of people in medieval Europe did not participate in the feudal system, which was largely reserved for fighting men.

Under feudalism, local political, military, and economic power was held by the lords. Each of them was subject to the lord above him, to whom they had sworn loyalty in return for **FIEFS** (land, its occupants and resources), and who could, at least in theory, demand service from them. Castles garrisoned by an elite cast of professional knights and men-at-arms, as well as local levies and sometimes foreign mercenaries, were the bases from which lords exercised their control.

Feudalism declined for a multitude of reasons. A major cause was the inheritance of fiefs, which compromised the system of lands being granted in return for oaths of loyalty. Strong national leaders, changes in warfare that reduced the importance of armored knights, and the phenomena of scutage and liege homage also contributed to the decline of feudalism. **SCUTAGE** was the practice of replacing military service with monetary payments. **LIEGE HOMAGE** was the practice of a vassal who had sworn oaths to more than one lord giving his primary allegiance to only one of them, thus eroding the basis of the feudal system. By the beginning of the fifteenth century, feudalism was for the most part dead.

Because the mounted knights that were at the core of the feudal system needed substantial economic support in order to arm, armor, and equip themselves, and needed to spend much of their time training for combat, substantial amounts of land and peasant labor were needed for their upkeep. Thus, feudalism was complemented by manorialism.

## MANORIALISM

**MANORIALISM** was an economic, social, and administrative system that defined the hereditary relationships between the peasantry and the nobility. While only the military and political elite of any given area was affected by feudalism, nine out of ten people in most areas were subject to the conditions of manorialism.

As a rule of thumb, writers should assume that more than half the people in most medieval European areas were bonded peasants—serfs—who had few, if any, rights or freedoms and were completely subject to the landed aristocracy. In some countries, particularly Mediterranean regions like Greece and Italy, outright slavery was widely practiced.

Manorialism had its origins in the last years of the Roman Empire, when laws were enacted binding farmers to the land. When Rome fell in the fifth century, Europe was thrust into a state of chaos, descending into the Dark Ages, and farmers were vulnerable to violent, invading peoples. Thus, they were largely willing to cede liberties in exchange for security, maybe even in the early years hoping that the times of trouble would pass and things would return to "normal." Crises were normal enough that manorialism solidified and was strengthened in the ninth and tenth centuries when new waves of invasions by Magyars, Muslims, and Vikings struck Europe. Manorialism reached its peak in the eleventh and twelfth centuries; in the following centuries, it began a prolonged decline that did not end in some areas until the twentieth century.

In general, manorialism was a hereditary system under which a lord owned or controlled the land, and then allotted portions of it to the individual peasants who resided under him. In exchange, the peasants paid the lord in crops, money, and labor. The specifics of manorialism varied from state to state (e.g., the proportion of their crop or yield; how much money, if any; how many days of labor per year; the size of land parcels).

Peasants throughout medieval Europe had severely abbreviated rights, especially by modern standards. Without the permission of their lord, peasants were not even allowed to travel or choose their own occupations. In eastern Europe, conditions like this persisted until the early years of this century. Lords had jurisdiction over many sorts of crimes committed on their lands and tried them in manorial courts. Such courts were a substantial source of revenue for the lords, who often stood to gain financially through fines and court fees regardless of the outcome of cases (or who might be tempted to sway the outcome of a case in a way favorable to themselves).

Conditions began to improve for the peasantry around the 1100s, in large part because of an agricultural revolution that was attributable to several factors. One was the implementation of a three-field farming system in which one field was used for summer crops, another for winter crops and another left fallow, increasing output and avoiding soil depletion. Another factor was improved irrigation systems. Technology, too, played a part in improved productivity, and implements like the wheeled plow, horse collar, clearing axe, and flail were of immeasurable value to medieval farmers.

Reclamation of land from the wilderness through the clearing of wooded areas and the draining of swamps contributed to greater availability of arable land, allowing for overall greater production. The Catholic church played a big role in such land reclamation as much of it was accomplished by monastic orders, who established their own manors, which were managed by abbeys and run much like their secular counterparts.

--------------------------------------------------------------------------------

# CHRISTIANITY

CHRISTIANITY was the predominant religion of medieval Europe and was a social and political force as important as feudalism and manorialism, and frequently more powerful than either.

Indeed, the role of the Church in day-to-day life, the importance of religion to most people, and their level of faith in general can scarcely be imagined by most people today. It was this level of faith that enabled the Church to muster entire communities to raise great cathedrals, the greatest works of architecture of the Middle Ages. Such centers of worship could take decades to complete, and thousands of laborers and craftsmen such as carpenters, glaziers, and masons would participate in their construction.

The Church assumed many of the administrative functions that the government of the Roman Empire had once fulfilled, such as the construction of public works and the colonization of wilderness areas. It also served as a repository of knowledge and literacy, which had been nearly expunged in the chaos of the Dark Ages. (Most people, even kings and nobles, were illiterate until the last centuries of the Middle Ages). Histories and other information were recorded in tomes by monks, who copied and illustrated them (a process called illumination) in monastery scriptoriums. This work allowed many works from antiquity to survive and produced many valuable works of art.

Medieval Europe was considered as the heart of Christendom because of the important role played by the Catholic Church in society. Nonetheless, in practice, the Christianity of the Middle Ages bore little resemblance to its modern counterpart and was intermingled at every level with elements from the violent, superstitious, essentially pagan world it was a part of. For example, many medieval Christian churches were built upon the sites of Roman, Germanic, even prehistoric pagan temples or worship sites. And, in Scandinavian churches, the iconography of statues of saints can be identified with that of the various Norse gods. Even today, at Catholic Easter masses in some rural villages in Belgium, handfuls of grain are ritually cast into a vat of green flames. Fantasy writers can put such phenomena to good use in their stories.

Veneration of the saints, frequently crossing the line into outright worship, was characteristic of medieval Christianity. Individual sects, cities, guilds, and even entire kingdoms chose patron saints and sought their blessings and special benefits through votive masses, adoration of relics, and special feast days (which frequently displaced Sundays as days of worship). Interestingly, the characteristics of patron saints often corresponded closely with those of the pre-Christian deities that the people in the same regions had worshipped.

That is not to say that people did not have a strong belief in God, only that they saw Him as an unapproachably powerful, frightening being that could not be reliably called upon to intercede in their daily lives. (After all, it is much easier to believe in a benign and sympathetic god if one lives in a benign and reliable world.) In fact, so feared was God in the Middle Ages that many people refused to take communion because of His ominous presence in the host. This phenomena became so widespread that in 1215, the Fourth Lateran Council was forced to make annual communion obligatory.

## THE SOCIAL ORDER

Titles of nobility are used to organize the upper echelons of an aristocratic society, and those used throughout Europe during the Middle Ages originate largely during the early Holy Roman Empire. Many were derived from Roman titles of rank, among them count and duke, while others were distinctly Germanic in nature, such as earl. Titles, especially the highest ones, were frequently linked to specific lands, powers, and responsibilities.

Historically, hereditary titles usually passed from father to son or, in the absence of a suitable male heir, from older brother to younger brother. However, in the real world this varied by region and even by title, and the whole system and its study is rather arcane. Writers can certainly create a simple, clear-cut system, or may decide a complex, even impenetrable system is of more use to them.

In the following section, the feminine construction of the various titles appears in parenthesis after the masculine form. Such feminine forms can variously refer to the wife of a titled individual who wields incidental, if any, power, or to a titled individual who rules in her own right. Historically, such women sometimes took power when their husbands died or when their reigning father or brother died without a suitable male heir (e.g., Queen Elizabeth II of England). In a fantasy milieu, women might more frequently be entitled to hold such positions, and hereditary titles could even pass from mother to daughter.

The head of a state was usually a king (queen) or emperor (empress), and even he was theoretically subject to the will of God, an idea expressed in the concept of "the divine right of kings." However, this was largely a device to check both papal interference into the business of monarchs and to implement unpopular policies by dismissing accountability toward the populace. Lesser nobles might be the rulers of smaller states. Such nobles, in order of precedence, include princes, dukes, marquesses, counts, viscounts, barons, baronets, and knights. Princes, dukes, or other nobles might be the rulers of relatively small cities.

It is possible for cultures to have aristocratic ranks beyond these. For example, German states also had the ranks of Furst (Furstin), Pfalzgraf (Pfalzgrafin), Landgraf (Landgrafin), and Freier (Freierin).

Writers should not forget that as colorful as aristocratic societies are, they are distinctly undemocratic. Even when measures that are perceived as democratic are instituted, such as the imposition of the Magna Carta, they are usually only intended by a lower echelon of the nobility to reduce the power of those above them, not to extend it to all segments of society. For example, when the Magna Carta was signed in 1215, serfs were worse off than they had been before the Norman Conquest.

On the other hand, nobles frequently shouldered great responsibilities. In a dangerous and often violent world, it was the nobility that was responsible for administering the subdivisions of states, raising armies, and leading troops into battle. Naturally, in many areas, the various ranks of nobility frequently came to lose their original meaning or level of responsibility. For example, in the prerevolutionary France of the eighteenth century, a marquis was not responsible for guarding a marc, or border area, as was originally the case.

In some states, including most of the monarchies that still exist today, titles of nobility are often granted as a symbolic but nonmonetary way to recognize and reward service to the state. For example, the Constitution prohibits the United States from granting titles of nobility, and in republican Rome, there was a fear of anyone who was in a position to proclaim themselves, or be proclaimed, king.

**NOTE:** Royal titles are not capitalized unless used in conjunction with a name, unless they are in German, which capitalizes all nouns. Some of these are rough equivalents of the listed English titles.

**prince (princess):** Whereas the child of a monarch is referred to as a prince or princess, in some states the children of a prince or the spouse of a monarch might also hold such a title. Princes, if not the head of an independent state, usually have few powers and no land, but might also hold some other title. For example, the oldest son of the monarch of England is also the Prince of Wales. A state ruled by a prince is called a principality.

(French **prince, princesse**; German **Prinz, Prinzessin, Furst, Furtin**; Italian **principe, principessa**; Spanish **principe, principesa**)

**duke (duchess):** Derived from the Latin *dux,* or "leader," the duke is usually the most powerful of the landed nobility beneath the monarch and is the highest title in the English peerage (i.e., the nobles entitled to sit in the House of Lords). A state or area within a state ruled by a duke is variously called a dukery, duchy, or dukedom.

In some societies, nonruling dukedoms have been bestowed upon princes in direct line of succession to the throne or upon generals who have won great victories in battle (such as the English generals Marlborough and Wellington). The first nonruling English duke was created by Edward III in 1337 when he made his oldest son, Edward the Black Prince, Duke of Cornwall.

Some states with many dukes distinguish the most powerful (or, for example, the siblings of the monarch) as "grand dukes." Grand dukes might wield great power within a state, as in Imperial Russia, or be the leaders of small states, such as the Grand Duchy of Luxembourg.

(French **duc, duchesse**; German **Herzog, Herzogin**; Italian **duca, duchesa**; Spanish **duque, duquesa**)

**marquess (marchioness):** Dating from the eleventh century, this title originally applied to lords who were responsible for guarding border areas, known as marches. In Germany, where the title Markgraf was bestowed upon counts who stood border guard for their monarch, such nobles could be further distinguished as Landgraf or Markgraf, depending on the sort of territory they controlled.

(French **marquis, marquise**; German **Markgraf, Markgrafin**; Italian **marchese, marchesa**; Spanish **marques, marquesa**)

**count (countess):** From the Latin word *comes,* "companion," a count is a powerful noble with authority over a province or similar area. The English equivalent is the earl, the oldest title in the English peerage. Derived from the Danish *jarl*, or "chieftain," the earl was originally the lord of a shire.

> (French **comte, comtesse**; German **Graf, Graefin**; Italian **conte, contessa**; Spanish **conde, condesa**)

**viscount (viscountess):** Meaning the lieutenant or deputy of a count, the title of vice-count was probably created in the Holy Roman Empire prior to the reign of Frederick I Barbarossa. In some states, high-ranking soldiers have sometimes been rewarded with the title of viscount.

> (French **vicomte, vicomtesse**; German **Vicomte, Vicomtesse**; Italian **visconte, viscontessa**; Spanish **visconde, viscondesa**)

**baron (baroness):** Barons are the lowest level of noble who are granted land directly from a sovereign, and their name is derived from this meaning. The title came to England during the Norman Conquest, where barons became the lowest level of noble entitled to sit in the House of Lords. Historically, the baronage relished the power they lorded over those below them, but chafed at royal control. It was the barons of England who took advantage of the weakness of King John Lackland by foisting the Magna Carta upon him. An area ruled by a baron is called a barony.

> (French **baron, baronne**; German **Baron, Baronin, Freiherr, Freiherrin**; Italian **barone, baronessa**; Spanish **baron, baronesa**)

**baronet (baronetess):** Baronets were originally English barons who lost the right of individual summons to Parliament in the fourteenth century. A hereditary order of baronets was created in England in 1611 by King James I and sold to gentlemen willing to set up plantations in Ireland. In 1624, baronets were also created for gentlemen prepared to settle in Nova Scotia. The title for the wife of such a noble would simply be "lady." Historically, only one woman was ever made a baronetess.

**knight (dame):** The term knight can be used many ways, and can refer to an individual honored with the nonhereditary title of knight; to individuals enrolled in an order of knighthood (see "Knighthood," page 164); or, used loosely rather than titularly, to refer to any armed and armored mounted warrior (e.g., any baron riding into battle might be referred to as "one of the king's knights").

It is with good reason that the rank of knight is associated with the mounted warriors of the Middle Ages, a class who enjoyed high social status. The French and German terms for a knight do, in fact, mean "horse-man," while the English word knight is derived from the Saxon word *cnyt,* or "attendant."

(French **chevalier**; German **Ritter**; Italian **cavaliere**; Spanish **caballero**)

Not all societies will have all of the listed titles of nobility, and they may not be as important in all societies. For example, in Imperial Russia, the tsar, or emperor, was at the apex of society. Below him were a vast number of princes and princesses, but because there was no law of primogeniture, as in many western states, the aristocracy was bloated, and many of these nobles were relatively unimportant and not in line for the throne. (A reading of some of Tolstoy's works will shed a lot of light on this subject.)

## ECCLESIASTIC TITLES

Writers should not overlook the role of ecclesiastic officials in medieval society. The pope at various points in time had his own armies, extensive lands, and a direct mandate from God that translated into great political influence over other monarchs. In short, he was a king as much as any other. Cardinals were not called "princes of the Church" without good reason. And powerful abbots might have controlled several manors, even a dozen or more, from their abbeys; in England, France, Germany, and Italy, such Church officials were often the equivalent of barons or better, and could wield great economic power within a state and political power at court.

In some states, political power was sometimes held jointly with ecclesiastic power. For example, the rulers of the mountain city-state Salzburg in Austria were called "prince-bishops." Military power might also have been wielded by churchmen, and there are numerous examples of bishops and priests of other ranks leading troops into battle. One of the earliest examples of this is depicted on the Bayeux Tapestry, the chronicle of the Norman conquest of England.

The basic hierarchy of the Church was based upon three sorts of church-men, priests and bishops, and the pope.

**abbot (abbess):** An abbot, from the Hebrew *abba,* or father, was the head of an autonomous community of monks. Such communities were usually founded by members of a monastic order, such as the Benedictines. In the

Church hierarchy, an abbot was on about the same level as a bishop and tended to have at least as much political power as a baron. The community he controlled was called an abbey, which consisted of one or more monasteries.

An abbot was expected to govern his monks with both compassion and firmness, and, as Christ's deputy, his flock was expected to show him reverence and obedience. Abbots were usually elected for life by the senior members of the community from among a pool of qualified candidates, an appointment that usually required confirmation from the papacy or head of the order.

Basilian monks usually called a leader of one of their communities a **hegumen**, while Russian and other eastern orders used the term **archimandrite**.

Like her male counterpart, an abbess was the head of one or more convents or cloisters of nuns. Historically, they did not tend to wield the same political power as abbots, who controlled powerful estates.

**archbishop:** Such churchmen were responsible for large areas, called provinces in England, with several bishops under them. For example, England has two archbishops—the Archbishop of Canterbury (the head of the Church of England) and the Archbishop of York. Such figures often had great influence, even beyond death. For example, when Archbishop of Canterbury Thomas Becket was slain by four knights of King Henry II, the site of his assassination almost immediately became a major pilgrimage center, and he was canonized a saint.

**bishop:** From the Greek word for "overseer," bishops were regional church leaders and had a cathedral as their seat. Cathedrals were among the most impressive and labor-intensive structures build in Europe during the Middle Ages, and they were indicative of the political, spiritual and economic power of a bishop who could muster the resources to have one built.

The ecclesiastic are governed by a bishop was known as a diocese; a political area ruled by a bishop was known as a bishopric.

**cardinal:** Originally, the term cardinal was applied to bishops whose diocese had been overrun by barbarians in the sixth century and who were subsequently assigned vacant diocese by the pope. Later, senior priests of certain parishes in Rome came to be known as cardinals. By the eleventh century, these churchmen had developed into the sacred College of Cardinals, and served as assistants and counselors to the pope. In 1059, cardinals became the church officers empowered to elect a new pope, and later in the eleventh century, bishops outside of Rome began to be appointed cardinals.

**deacon (deaconess):** Such ordained churchmen, immediately subordinate to priests, were responsible for serving as their assistants in charge of the purification ceremonies connected with preparation for baptism and charged with the care of the poor and unfortunate.

Deaconesses, probably ordained just like their male counterparts, were principally responsible for assisting at the baptism of women and in helping them to prepare for that sacrament, and also administered to the women of Christian communities. In western Europe, such female officers were active until about the eleventh century; in eastern Europe, they continued to function for somewhat longer, and among certain sects in the Middle East, served throughout the Middle Ages.

**pope:** Head of the Catholic Church. During the Middle Ages, the pope was also the head of western Christendom. (In the east, the patriarch of Constantinople was generally acknowledged as the supreme authority.) The pope was believed to be in a direct line from Saint Peter, who was believed to have received his authority directly from Christ. The seat of his authority was Rome as opposed to Vatican City, a relatively modern state.

In addition to the direct political authority the pope wielded over Rome and its environs, essentially as a king, he also had much influence over other states. For example, the pope crowned the heads of the Holy Roman Empire and could call upon the monarchs of Europe to launch crusades—and not just upon Muslims in the Holy Land, but also heretical communities within Europe itself, as in the case of the Albigensians of southern France, who were largely annihilated by a force of Norman crusaders.

The pope could also excommunicate individuals or even entire countries, making them ineligible to receive the sacraments until reconciled with the Church. To most modern minds, this holds little meaning. To the medieval man or woman, such a prospect was horrible and held the threat of eternal damnation. Of course, the power to censure secular rulers through excommunication could backfire with dire consequences.

For example, after being excommunicated for divorcing his wife without papal consent, King Henry VIII of England, once called "Defender of the Faith" because of his devotion to the Church, founded the Church of England rather than beg the pope for mercy.

## KNIGHTHOOD

Knights were frequently organized into orders of knighthood, many of which were fraternal or military associations of armed, armored, and mounted expert soldiers fervently dedicated to God or some other noble cause. Just as such organizations can evoke colorful and powerful images of their role in history, so too can they be used to evoke powerful images in works of fantasy.

Some orders of knighthood owed allegiance to a specific sovereign, others received support from a variety of sources (e.g., the Hospitalers received men, money, and material from several Christian states), while others were wholly independent and even established states for themselves (e.g., the Teutonic Knights, who carved the state of Prussia out of pagan eastern Europe).

The head of an order might have one of several titles, including Grand Master, Knight Grand Commander, and Knight Grand Cross. The second highest member of an order was usually styled Knight Commander. Various other members might have held titles that denoted some office within the order, for example, Sergeant-at-Arms. Most of the other members of an order would likely simply hold the title of Knight.

Most orders of knighthood were very religious and ritualistic, like militarized sects, and many even had a cultlike quality, with complex initiations, sacred mysteries, and increasing degrees of arcane knowledge.

Among the oldest and most distinguished of the historic orders of knighthood are the Sacred Military Constantinian Order of the Knights of Saint Catherine of Sinai, founded in 737; the Equestrian Order of the Knights of the Holy Sepulchre of Jerusalem, founded in 1113; the Order of the Garter, founded in 1348; and the Order of the Golden Fleece, founded in 1429.

The following orders were especially representative, colorful, or influential. All were formed in the Holy Land during the Crusades, but each evolved in different ways and is remembered for different accomplishments.

**HOSPITALERS** were members of the Knights Hospitaler of Saint John of Jerusalem, an order formed by crusaders in the eleventh century for clergy attached to a hospital that tended to sick and needy pilgrims to the Holy Land.

In the twelfth century, the order was recognized and began to participate in military operations on behalf of the Latin Kingdom of Jerusalem. In 1187, Jerusalem fell to the Muslims and the order moved to Acre, a fortified coastal city, from which it continued to care for the sick, patrol the roads, and crusade against the infidels. In 1291, Acre fell and the Hospitalers moved to Cyprus. A few decades later, in 1310, it moved to the Greek island of Rhodes, which it ruled as an independent state until it was conquered by the Ottoman Turks in 1522.

Holy Roman Emperor Charles V gave the island of Malta to the order in 1530. They successfully defended it against repeated and numerically superior assaults by Turkish forces, and remained there until 1798, when Napoleon Bonaparte ejected them from the island. After that, the Hospitalers entered a period of decline. Nonetheless, they still exist today, as the Sovereign Military Order of Malta.

**KNIGHTS TEMPLAR** were members of the Poor Fellow-Soldiers of Christ and the Temple of Solomon, who were also formed during the Crusades. Many nobles joined the order, and it quickly became a powerful, rich, proficient military organization. A grand master and a general council presided over the order, which was divided into knights, sergeants, chaplains, and craftsmen.

Distinguishing characteristics of the knights included white cloaks emblazoned with red crosses, round churches, and commanderies that they often used as banks. Indeed, after 1291, when the European crusaders were driven from the Holy Land, the main worldly pursuit of the Templars became banking and moneylending. Such was their financial influence upon the nations of Europe that they drew the envy and enmity of both secular rulers and clergy.

Beginning in 1307, monarchs in France, England, and Spain raided and shut down the Templar headquarters. They arrested the knights and charged them with heresy, immorality, and witchcraft, and sought to support these charges with confessions extracted by torture. The pope initially championed the Templars, but eventually renounced them for cynically political reasons. In 1314, the leadership of the Templars was burned at the stake in Paris. The charges against the Templars now appear to have been largely fabricated, and the order driven to extinction because of their success rather than their crimes.

The **TEUTONIC KNIGHTS** were founded in 1190 as the Brothers of the Hospital of Saint Mary of the Teutons in Jerusalem for the purpose of serving in a hospital during the siege of Acre during the Third Crusade. Despite its origins as a crusader order in the Holy Land, the knights forged a name for themselves thousands of miles away in Germany.

Within a decade, the Teutonic Knights had become a military order of nobles who took vows of chastity, obedience, and poverty. In the thirteenth century, they relocated to Europe and began the work it became known for: unrelenting warfare against the pagan peoples of eastern Europe. Moving eastward, the knights conquered and colonized the state of Prussia, playing an important role in the expansion of German culture and influence.

In 1237, the Teutonic order merged with the Livonian Knights, an order that had carved out a domain for themselves along the Baltic coast. This combined order continued its eastward expansion, but in 1240 was defeated by a force led by Russian national hero Alexander Nevsky (who, incidentally, was a sworn vassal of the Mughal Empire, which at that time held Russia in the "Mughal yoke").

For the next two centuries, the order continued to war against Lithuania, Poland, and Russia, but suffered as many defeats as victories. The order ceased to exist as a military force in 1525, when its grand master converted to Lutheranism and declared the militarized monastic state of Prussia a secular duchy.

## POLITICAL ENTITIES

Throughout the Middle Ages, a great variety of political entities were founded, existed, and disappeared. In addition to innumerable tiny kingdoms, principalities, and lesser states, several significant states and organizations emerged. Descriptions of the following entities are not intended to give a complete view of medieval Europe, but rather to give writers ideas for the kinds of organizations that might have a place in their worlds.

The **HOLY ROMAN EMPIRE** governed most of Germany, Burgundy and Italy for almost one thousand years, from A.D. 962 to 1806. Many of the great institutions of the Middle Ages were either founded within this great state or greatly influenced by it. Two great precepts provided the moral foundation of the empire: the idea of a hierarchical political organization with a single ruler at its head, and the idea that all Christians were united.

In 800, Charles the Great—Charlemagne—became emperor of what he called the Roman Empire when he was crowned by the pope in Rome. This state, an ostensible restoration and continuation of the empire that fell more than three centuries earlier, lasted until 925, when it fragmented into a series of successor states.

In 962, Otto I of Germany and Pope John XII collaborated to resurrect Charlemagne's Roman Empire (the adjective "Holy" was added in the twelfth century to emphasize its ostensible importance to Christendom). All of the successive Holy Roman Emperors were similarly kings of Germany, elected to the post by the region's princes.

Although the Holy Roman Empire was not really an empire, holy, or Roman, its kings often had great influence throughout Europe, in no small part because of the respect for the concept of the empire and its leader. Because of this, German kings expended much financial and political capital to see themselves elected to the post and crowned in Rome.

The Holy Roman Empire declined with the end of the Middle Ages and was broken up by Napoleon Bonaparte in 1806 when he conquered Germany.

**CRUSADER STATES**, many no larger than fortified cities and their environs, were founded throughout the Holy Land, the Levant (modern-day Lebanon), Syria, and Asia Minor (modern-day Turkey) by western European Crusaders in the eleventh, twelfth, and thirteenth centuries. Among the most significant of these were the Latin Kingdom of Jerusalem and the Latin Kingdom of Constantinople.

The Latin Kingdom of Jerusalem was founded in 1099 by the commanders of the First Crusade and included Palestine (modern-day Israel), Beruit, and Antioch. The Crusaders elected Godfrey of Bouillon the first king of Jerusalem, although he used only the title "Defender of the Holy Sepulchre." Jerusalem itself was lost to the Muslims in 1187, and the Latins were unable to recapture it, despite financial aid from Europe and the professional military assistance of various orders of knighthood. The kingdom was gradually whittled away and finally collapsed in 1291, when the fortified port city of Acre fell to the Muslim Mamelukes of Egypt.

The Latin Kingdom of Constantinople was founded in 1204 when a force made up of French and Italian Crusaders overran and sacked the capital of the Byzantine Empire, and chose Count Baldwin IX of Flanders to be Emperor Baldwin I of Constantinople. Dependent on French and Italian financial aid and requiring Venetian naval support, the state functioned as little more than a military camp during the six decades of its existence. It was also reviled in some circles because it had been established at the expense of the greatest Christian, albeit Orthodox, state in the east. In 1261, soldiers of the Byzantine emperor in exile recaptured the city and ejected the remaining Latins.

The **HANSEATIC LEAGUE** was a commercial alliance of Baltic and North Sea German cities that was gradually formed between 1250 and 1350. Leading members of the league included Danzig, Hamburg, Bremen, and Riga, and the Teutonic Knights and the state of Prussia also cooperated with it. The league maintained offices (kontors) in non-German cities that included Bergen, Bruges, London, and Novgorod, where its merchants lived and traded.

Essentially a coalition of regional groups, which met regularly in a diet from 1356 to 1669, some two hundred different cities were members of the organization throughout its history, and about three dozen were part of the organization at any given time. Accomplishments of the league included suppressing piracy, defending members against aggression, lobbying for passage of beneficial commercial laws, preparing charts and other navigational aids, and obtaining valuable concessions for its members.

Enemies of the Hanseatic League included Denmark, which the league defeated in naval combat in 1370, and in the later Middle Ages, the Netherlands and England, which competed against the league commercially and curtailed its rights in their territories.

The league began to decline after 1500, and although never officially disbanded, effectively ceased to exist after 1669.


## PERIPHERAL CULTURES

Beyond the borders of western Europe and its institutions of feudalism, manorialism, and Christianity, lived many other peoples. To the fantasy writer, these peoples and their lands represent a source of colorful characters, stirring legends, and exotic settings for adventures.

There were the pagan peoples, among them the Saxons, the Picts, and the Vikings. There were also the Muslims, among them the Saracens and the Moors. Throughout the Middle Ages, all of them were the antagonists of the English, French, Spanish, and Germans of Christendom.

Of course, the way such foreign peoples were perceived in contemporary literature and society does not necessarily reflect their true natures, and writers may wish to take this into account. For example, many medieval Europeans believed Islamic culture was a Satanic inverse of Christendom, with an antipope as its head and similarly evil counterparts to all other elements of their own society. Not only was this not true, but many informed rulers and scholars in western states found much to admire in Muslim culture, arts, and science.

Several of the more interesting and influential of these peripheral peoples are described below.

The **MAGYARS** were a people who originated along the Volga River in northeastern Europe and adopted the many habits of Turkish tribes they encountered, including their equestrian ways. In the late ninth century, they conquered the Carpathian Basin and then began to launch destructive raids westward into Germany. The mounted Magyar raiders moved further and further west until King Otto I, founder of the Holy Roman Empire, met and defeated them at the Battle of Lechfield in 955. Soon after, the Magyars converted to Christianity and established the Kingdom of Hungary.

The **MOORS**, Muslim Berbers from North Africa, invaded Spain in the eighth century and occupied it for several hundred years. In the late fifteenth century, the Christian monarchs Ferdinand and Isabella systematically drove the Moors from Spain, but they were able to hang on in a few fortified cities until the seventeenth century. Moorish troops also invaded France several times early in the Middle Ages, but were always driven back. (A Moorish cavalry army was defeated in 732 by the French infantry under Charles Martel, who ordered his troops to aim the blows of their heavy axes and swords at men and horses alike.)

The **MONGOLS** swept into Europe in the thirteenth century, threatening Christendom and Islam alike, and even causing the two to briefly unite. Under Ghengis Khan, Mongol cavalrymen conquered much of the Old World, and by the time their great leader died in 1227, their empire stretched from the Black Sea to the Pacific Ocean and from Siberia to Tibet. As with Charlemagne's empire, however, that of the Great Khan could not long survive his death and was divided amongst his sons. By the fourteenth century, most of the Mongol successor khanates, or kingdoms, had collapsed, and by the beginning of the fifteenth century, their act upon the world stage had ended.

The **NORMANS** were the descendants of Viking raiders who settled along the coast of northern France in the tenth century. In 1066, the Normans, under their leader Duke William, conquered England and established a kingdom on either side of the Channel. A tough, martial people, the Normans were called upon by various popes to engage in several crusades, sold their services as mercenaries throughout Europe and the Mediterranean, and conquered Sicily.

The **PICTS** were a mysterious people of unknown origin who lived in Scotland from ancient times and battled the Romans along their northern frontier and eventually harassed the English. Covered in blue paint and specializing in ambuscade, Picts are a constant enemy of the noble Prince Valiant. They reached the peak of their power in the mid-eighth century under King Angus, and a century later formed a unified kingdom with the Scots.

The **SARACENS**—as Muslims in general, especially Arabs and Turks, were referred to throughout western Europe and the Byzantine Empire—represented one of the most persistent and real threats to Christendom. Turkish soldiers of the Ottoman Empire (founded in the 1300s) conquered the Byzantine Empire, the seat of Orthodox Christianity; overran most of southeastern Europe; and menaced Sicily, Italy, France, and Austria, being stopped at the gates of Vienna every few centuries. Saracens were also the major opponents of the Crusaders and the villains of popular literature and lore, as in the *Song of Roland*, the quintessential heroic poem of the Middle Ages (even though in reality, Basques killed the figure Roland is based on).

The **SAXONS** were a fierce Germanic people who conquered many of their neighbors and by the fifth century A.D., occupied Britain and what is now France and northwestern Germany. During the sixth, seventh, and eighth centuries, the Saxons warred against various French kingdoms. Charlemagne led almost annual campaigns against the Saxons for thirty-two years in an attempt to end their dark pagan practices, which included human sacrifice. Although the Saxon chieftain Widukind opposed the Franks stubbornly, Charlemagne eventually defeated them through warfare, mass deportations, and executions.

The **VIKINGS**, natives of the Scandinavian countries of Denmark, Norway, and Sweden, and colonizers of Iceland, were certainly the best known, most colorful, and most feared of the European pagan peoples. From the ninth to the twelfth centuries, the Vikings raided and traded along the coasts and rivers of England and Ireland, penetrated into Russia, and even made incursions into the Mediterranean, Middle East, and North America. Landing along unprotected shores in their dragon-prowed ships, the raiders would sack and burn local villages, take slaves, and sometimes even capture horses and raid inland.

## TERMS

The following terms cover many aspects of life in the Middle Ages, including the legal system that regulated people's lives under manorialism, and major events and phenomena.

**ad censum:** Term for the status of serfs who pay their rent money rather than labor. Such a tenant was referred to as a *censuarius* (pl. *censuarii*).

**ad opus:** Term for the status of serfs who owe payment to a lord in the form of labor.

**amercement:** a fine

**assart:** An area of wasteland or swamp that is reclaimed for agriculture.

**assize of bread and ale:** A royal law setting prices and standards.

**bailiff:** The chief official on a lord's manor.

**balk:** A raised strip of land left unplowed so as to separate the tracts assigned to serfs.

**beadle:** A manorial official, usually an assistant to a reeve.

**bondman:** A serf.

**boon-work:** The obligation of peasant tenants to provide special labor for a lord, primarily for his harvest.

**bylaws:** Rules made by open-field peasants to govern farming and grazing.

**cellarer:** The official of a monastery responsible for provisions.

**champion country:** Open country, which in the Middle Ages in northern Europe and England was settled by compact villages that were surrounded by their own fields. From the French *champagne*, or "open field."

**charter:** An official document, such as a grant of privilege or a deed.

**chevage:** A payment made annually by a serf living outside the manor.

**communitas villae:** A term used to refer to the community of the village.

**corrody:** An old-age pension that provided room, board and incidentals, often purchased from a cloister for an annual premium by peasants.

**cotter:** The tenant of a cottage, who usually owned little or no land.

**Crusade:** A holy war called by the pope that was participated in by the military powers of Christendom. Nine Crusades were launched against the Muslims in the Middle East from 1095 to 1272 in an attempt to drive them from the Holy Land. Most were partially or wholly unsuccessful, largely because of a lack of cooperation between Europeans from opposing states. From the twelfth through the fifteenth century, numerous Crusades were launched against pagans and heretics in Europe.

**curia:** A courtyard.

**custumal:** A document listing the rights and obligations of serfs.

**Dark Ages:** A term for the period from the fall of Rome in the late fifth century A.D. through the ninth or tenth centuries, by various accounts. Although widely considered a period of decline, it was nonetheless a period characterized by some political, social, and technological developments.

**demesne:** The portion of a manor cultivated directly on behalf of a lord, through the obligatory labor of his tenants.

**dies amoris:** An opportunity given to litigants to reconcile their differences. Also known as **love-day**.

**distraint:** An arrest or summons to court.

**essoin:** A delay permitted to a defendant in a court case, or an excuse for not appearing in court.

**estate:** The sum total of a lord's holdings, often consisting of several manors.

**extent:** A document listing the lands, rents, and services of manor.

**eyre:** A royal circuit court.

**farm:** A lease.

**fief:** Land granted to a vassal in return for services, usually military in nature.

**frankpledge:** A legal device under which every member of a tithing was responsible for the conduct of other members. An English system that predated the Conquest.

**furlong:** A subdivision of an arable field.

**gersum:** An initial fee for taking possession of a tenancy.

**glebe:** Land designated for the support of the parish church.

**gore:** An odd-shaped piece of arable land created by irregular terrain or the convergence of plowed strips.

**hallmote:** A manorial court of justice.

**hamlet:** A small, agricultural settlement that lacked some of the characteristics of a village, such as permanency. Such communities were typical of the Dark Ages and in frontier areas, or during times of political unrest.

**hamsoken:** An assault upon a victim in his own home, considered more serious than an attack upon neutral ground.

**headland:** A small section of land left at the end of plowed strips used for turning the plow around.

**heriot:** A death duty paid to the lord, usually in the form of the deceased's best animal.

**hide:** A variable unit of land, in theory 120 acres, used for the purposes of tax assessment.

**house hire:** The rent paid by a serf for his house. Also **heushire**.

**hue and cry:** A system under which all within earshot were required to try to apprehend a suspected criminal.

**hundred:** An administrative division of an English county theoretically consisting of one hundred hides.

**hut, sunken:** Characteristic of the early Middle Ages, the sunken hut was the smaller of the two basic peasant structures (the other being the longhouse). Used as dwellings, workshops, and storage rooms, such huts were dug up to a yard into the earth and roofed with A-frame structures of wattle and daub or thatch, and were usually about ten feet wide by twenty feet long.

**infangenthef:** The right of a lord to prosecute a thief caught on one of his manors and to confiscate his possessions upon execution.

**leirwite:** A fine levied against an unmarried woman for sexual misconduct.

**longhouse:** One of the two basic sort of structures built by peasants throughout the Middle Ages (the other being the sunken hut). Village longhouses tended to be some twenty to fifty feet long and perhaps fifteen feet wide, with wooden frames, wattle-and-daub walls, and thatched roofs. They were not very sturdy, and hoodlums often broke into houses simply by battering through a wall. Also **byrehouse**.

**Magna Carta:** The document signed under duress by King John Lackland of England in 1215, guaranteeing various political and social liberties to freemen and the nobility. Considerably more than half the population were not freemen, however, and thus did not benefit at all from the "Great Charter."

**manor:** An area consisting of a lord's demesne and the land allotted to his serfs.

**merchet:** A fee paid to a lord by a serf when his daughter married.

**messor:** A minor manorial official, the assistant to a reeve. Also **hayward**.

**messuage:** A house and its yard.

**Middle Ages:** The period in Europe between antiquity and the Renaissance, generally reckoned as the millennium from the fall of Rome in A.D. 476 to the fall of Constantinople in 1453.

**mortuary:** A death duty paid to the parish church upon the death of a serf, typically his second-best beast. Compare with **heriot**.

**multure:** A portion of flour kept by a miller as payment for grinding grain.

**Norman Conquest:** The 1066 invasion of Saxon England by Duke William of Normandy, possibly the most formative event in the nation's history. The Normans defeated the Saxons at Hastings and established a Norman dynasty.

**open-field system:** An agricultural system of northwestern Europe and England characterized by nucleated agricultural communities; i.e., compact villages where farmfolk dwelled, surrounded by their fields.

**pannage:** A fee paid by peasants to a lord to allow their pigs to forage in a wooded area.

**pinfold:** A lord's stockade for stray animals.

**pledging:** A legal device by which one peasant guaranteed the conduct of another (e.g., the payment of a debt, appearance in court, good conduct).

**plague:** Various epidemics ravaged Europe throughout the Middle Ages, especially in areas of relatively dense population. Major visitations of the plague began in A.D. 767 and reached a horrifying peak in the Black Death (bubonic plague) epidemics of the fourteenth century, which slew from one-quarter to one-half of the continent's population. Fleas, borne by rats, carried the diseases.

**quarter:** A unit of volume equal to eight bushels.

**reeve:** The main manorial official under a bailiff, always a serf.

**ring:** A unit of volume equal to four bushels.

**seisin:** Legal ownership of a property.

**selion:** A narrow strip of plowable land, up to several hundred yards in length.

**serf:** A manorial peasant with obligations that included merchet, tallage, and week-work.

---

**steward:** The supervisor of a lord's manors and the chief official of his estate. Also **seneschal**.

**tallage:** A tax levied annually by a lord upon a serf.

**tally stick:** A notched stick used by a reeve to account for a manor's deliveries, expenditures, production, and receipts.

**tithe:** A payment to a church equaling one-tenth of agricultural produce, sometimes including a monetary levy for other things such as livestock.

**tithing:** A unit of ten or twelve village men mutually responsible for one another's conduct.

**toft:** The yard of house in a village, usually facing the street, surrounded by a fence or ditch and containing pens and buildings for animals and their fodder.

**tota villata:** A term for the body of all the people in a village.

**village:** A permanent, organized farming community of the Middle Ages that also included some craftspeople, which began to appear from about the tenth century onward. From the Roman *villa*, the agricultural estates that were the center of many settlements in the early Middle Ages (circa A.D. 500 to 900). In England and northwestern Europe, the village buildings tended to cluster around the manor house and the church and were surrounded by fields. In Mediterranean countries, the village tended to be built within the walls of fortified hilltops, with fields, vineyards, and animal pens on the plain below.

**villein:** Term used in England for a serf.

**virgate:** A unit of land, ranging in size from eighteen to thirty-two acres, ostensibly sufficient to support a peasant family.

**wardens of the autumn:** Officials appointed by peasants to help oversee harvest work. A similar official appointed by a lord was the reap-reeve.

**wardship:** The right of guardianship exercised over a minor by a lord.

**wattle and daub:** A lattice work of wooden sticks coated with clay and used for the walls of peasant huts throughout medieval Europe.

**week-work:** The main labor obligation of a manorial serf.

**woodland country:** Forested areas that in the Middle Ages were settled by isolated farmsteads, hamlets, and non-nucleated or spread out villages. Woodland areas were often settled as a first step in clearing them for more intensive agriculture.

**woodward:** A manorial official in charge of a lord's wooded areas.

---

# CHAPTER 2
# World Cultures

### by Michael J. Varhola

Fantasy cultures can be as varied, colorful, and exciting as the real world and more so, if writers make the effort to craft these most critical backdrops. Nonetheless, many fantasy novels today seem to be set in an unending series of northern European countrysides; the villages, castles, and taverns inhabited by Germanic, English, or Scandinavian peoples; the forests, streams, and caves haunted by trolls, orcs, and goblins. Think twice before doing the same with your novel because you are covering ground many other writers have already visited and will continue to tread.

Beyond Europe, however, there are thousands of potential world cultures to use for inspiration or as a base for your fantasy cultures. Several cultures are profiled on the following pages. One intent of these profiles is to hint at the great variety of foreign cultures available to writers from every inhabited part of the world and from every period of human development. Another intent is to inspire and guide writers to seek out more information about these exciting cultures and incorporate them into their own worlds.

Writers should consider what point or points in a culture's development they are going to portray. Each has its particular allure and interesting characteristics. Cultures cannot remain static for long and are constantly changing, expanding, and contracting. Is the culture in the ascendant, with dynamic leaders striving to carve a place in a world of dangerous competitors? Is it a strong, powerful state, secure against all but the most dangerous enemies?

Is it an ancient, now-decadent culture with indifferent leadership and on the brink of imminent decline? Or has that decline already begun, with collapse from the inside being hastened by aggressive outsiders?

If you know the story you want to write, you can pick cultures with a history that fits your ideas. Similarly, the history of a particular culture can go a long way toward inspiring story lines, events, and characters.

Several fascinating cultures are profiled in the following chapter to inspire you to use them or find others more suited to your needs.

## RESOURCES

More information is available to writers today than at any other time in human history. In fact, this creates a problem of not knowing just where to start or what to choose.

Despite the vast resources of the World Wide Web, good old-fashioned books are probably still the most accessible resource. Most writers know how valuable bookstores and public libraries can be in finding good source material. You should be careful, however, not to neglect two ends of this spectrum.

Children's books often make great introductions to an unfamiliar subject. So what if a book on the Roman Empire is written at a seventh-grade level? If you don't know anything about the subject to start with, the clear outline, simple prose, and pictures will all be refreshingly easy to digest. And fantasy writers might not need much inspiration beyond this.

University libraries are the other end of the spectrum and can provide books of a specialty level that will not generally be found in a public library or mall bookstore. Writers can explore this venue when greater detail is needed on a specific subject.

Books that focus on specific arts or sciences of a culture can be of use to writers who want protagonists with special backgrounds or skills. For example, a book on Inca record-keeping techniques could be quite instructive to a writer creating a character who is an Inca imperial governor.

Reprints of original epics and texts can be incredibly instructive, of an ideal if not always of a reality. Such texts are of immeasurable value when creating fantasy worlds. For example, the Hindu epics *Mahabarata* and *Ramayana*, Chinese philosophical works like Confucius's *Analects,* or Aztec codices.

Periodicals can also be a good source of material. One of the best is *National Geographic,* which typically features aspects of one or more world cultures in each issue.

## AFRICA

Africa is now widely considered to be the cradle of humanity, so it is appropriate that some of the oldest and richest human cultures should have originated there.

Many of these cultures veritably demand to be incorporated into the milieux of fantasy worlds. Among these are tribes of pastoral cattle herders in east Africa, forest kingdoms in west Africa, mountain peoples in Ethiopia, and the riverine cultures along the Nile (Blue and White), the Congo, and the Zambezi.

One of Africa's greatest cultures, New Kingdom Egypt, is profiled here.

### Egyptian (New Kingdom) Culture

What we think of as ancient Egypt lasted nearly four millennia, beginning around 3500 B.C. and continuing until about 30 B.C. Historians divide those thousands of years into ten broad periods and these periods into more than thirty different dynasties.

The New Kingdom, comprised of the eighteenth, nineteenth, and twentieth dynasties, is in many ways the most interesting period and was characterized by dramatic social and political change and by the transformation of Egyptian culture from a simple riverine kingdom into a complex militarized empire.

At the beginning of the sixteenth century B.C., the kings of Egypt were subject to a militarily powerful people called the Hyksos. These people dominated the Nile river valley and occupied the northern part of the country, holding in vassalage the Egyptian nobility. Egyptian kings of the seventeenth dynasty rose up against the Hyksos, leading a war of liberation against them and their native allies and overthrowing them after several years of savage warfare. Amosis became the first king of the eighteenth dynasty (1570–1320 B.C.).

### Arts and Sciences

Egypt's great pyramids are what it is best known for architecturally, but they were old when the forefathers of the eighteenth dynasty were driving out the Hyksos. Egypt's last pyramids were completed about one thousand years before the advent of the New Kingdom. New Kingdom architecture is just as significant and even more varied than that of earlier periods.

During this period, the dead were interred not in pyramids, but in smaller, personal tombs. Nonetheless, pharonic tombs were still very elaborate, consisting of chambers excavated from the solid rock of hillsides, their approaches augmented by temple complexes and columned galleries. Walls were decorated with images of mythological and historical events, carved in sunken relief (as opposed to the low-relief figures of earlier periods).

Prior to the overthrow of the Hyksos, Egyptian culture was sophisticated and civilized, but, metallurgically and militarily, it was still in the Stone Age. Their acquisition of Hyksos bronze-working skills brought them up to par technologically with some of the other great cultures of the ancient world. A growing sense of national identity also helped to elevate their position in the international scene of the day.

Pictograms called hieroglyphics were used throughout Egypt for, among other things, record keeping, religious texts, and tomb inscriptions.

### Government

The pharaoh, a semidivine king wielding absolute power, sat upon the throne of Egypt and served as the ultimate military, secular, and religious overlord. Three of the most well-known pharaohs reigned during the New Kingdom: Ramses II, widely identified as the pharaoh of Genesis in the Bible; Tutankhamen, who was laid to rest in the richest royal tomb to survive into the twentieth century; and Hatshepsut, a rare and powerful female pharaoh who ruled for twenty-two years.

As the New Kingdom evolved into a militarized state, a bureaucracy evolved to oversee such things as weapon and equipment manufacturing centers, arsenals, military levy and payroll lists, acquisition and breeding of horses, and the construction of border fortifications.

### Military

Three broad arms comprised the Egyptian army during the New Kingdom: Egyptian chariotry and infantry, and auxiliary foreign troops, for example, Nubian archers or Canaanite peasant levies. Prior to and during the early days of the New Kingdom, chariots were rare and highly prized, and often acquired from a defeated enemy force after a battle. Chariots were crewed by two soldiers. The archer was heavily armored in a coat of scales and armed with a composite bow. The driver was lightly armed and had little or no armor but may have had a large shield mounted on one arm. Chariot runners, lightly armored infantrymen, were assigned to chariots and detailed with dispatching the crews of disabled enemy chariots.

The weapons and equipment of infantrymen evolved during the New Kingdom, reaching a characteristic point during the nineteenth dynasty (1320–1200 B.C.). Such foot soldiers wore the familiar striped headcloth or a simple round helmet, carried large rectangular shields that were rounded on the top, and wore armor made of bands of linen across the chest and the nonshield arm. Their wood-and-bronze weapons included hand axes; two-handed, weighted mace axes; spears; throwing sticks; and Khopeshes (heavy, curved swords).

Archers became more important during the New Kingdom, eventually being armed with powerful composite bows in place of simple stave bows. The effectiveness of such troops in battle was greatly enhanced when they were formed in mass. They wore no armor and were kept from close combat with the enemy.

Egypt's borders had traditionally extended only a few miles to either side of the river and along the coast at the mouth of the Nile. During the New Kingdom, Egyptian forces extended these borders into neighboring areas, largely to act as a buffer for the Nilotic homeland. Egyptian armies campaigned south into the Sudan, north into the Levant (modern-day Lebanon), and as far east as the Tigris-Euphrates river valley (in modern-day Iraq).

After the overthrow of the Hyksos, military challenges for the New Kingdom included a long-term war with the Kingdom of Mittani to the north, clashes with the Hittites of Persia to the east and the Libyans to the west, and a major land and sea invasion by the "Sea Peoples," a coalition of eastern Europeans and Asians. Defeated by Ramses II during the twentieth dynasty (1200–1085 B.C.), the remnants of these people settled along the coasts of what is now Israel and became known as the Philistines.

### Economy

Egypt's economy was based on intensive agriculture within the lush Nile River valley. Traditionally, farming villages that were clustered around temple or palace complexes, rather than urban areas, were the centers of communal life.

As the militarized society of the New Kingdom developed fortified palaces, border fortifications and enclaves of craftsmen specializing in critical skills (e.g., chariot makers, bowyers, and fletchers) became increasingly vital.

Egypt also engaged in trade with a wide variety of states, including Somalia and southern Arabia along the Red Sea, and Crete, Phoenicia, and Syria in the Mediterranean Sea. And, as a burgeoning imperial power, goods flowed into New Kingdom Egypt from the lands under its control, mostly via specially built coastal and riverine trading vessels. For example, at least three sorts of wood were used for Egyptian war chariots, most of them coming from the Levant, or Lebanon, and many of the spices used for perfumes and embalming were sent from Yemen, in southern Arabia.

## Religion

A pantheon of humanlike gods, many of them with animal heads, was worshipped by the ancient Egyptians. Among the most important in the New Kingdom were Amun, god of Thebes; Ra, god of the sun; Set, god of death; and Montu, god of war. The pharaoh was often associated with Amun and Ra, and increasingly with Montu.

Worship of Egyptian gods spread throughout the ancient world, where they were sometimes revered under different names, for example, the goddess Isis was worshipped in Greece as Aphrodite, and later in Rome as Venus.

Egyptian rulers showed devotion to their gods through the construction of massive temple and tomb complexes that required thousands of craftsmen and many years to build. Egyptians believed that properly preserved dead lived on in the afterlife, and the noble and wealthy were embalmed in an elaborate ritual process that lasted several weeks. They also believed that objects buried with the dead could be used by them after death.

One pharaoh, Akhenatan, attempted to impose upon Egypt the worship of a single god, Aten, the sun-disk. His monotheistic reforms did not long survive his death.

During the New Kingdom, the priesthood grew rich and powerful, coming to own a third of the country's arable land. Because they were appointed by the king, however, they could not easily pose a challenge to him.

# ASIA

To ancient and medieval Europeans, Asia was a vast, mysterious, fabulous place, full of innumerable foreign kingdoms, peoples, and religions. This impression, while not always accurate in specifics, was generally very true.

The largest continent is home to perhaps the greatest variety of cultures, heroes, gods, and kingdoms, some of them truly alien to the people of the West. Indeed, Asia is ripe to bursting with rich material for the fantasy writer. Japanese cultural elements have become popularized and familiar, but little is known by most of us about other Asian cultures.

These seem almost uncountable and include Buddhist kingdoms of Tibet, Indonesia, and Cambodia; the Hindu peoples of India; the Muslims of Pakistan and Afghanistan; the nomadic Mongol shamanists of the central Asian steppes and deserts; and the Indo-Sumerian city dwellers of the Indus River valley.

Two Asian cultures, Chinese and Mughal, are profiled here.

## Chinese Culture
## (Early Imperial Period, 221 B.C.-A.D. 618)

Chinese written history goes back more than three thousand years, and people have lived in China for tens of thousands of years. China's history can be divided into four broad periods: the Age of Conflict (1500–221 B.C.), the early imperial period (221 B.C.–A.D. 618), the Golden Age (A.D. 618–1368) and the late imperial period (A.D. 1368–1911).

In the centuries prior to the Early Imperial Period, China was divided into a dozen warring states. One of them, Qin, defeated the others during the fourth and third centuries B.C., unifying the country in 221 B.C. After this, China was periodically divided by internal conflict and split into as many as three opposing kingdoms, but the ideal of a unified country under a single emperor persisted.

### Arts and Sciences

Some of the world's greatest art, literature, and architectural wonders were created in China.

Bronze casting was an important art form from about 1000 B.C., and produced beautiful, intricate vessels and implements decorated with abstract designs and animals. Ordinary people never used bronze, however, and such items were reserved for the rituals of the imperial court and temples.

A written language of pictorial figures similar to modern Chinese writing was developed during this period and used for preserving everything from government records to the works of philosophers. This development was accompanied by the invention of bamboo paper around the first century A.D., followed by block printing.

Medicine was advanced by ancient standards, and acupuncture was one of the medical disciplines developed during the early imperial period.

Architectural and engineering accomplishments of the age were extensive. Imperial engineers built bridges and roads, linking the far corners of the country. Among the architectural feats of the period still evident today are the Great Wall and the Grand Canal. During the early imperial period, sections of defensive line in the northwest were connected to form the Great Wall, a fifteen hundred-mile-long barrier intended to hold back the dreaded Xiongnu (Huns). The Grand Canal, flowing one thousand miles from Beijing in the south to Hangchow in the north and linking the Yangtze and Yellow rivers, is still used today.

Chinese cities tended to be symmetrical, walled, laid out on gridplans of straight streets, and filled with square and rectangular buildings. Buildings were usually of red brick and roofed with green-glazed ceramic tiles.

## Government

Imperial Chinese society was structured into a rigid hierarchy, the earthly head of which was the emperor, the "Son of Heaven," who ruled with absolute power. Ministers, officials, and a system of bureaucrats assisted the emperor in running the great country, and aristocratic, military, and religious factions surrounded him, seeking to forward their own interests and creating continuous court intrigue.

Qin Shihuang was the first emperor of a unified China. He had a reputation for evil and cruelty, but also for efficiency and lawfulness. He instituted standardized weights and measures and built roads throughout the country. Scorning Confucianism, he championed a philosophy called legalism that advocated a system of rewards and punishments for various sorts of behavior. After his death, chaos racked the country for eight years.

The hierarchical nature of Chinese culture was largely based upon the teachings of Kung-Fu-tzu (Confucius), who traveled throughout the warring states of China during the Age of Conflict (1400–221 B.C.) advising kings to rule by setting a good example for their people. His book *Analects* influenced Chinese leaders and scholars for two thousand years. He taught that children were subject to parents, wives subject to husbands, and younger people subject to older people.

### Military

Unification presented China with different military challenges from those of the warring kingdoms, including quelling uprisings and defending frontiers from foreign invaders. Foremost among the latter were the Xiongnu, against whom several determined military expeditions were led.

Infantry formed the basis of contemporary Chinese armies, augmented by smaller forces of chariotry and cavalry. Forces formed for a special purpose might have a different composition, however; for example, expeditions into the western steppes were made up mostly of cavalry troops. Chariots were typically crewed by three warriors; a spearman, a driver, and an archer or crossbowman.

Armor consisted primarily of coats of leather or linen, enhanced with scales or whole plates of bronze or iron for the best-equipped troops, and augmented by shields and helmets. Weapons included straight, single-edged swords; crossbows; composite bows; and bamboo-hafted spears.

### Economy

The vast majority of Chinese were farmers who worked the valleys of the Yellow and Yangtze rivers. Others were tradesmen, bureaucrats, or soldiers who dwelled in towns. The entire country, especially the rich south, paid taxes in the form of grain and manufactured goods to support the government and the army.

Trade was facilitated by the roads, canals, and rivers of the empire, and flourished under the stable conditions of a unified government. Among the most important trade routes was the Silk Route, which stretched from Changan in the middle of the country all the way to Persia (modern-day Iran).

### Religion

Confucianism, Taoism, and Buddhism represent three of the main religious or philosophical movements that had an influence on Chinese history. Their various factions represented them at court, and strove to curry and maintain imperial favor.

Confucianists believed that the earthly bureaucratic hierarchy of the empire was simply an imperfect model of a heavenly hierarchy, and that all people had a divinely ordained duty.

Taoism developed about the same time as Confucianism, but in opposition to it. It was formulated by Lao-Tzu, who in his Tao, or way, said that wise men do not try to change the world, but rather do nothing and seek harmony with nature. Monasticism flourished amongst Taoists, and great monasteries, often supported by pious patrons, were built throughout the country.

Buddhism, an import from India across the Himalayas, brought a pantheon of deities and supernatural beings to augment those of the existing Chinese religions. It, too, leaned toward monasticism.

## Mughal Culture

Hordes of Islamic Turco-Mongol soldiers swept into India in the early sixteenth century, conquering vast territories, subjugating the local Hindu people, and establishing one of the most colorful and durable empires ever seen. Established in 1526, the Mughal Empire began to wane in the early 1700s, eventually became a puppet state of the British, and collapsed in 1858. It is possible that no other empire has exceeded the luxuriousness, wealth, or absolute power of the Mughals.

The forces that for over a century dominated most of India were descended from Mongols, who had in centuries past settled in Turkey and converted to Islam. Under Babur, a nationless military adventurer descended from both Tamerlane and Genghis Khan, these people conquered Afghanistan in the early sixteenth century. In 1516, Babur made his first raid into India, and in 1526, he invaded in force, deposing the ruling Islamic dynasty and establishing the Mughal empire.

Mughal life revolved around the court and opulent, elaborate, sometimes labyrinthine palaces and **zenanas**, or harem precincts, which were the settings for the intrigues, assassinations, and coup d'etats that plagued the Mughals throughout their reign. Mughal emperors, **padishahs**, along with their officials and supporters, had to constantly be on guard against poisoning, strangulation, or other forms of assassination.

### Arts and Sciences

Although descendants of a people who excelled at destruction rather than creation, the Mughals became great patrons of poetry, painting, and architecture.

Tomb architecture is what the Mughals are best remembered for, most notably the Taj Mahal; several other tombs, less well-known outside of India, remain notable sites to this day.

---

The Mughals were also a very literate people. A well-administered empire, the Mughals employed innumerable scribes and record keepers, leaving behind a detailed, if somewhat narrow, record of their reign; for example, women were rarely mentioned at all, and those who rose to positions of power, such as the Nur Mahal, wife of the emperor Jahangir, tended to be vilified for their efforts. The padishahs were multilingual, enjoyed creating poetry, and kept detailed memoirs, mostly in Persian.

Poetry was highly regarded, and valued cup-companions of the emperor were expected to entertain him with verse. Spontaneous couplets ranked especially high.

Indian miniature painting reached its height under the Mughals, and accurate likenesses of all the emperors and many of their officials survive to this day.

## Government

The padishah was an absolute dictator, epitomizing the eastern despot. The earliest Mughal emperors were able military commanders and administrators, and created a stable government and an extensive bureaucracy that allowed the empire to be maintained by the increasingly indolent, less capable emperors that followed them.

By modern standards, the best of them were excessively cruel and authoritarian, routinely torturing to death enemies and engaging in entertainments that included massive hunts and forcing unarmed men to fight dangerous animals. Invariably, however, the padishahs seemed to have had dual personalities. For example, Shah Jahan apparently murdered two of his brothers on his way to the throne and rebelled against his father, Jahangir, multiple times. Nonetheless, he was a brilliant intellect who so loved one of his wives that he constructed one of the world's great monuments to passionate romance, the Taj Mahal.

**SUBADARS** (provincial governors) controlled the various **SUBA** (provinces) of the empire, which were divided into **SARKARS** (districts) administered by **FAUJDARS. GHATWALS** administered small frontier districts.

## Military

As befitted a people descended from Mongols, elite troops of aristocratic cavalrymen were at the heart of the Mughal military system. Cavalry armor and arms included mail, swords, axes, maces, lances, and composite bows.

Secondary formations included armored war elephants, matchlockmen, and slow, unwieldy artillery trains that tended only to be useful in sieges. Huge, elaborate fortresses housed their troops and watched over the country.

Defense of the empire was a constant concern and necessitated keeping able generals and thousands of soldiers in the border regions. In the north, Afghan tribesmen kept the frontier in a state of almost constant warfare (as they have for so many other conquerors), and Persia periodically attacked, as they did during the reign of Jahangir, capturing the fortified city of Kandahar. In the south, unruly Rajput lords schemed away in their hilltop forts, ever ready to seek personal gain by striking a bargain with a likely pretender to the throne. In the eighteenth century, the powerful Maratha caste arose and began to gnaw away at Mughal territory.

### Economy

Mughal government heavily taxed its subjects, taking from the vassal Hindu population a third of its agricultural produce. Trade goods from China, East Africa, and the Middle East flowed into Mughal India, and direct trade with European powers began in the sixteenth century. Currency included gold **MURHS**, silver **RUPEES,** and gems, notably sapphires and rubies. The complex financial affairs of the empire and the major provinces were overseen by civil officers called diwans.

### Religion

The Mughals were Muslim, and perhaps more than anything else, this separated them from the subject Hindus, whom they considered pagans. Nonetheless, the Mughals allowed them to worship unmolested, and Akbar, greatest of padishahs, even tried to unite Hindus and Muslims through a new religion of his own called **DIN ILAHI**, Divine Faith.


## MESOAMERICA

Mesoamerica, that expanse of land extending north from what are now El Salvador, Honduras, Belize, and Guatemala through southern and central Mexico, was home to the most sophisticated pre-Columbian peoples of the New World, among them the Maya, Aztec, Olmec, Mixtec, Toltec, and Zapotec.

All the Mesoamerican peoples were products of a shared cultural tradition that included similar art and architecture, agricultural systems, and religious

---

beliefs. These people carved their civilizations from the vast rain forests of the Yucatan Peninsula, the rugged mountains of the Pacific coast, and the scrublands of central Mexico.

Two Mesoamerican peoples, the Maya and the Aztec, are profiled here. Several others are described briefly in the chronological order of their ascendancy.

## Mayan Culture

Mayan culture flourished in the Yucatan Peninsula of southern Mexico beginning around A.D. 300, with more than a dozen of their huge city-states rising up from the steaming rain forests. Many Mayan cities, among them Copán, Palenque, and Tikal, were huge by ancient standards and home to as many as fifty thousand people.

Endemic warfare and climatic changes that began around the middle of the ninth century coincided to bring about the decline of Mayan culture. Many cities were abandoned, and the recording of dates on stone tablets ceased, the last in 889. Life shifted to a few rival cities in the north and south of the area once dominated entirely by the Mayan states. These remaining cities held out against various successor peoples for several centuries, but most were conquered by the Spanish conquistadors in the early 1500s. Their final stronghold, Tayasal, fell in 1697.

### Arts and Sciences

The Maya were the only New World people to develop a complete written language. Such writing was composed of both pictograms and symbols that represented sounds. By connecting these sound symbols appropriately, the Maya could write any of their spoken words.

Most Mayan books, or codices, were religious texts that Mayan kings believed they could use to predict the future. Hundreds of such bark-paper books were destroyed by the Spanish when they conquered the remaining Maya in the 1520s. Now only a handful of these texts remain.

Mayan astronomers were experts at their craft, gauging the movements of heavenly bodies for religious purposes. They were able to predict eclipses and the movements of the planet Venus.

## Government

Mayan society was not unified and individual cities were ruled by their own kings. Such kings were called **ahaw** (lord) or **makina** (great sun lord), and served both as military commanders and priests. Mayan kings of note, whose names come down to us from monuments and inscriptions, included Shield Jaguar and Bird Jaguar of Yaxchilan and Pacal of Palenque.

Mayan kings served their people by performing critical religious ceremonies that usually involved drawing their own royal blood, which was believed to have special powers. Other duties included human sacrifice to their gods, usually of prisoners captured in war.

Mayan kings led their troops into war and gained prestige for the capture of enemy warriors. However, they ran the risk of being captured themselves and becoming a prime human sacrifice in their turn.

## Military

For many years, scientists believed that the Maya were a naturally peaceful people. Evidence has come to light in recent years, however, that a continual need for human sacrifice drove the Maya into constant warfare against each other.

Mayan warriors wore costumes and face paint calculated to terrify their opponents and went into battle howling and blowing war trumpets. Capturing enemy soldiers rather than slaying them was the primary goal of such conflicts, and warriors were respected for the number of enemies they had taken in battle.

The planet Venus was identified with the god of war, and its seasonal appearance marked the annual start of Mayan intercity warfare.

## Economy

Most Mayans were farmers, growing corn, squash, and beans in forested areas cleared using slash-and-burn agriculture. Such commodities, along with luxury goods and currency in the form of cacao beans, were traded amongst the Maya.

Jade was the most precious material known to the Maya and was used to make ceremonial and religious accoutrements for the nobility and priesthood.

## Religion

The Maya believed in dozens of gods who governed the various aspects of nature, and who were able to both create and destroy. The sun god gave warmth and light, but could also bring drought; the rain god brought water, but could also inflict floods; the war god brought victory, but could also impose defeat.

The gods were placated with their favorite foods, notably corn cakes, meat, and human blood. Incense made from the sap of the copal tree was burned during offerings to the gods. Rituals also included pageants in which priests dressed like the gods and danced to music.

Prominent among the Mayan gods were Ahaw Kin, the god of the sun, who entered the underworld at night and was transformed into the jaguar god of war; Tlaloc, god of rain, who was worshipped by many other Mesoamerican peoples, including the Aztec; and Ym Kaax, the god of the staple food corn. Many other gods were also worshipped, some specific to certain areas or cities; many of them are now nameless, their identities lost to the ages.

## Aztec Culture

In the early fourteenth century A.D., the Aztecs were a migratory people who eventually settled on several islands in Lake Texcoco in central Mexico. Here, by 1325, they began building their capital, the city of Tenochtitlán (modern-day Mexico City), which was joined to the mainland by several causeways. From this secure base, the Aztecs began to expand to neighboring lands, seeking farmland, prisoners to sacrifice to their gods, and wealth. They established an empire that lasted some two hundred years.

In 1519, Spanish conquistadors under Hernando Cortés landed on the Mexican coast east of Tenochtitlán, on the day and year it had been predicted the god Quetzalcoatl would appear. Cortés was identified with this deity and was thus able to rule the Aztec through the reigning king, Montezuma II. He ultimately plunged the empire into civil war and left it utterly destroyed by 1525.

### Arts and Sciences

The Aztecs had strong engineering abilities and built great cities full of palaces, temples, and public areas. Aztec cities did not tend to be walled, and siege warfare was not common. However, Aztec cities were deliberately laid out with convoluted street plans that could be used to confuse, trap, and ambush invading armies. Temple and palace precincts within cities were often walled citadels, and pyramids and other tall public structures could be used as firing platforms by defending archers. Thus, entering Aztec cities was not hard, but taking or holding them proved to be very difficult (even for the Spanish, who were more than once almost annihilated in brutal street fighting).

Huge pyramids often served as tombs for Aztec rulers, and "god houses," small temples, were built on top of them as a place where the deceased noble or various gods could be honored.

Other prominent public structures included game courts for **HACHTLI**, a brutal game played with a rubber ball between two teams of warriors (the Maya played a similar game). Such I-shaped courts had walls about eight feet high set with a vertical stone ring through which the ball had to be maneuvered using only elbows, hips, and legs.

Aztec astronomers carefully measured time. Time passed in cycles of fifty-two years, and each year was divided into eighteen months of twenty days each, each of these days having its own name. Time was reflected on huge, carved stone calendar wheels, some more than thirteen feet in width.

### Government

Head of the Aztec empire was the **TLATOANI**, or emperor. Upon the death of an emperor, the army commanders and chief priests chose a successor, usually from among the most qualified members of the royal family. Aztec rulers tended to be wise priests and skilled warlords.

A large staff of soldiers, priests, and administrators worked for the emperor and ensured that his commands were carried out, and a bodyguard of two hundred chieftans saw to his personal security.

### Military

Aztec methods of warfare were highly stylized but nonetheless brutal. Capture of enemy soldiers was important to the Aztec, who typically had such prisoners killed in ritual combat.

Battles were usually fought between opposing lines of brightly clad Aztec soldiers, with the most experienced soldiers in the front ranks. Levies and veteran soldiers, including knights and shock troops, **CUAHCHICS**, were all identified by distinctive uniforms and commanded in battle by captains and generals.

Armor for common troops was the **ICHCAHUIPILLI**, a heavily quilted cotton vest. A padded cotton body suit, **TLAHUIZLI**, was worn by veteran soldiers. These came in a great variety of colors and patterns, and were determined by experience, status, and unit. For example, two elite units were the Eagle Knights and the Jaguar Knights, both of which wore stylized wooden helmets decorated to look like their totem animals. Shields were used by all sorts of troops and were made of wood covered with hide and decorated with colored cloth or feathers.

Aztec weapons were made of wood and stone. Most fearsome of these was the **MACAHUITL**, a sword-shaped, hardwood club whose edges were armed with rectangular obsidian blades (freshly chipped obsidian is sharper than surgical steel). Another weapon favored by the Aztecs was the **TEPOZTOPILLI**, a hafted weapon like a spear whose head was armed with pieces of obsidian. Bows, slings, and atlatls were also used, the latter to hurl large darts with great velocity.

### Economy

The Aztec's primary crop was corn, which was used to make tortillas, their staple food. Because the early island-dwelling Aztecs initially had limited farmland at their disposal, they developed **CHINAMPAS**, large floating wicker baskets filled with earth in which they grew plants, including trees.

Merchants called **POCHTECA** extended Aztec trade throughout Mesoamerica and to the lands beyond (as far north as the Mississippi River valley). They also served as spies, bringing back information about rival cities. Because the Aztec had no beasts of burden and did not use the wheel as a tool, all of the pochteca's wares had to be carried on the backs of porters.

### Religion

Aztec gods gave their people what they needed to live but demanded human sacrifice in return. Their chief deity was the sun god Huitzilopochtli, who battled the moon and stars every day but needed human blood for strength and would be defeated without it. Thus, the Aztec world believed the world would end if they did not make sacrifices, a belief that made warfare a perpetual way of life. Other important gods included Ixtilton, Huitzilopochtli's lieutenant, and Quetzalcoatl.

Sacrificial victims were frequently treated as honored guests for a time, after which they fought ritual combats or played games of hachtli, often willingly. Survivors were then executed upon the temple altars.

Aztec priests painted their bodies all black and never cut or washed their hair. They often fought on the battlefield as elite warriors.

### Clothing

Aztec clothing tended to be simple. Men wore loincloths and decorated capes held in place by a shoulder knot. Women wore knee-length fringed skirts and colorful ponchos. Both sexes wore sandals or went barefoot. The cloth or pattern an Aztec was allowed to wear was determined by his rank, a stricture constantly challenged by the newly wealthy pochteca merchants.

Pendants worn through the nose were popular with men, as were decorative spikes or knobs worn through the skin below the lower lip. Women favored makeup in the form of bright patterns pressed on the face with ceramic stamps.

## OTHER MESOAMERICAN CULTURES

### Olmec

The Olmec are among the most ancient of the Mesoamerican peoples, becoming fully established by about 1200 b.c. and flourishing until about 400 b.c., when they broke up into smaller communities.

Centered along the southern Gulf coast of what is now Mexico, the Olmec were Mesoamerica's first complex culture, and many other regional peoples ultimately traced their ancestry back to them. Olmec communities were characteristically built in marshy areas on raised clay platforms that included stone paving and drainage systems.

Of all Mesoamerican art, that of the Olmec is perhaps the strangest, and includes colossal carved basalt heads, often as much as ten feet tall and twenty tons in weight, and weird jade depictions of were-jaguars and people with broad, fleshy features (unlike those of other local peoples), many with cleft skulls.

### Toltec

The Toltecs migrated into the Valley of Mexico in the seventh century a.d. during the waning of the Mayan power and after the collapse of Teotihuacán. They dominated central Mexico from the tenth to the mid-twelfth century a.d., establishing their capital at Tula, the northernmost of any built by Mesoamerican people.

Droughts weakened the Toltec in the twelfth century, and Tula was overrun by displaced peoples around 1150. Some of the surviving Toltecs fled to the Valley of Mexico, and many Aztecs were later proud to claim a Toltec lineage.

The Toltec had strong contacts with the Maya of Chichen Itza, as evidenced by similarities in art and architecture. They also established trade routes that stretched from what is now Costa Rica to the American Southwest.

## Zapotec

Zaptoec culture was centered in what is now Oaxaca state in modern-day Mexico on the hilltop capital of Monte Albán, a site founded around 500 B.C.

By about A.D. 300, the Zapotec had developed one of the greatest Mesoamerican civilizations, and it flourished until around A.D. 800, when the metropolis of Monte Albán was home to about sixty-six thousand people. After this time, the focus of the Zapotec culture shifted to smaller towns and the capital began to decline, but was never completely abandoned.

Mixtec invaders conquered most of the Valley of Oaxaca during the thirteenth and fourteenth centuries, after which the center of the Zapotec civilization shifted southward to the Tehuantepec region, where it remained independent until the Spanish conquest.

Zapotec art included the oldest hieroglyphic inscriptions yet found in Mesoamerica, many temples, and painted tombs that contained funerary urns in the form of Zapotec gods.

## Mixtec

The Mixtec established several city-states in the seventh century A.D. in the mountainous Oaxaca region of southern Mexico. For many centuries, the Mixtec did not intrude much upon the affairs of their neighbors, but in the thirteenth and fourteenth centuries, strengthened by various political alliances and diplomatic marriages, the Mixtec conquered most of the Valley of Oaxaca and displaced the Zapotec. Mixtec soldiers tended to use the atlatl and sling more than other weapons.

The Aztec in their turn conquered most of the Mixtec lands between 1486 and 1519, and later defeated them completely with the help of Zapotec and Spanish allies.

Mixtec artisans were among the most skilled of Mesoamerica, and created turquoise mosaics, gold jewelry, painted manuscripts, and stone carvings. Many of the richest archaeological finds from Mexico were fashioned by Mixtec craftsmen.

# NORTH AMERICA

Our own continent is home to a great diversity of colorful cultures, some of which are familiar to us, corresponding in part to the popular images we have of Indians. From the wigwam building woodland Indians of the East Coast, to the tipi-dwelling buffalo hunters of the Great Plains, to the whale-hunting totem-pole carvers of the Pacific Northwest, North America provides ample cultural material for the fantasy writer. An added benefit to adapting these cultures is the wealth of resources available, including published literature, historical sites, and the living legacy of Indians themselves.

As Indian cultures that predate contact with Europeans are most appropriate to a fantasy setting, writers should be careful to separate indigenous aspects of Indian culture from those that were formed by such contacts. For example, although the Plains Indians are thought of as great equestrians, horses were brought by Spanish explorers and colonists and were unavailable before the seventeenth or eighteenth centuries. Similarly, the familiar tomahawks of the woodland Indians were trade items brought by Europeans. A bit of research in this area can be both instructive and surprising.

Innumerable books on American Indians can provide general leads on the most well-known Indian cultures. One which is not well known is also one of the most exotic, the culture of the Mississippians.

## Mississippian Culture

From around A.D. 700 to 1500, a sophisticated people known to us as the Mississippians flourished in the great river valleys of North America, practicing agriculture on an intensive scale and building great cities of earthen mounds and pyramids. In many ways, their culture was similar to those of the great civilizations of Mesoamerica.

Introduction of corn to the region more than two thousand years earlier, in the sixteenth century B.C., allowed the indigenous hunter-gatherers to settle down and practice agriculture in the valleys of the Mississippi, Ohio, Tennessee, Arkansas, and Red rivers. The urbanized civilization of the Mississippians evolved from this culture and reached its peak around A.D. 900 during a period of global warming that provided the conditions for even more intensive farming.

Mississippian culture reached its height between A.D. 1100 and 1200, when climatic changes led to widespread drought; this climatic episode lasted until about 1550. These devastating changes led to malnutrition and starvation. This, combined with resulting social chaos and war, a likelihood of diseases or parasitic infestations spawned by overcrowded living conditions, and Old World diseases spreading ahead of European explorers, decimated the native populations and ultimately destroyed the complex Mississippian culture.

Early sixteenth-century French explorers visited some Mississippian cities and contributed to what we know about them. However, when Hernando de Soto ventured up the Mississippi in 1541, all he discovered was ruined cities and abandoned fields. Mississippian culture had disappeared.

### Arts and Sciences

Mississippian towns are their most enduring legacy, which in layout were amazingly similar to those of Mesoamerica. Huge earthen mounds, the largest precolonial structures in North America, were the central structures of these towns. Some two dozen flat-topped mounds clustered around a central rectangular plaza. Cahokia, the most prominent Mississippian site, contains more than one hundred mounds, the largest of which is one hundred feet high and contains more than twenty-one million cubic feet of earth. Many mounds were surmounted by temples, and the mausolea of the social elite. Timber longhouses with thatched roofs were also characteristic of Mississippian towns.

The Mississippians had standard units of measurement and a working knowledge of mathematics and astronomy, all of which was applied to the layout of their cities and placement of their mounds. Nonetheless, they did not have a written language.

### Government

A stable economic base resulting from the surplus allowed powerful chiefs to consolidate villages into states centered on temple towns, and to levy taxes for public works, like the temple cities. These mound cities served as administrative centers where tribute and grain surplus were brought and food distribution took place.

A complex social order developed, and four distinct castes developed, those of the warrior, priest, artisan, and farmer.

## Military

Collapse of the Mississippian culture led to social chaos and warfare; during the period A.D. 1200–1300, as many as 30 percent of adults may have been killed by warfare. By 1200, all cities and many villages were defended by twelve- to fifteen-foot-tall walls and shooting platforms. Mounds were also pallisaded and used as redoubts. Weaponry included bows and arrows from around A.D. 800; stone-headed axes and clubs were also used.

## Economy

Rich alluvial soil, excellent climatic conditions, and a new hardy strain of corn produced an annual crop surplus, which allowed village populations to explode from a few hundred to as many as ten or twelve thousand. Diet was nearly 90 percent corn, supplemented with nuts and game.

Labor became specialized, and artisans crafted arrowheads, shell beads, and a type of pottery traded up to thousands of miles away.

Trade existed with peoples in Canada, Wisconsin, Virginia, Montana, and the Rockies, Ohio, Pennsylvania, Florida, and the Gulf Coast, and Mexico. Valued commodities such as marine shells, obsidian, jade, mica, quartz, pipe-stone, copper, and silver, and the teeth of alligators, sharks, and bears, all flowed into Mississippian towns.

The collapse of the agricultural system resulting from climatic changes eventually destroyed Mississippian economy, necessitating a partial return to hunting and gathering.

## Religion

The Mississippian mounds were at the center of a complex, widespread religion now referred to as the Southern Cult. It may have had Mesoamerican influences, and was at least in part a death cult; for example, upper-caste dead were left in mortuary houses on central mounds until partially rotted, when they were given elaborate funerals.

Ritual objects found in burial sites and on mounds include disk-shaped gorgets of shell; monolithic axes and maces of dense, polished stone; carved wooden masks; and pottery heads.

Once the agricultural system degenerated, the Mississippian temple cities disappeared, along with the state religion.

# OCEANIA

Oceania, the island world of the Pacific, is home to a variety of exotic cultures that can be divided into three broad groups. Micronesians, living on the tiny coral atolls of the western Pacific, clad in sea urchin armor and wielding weapons edged with shark teeth; pygmylike Melanesians, dwelling in the mangrove swamps and mountain forests of New Guinea; and Polynesians, inhabiting the islands of Hawaii, Tahiti, and New Zealand.

It is a Polynesian culture, the Maori, that is discussed here.

## Maori Culture

Around A.D. 900, a Polynesian people arrived at a pair of large, temperate islands far to the south of any known to them. Those islands are today known as New Zealand, and its first human inhabitants as the Maori.

As North Island has a warmer climate that supports agriculture, it became densely settled. South Island is colder, and the Maori there dwelled in smaller groups and lived primarily as hunter-gatherers. Settlements along the coasts were typical, and inland areas were settled where game was initially plentiful. Precolonial Maori population ranged between 100,000 and 250,000.

Maori culture until about A.D. 1350 is referred to as archaic. After that time, many natural resources had been depleted and several game species had been hunted to extinction. From the late fourteenth century onward, warfare increased dramatically, as did the building of fortifications. This is then referred to as the classic period of Maori culture.

### Arts and Sciences

Traditional Maori arts included chants, dances, songs, wood carving, and tattooing. Carving was used for meeting houses, great canoes, and weapons. Warriors wore tattoos in swirling blue and black patterns on their faces and buttocks.

Poetry and storytelling were highly regarded amongst the Maori, who were not a literate people but did have a strong oral tradition of myths and legends. Their language is part of the Austronesian family, related to Tahitian and Hawaiian.

### Government

Kinship ties were the primary force upon which Maori society was organized. The basic social unit was thus the **WHANAU**, a family group of three or four generations that dwelled together. Several whanau with common ancestry comprised a **HAPU**. Such "subtribes" owned valuable assets like canoes and controlled a specific area of land over which it exercised hunting, foraging, and fishing rights. Several hapu in their turn made up one of about fifty large tribes, each member of which was descended from a common ancestor, usually a hero with great powers. Within these social units, Maori culture was divided into three social classes: the aristocracy, commoners, and slaves captured in war.

### Military

By 1350, the Maori were building hill forts called **PA**. These were usually constructed on a piece of high ground or, more dramatically, by terracing the slopes of an extinct volcanic crater; some were also built on level ground or in marshes. Pa were typically composed of ditches, earthen banks surmounted by wooden palisades, and raised fighting platforms from which missile weapons could be hurled. Dwellings, storehouses, and sometimes cultivated areas were clustered within the pa around a central open space, or **MARAE**.

Many warriors went into battle naked, while other wore flax coats, short capes, or simple waist-blankets. The most characteristic Maori weapon was the **PATU**, a short, broad, tear-shaped club that came in many variations and was made from a variety of materials, including polished black or green stone, wood, and whalebone. Other weapons included darts; the **TEWHATEWHA**, a two-handed wooden war club with a beaklike head; and a fighting stick called a **TAIAHA**, which at a glance might have looked like a small spear. The Maori were very adaptable in warfare and adopted weapons like shotguns, muskets, and hatchets for their wars with the British.

Cannibalism was practiced among men, women, and children killed in the course of warfare. This was done not so much for their value as food but because of a belief that supernatural power could be conveyed by consuming the remains of enemies (relatives were buried with elaborate funerary rites).

### Economy

Maori dwelt in villages and practiced small-scale farming, mostly of sweet potatoes. Diet was augmented by fishing, hunting, and gathering. Game included at least thirteen species of **MOA**, heavy, flightless land birds ranging in size from a few feet to more than three yards in height, and the kiwi, a small bird with rodentlike habits.

Stone of various sorts throughout New Zealand was traded extensively among tribes, especially obsidian, chert, argillite (for adzes), quartzite, ortho-quarzite (for blades), and greywacke. South Island greenstone became a favored stone for status items like ceremonial clubs and ornaments.

### Religion

The Maori believed in a pantheon of nature gods, which included major deities like Rangi, god of the sky; Papa, god of the earth; and Tane, god of the forests. Priests, or **TOHUNGA**, consulted major gods prior to important occasions, such as warfare or the construction of a canoe. Commoners were more likely to commune with ancestral spirits or local minor deities, like Maru, a god of war.

How **TABU**, or spiritually powerful, someone or something was was very important to the Maori, and very complex and difficult for others to understand. All men were tabu to some extent, based upon factors like their lineage and how many enemies they had defeated (women were tabu only when menstruat-ing or during childbirth), and the status of warriors and priests was measured according to how tabu they were. Great priests and chiefs were so tabu that food they touched could kill commoners eating it and paths traveled by them could not be used by anyone else.

## SOUTH AMERICA

South America was home to some fourteen million natives in the years just prior to the arrival of Columbus. The ancestors of these people arrived on the continent around 12,000 B.C., and settled in the lowland jungles of the Amazon River basin, along the shores of the Caribbean and throughout the Andes mountain range. The continent's greatest cultures evolved along its west coast and included the Nazca, Moche, and Chimu. Most successful and well-known, of course, were the Inca.

### Incan Culture

Largest of the pre-Columbian states, the Inca rose from an obscure tribe to an empire in less than a century. Around A.D. 1300, they settled high in the Andes mountains and built Cuzco, their capital. In 1438, Pachacuti Inca ascended to the throne and began to subdue neighboring peoples; his son

Topa continued in his footsteps, conquering the northern Peruvian kingdom of Chimor. Eventually, the Inca empire stretched along two thousand miles of the South American coast, spreading inland an average of about two hundred miles and encompassing a third of the continent's population.

The Inca learned much from other highland peoples, especially the conquered Chimu. When Spanish conquistadors under Francisco Pizarro encountered them in 1522, the Inca empire under Atahualpa was still growing and represented a sociopolitical system that had evolved over five thousand years.

## Arts and Sciences

Amazingly, even though they developed an indisputably great civilization, the Inca had very few of the characteristics normally associated with a civilized people. Things they lacked included the wheel and written language.

Nonetheless, the Inca undertook huge public works and left behind a durable legacy. Massive citadel, temple, and fortress complexes, formed of perfectly fitted, irregular blocks of stone weighing several tons each, are the most obvious remnants of Inca engineering ability. Just as impressively, they linked their empire with some twenty-five thousand miles of interconnected mountain and coastal roads, overcoming ridges with tunnels, marshes with causeways, and the rifts and chasms of the Andes with suspension bridges up to seventy-five yards long. These bridges are still built by Peruvian villagers, who construct them in a mere three days using nothing but rope made from twisted grass, anchoring the ends of the bridges in ancient stone sockets carved by Inca craftsmen.

## Government

Incan government was pyramidal, a strict hierarchy that ensured government control at all levels of society; at its apex was the Sapa Inca, who wielded absolute authority in political, military, and religious matters. The aristocracy consisted mainly of the emperor's relatives and served as his councilors and provincial governors. Government officials, some of them highly specialized, were all accountable to the Sapa Inca, either directly or through those above them.

A form of record keeping known as **QUIPUS** allowed information to be kept on things such as tax revenue and turnout for public projects or military duty. The quipus, a cord with knots in significant numbers, patterns, and colors, was a document that allowed information to be stored and transferred, and was read and interpreted by officials called **QUIPUCAMAYOC**.

--------------------------------------------------------------------

Couriers, **CHASQUIS**, ran along the roadways to deliver official messages; they ran 6 ½-minute miles, and in relays could cover 1,250 miles in five days.

Two of the main weaknesses of Inca government were that there was no clear line of succession to the throne and authority collapsed when the Sapa Inca died.

### Military

A standing army of up to ten thousand men formed the core of the Inca military, acting as a cadre for an agrarian militia that could be activated when needed.

Primary Inca weapons were a stone-hurling sling of plaited llama hair and the **MACANA**, a mace with a star-shaped head of stone or bronze. Other weapons included a double-edged hardwood weapon like a two-handed sword, stone- and bronze-headed axes, and throwing spears with metal or fire-hardened wooden heads. Soldiers' uniforms consisted of their regular clothes, augmented by helmets, quilted cotton coats, shields, and slats of iron-hard wood hung from the back of the neck to protect the spine.

Depots of weapons and supplies were set up along the well-maintained Inca road system. The main purpose of this road system was to allow rapid movement of large bodies of troops. Discipline and the ability to quickly move well-supplied armies was one reason the Inca were able to defeat enemies against which they were superior in neither weapons nor tactics. Battles between the Inca and their foes were chaotic messes, opening up with volleys of slung stones, followed by hurled spears and then close combat with maces, clubs, and axes. Inca disorganization in battle, along with ritualized patterns of campaign and prescribed times for attacks, made them unable to withstand the brutal efficiency of the Spaniards.

Defeated but still hostile peoples were relocated to the Inca heartland, while loyal subjects were sent to live as colonists, **MITIMAES**, to conquered areas.

### Economy

Heavy taxation allowed the Incas to maintain a standard army, fight wars, and undertake huge public works projects. A tax of about 66 percent was levied on produce and manufactured goods, and the **MIT'A**, an obligation to provide labor, was levied on the masses.

The superior road system also allowed efficient transport of goods, transported on the backs of llamas and people. Levied goods were transported to and stored in government supply centers, some of which were massive; the granaries at Huanuco Pampa could hold up to thirty-six million liters of grain. Such centers also served as manufacturing centers for the production of goods such as textiles, tools, or pottery. Such goods were highly standardized throughout the empire, and show little individual variation.

## Religion

The Sapa Inca was believed to descend from the sun god, and the main state religion was the cult of the solar deity. Common people were allowed to worship local rocks and streams, so long as they also propitiated the sun god. Viracocha, the creator god, was the chief deity and the one worshipped by the aristocracy.

Temples were filled with gold and silver ornaments and statuary, most of which were melted down and shipped back to Spain as ingots after the Spanish conquest.

# CHAPTER 3

# Magic

## by Allan Maurer and Renee Wright

The ancient occult sciences retain their power to entrance us even in this age of science and skepticism. In contemporary stories, nailing a few elements of magical lore into a solid timber of realism can provide the essence of a fantasy plot. From the most primitive tribes to the most sophisticated modern city, humankind believes in magic. We mutter spells (knock on wood), curse in holy names, conduct miniature rites (throwing spilled salt over a shoulder). So, too, in all times and places, both professional and amateur wizards, witches, shamans, and magicians attempt to discover magic's secrets.

## HISTORY

Magic differs from religion primarily in intent: Religion is an appeal to the gods; magic attempts to *force* their aid. The nature magic of pagan religion goes back to prehistoric times. The word "magic" probably derived from the Greek word *magein*, the science of the priests of Zoroaster (Assyrian/Babylonian), or from *megas*, Greek for "great." Early Middle Eastern civilizations created a divide between the high magic of the priests and the low magic of the people, which persists to this day. The Chaldeans refined and shaped astrology, oracles practiced from holy temples, and harvest rites became public functions. But less exalted magicians practicing in small towns, the countryside, or the neighborhood offered inexpensive protection against the Evil

Eye, explained dreams, foretold the future, and sold amulets, talismans, and other magic wares.

Ancient Babylonian and Egyptian magic systems were among the earliest known, already thousands of years old when Athens flourished in 400 B.C. or the Caesars reigned in A.D. 1, and many of their secrets are still sought. The mystery religions of ancient Greece and Rome, themselves descended from the savage primitive rituals of harvest and hunt, degenerated into the magic of the Middle Ages, which the Christian Church condemned as witchcraft. At the same time, the Church appropriated pagan holidays and a pantheon of saints, many borrowed from the Olympian collection of ancient gods and goddesses. As religions succeed each other, they often demonize their predecessors. Old Testament Hebrews made demons of hell of Babylonian, Egyptian, and other Middle Eastern deities, both male and female. The magician practicing black craft depends upon who tells the story: Most of us are familiar with the version of Moses vs. Pharaoh's magicians in Exodus (they turned their staves to snakes; Moses turned his into a bigger snake, which ate theirs). In the Egyptian version, according to witchcraft researcher Margaret Murray, "the wise priest of Egypt defeats the miserable foreign sorcerer whom he had saved from the water when a child."

European magic before the Crusades remained largely a hodge-podge of ancient religions and surviving folk magic. Following the Crusades, oriental theories and practices modeled on those practiced by the Sufis, Byzantines, and Moors of Spain created European high magic. Secret societies and secret sorceries flourished, based on Alexandrian Neoplatonic ideas, the Hermetic books, and the Hebrew Kabbalah. Basic principles included the Hermetic tablet's injunction: "As above, so below"; the idea that everything in the universe is associated through a series of secret connections between numbers, letters, the heavens, the elements (earth, air, fire, water), etc.; and the conviction that one could magically tap the infinite creative power of the universe. The refined development and application of the magician's imagination played an active role in medieval ritual and high magic.

At all times and places, however, the low magic of necromancers, who called upon the spirits of the dead, invoked hosts of demons and peddled love potions and talismans, coexisted with both established religion and ceremonial high magic. During the medieval era, both deeply superstitious and religious

---

in a way difficult for most people to imagine today, some magicians practiced a black art that was essentially a desecration of Christian rites, symbols, liturgy, biblical passages, and holy sites. Muslims who practice black magic do the same things with Islamic religion. These practices survive today, but should not be confused with pagan witchcraft or Wicca, which are revivals of the ancient world's mystery religions (Rome, Egypt, Babylon, Greece) and have nothing whatsoever to do with Christianity.

## The Force

All magic shares certain general features. The concept of **MANA**, a magical force in virtually everything, has been called the "mother idea of magic." This idea of a universal force latent in all creation is common to primitive peoples: mana is called **MANITOU, POKUNT,** and **WAKAN** by various American Indian tribes; ancient Peruvians called it **HUACA**; in Mexico, it is called **NAGUALISM**; and in Lake Tanganyika, it is called **CHURINGA** or **BOOLYA**. Larry Niven wrote a series of popular novellas speculating that this force, which our mythology and legends suggest was once much more powerful than it now seems, could be used up. He called the first story *When the Magic Goes Away.* Story ideas lurk everywhere in this material.

The ability to tap this magical force, or mana, is almost always extremely limited. Everywhere, tradition binds magic, ruling its access and use, and magical power traditionally lies in the knowledge of spells and rites. Sometimes it is invested in the person of the wizard. The rules of magic are limited, but it has many classes of practitioner.

## Two Worlds

Most magical systems assume there are two worlds. One is the material, everyday, mundane world of reality in which experience and practical knowledge work. The other is a supernatural world, usually accessible only through a medium, the wizard/witch/wise one. Primitive man, for instance, nearly always recognized a natural and supernatural order. He applied knowledge of soils and planting times or where the fish or game were found, but performed magic to ensure good weather and protect himself from accidents.

Magicians attempt to control the unknown: the weather, abundance of crops or hunt animals, the course of a love affair, or the outcome of a battle.

Magic gives a house sturdiness after it is built with conventional means. Magical rites promote an abundant crop, but seeds are still planted.

## PRINCIPLES OF MAGIC

The principles of **SYMPATHY** (homeopathy and contagion) and **ANTIPATHY** guide virtually all human magic. They are widely applied in language, actions, and even the magician's "inner state" or thoughts.

### Sympathetic Magic

Sympathetic magic relies on the ancient idea that if one thing resembles another, the two are magically connected. The two principle types of sympathetic magic are: **HOMEOPATHY** (like affects like) and **CONTAGION** (things once in contact, even tenuously, retain a connection even though widely separated).

Sympathetic principles affect all aspects of magic. Words of a spell draw upon this principle. Strong things are mentioned to impart strength; fast things are cited to impart speed. To make a household sleep like the dead, the magician uses grave dirt or the bones of the dead, placing them on the roof or in the home of intended victims. The magician cures "yellow" jaundice by banishing yellow. He paints the patient yellow then washes the color away. He brings in yellow birds then shoos them away. (Antipathy is also used. Other colors drive out the yellow; the patient drinks water mixed with the hair of a red bull and sits on the skin of a red bull.)

Imitation of successful hunts, fishing expeditions, and harvests form the basis of many primitive rituals. African tribal and American Indian dances mimic the animal and the hunter and their interplay. Prehistoric cave paintings in Ariege, France, show a man clothed in a stag's skin with antlers on his head. A prehistoric Egyptian carved slate shows a man disguised as a jackal. Shamans, wizards, and magicians throughout time have relied upon animal familiars, vision quest guides, and totems.

In planting societies, dancers poked the ground with sticks imitating real planting, a movement you still see some in European country dancing. Ritual movement and dancing played multiple roles in magic, ranging from tribal celebrations and occasions to solo dance by shamans.

The sympathetic principle governs performance of rites. If a wizard intends to magically harm a person with his wand or staff by "pointing" in the direction of his enemy, he must emotionally and even intellectually believe and feel he is thrusting the wand as a sword into the enemy's belly and twisting it. He must "act" as if performing an actual stabbing. The similarity of one's actions in a magical rite to the same actions in real life is an important part of making the magic work. Thus, sympathetic relations may involve color, sound, meaning, physical resemblance, and the state of the magician's mind and attitude.

## Homeopathy

The most common type of sympathetic magic is homeopathy. Homeopathy means like affects like. Some call it imitative magic. A magician might administer a potion that includes animal liver to a patient with liver pain.

Homeopathy is the basis for making an image of an enemy and sticking pins in it to cause her pain, discomfort or death, one of the most widely practiced forms of magic. One of the earliest records of this charm is in the trial of women and officers of the harem of Ramses II in Egypt in 1100 B.C.—they made images of the Pharaoh with magical incantations. Familiar to us in the form of the voodoo doll, the practice of making stone, wood, cloth, or wax images and puppets in the likeness of enemies was practiced by the ancient Greeks, who inherited much of their magic from the Egyptians and other Middle Eastern regions.

North American Indians draw figures of a person in sand, ashes, or clay, then poke the image with a sharp stick, shoot an arrow into it, or run a needle through its head or heart. Peruvian Indians mixed fat with grain to form images of people they wanted to harm, then burned the effigy on a road the victim traveled. A Malay version includes nail parings, hair, eyebrows, spittle—enough pieces of the intended victim to represent the whole body—and combines them with bee's comb wax in a figure scorched over a fire for seven nights while saying: "It is not wax that I am scorching/It is the liver, heart, and spleen of (victim's name) that I scorch" (from Frazer's *The Golden Bough*).

Making images can work for good as well as evil. In Sumatra, a barren woman holds a wooden doll of a child in her lap to encourage one to grow in her womb. In some cases, the father of a large family recites spells while the woman holds a cotton doll to her breast; in others, a wizard enacts a mock birth with a large stone tied to his stomach.

Homeopathic magic resembles the pretend games of children, often right down to the sincerity of the pretending, which is necessary to make the magic work. Magicians sometimes resort to "tricks" intended to convince others of their power, the belief necessary to working their "real" magic.

## Contagion

Contagion is the concept that anything once in contact with something else retains a magically useful connection to that thing even if the two become widely separated. Often contagion combines with imitative and homeopathic principles in spells and rites. A wizard making an image of any enemy would want items once in physical contact with the person: nail clippings, hair, teeth, clothing. Today, superstitious (or careful) people still guard their nail and hair clippings, pulled teeth, and intimate apparel. One occult author recalls her mother "keeping a jar full of my nail clippings from infancy on."

Contagion can work to the good of the practitioner, too. Placing an extracted tooth where a mouse or rat could get it would impart the strength of the rodent's teeth to its former owner when gnawed. In many parts of the world, the umbilical cord and the afterbirth are thought to retain such a powerful connection to the child even after removal that what happens to them may determine the child's entire fate. If properly preserved—buried in the sand, for example—the child will be prosperous; if not, he will be doomed. Or to make a child a good climber or hunter, the umbilical cord might be hung from a tree.

Frazer notes the "relation ... believed to exist between a wounded man and the agent of the wound." Melanesians, for example, keep an arrow that wounded a warrior in cool leaves to combat inflammation. His enemy, meanwhile, knowing he inflicted the wound, drinks hot, burning juices and chews irritating leaves to inflame it. He twangs his taut bow string to pain the wounded enemy. This belief led to the widespread idea that to keep a human or animal wound from a blade or puncture from becoming infected, one must clean and oil the knife, scythe, or nail that caused the harm. This idea is based on the notion that the blood on the weapon continues a connection with blood in the body.

In the New Hebrides, obtaining a cloth someone used to mop his sweat gave the wizard power of death over the hapless victim. The magician would wrap the cloth with leaves and twigs of a specific tree and burn them. In Prussia, it was thought that if you couldn't catch a thief, you could snatch a piece of his clothing and make him sick by beating it.

Less tangible connections also offer magicians the power of contagion. In Mecklenburg, Germany, it is believed that driving a nail into a man's footprint will make him lame. A German hunter might drive a coffin nail into an animal's footprint, believing it will hobble the quarry. Many American Indian and African tribes follow similar customs, throwing dirt from an animal's tracks in the air to bring the quarry down, or placing charms on the tracks to magically slow or cripple the beast.

In France, a witchhunter might follow a suspect and drive a knife into her footprint, thinking that if she is a witch, she will not be able to move until the knife is withdrawn. In Bohemia, a peasant girl might plant a marigold in earth she dug from the footprints of a man she loves, hoping love will bloom with the flower. The ancient Greek Pythagoreans recommended smoothing away the impression of your body when you rise from bed as a precaution against magic, so even the most tenuous connection could be magically useful.

## Antipathetic Magic

Antipathy is what some anthropologists call benevolent charms or the white magic that overcomes black. Holy water drives away devils, for example. A sounding bell does the same. A silver bullet slays a werewolf, and a vampire cannot see himself in a mirror because of its silver backing. Red berries or thread, because of their bloody color, counter witchcraft. Garlic repels vampires. Making the sign of the cross or other protective gestures drives off demons, as do protective talismans. These examples act in antipathy, or counter to, evil or black magic.

## Taboos

Taboos prevent magical contamination. Magic, particularly among primitive peoples, whether African, Polynesian (such as the Maori of the previous chapter), or American Indian, is a highly practical affair. Generally, they are protection against the unknown. Taboos restrict contact between the tabooed person (a king, a woman during childbirth, a warrior before his first battle) and others. They require purification or protective rites, often including bathing, shaving the head, marking of the body by a magician, incense, fire, or water.

Touching a king, his clothes, or his food is often taboo among primitive peoples. Warriors going to their first (or first several) battles are taboo, often in the same manner as menstrual women are taboo. Rules for both include unapproachable seclusion, taboos against scratching the head or any other part of the body with fingers, sexual abstinence, and minimal handling of food and their containers. The seclusion sometimes requires a man to build a separate hut for a bride in childbirth.

Taboos surround contact with strangers, with both sides performing obligatory rites: fire and incense greet them to drive away evil spirits; the visitor may carry lighted sticks or bark for the same purpose; on returning home, a traveler must bathe and visit a shaman/magician for cleansing, which frequently includes receiving a visible mark on the forehead or otherwise highly visible spot.

Taboos on eating and drinking may be particularly rough on kings, who take extraordinary precautions. The mouth may be a door to the soul, and food, which comes into contact with preparers and may not be completely consumed, may easily be magically (or actually) acted upon. Taboos force eating meals behind locked doors to prevent the soul's escape and being hidden from view, even in public, where, in some primitive societies, a cloth is held up to shield a king taking his meal. Since, by sympathetic contagion, the leftover food one leaves or the dishes one eats from retain a connection to the consumer, leftovers (even bones) are burned, buried, or thrown into the sea to prevent sorcerers from obtaining them. A sorcerer keeps his eyes open for such refuse, particularly bones of birds, animals, or fish consumed by people. He can concoct deadly charms with them.

A primitive might eat many animals or plants in order to share their qualities, for example, eating a rabbit to gain speed or an elk to gain strength, but he must not eat others so as not to share them.

Sympathetic and homeopathic principles govern many taboos: boys of a fishing tribe are forbidden to play cat's cradle lest they entangle their hands in fishing nets as adults; warriors may not eat a cock that dies while fighting, lest the same happen to them. Women at home during the hunt often face many taboos, such as being forbidden to kill any male animal while the warrior is gone or he may die.

Mourners or others who have contact with the dead; people leaving and entering houses; women at childbirth as well as menstruation; those who kill another person; hunters and fishers, who must propitiate the animal spirits just as warriors must propitiate the ghosts of their dead enemies; are all heavily tabooed.

## WHAT MAGIC DOES

Anthropologist Bronislaw Malinowski (1884–1942), who identified many of these common features, said all magic has one of three functions: to produce, protect, or destroy.

Magicians, wizards, and so on accomplish these ends via three elements. They are:

1. Spells, incantations, invocations, enchantments (what is said)

2. Actions taken: rites, gestures, use of magic tools (what is done)

3. Conditions of the practitioner, which requires precise, arduous preparation and might include:
    Purification by fasting
    Meditating in solitude
    Dancing
    Drumming
    Staring into flames
    Inhaling smoke
    Ingesting drugs
    Enduring pain
    Intense sweating

After ritual self-purification, the magician recites the spell, almost always accomplished by an action or rite that is intended to carry the magic to its intended object. Usually, continued and unbroken attention to the proper state of mind is necessary for a magician's powers to work. In higher magic, a trained imagination brought to intense concentration may be required.

Let's take a closer look at each of the elements of the magical act.

### Spells, Incantations, Invocations, Enchantments

The first element of magic is what is said. Words themselves retain a magical ability to affect us even in our enlightened era. Many people still have difficulty separating their reactions to words from their reaction to what the words symbolize. Cursing involves invoking the names of deities, saints, or devils: holy names or their devilish counterparts, whether in casual speech or magic spells.

The spell is associated so strongly with magic that in some primitive societies, the word for magic and the word for spell are the same. Usually a spell must be spoken exactly, without the slightest deviation from text and with proper pronunciation or intonation. Everywhere, the spoken part of a magic act is of supreme importance.

Spell books, such as the grimoires of the Middle Ages, required debilitating purifications on the magician's part, extreme care in making tools, and letter-perfect recitation of enormous lists of words of power, holy names, and turgid prose. Among Polynesians, a single slip during the most sacred ritual might cause the death of the practitioner by supernatural causes. Spells are governed by tradition rather than creativity. Altering a spell defuses its magic. Ancient Egyptian magic, **HIKE**, worked through spoken formulas that had to be recited exactly as proscribed at a particular place and time. Egyptians credited mispronounced words with all instances of magical failure.

The language of spells relates directly to an associated ritual and desired effect. To confer speed to a canoe, for instance, a spell cites birds on the wing, the lightness of a seagull on water, the floating ability of certain woods, onomatopoeic words that sound like speed.

Spells use cryptic, archaic language; lists of ancestral names, holy names, demon names, and spirit names; and stories of mythological events, all in precise order and pronunciation, often known only to an elite group of initiates. The difficulties of meeting the stringent requirements for preparation and performance were cited as reasons why magic failed to work. In one of the most moving fantasy short stories of the mid-1970s, Tom Reamy's award-winning "San Diego Lightfoot Sue," a forty-five-year-old woman falls in love with a teenage Kansas lad and wants him to see how she looked at fifteen. The daughter of a witch, she performs a rite that goes wrong. Witnesses see only a green fire that consumes her—virtually the only fantasy element in the story. The archetypal power of this stuff works even in small fictional doses. A single magical idea that spells are dangerous to the magician if not performed properly continues to inspire tales in every medium.

The need for exactness in spells and rites supplies a basis for much humor in modern fantasy with mistakes responsible for all sorts of consequences, from the humorous sort practiced by Samantha's senile aunt on television's *Bewitched*, to the gruesomely macabre. Humor, fantasy and horror often compliment each other in fiction, perhaps because our human reaction to horror and the fantastic is often nervous laughter. In fiction, certain authors always made a living combining humor and horror, and humor and fantasy. At least two twentieth-century cartoonists, Gahan Wilson and Charles Addams, never strayed far from their successful mix of the two. Film and TV scripts combine fantasy, horror and comedy in an almost distinct genre in which the fantasy element—a genie, ghost, witch, magician—serve entirely comical purposes (*Buffy the Vampire Slayer*, *I Dream of Jeannie*, *Death Becomes Her*). So don't be overly surprised if the Grim Reaper in your story turns out to have a sense of humor.

## Black and White Magic

Magic in all times has served both positive and negative purposes, which are sometimes referred to as white magic and black magic. Magic itself is neutral; it is the application to which it is put that characterizes it. In the case of Christian, Islamic, or other religious "black magic," official church rites are often reversed, as in the Black Mass or saying the Lord's Prayer backwards. Necromancy—calling upon the spirits of the dead—is also characterized as black magic.

When one religion succeeds another, as Christianity has pagan worship of multiple gods and goddesses, the priests, wizards, or wise men/women of the former (paganism) are characterized as witches and black magicians by the current religion. (Many of the gods and goddesses became Christian saints, and pagan festivals became Catholic holy days.) Hebrew tribes worshiping their God, Yahweh (later Jehovah), did the same to the many Babylonian, Persian, Egyptian, and other Middle Eastern deities, going so far as to make devils of former deities such as Baal.

The black magic of the medieval era, with its grimoires and their impossible-to-fulfill requirements, is generally considered silly by modern magicians. But at the same time, magicians practice various high-magic systems imported from the East, where they mix oriental ideas with those surviving from pagan times. (We'll cover this in greater detail later.)

## Rituals, Rites, and Wrongs

Nearly all spells are accompanied by actions. These "rites" generally require the same exactness on the performer's part as the reciting of spells. The main purpose of a rite is to carry the magic of the spell to its desired object.

Rituals are ceremonial acts for religious or sacred purposes. They have various, frequently overlapping purposes: to placate, propitiate, supplicate, honor, obey, or call forth the gods, goddesses, spirits, or demons; to initiate passage into adulthood, entrance into a secret society, or entrance into a mystical vocation such as magician or shaman (all three may be ecstatic in nature, requiring taking drugs, fasting, lonely ordeals in the wilderness or jungle, pain, sleep deprivation, and other means of altering consciousness); to mark transitions or passages; to encourage fertility, healing, or cleansing; to protect home, family, children, or warriors; to banish wrongdoers.

### Elements of Ritual

The elements of ritual vary according to the type of magic practiced. Those required for ritual and ceremonial magic are covered in more detail in that section. Among the common features of ritual in all magic are:

- Reciting holy names, the names of God, spells, chants, or prayers
- Dancing and other movement, particularly ritualized postures and gestures
- Costumes, masks, fetishes
- Incense, smoke, candles, fires
- Offerings, sacrifices
- Feasting or fasting
- Purifications
- Use of sacred objects, relics, tools, images, symbols

Ceremonial rituals include making the familiar magic circle, and within it, the triangle of the art. Magicians must remain inside the circle or lose their protection from the entities they summon.

### Meditative Magic

Meditation is an element of magic from the shamanism of primitive tribes to the most esoteric ceremonial magic. It is used to cleanse the body, mind, and soul, and to connect to the creative force of the universe through altered consciousness. Meditating on the Tree of Life forms an important aspect of Kabbalah.

Some magical systems, such as Hawaiin Huna and Islamic Sufi, actually do their primary work through meditation and associated mental activity—imagination, visualization, and concentration. This might be achieved through self-deprivation of food, sleep, or company; drumming; drugs; or dancing.

In Sufi practice, whirling is one way to achieve an ecstatic state in which magic of a psychic nature can be performed. Since Sufis who follow pious poverty are called "dervishes," those who spin their trances are called "whirling dervishes." Fantastic literature and poetry from Rumi to *Arabian Nights* are cited as "quintessential Sufi texts." Since each Sufi adept teaches from his own system, no single Sufi approach to mysticism exists. Orders included not only the Whirling Dervishes, but also the Howling Dervishes, Shaven Dervishes, and Silent Dervishes. Islamic black magic works much the same as Christian-inspired black magic: holy objects, places, garments, symbols, rituals, and the Koran are desecrated, recited backwards, or otherwise profaned for dark magic purposes.

## RITUAL AND CEREMONIAL MAGIC

Ritual magic is the performance of ceremony to obtain material and spiritual power. Ceremonial magicians may follow one of two paths. In one path, the magician spends years of study and preparation learning the secrets of the Kabbalah, the Hermetic books, or a master's teaching until he learns to discipline his will and imagination, leave his physical body, and work magic on the "astral plane."

This astral plane holds, in hidden planes, worlds of beauty and awesome terror. It is a literal twilight zone containing the highest dreams and darkest nightmares. The shaman travels there in a vision quest or to fight demons making a tribemate ill. The mystic ascends there after disciplining and training his imagination and will. All of the higher occult experiences occur here. The geography of this astral world and means of access to and travel through it supplies the material taught by many esoteric schools of occult science.

The magician ascends the multiple planes by various rituals, but one must be fit to receive these teachings. Magicians map out some areas in this unimaginably vast territory, describing inhabitants, their living space, the language they speak. The student ascends the planes as he rises in grade and learns the spells, names of guardian angels, smells, colors, and other symbolic aspects of the planes. He learns which demons inhabit the plane, which he defends against with the proper protective spells and rituals.

The simplest method of astral out-of-body travel is through visualization training. The student begins by relaxing in a prone position and imagining his astral body rising from his physical body. With training, visualization is intensified until the magician's consciousness transfers to the astral "watcher."

Other methods, such as meditating on the paths of the Kabbalistic Tree of Life, follow a specific protocol, and traveling unprepared or leaping ahead of one's knowledge is considered dangerous and foolhardy.

Eliphas Levi's volume, *Dogma and Ritual of High Magic* (1856), proved hugely influential on the modern practice of this type of ritual, leading directly to the Order of the Golden Dawn and many other schools of modern ceremonial and ritual magic. The tendency of modern magic, however, has been to bring various systems of magic and occult science together in a synthesis that combines multiple schools. While not true of all modern magicians, many dispense with the more complicated requirements of traditional ceremonial magic in favor of simpler but no less volatile systems.

Following the second path, a ceremonial magician may draw his magic circle, his pentagram of two triangles, and call forth deities, spirits, demons, and the dead following directions from a grimoire or magic texts such as the medieval *The Key of Solomon*, which names hundreds of Greek, Roman, Egyptian, and various other gods, demons, and spirits. The paraphernalia required to follow this path and the preparations of the magician are described in arduous detail in spell books. But this concept did not originate in the Middle Ages. Works from the great library of Assurbanipal reveal that grimoires full of spells were common fifteen centuries earlier. Babylonian grimoires included **UTUKKI LIMNULI** (evil spirits), **LABARTU** (hag-demons), and ceremonial texts such as the **MAKLU**, which contained eight tablets of incantations and spells against wizards and witches (making images of their enemies and destroying them is a major element). Another sixteen tablets on exorcism of evil spirits names demons, goblins, and ghosts.

This style perhaps reached its highest development when MacGregor Mathers (a Golden Dawn member) translated into English *The Book of the Sacred Magic of Abra-Melin the Mage*, allegedly a fifteenth-century guide but more likely an eighteenth-century work. It did away with most complicated ritual and paraphernalia required by European ceremonial magic. Abramelin magic supposes the material world is created by evil spirits that the magician can control after he attains the help of his guardian angel. (This is an ancient magical idea. The Golden Dawn magicians believed the magician's "guardian angel" was actually his own true self.) Discovering this, the magician can force the spirits—which may be recognized as materializations of archetypal ideas inside his mind or aspects of himself—to do his bidding. The book includes a large number of magic squares, letter arrangements that represent and empower the magician's wishes. Abramelin magic fascinated Aleister Crowley, who warned that it was extremely dangerous to use without proper preparation.

Both paths may be dangerous to the life and soul of inadequately prepared magicians. One practicing magician says, "It's like a dark force and a good force. The dark force, calling up demons, is quicker, but you pay a toll. It's dangerous and costly to the magician spiritually. The other path, meditating on the Kabbalistic Tree of Life, say, is slower, but still dangerous if you do not do it right."

Both paths also evolved from ideas already old in Egypt when written down in ancient Greece. The occult sciences proceeded from these ancient moorings in sympathetic magic, the study of stars and rites for the Egyptian dead, to the Neoplatonic ideas of Plotinus of Alexandria in A.D. 233, who sought "the ideal reality which exists behind appearances." This idea—similar to Plato's concept of elementary ideas, hence the "Neoplatonic" label—led Plotinus and his followers, Porphyry, Iambilichus, and Proclus, into out-of-body magical practice where they encountered gods and demigods, malignant daemons and genii. While in an ecstatic, meditative, out-of-body state achieved through austere living and careful preparation, the Neoplatonists believed evil genii and daemons might pursue and capture them if the philosopher/magicians did not escape by returning to their physical bodies.

Gnostics, who sought **GNOSIS**, or secret knowledge, further developed and refined Neoplatonic and other oriental magical ideas. Simon the Magus, mentioned in the Acts of the Apostles in the Bible, was a Gnostic magician (and the Bible relates only the canonical Christian version of his story). Gnostics were declared heretical by the Catholic Church as it solidified its accepted theology.

### The Hermetica

The Hermetica, according to occult tradition, is forty-two books written by various authors but attributed in a convenient fiction to Hermes Trismegistus, "Thrice Greatest Hermes," a combination of the Greek god and Egyptian god of wisdom, Thoth. The secret knowledge in these works are dense with occult symbolism. Their basic idea suggests that the universe is a whole and is connected via a complicated system of correspondences, which is the import of the statement from the Hermetic work, the Smaragdine Tablet: "As above, so below." Legend says the Hermetic books contain fragments of the magic secrets of ancient Greece and Egypt, which were originally contained in books lost when the library of Alexandria burned, destroying much of the collected knowledge of the ancient world. They include *The Divine Pymander* and the *Vision*, which mix esoteric thought from dynastic Egypt with instructions for the spiritual development of the soul.

## Medieval Magic

European high magic kept a low profile after mainstream Christianity conquered the West in the fourth century. The thirty-sixth Canon of the Ecumenical Council at Laodicea in A.D. 364 forbids priests and clerks to become magicians, enchanters, or astrologers. It was merely the first of many canons to follow forbidding various magical practices as the Church decided that magic and Christianity were largely incompatible. Most magic practiced in Europe prior to about the twelfth century was the nature religion based on herbs and stones, the moon and stars, and cultural superstition or remnants of the ancient mystery religions. The Church regarded both as witchcraft or black magic.

When the Crusaders returned from the Middle East, they brought with them oriental ideas of theosophy (from the Greek, *theos*, meaning "god" and *sophia*, meaning "wisdom") that claims one can know the nature of the deity absolutely through proper preparation, study, and ritual. Magical systems in the Middle East, practiced by the Byzantines, the Moors of Spain, and the Arabs, drew upon the Alexandrian Neoplatonic ideas. Paracelsus and Agrippa together virtually outlined medieval high magic principles between them.

Paracelsus (born in 1493 near Zurich) wrote several tomes outlining his complex ideas, which first outlined the astral body concept, established connections between the body and the planets, and preached the importance of the willed imagination. "It is possible," he wrote, "that my spirit, without help of my body, and through an ardent will alone, and without a sword, can stab and wound others. It is also possible that I can bring my adversary into an image and then fold him up and lame him at my pleasure. Resolute imagination is

---

the beginning of all magical operations."

The primary influences of Agrippa were due to the stories told about his own adventurous life. He was born Agrippa von Nettesheim, Henrich Cornelius (1486–1535). A German soldier, physician, alchemist, astrologer, and magician, Agrippa knew eight languages and traveled Europe widely as a soldier and in service to noble patrons. His defense of magic, *De occulta philosophia* (1531), and the tales surrounding his life (he made enemies freely, particularly among the medieval monks), made him one of the major figures who contributed to the medieval fascination with high magic. Agrippa regarded magic as "the true road to communion with God," linking his mysticism to Neoplatonic ideas and modern magic alike.

Legend said Agrippa always traveled with a familiar in the shape of a large fearsome black dog. He paid his bills with money that looked normal but later turned to worthless shell. Agrippa, it was said, used a magic glass to view distant times and places, once spying his mistress weeping over the absence of another lover. One of the most famous stories says a boarder in his home convinced Agrippa's wife to let him enter the learned man's museum. The boarder found a book of spells and began to read. He ignored a knock on the door and went on reading. Finally, a demon burst through the door and asked why he had been summoned. Terrified, the boarder could not answer and the demon strangled him. Agrippa returned at that moment and, fearing he would be charged with the boarder's murder, persuaded the demon to return him to life. People saw the boarder walk through the marketplace, and after he died when the demon spell wore off, they thought he did so of natural causes. Agrippa's life is a prime example of the power of stories to heighten the power of a magician, for he was actually a relatively harmless alchemist/astrologer with a wide correspondence that accounted for his worldwide knowledge others attributed to his magical familiar.

### Power Animals

Very early on, humankind recognized the powers of the animals that shared the earth, and the ability to "talk to the animals" became a basic skill of shamans and magicians worldwide. Many tribes, peoples, and societies trace their origins to a founding totem animal, often associated with a god, and hold that animal sacred. Animal powers are often invoked through dances imitating their movements and musical instruments imitating their cries.

Acquiring an animal guide or familiar is important in many kinds of magic and spiritualism. The Native American sought this animal spirit guide during a vision quest while alone in the wilderness, or on a spiritual journey assisted by hallucinogenic drugs, such as peyote. Western magicians gained the aid of a familiar through meditation and invocation, wearing masks and practicing shape-shifting.

**Alligator or Crocodile:** aggression, survival, reason (Egypt)

**Ant:** group-minded, hard worker, wisdom (Muslim); sacred to harvest goddesses

**Ass or Donkey:** stubbornness, obstinacy, symbol of opposites; sacred to Greek god Dionysius

**Bat:** good fortune, great happiness (China), rebirth, guardian of the night, cleanser, guide to past lives

**Bear:** power, adaptability, knowledge of the healing power of herbs, brings balance and harmony on the astral plane

**Beaver:** builder, gatherer, concentration, harmony in group work

**Bee:** purity, queenship, wearer of veils

**Boar:** courage, protection; fertility; symbol of the Lord of Earth; sacred to the Greek god Adonis, the Hindu god Rudra, and the Egyptian god Set

**Buffalo or Bison:** sacredness, fertility, abundance, symbol of spirit

**Bull:** fertility, strength; associated with many gods and used in rituals in many religions or cultures including Egyptian (the Apis and Serapis cults), Cretan (the Minos cult), Celtic, Sumerian, Hindu, and Mithraic

**Butterfly:** metamorphosis, carefree, transformer, love (China)

**Cat:** a strong protector, seer of spirits, independent and self-assured, seeking for hidden information, shape-shifter, sacred to Egyptian goddesses Bast and Pasht

**Cow:** love, abundance, nurture, contentment; represents goddess in many religions

**Coyote:** prankster, shape-shifter, illumination, opportunist, insightful, playful

**Crane:** solitude, independence, intelligence, astral travel to learn deeper mysteries

**Crow:** trickery, boldness, prophecy, shape-shifter, keeper of the sacred law, omen of change

**Deer:** *see* Doe, Stag

**Doe or Hind:** gentleness, loving-kindness, swiftness, alertness, bearer of messages

**Dog:** loyalty, companionship, keen hearing and tracking skills, a guard from approaching dangers

**Dolphin:** kindness, playfulness, link to ocean

**Dove:** communication through spirit; messenger to spirit world; peace, gentleness, love

**Dragonfly:** flighty, carefree

**Eagle:** connection to the Creator, divine spirit, wisdom, swiftness, keen sight

**Elephant:** confidence, patience, removal of obstacles, ability to learn

**Elk:** strength, agility, freedom, sensual passion

**Ermine:** purity

**Fish:** abundance, prosperity, harmony; loving companions or children

**Fox:** cunning, provider, intelligence, stealthy, able to make fools of pursuers

**Frog:** transformation, resurrection (Egypt), link to water element, beginning of new cycle; sacred to Hecate

**Goat:** wild energies, removal of guilt, independence; associated with Hindu Agni; Sumerian Marduk; Palestinian Ba'al; Greek Dionysius, Athene, and Pan; Norse Thor; Christian Satan

**Goose:** new beginnings, happy family life

**Grasshopper:** nobility (ancient Greece)

**Hare or Rabbit:** alertness, nurturing, hidden teachings, intuitive knowledge, transformation

**Hippopotamus:** birth of new ideas, righteous anger, protection of the family

**Horse:** stamina, mobility, strength, companion for astral travel

**Hummingbird:** messenger, able to stop time, happiness, love

**Jackal:** seeker of mystical knowledge, explorer of past lives; sacred to Egyptian god Anubis, "Opener of the Way"

**Leopard, Panther, or Cougar:** leadership, courage, swiftness, perseverance, gaining confidence for astral travel

**Lion:** strength, courage, energy, royalty, family ties

**Monkey:** ingenuity, clever solutions; sacred in China and Japan; symbol of Egyptian god Thoth

**Moose:** headstrong, unstoppable strength, longevity, shared joy, wisdom in solitude

**Mouse:** secrets, shyness, ability to remain inconspicuous, attention to details, stealth, trust, innocence

**Otter:** finding inner treasure, gaining wisdom, enjoyment of life, a trickster; sacred in ancient Peru and to the Celtic god Cernunnos

**Owl:** wisdom, truth, patience, keen sight, guide to the underworld, clairvoyance

**Peacock:** all-seeing awareness, dignity, sacred to the Roman goddess Juno

**Pelican:** self-sacrifice

**Phoenix:** resurrection, renewal

**Pig:** *see* Sow, Boar

**Porcupine:** minds own business, trust in spirit, guards privacy; to Native Americans, a symbol of faith and trust

**Quail:** good luck, courage, victory

**Ram:** virility, fertility; sacred to Celts and Muslims; symbol of Indian fire god Agni and Phoenician god Baal

**Rat:** symbol of fertility and wealth in China

**Raven:** trickster, teacher, hoarder, spirit messenger, change in consciousness, help with divination

**Salamander or Lizard:** understanding dreams, mental creativity, transformation

**Salmon:** instinctive, persistent, determined, spiritual knowledge

**Scarab:** Egyptian beetle, symbol of the sun and creation

**Scorpion:** keeper of the house of the dead, revenge

**Seahorse:** confidence, grace

**Sheep:** timidness, ability to keep your balance; *see also* Ram

**Snake:** transformation, shrewdness; symbol of rebirth, immortality; associated with many gods

**Sow:** female pig associated with the Crone goddess, deep earth magic, knowledge of past lives

**Spider:** creativity, weaver of pattern of life in both ancient Mediterranean and Pueblo Indian mythology

**Squirrel:** preparing for the future, foresight, warning, changes, spiritual watchdog

**Stag:** Lord of the underworld, understanding of the cycle of death and rebirth

**Stork:** carrier of souls, fertility

**Swallow:** bird of springtime, flowering, and love

**Swan:** grace, balance, innocence; symbol of the Muses and Valkyries

**Thunderbird:** Native American bird of lightning, bringer of rain and other heavenly gifts

**Tiger:** swift action, strength and willpower in a difficult situation; associated with gambling, the wind, and the elements in the Orient

**Turtle:** creative source, self-contained, long life, patience, spiritual shield, relaxation

**Vulture:** carriers and defenders of the dead, prophecy

**Whale:** wisdom, music, long life, telepathic abilities, providence

**Wolf:** loyal, successful, leader on the astral plane, hunting and seeking, strong protection

**Wren:** sacred bird of the Druids, form of the Fairy Queen

## SECRET SOCIETIES

### Rosicrucian Brotherhood

A Rosicrucian Brotherhood published a series of pamphlets in Germany between 1614–1616 claiming to have mystic secrets. Many doubt whether any seventeenth-century Rosicrucian Brotherhood ever existed, but it became fashionable among those who styled themselves magicians to imply they knew Rosicrucian secrets. Modern Rosicrucian groups have only a tenuous link with those of the past. Within the occult community, many believe if such a group existed, only a few adepts passed on whatever secrets they possessed orally to a few who succeeded them, and so on. Some people who claim to be Rosicrucian say they are doing exactly that.

The nineteenth-century Rosicrucians are particularly interesting. The English Rosicrucians (formed in 1866) included three founding members of the most famous modern magical society, the Hermetic Order of the Golden Dawn, and were mostly occultists.

French Rosicrucians were mostly artists and literary men. The Grand Master of the Rose-Croix in 1885, Josephin Reladan, who called himself Sar ("King" in Assyrian) Merodack (a character in one of his novels), and his associate Marquis Stanilsas de Guaita together created the Ordre Kabbalistique de la Rose-Croix. These two found themselves embroiled in a magical battle with the novelists J.K. Huysmans, author of the novel about decadent French black magic, *La Bas*, and with the Abbé Boullan, a former Catholic priest and magician. Boullan, investigated by the Church for unholy and carnal cures of nuns, murdered a child and practiced sexual mysticism of an unpleasant sort. Stanislas de Guaita stayed with the Abbé in 1886 and left with the text of one of Boullan's magic rituals. Soon afterward, Boullan suffered several heart attacks, which he blamed on sorcery by de Guaita. When Huysmans visited Boullan during work on his novel about magic in nineteenth-century *fin de siècle* Paris, he found him conducting magical rites directed against de Guaita. A letter condemning Boullan to death by "the fluids" arrived while Huysmans was there, and he thought himself under attack by magic as well.

Huysmans returned to Paris and accused de Guaita of magical murder, but was challenged to a duel, apologized, and retracted the statement. De Guaita, a decadent, sinister character, wrote several lengthy works on magic. His own experiments included heavy drug use—hashish, morphine, and cocaine—and he died young and blind.

## The Freemasons

Although the Freemasons trace their legendary lineage to the architect of Solomon's temple, who was killed by workmen because he would not reveal the secret "word of God hidden in the temple structure," they were the remnants of a medieval stonemasons guild until the mid-1800s. The secret initiation rite, however, dramatizes the story of Hiram Abiff, the architect skilled in bronze work sent by the King of Tyre to Solomon to work on his temple. Masonic initiates die as Hiram and are reborn as Masons in a ritual drama some trace to the Egyptian mystery school of Isis and Osiris, who also fell to thugs and were resurrected. Followers of the Isis cult were called "the widow's sons," and Masons are the "sons of the widow."

Sufi mystics believe the architects of Solomon's temple were Sufis who incorporated holy words of God as numeric equivalents in its measurements, so an Arabic influence seems likely. The Saxon king Aethelstan (A.D. 894) brought Masonry to England after learning it from Spanish Moors. No one knows why, but the stonemason guilds, who initially kept the techniques of their craft secret, began admitting "speculative" members. The first important speculative member was Elias Ashmole (1617–1692), an astrologer, kabbalist, alchemist, and Rosicrucian, among other things.

Speculative freemasonry adopted the tools of the craft as symbols (the square, compass, plumb line, and level), grades (Entered Apprentice, Fellow

Craft, Master Mason), rules of secrecy, and member recognition methods from the medieval guilds. Members wear white leather aprons like those builders once wore. Blue and gold are the ritual colors. Meetings are held in lodges or temples decorated with Masonic symbols and with checkered black-and-white floors, which symbolize man's dual nature. Two important Masonic symbols appear on the back of the U.S. dollar bill: the Great Pyramid of Giza and the all-seeing eye of the great architect associated with Horus, son of Isis and Osiris. Numerous American Founding Fathers were Masons, including John Hancock, George Washington, and Benjamin Franklin.

During both the eighteenth and nineteenth centuries, Masonic groups were infused with mysticism by the German Rite of Strict Observance; the French groups were inspired by the Compte de St. Germain, who performed ancient rituals, and the Egyptian rites of Count Cagliostro. The Ancient and Accepted Rite of the Thirty-Third Degree evolved from these. Only Master Masons are allowed to reach for these higher states, which they say leads to "a mystic union with God." The Vatican condemned anyone joining a Masonic Lodge to excommunication in 1917, and the Greek Orthodox church condemned it in 1933, calling it reminiscent of heathen mystery cults.

## Levi's Laws of Magic

Despite the increasingly scientific and materialistic world view that prevailed during the eighteenth-century Age of Reason, the nineteenth century saw a revival of interest in ritual magic. It began with Francis Barrett's *The Magus, or Celestial Intelligence*, published in 1801. The man who virtually created the mindset for modern magic, however, was Eliphas Levi, who penned *Dogma and Ritual of High Magic* in 1956.

Levi outlined what he called the "three fundamental laws of magic." Levi's first law stated that human will was a force as material as steam or a "galvanic current." Levi maintained that all the tools of the magic art—geometrical figures, candles, incense—served only, but necessarily, to concentrate the magician's will.

Levi's second law posits the existence of astral light, a mystic medium like ether scientists once thought existed in the vacuum of space. Some magicians believe they have access to all that ever happened or will happen from the so-called "Akashic Record," in this astral domain. Madam Blavatsky, the famous founder of the Theosophical Society, claimed to "read the astral light" to draw upon the Askashic Record.

Levi's third and most important law updates the medieval and Hermetic idea that correspondences exist between the macrocosm, the universe, and the microcosm, the individual person. The soul of the man, Levi said, is the "mirror of the universe."

Levi said anything present in the universe is also present in the person and can be invoked through a knowledge of the correspondences: A force personified as Hermes corresponds to wisdom. The magician can call up this cosmic force into his own soul or call down the force and project it into a magic triangle, where it materializes if a "material basis" such as blood or incense is provided. These personifications of cosmic forces generally are archetypal and include deities, demons, and spirits of all times and places.

## The Golden Dawn

The Order of the Golden Dawn was founded in 1886–1887 by Dr. William Wynn Westcott, a London coroner, Samuel L.M. Mathers, an "eccentric pseudo-Highlander of no identifiable occupation," and Dr. William Woodman, a physician. The membership and teachings of the Golden Dawn exerted a powerful influence on all of the following magical movements and, indeed, has never been equaled. Its members included not only Crowley and W.B. Yeats, but later, classic fantasy writers Arthur Machen and Algernon Blackwood. Magicians such as Mathers and A.E. Waite reintroduced the tarot to magical practice and, along with Crowley, codified and modernized occult practice, sewing many threads into one complex fabric. The Golden Dawn established a magic school complete with examinations. The Golden Dawn tradition continues in England where two temples survive.

Among other activities, the Golden Dawn added a fourth law to Levi's, that of the trained imagination, which they felt necessary to direct willpower. The Golden Dawn also expanded Levi's correspondences into an elaborate system that, according to the *Encyclopedia of the Unexplained* (edited by Richard Cavendish), connected "every Egyptian, Greek, and Roman God, every spirit name in *The Key of Solomon*, and other medieval grimmores, every name in the Jewish and Christian Angellologies, to the twenty-two paths and sefiroth of the Kabalistic Tree of Life. To each of them were attributed colors, animals, precious stones, scents, magical formulae, and so on." To evoke the proper force,

---

the magician looks up a table corresponding to it and designs his ritual to fit. Cavendish includes a lush description of a Golden Dawn ceremony following this system in which four magicians stood inside an octagon drawn in orange-yellow chalk. A lamp burning olive oil and snake fat was at each octagon angle. Outside the figure was a triangle where the spirit should appear. Incense of mercury smoldered in a censer. A mercurial "hell-broth" bubbled in a cauldron heated by an alcohol lamp that contained a preserved snake. The mercurial spirit was supposed to form from the mercury smoke. Florence Farr, the magician, spoke:

"Accept of us these magical sacrifices, prepared to give Thee body and form ... the heat of the magical fire is my will enabling Thee to manifest Thyself in pleasing form before us ..." and she went on to name which of the magical elements formed which parts of the spirit as another magician threw that element into the cauldron and Farr invoked a magic word. One of the participant's papers included a parchment allegedly consecrated by "being placed on the spirit's head after he materialized."

Many Golden Dawn members freely used various drugs. (Crowley eventually became a heroin addict.) They fought amongst themselves over a variety of matters.

## DIVINATION

Foretelling the future always formed a significant part of a magician's job. Reading omens, the stars, the cards, a palm, or bumps on a head; casting runes, yarrow stalks, dice, bones, coins, or sticks; peering into crystal balls, teacups, or animal innards; and talking to spirits, the dead, and psychics via telephone hotlines, all have the single purpose of glimpsing the future.

Many of the oldest and most developed branches of the magician's art involve divination, among them astrology, tarot, I-Ching, casting the runes, and prophet (psychic) predictions. Signs and portents of the future are everywhere for the knowledgeable and talented oracle—in the air, earth, fire, water, sticks, stones, and bones.

Below, we list the best-known and many lesser-known methods of divination with a brief description. Their very number and variety illustrates the importance of this field of magical practice.

**aeromancy:** Divination from the air and sky, such as cloud shapes, comets, or sky color. Comets in particular inspired prophets of ancient and modern times.

**alectryomancy:** A black hen or white gamecock pecks corn grains from a circle of letters forming words or names that the prophet interprets. Recite the alphabet at daybreak, noting those letters that coincide with a rooster crowing.

**aleuromancy:** Fortune cookies. Answers to questions rolled in dough and baked. Random choice comes true.

**alomancy:** Fortune-telling by salt. Throwing some over your shoulder to avoid bad luck and other modern superstitions are reminders of this ancient practice.

**anthopomancy:** Prophecy through human sacrifice.

**arithmancy:** Divination through the use of numbers.

**astrology:** Divination by the positions of the heavenly bodies.

**augury:** Interpreting signs and omens, but also fortune-telling in general.

**austromancy:** Divination by reading the direction and force of the winds.

**axiomancy:** An axe answers questions by its quivers when hacked into a tree.

**belomancy:** Tossing or balancing of arrows.

**bibliomancy:** Divination with books opened randomly, and many other methods.

**capnomancy:** Interpretation of smoke rising from a fire.

**cartomancy:** Divination with cards.

**catoptromancy:** Turning a mirror to catch lunar rays.

**causimomancy:** Studies how objects burn in a fire. An object that burns slowly or not at all indicates good tidings.

**cephalomancy:** Reading the head of a donkey, goat, or other animal.

**ceraunoscopy:** Interpreting the bubbles that form when hot wax is poured in water.

**chiromancy:** Divination by reading the lines of the hand. Combined with chirognomy, or reading the shape and structure of the hand, we get modern palmistry.

**cleromancy:** Casting lots using stones, sticks, or other objects.

**clidomancy:** Dangling a key that answers questions by turning one way to say yes, another way to say no. Only one of the many forms of radiesthesia, where any object on a string or chain may be held between two fingers and questioned. If the dangling object circles, it means yes. If it goes back and forth, it means no. Different movements are sometimes assigned to yes and no, but the principle remains the same.

**crominiomancy:** Divination from onion sprouts. (It'll bring tears to your eyes.)

---

**crystallomancy:** Scrying, or crystal gazing.

**cyclomancy:** Fortune-telling via a turning wheel.

**dactylomancy:** A dangling ring answers questions. Another form of radiesthesia.

**demonomancy:** Demon-aided future seeing.

**dendromancy:** Studying oak or mistletoe parts for signs.

**geloscopy:** Divining the future from laughter. For happy wizards only.

**gyromancy:** People will walk in a circle and spell the prophecy by marking where they stumble.

**haruspicy (also Hieromancy, Hieroscopy):** Prophecy by inspecting the innards of sacrificed animals.

**hippomancy:** Interpreting the neighing and hoof stamping of horses.

**hydromancy:** Divination by interpreting the color, flow, ripples, and other shapes in water. Led to tea reading.

**ichthyomancy:** Fishing for clues to the future by examining the entrails of fish (pun intended).

**lithomancy:** Precious colored stones are spread on a flat surface with the brightest color indicating the future: red—happiness in love; yellow—disaster; purple—sadness; black or grey—misfortune; green—hope realized; blue—good luck. Colored beads may be used.

**margaritomancy:** Pearls under a pot (it is said that they bounce when a guilty person approaches).

**meteroromancy:** Telling the meaning of meteors, which have long been considered potent omens.

**moylbdomancy:** Foretells future events through interpretation of the hissing of molten lead.

**myomancy:** Omens made by the sounds or signs of mice.

**oculomancy:** Determines events by looking deep into your eyes.

**oinomancy:** Like hydromancy, except wine is examined for future omens.

**oneiromancy:** The interpretation of dreams.

**onychomancy:** Symbols and signs revealed by sunlight on fingernails.

**oomnatia (also Ooscopy, Ovimancy):** Inspecting eggs for omens and signs, a quite ancient divinatory technique.

**ophiomancy:** Serpents used for divination.

**ormnithomancy:** Birds and their actions tell the tale.

**pegomancy:** Spring water and its bubbles are used for divination.

**pessomancy:** Signs seen in pebbles.

**phyllorhodomancy:** Ancient Greek practice of slapping rose petals against the palm and judging the future by the loudness of the clap.

**psychometry:** Obtaining impressions from physical objects.

**pyromancy:** Fortune revealed by interpreting flames.

**rhabdomancy:** Use of a wand or stick to divine the future. This practice led to radiesthesia.

**rhapsodomancy:** Divination with a book of poetry that is randomly opened; the passage read as an omen or guide.

**sciomancy:** Spirits tell the future.

**sideromancy:** Studying the shapes of straws burned on a hot iron.

**sortilege:** Casting lots (sticks, runes, dice, stones, coins).

**spodomancy:** Signs read in cinders, ashes and soot.

**stichomancy:** The random opening of a book in hopes the passage will portend the future.

**tephramancy:** Burning tree bark and reading the signs in the ashes.

**tiromancy:** Examining cheese for omens and signs.

**xylomancy:** Divining from the size and shape of pieces of wood randomly collected, or burning the pieces and observing which flame first.

## BUILDING YOUR OWN MAGICAL WORLDS

One effective way to create a magical world of your own is to think of yourself as a folklore collector in that world. You will probably not include all of your background material in your actual writing, but even what you do not use will help give your work a solid suspension system—a way to help readers suspend disbelief while they are in your fictional world.

Remember that stories—as legends, mythologies, or anecdotes—invest virtually every item and action of a magician's, wizard's, or witch's repertoire with meaning and power. The stories themselves are frequently part of a wizard's secret knowledge, which he passes on only to initiates. Other stories are tribal property, but no less holy, honored, and valued.

*The Handbook of Folklore*, by Charlotte Burne, suggests questions folklore collectors ask about any society's magic art. Writers creating fantasy worlds should do the same. For example:

- What are the names for magic users (wizards, witches, charmers, magicians, shamans)?

- Are stories told about famous magicians?

- Are magicians males, female, or both?

- What rewards does a magician receive for success?

- Is the magician punished for failure?

- Does the magician do good (white) magic or evil (black) magic or both?

- Are society's good magicians and evil magicians separate individuals, such as the **SORCHELEUR** and **DESORCHELEUR** of the Channel Islands?

- How does a magician attain his powers (initiation; instruction; inheritance; preparation through fasting; solitude; trance or drug states; or direct transfer from another magician, deity, demon, or spirit)?

- What is the magician's social and/or political status? (In most primitive societies, the magicians are accorded status second only to the chief; however, in some they are accorded respect while alive, but are buried in the hollow of a dead tree or otherwise ignominiously disposed of after death.)

- Do the wizards/magicians form a craft, guild, or society?

- Do they assemble secretly and meet with demons or other spirits?

- Are the magicians members of an outcast group, such as Gypsies, or do they belong to the tribe or community?

- Is any country, area, district, or people particularly powerful?

- What are a wizard's powers?

- Are a magician's powers general, or specific and limited? Powers the magician/wizard/witch/sorcerer might have:
    Prophecy
    Divination
    Controlling the weather

Healing

Laying or countering curses

Making amulets, talismans, or both

Conducting public and/or private rituals

Exorcising demons

Shape-shifting into animals, spirits, shapes, or things

Traveling through the air

Raising or stopping storms

Causing earthquakes

Becoming invisible

Calling up demons or spirits

Talking to demons, spirits, deities, or the dead

Kidnapping souls

Transforming men into beasts

Avenging injury

Causing illness or death

Affecting others' bodily functions

Bringing rain to crops, fish to nets, or game to hunters

Making a house solid, safe, and stable

Giving swiftness to a canoe

Making charms to win a lover, harm an enemy, protect from harm, confer beauty, bring good fortune

Making an arrow, dart, spear, knife, or other weapon hit its intended target

Protecting against bad fortune

Providing a bountiful harvest

Inflicting pain or injury

Giving skill in war, games, or the hunt

Calling up or repelling spirits or demons

Casting out or exorcising spirits or demons

- Does the magician have animal familiars? If so, which animals? Is the magician identified with a certain animal? How does the magician acquire an animal familiar or guide?

## Magical Rites

Continue to imagine yourself as a folklorist collecting data in your imaginary world, and ask these questions regarding the rites your world's wizards/witches/magicians may conduct:

- What is the what, when, where, how, and why in each case?
- Are the rites performed in public or secretly?
- What is their purpose?
- How are the magician and his assistants dressed? What sort of apparatus is present?
- What is the meaning and purpose of each item?

### Preparations for rites

- Purifying ceremonies (sweat lodge, fasting, meditation, vision quest)
- Divining omens
- Drawing magic pentagrams or circles

### Gestures

- Are gestures used, such as the two-fingered "horns" or the sign of the cross?
- Does the magician dance?
- What symbolic gestures are used, such as trying and untying knots to symbolize binding or loosening?

### Sounds made in magical rites

- Chanting, singing, muttering
- Percussion: drums, hollow logs, gourds
- Rattles, bull-roarers, rainsticks
- Flutes, bells, stringed instruments (often one to three strings as in the berimbau or kora)
- Spells, magic words, formulas
- Recited names

### Materials used

- Blood, entrails, eyes, feathers
- Other human or animal body parts
- Roots, herbs, flowers, other vegetable matter
- Air, water, fire
- Iron

- Salt
- Earth
- Wax

At all times, folklorists are cautioned, "Note the colors, numbers, odors in the rites." One national magazine editor told his assistant, "You can always spot amateur stories. There's no smell in them." Scent is often an integral part of magical rites and ceremonies in the following forms and more: incense, herbs, fire, smoke, alchemical reactions, sweat, blood, burning candles.

## Magical Practices

The folklorists visiting your world would also want to know which magical practices are used to:

- Kill enemies
- Injure enemies
- Blight crops
- Injure domestic animals
- Harm others' property
- Make themselves or others invisible
- Cause sleep
- Bring luck in games, sports, business, life in general
- Bring success in games, business, travel, love
- Avert evil in travel
- Protect houses, animals, crops; property from theft, sorcery, fire, the weather
- Preserve beauty, loyalty, marital fidelity, or wealth

## WRITTEN IN THE STARS

"As above, so below" expresses a basic tenet in the world of magic. Astrologers study the movement of stars and planets to determine their relationship to events on our planet. Many stories are written in the stars.

*Astrologer* and *magician* once meant the same thing in the ancient Middle East, where Chaldean astrologers/magicians guided state affairs. As recently as the Reagan administration, astrologers have been called on for the same services right here in the United States.

------------------------------------------------------------------------------

Today, practicing magicians use astrological lore to determine the best times to cast spells and make amulets. For instance, a spell to gain love might be performed on Friday (the day of the week ruled by Venus), when the planet was in favorable aspect in a favorable sign (Libra, Taurus or Pisces). An amulet made of copper, a metal sacred to Venus, might be used. A spell for prosperity, on the other hand, would best be cast on Thursday (Thor or Jupiter's Day) using tin.

Our current system of astrology derives from the Chaldean and Babylonian systems as revised by Greek, Renaissance, Victorian, and New Age sages. Based on twelve signs associated with constellations on the ecliptic (the path of the sun and moon across the sky), the system organizes a number of correspondences that can prove helpful in designing a fictional character.

Using astrological aspects as the basis for character development, a writer can create conflict within a particular character through an affliction or malefic influence in the chart. A passive Cancer with Gemini rising, for instance, might seem to have a dual personality and suffer from periodic rages, thanks to a poorly aspected moon in Taurus. Other planets might add further complications. Or, simply read the appropriate horoscopes in books or papers.

An author of *Star Trek* novels and her own science fiction series said she learned to characterize by reading Linda Goodman's book, *Sun Signs*, a popular treatment of astrology. The conflicting character traits of those born under astrology's sun signs suggest many a story.

None of this astrological detail needs to reach the page except for how it affects your characters' behavior. Consider creating an astrological chart for each main character to provide a detailed background of character traits and personal preferences. New computer programs make charts easy to cast and can easily determine such significant, but often overlooked, aspects as the "part of fortune." Or again, use published horoscopes for this work.

Star-crossed lovers are a prime component of fiction. Water and earth signs are considered poor matches for fire and air signs, and individual charts can place many complications in the most perfect of love stories.

Placing each planet within a chart and its relationship to all the others provides a powerful way to analyze (and design) a personality. Major attention is usually focused on the characters' sun signs, moon signs, and rising signs.

Comets and asteroids play important parts both in an astrological chart and in the actual history of a planet. For example, a comet is the source of the destructive "thread" that threatens Anne McCaffrey's world of Pern. In the earth's history, the appearance of a comet has traditionally marked an important event—the birth of a hero—or warned of an impending disaster—plagues, famines, wars, or the deaths of kings.

## Exploring New Worlds

Fantasy writers add an extra element of reality to their works by working out the details of the astrology and astronomy of the worlds they create. J.R.R. Tolkien's work provides an excellent example of the use of the heavens in fantasy fiction. The stars of Elbereth and Earendil serve as visible reminders of the distant past, still remembered by the elves of Middle-earth.

The following are some options in designing the heavens of a fantasy world:

- Use the stars of Earth, either the familiar constellations of the current day, or one of the systems used by other "star-struck" cultures, such as the Mayan, Polynesian, Chinese, or Native American.

- Use the stars of Earth, giving them new names, histories, meanings, and associations.

- Create a new planetary system and star field for the fantasy world.

Traditional astrology is based upon the stars and planets as observed from our world. In designing the heavens of a fantasy world, consider these elements:

**THE PRIMARY STAR.** The primary star is the fantasy world's sun. Determine: its name, color, and classification (red giant, white dwarf); its close neighbors (is it two-star system?); its behavior (periodic sunspots, pulsations); whether the star is seen as the center of the system or the planet itself is considered the "center of the universe."

**OTHER PLANETS.** Planets closer to the primary appear as "morning" and "evening" stars, rising close to dawn and sunset.

**FIXED LIGHTS.** Stars seem to remain relatively fixed in position. The brightest stars are usually named and included in constellations that reflect historic or legendary figures and events. Stars can be used to fix specific dates in the year: the Egyptians based their year on Sirius, marking the annual Nile river flood; the Hopi based their ceremonial calendar on the Pleiades.

--------------------------------------------------------------------------------

**SATELLITES OR MOONS.** Besides creating the tides, the Earth's single moon played a determining part in measuring the length of the year. The lunar year varies from twelve to thirteen months before the moon repeats its solitary journey across the star field. More moons would create a more complex situation.

**THE LENGTH OF THE PLANET'S YEAR.** This is the time it takes a planet to circle its star. Our current solar calendar, diving the year into twelve months of varying length, evolved from the earlier lunar year. Its advantage is that it "fixes" the seasons, so that the same events and weather occur at the same times each year. Many religious calendars remain at least partially oriented to the moon.

**THE POLE STAR(S).** The axis of the earth points north and south toward "still" spots that do not rotate as most stars seem to. The North Star (Polaris) is currently the pole star of the northern hemisphere. Because the axis of our planet wobbles, the pole star changes, a phenomenon known as precession of the equinoxes. This precession divides the history of the earth into cosmic ages of about 2,150 years each. We're currently leaving the Age of Pisces for the Age of Aquarius. The earliest horoscopes were most likely cast in the Age of Taurus, some six thousand years ago.

**THE GALAXY.** The Milky Way, our spiral-armed galaxy, appears in the summer sky as a foggy white ribbon. Many cultures associated it with the milk of a moon cow goddess.

Astronomical lore accumulates throughout history, much of it remaining in language as folk sayings or adages. Two examples:

- When two full moons occur in the same month, it's called a "blue moon." This is the origin of the saying, "once in a blue moon."

- The forty days following the helical rising of Sirius, the Dog Star, are called "dog days," usually the hottest days of the year.

### Other Astrological Systems

Although our present-day twelve-sign astrological system has deep roots—it's based on the Babylonian base twelve numerical system, which was used for all sacred calculations—other systems are possible. Inscriptions indicate that the ancient Babylonians originally recognized eighteen zodiac signs. Some historians contend that the twelve-sign system was originally a thirteen-sign system in some cultures, such as the Celtic/Druid, and was suppressed when solar religions replaced lunar religions in much of the western world. James Vogh, in *Arachne Rising*, suggests Arachne, the Spider, as the missing sign of the zodiac, positioned between Taurus and Gemini and associated with the constellation Auriga. Other cultures have configured the stars differently, seeing different constellations and different truths.

Extensive information on the star systems and astrology of these cultures can be found in anthropological works or, in some cases, current nonfiction books. Here's a brief rundown on the general form of some of the systems developed by other cultures.

### Chinese

Chinese astrology placed emphasis of divining the future and determining the proper times to act. The twelve animal signs familiar from restaurant place mats come from a system based on the orbit of Jupiter, which takes about twelve years to orbit the Sun. The twelve signs are the Rat, Ox, Tiger, Rabbit or Cat, Dragon, Snake or Serpent, Horse, Sheep or Goat, Monkey, Cock, Dog, and Pig or Boar. Each sign lasts a full year and begins on the second new moon after the winter solstice, which is the generally accepted New Year in Asian countries and usually falls in late January or early February. Works on Chinese astrology delineate the qualities of each sign and compatibility between signs. The much older Chinese system based on the phases of the moon assigns each day to one of twenty-eight named lunar mansions, each regarded as favorable or unfavorable for certain activities. The twenty-eight are grouped into four categories, each with seven mansions: the Green Dragon of spring, beginning with each new moon, followed by the Black Tortoise of winter, the White Tiger of autumn, and the Red Bird of summer.

### Olmec

Beginning with the Olmec civilization (circa 600 B.C.), Central American societies followed sophisticated astrological systems based on the numbers 13 and 20. Each of twenty signs, called **TONALLY** by the Aztec, ruled a single day; another cycle of thirteen ran concurrently, so each day had both a name and a number that provided a key to personality and the analysis of events. Thirteen cycles of twenty days made up the 260-day astrological year. Longer cycles were based on the Jupiter/Saturn 7,200-day cycle (twenty tun, the 360-day civil year), called a **KATUN**. A creation epoch included 260 katuns, about 5,125 years, one-fifth of a precession cycle. The Harmonic Convergence of 1987 signaled the beginning of the last katun of the fifth and final cycle of creation, according to Mesoamerican calculations.

Astrological systems can also be based on completely imaginary planets. Uranian astrology, for instance, posits the existence of eight hypothetical "trans-Neptunian" planets: Cupido, Hades, Zeus, Kronos, Appolon, Admetos, Vulcanus, and Poseidon.

## Other Uses for Astrology

Though today astrology is mostly used for personal prediction, character analysis, and relationship compatibility study, other societies have used the study of the stars and planets for a variety of purposes. To:

- answer a question, using a chart cast at the moment the question is asked (horary astrology)

- determine the best time to carry out a particular activity—marriage, planting, beginning journeys, opening a business (electional astrology)

- predict and guide the course of nations

- predict natural disasters

- predict economic cycles (astroeconomics)

- diagnose and suggest treatment for disease

- choose the best time to plant and harvest crops

- diagnose and treat emotional or behavioral problems (astrotherapy)

- determine the most beneficial place to live (locational astrology)

- predict the weather (astrometeorology)

Besides birth, or natal, charts (cast from the moment a child takes its first breath), other charts can be cast for important occurrences in an individual's life:

- So-called death charts, calculated on the time of a person's death

- Decumbiture charts, calculated for the moment one goes to bed at the start of an illness

- Conception charts

- Compatibility charts, which overlay two natal charts to determine how they will relate, either in love or business

# CHAPTER 4

# Witchcraft and Pagan Paths

## by Allan Maurer and Renee Wright

Although primitive societies often use the word "witch" for any person in touch with the supernatural, the association in Western culture is usually with people working magic in secret. The Indo-European root word "weik" has to do with religion and magic and is related to another word, "weik," which means to bend or change. Thus a witch was one who could bend or change reality. In Old English, "wicca" was a male witch, "wicce" a female. Although witches today sometimes refer to their order as "the Wise," Old English "witan," which means to know, is unrelated.

The Roman Catholic Church tolerated witchcraft and minor sorcery for many hundreds of years, dismissing them as delusion and superstition. The witch trials and burnings began in earnest in the 1300s as witchcraft became associated with heresy and witches were believed to have made a "pact with the devil." Persecution continued until the 1700s and killed an estimated twenty million people, better than half of them women.

## HOW TO RECOGNIZE A WITCH

During the Inquisition's five-hundred-year-long reign of terror, the accused witch was stripped naked, shaved, then examined for signs of witchcraft. These included:

- The Devil's Mark: Sometimes a scar, mole, or birthmark. The mark was variously described as a mole, wart, birthmark, pimple, pockmark, cyst, liver spot, wen, insect bite, ulcer, or any other blemish. If nothing was visible on the body, the witch was "pricked" all over in search of the insensitive spot where the devil had given his binding kiss.

- The Witch's Mark: Any protuberance on the body, considered to be a "supernumerary teat" sucked by demons and familiars.

Other signs that someone was a witch that were accepted by the Inquisition included: talking to yourself; talking to animals; keeping a black animal (especially a cat or lamb); being too fond of any animal; spinning around; having freckles, red hair, or "unusual" eyes. According to Reginald Scot, a disbeliever, those most likely to be accused were the "old, lame, blear-eyed pale; wrinkled, poor, sullen, superstitious; lean and deformed; doting, scolds, mad." Any unusual behavior was enough to invite suspicion, especially in the wake of accidents or illness. The Witch of Newberry was executed for surfing on a board in the river.

Failing the discovery of any marks, the accused witch might be subjected to trial by fire, being forced to hold red hot irons (the innocent would not be burned); trial by water, a practice called "swimming the witch" (the innocent sank); or trial by weighting the witch against the weight of a Bible (guilty if the witch weighed less than the massive books of the day).

Today, anthropologists recognize several types of witchcraft. A good discussion of them can be found in Isaac Bonewits's *Real Magic*. He recognizes four types of witchcraft: classical, gothic, family or traditional, and neo-pagan.

## CLASSICAL WITCHCRAFT

Classical witchcraft refers to the primitive, so-called "low" magic found among most peoples where adepts cast spells; make potions (and poisons); and practice divination, herbalism and, often, various types of healing and medicine, especially midwifery. It survives today in a variety of shamanic practices around the world.

## Shamanism

Shamanism is mostly solo magical work, though shamans usually apprentice and endure many years of training. After an initial vision quest to find an animal familiar, the shaman will continue to go into a trance through various means (solitude, drugs, drumming, dancing) to work his magic. The shaman does much of his magical work on an astral plane not unlike the one ceremonial magicians seek through Hermetic wisdom, meditating on the Kabbalah's Tree of Life, or the other methods discussed in the previous chapter.

This oldest of pagan paths is enjoying a modern revival thanks to the works of Mircea Eliade, Michael Harner (the father of neo-shamanism), and others.

Harner proposes a Shamanic State of Consciousness (SSC) in which the shaman is able to travel into the underworld or into the branches of the World Tree to discover his power animal. The shaman enters a trance through one of several methods: rhythmic drumming, chanting, rattling, meditation practices, dancing or swaying, or the use of hallucinogens. He then calls upon his power animal to guide and protect him on his journey to the spirit world. Once he arrives there, if he's involved in healing, he battles the offending spirits, or if he is divining, he asks for spiritual assistance.

Many modern shamans are influenced by Carlos Castenada's series of books on Don Juan. The books detail the initiation of Castenada into the shamanistic practices of the desert Native American tribes, including a full description of a peyote ceremony and much "energy work" with the strands of power said to surround every individual and connect him with all others.

Serge King, in his book *The Urban Shaman*, outlines a shamanism based on the ancient beliefs of Hawaiian **HUNA**. The Huna shamans claim the ability to heal instantly, to change the weather, and many other seeming miracles through the application of a pragmatic creed. The principles of Huna are:

- Ike: the world is what you think it is
- Kala: there are no limits
- Makia: energy flows where attention goes
- Manawa: now is the moment of power
- Aloha: love is being happy within
- Mana: power comes from within
- Pono: effectiveness is the measure of truth

Hawaiian Huna teaches meditative and thinking practices that resemble modern neurolinguistic programming techniques closely, and psychologists and neurolinguistic practitioners have studied this Polynesian system.

A **KAHUNA** is a master who, through proper cleansing of his mind, body, and spirit, attains control of psychic powers latent in everyone. He heals by placing on hand on a patient's power spot (base of the spine, top of the spine at the neck, top of the head, or some such spot) and another on the troubled body spot. The kahuna keeps his mind connected to both of his hands so the energy may stream through them. Huna, by and large, is mental discipline.

## Northern Traditions

Norse, Icelandic, Germanic, Teutonic, Frisian, Latvian, Lithuanian, and Estonian religious traditions all survive among some groups to the present day. The northern traditions usually give far less emphasis to the goddess and more to the values of the warrior than other pagan traditions. Adepts study shamanism, artistic skills, writing in runes, the martial arts, and brewing to achieve goals of honor, honesty, courage and duty to family.

**SEIDR** is the oldest of the Norse traditions and is based on many shamanistic practices. The chorus sings a sacred song that induces a trance in the prophetess, called **VOLVA** or **VALA**. Frey and Freya of the Vanir are the principle deities. Adepts reportedly practice sexual magic.

Iceland has the distinction of being the only European country where paganism enjoys equal status with Christianity as the state religion. Iceland's literature preserves much of the mythology of the north, in the prose and poetic eddas, plus various sagas.

## Native American Traditions

Each tribe has its own name for the Great Spirit, though beliefs have much in common. In recent years, the language of the Sioux, the last tribe to be conquered, has been adopted as a kind of religious lingua franca. The Sioux revere T'Tanka as the Great Spirit and Watantanka, the Buffalo, as his sacred animal. Most tribes have a great reverence for Mother Earth and are ecologically active.

Important Native American sacred figures include White Buffalo Calf Woman, Thunderbird, Coyote, Raven, and Kokopelli. Rituals include the sweat lodge; the pipe ceremony, where tobacco is offered to the four directions; the

--------------------------------------------------------------------------------

vision quest, a wilderness experience in which initiates seek their power animal; and the sun dance. Personal talismans, amulets, and herbs are often carried in a medicine bag around the neck. Sacred shields depict scenes from the warrior's vision quest.

The Sioux prophet Black Elk foresaw a world in which the peoples of all nations joined in a great hoop around the Tree of Life, but the time of the prophecy's fulfillment has not yet come. His book, *Black Elk Speaks*, outlines his vision and the pipe ritual.

### African Traditions

African religions went underground in the slave cultures of the Americas. The African gods acquired the names of Christian saints. Common elements included drumming and dancing to induce trance, blood sacrifice, and possession by spirits of the gods, called **LOAS**. Initiates usually wore white.

**VOODOO** from Haiti (where it's spelled in the French manner, *vodoun*), incorporates Dahomean, Ibo, and Mago tribal influences. Initiates acknowledge a Supreme Being, Gran Met, who is considered remote, but worship a huge pantheon of lesser gods called loas. Principle loas include Danbhala, the Great Serpent, the oldest of the ancestors; Maitress Erzulie, the moon; her husband Legba (called "Papa"), the sun, who governs all entryways and fences, including the spirit gate; and Baron Samedi, god of death and the graveyard, who wears dark glasses, drinks alcohol, and smokes cigars. During ceremonies in the **HOUNFOUR**, or "holy of holies," the summoned spirits "mount the horse," possessing their chosen devotee who retains no memory of what happens during the possession.

**SANTERIA** developed in the Spanish-speaking areas, especially in Cuba. The African influence comes largely from the Yoruba tribe of Nigeria, whose language is still used in liturgies. **SANTEROS** and **SANTERAS** join with the high priest, called **BABALAWO**, in worshipping the **ORISHAS**, ancestor spirits led by Obatala, the oldest ancestor depicted as a white man on a horse, and his wife Oddudua, a black woman usually depicted breastfeeding an infant. (Orisha is a popular name for the African traditions in the United States, especially Santeria. It means "the deities.") Coconuts and herbs play important parts in Santeria. Divination methods include reading a throw of seashells or the meat of a coconut. Babalawos, who are always male, consult the Table of Ifa by throwing sixteen shells onto a straw mat. The pattern of the shells determines each person's orisha, plant, birthstone, and animal. The ceiba tree is the cult's most holy plant, thanks to its ability to attract spirits, and water is used to ward off evil spirits.

**MACUMBA** came from similar Yoruba roots in Portuguese-speaking Brazil. Some elements of the tribal religions of the Amazon are mixed in as well. The three types of macumba are candomble, umbanda, and quimbanda. **CANDOMBLE** is very similar to Santeria, except that the priests are often female. The orishas are most often known by the names of their associated saints. The year's biggest ceremony honors Yemanja, goddess of the waters and an aspect of the Virgin Mary, on January first. Over a million celebrants, dressed in white, wade into the surf at dusk and launch small boats loaded with candles, flowers, and figures of the saints out to sea. **UMBANDA** is a recent religion mixing elements of the African tradition, especially spirit possession, with elements of Hinduism and Buddhism, and is aimed at spiritual healing of previous incarnations through communication with the spirits. **QUIMBANDA** is the black magic tradition, calling upon King Exu, the dark lord.

### Earth Magic

James Lovelock's book *The Gaia Hypothesis* presents the idea that all the living matter on earth, in the air, in the oceans, and on land are part of a system that acts as a single, living biosphere controlling things like temperature and the composition of the atmosphere. The goal of many New Age pagans is to awaken Gaia's planetary mind, a concept much used in science fiction.

Traditional Earth magic has always operated from this perspective, studying the powers of Earth as a holistic organism. Earth magicians study dowsing, ley lines, stone circles, and sacred sites. Their rituals are intended to correct energy imbalances caused by bad planning. These imbalances are believed to create a "black stream" of energy associated with illness, accidents, and poltergeist activity in the area. In China, Earth magic is called **FENG-SHUI.**

**SHINTO,** the official religion of Japan, shares many of the concerns of Earth magic. Anything unusual in nature is considered "kami," or divine, and worshipped. Japan is dotted with Miya shrines next to odd rocks and trees. The Japanese "Way of the Gods" is a fertility cult, involving purification rites and ancestor worship. Onogor is the Central Pillar of the Earth; Amaterasu, the sun goddess.

### Ritual Magic

Based on the rites of the Golden Dawn, medieval grimoires such as *The Key of Solomon*, and Aleister Crowley's writings, ritual "magick" (Crowley's spelling) tends to be complex with many formal details including robes, tools, temple decorations, and verbal formula that must be recited precisely.

**THELEMIC MAGICK** was Crowley's own system of ritual magic, including many sexual rites. It's named for his "abbey" in Thelema, Sicily. The authorities threw Crowley and his friends out of the country after only a few years.

**ENOCHIAN MAGIC** is a ritual with an entirely different pedigree. It's based on a secret language revealed by angels to John Dee, Elizabethan England's greatest magus and alchemist. The language seems to have no antecedents, but the spells that form part of it are said to have exceptional power to summon spirits. Dee and his scryer, Edward Kelley, used the calls or "keys" to invoke angels before scrying in a crystal egg or black obsidian mirror. The Order of the Golden Dawn and Aleister Crowley, who claimed to be Kelley's reincarnation, made use of the calls.

## GOTHIC WITCHCRAFT

Gothic witchcraft is the sort confessed to by the witches tried by the Inquisition. Their witchcraft was a form of Christian heresy with many holy Church symbols and practices reversed or defiled, as in the **BLACK MASS**. Witches were believed to make a pact with the devil. Other elements of Gothic witchcraft: secret meetings at night, orgies, child sacrifice, cannibalism, the desecration of the Eucharist and crucifix, and the "ride by night," usually through the air. Accused witches "confessed" to most of these rites under torture in hopes of a more lenient execution. The charges bore a strong resemblance to the accusations brought against heretics throughout the history of Christianity. The Gnostics of the third century A.D., for instance, were accused of the identical set of crimes.

Some perversion of the Christian rites undoubtedly occurred in the Middle Ages and the Renaissance, probably at first by renegade priests who would perform the requiem mass (called the Black Mass at the time) for a person still alive, thus cursing him. It's impossible to discover the extent of these practices and their continuance to the present day, because they quickly made their way into literature, becoming a branch of pornography, especially in France. An outbreak of actual black magic, complete with masses said on the body of a nude woman and child sacrifices, seems to have occurred in 1678 during the reign of Louis XIV, under the patronage of his mistress Madame de Montespan.

Though today most practitioners of "The Craft" follow "the right-hand path" (white magic), some seek "the left-hand path" of black magic. Most are solitaries, but some belong to organized groups.

### Satanism

Anton La Vey's Church of Satan is the present-day descendant of the anti-Christian cults. The press has accused it of blood sacrifices, both animal and human, and sexual orgies, but little has ever actually been proved. La Vey's disciples follow an inverted gospel: "Blessed are the strong for they shall possess the Earth. If a man smite you on one cheek, smash him on the other!"

Other black magic cults prefer the spelling "Shaitan," and follow pre-Christian, often Babylonian or Persian, practices.

## FAMILY OR TRADITIONAL WITCHCRAFT

Family or traditional witchcraft involves secret traditions passed down through families, usually from mother to daughter, but sometimes apprentices. It is a religion of hearth and home, perhaps preserving various domestic rites performed by women in ancient times. Several modern witches, including Sibyl Leek and various Gypsies, claimed this traditional form of witchcraft. Typical elements include: worship of Mother Earth, the oak, or another tree used to represent the male principle; the use of kitchen implements as tools of magic, such as brooms or cauldrons; the primary practice of agricultural magic, to "work" the weather for the benefit of the crops; and simple divination used for seeing future husbands, children, and the like.

STREGA is the path of witches following an Italian tradition. They use red chili peppers on their stalks as wands. The peppers are decorated with either a male or female crown. The path is strongly matriarchal and uses much traditional herbal knowledge. Paraphernalia includes a tiny bronze sickle to harvest herbs.

------------------------------------------------------------------------

## Gypsy Magic

The wandering Gypsies may have set out originally from India. Many of their beliefs and practices derive from rites originally native to the civilization of the Ganges Valley (circa 1000 B.C.). On their travels through Europe, they made their living by fortune-telling. Favorite Gypsy methods of divination include: gazing into a crystal ball, palmistry, reading tea leaves, tarot cards, bumps on the head (phrenology), lines on the face (metoposcopy), dice, or dominoes. The apple is often used by Gypsies in rituals, and marriages are solemnized by jumping a broom.

# NEO-PAGAN WITCHCRAFT

Although ancient pagan beliefs survive in holiday customs, folk beliefs, and popular sayings, there is little evidence of the survival of an organized pagan religion of witchcraft such as Margaret Murray wrote about in her 1921 book *The Witch Cult of Western Europe*. Neo-pagan witchcraft is a modern development, rising from folklore and literature with only intellectual ties to ancient practices. Influenced by studies of anthropology, the neo-pagans seek to rebuild a culture linked to earth and its seasons, a link lost in the development of modern civilization. This loss, many believe, depletes our quality of life and endangers the future of our planet. Today, neo-pagan witchcraft falls into three basic categories: Wicca, a revival of ancient goddess worship; revivals of other traditional religions and mystery cults; and New Age neo-paganism, based on modern works of fiction or philosophy.

## The Literary Background of Wicca

Charles Leland's *Aradia, or the Gospel of the Witches*, published in 1899, began the modern renaissance of witchcraft. (Aradia was said to be a daughter of Diana and Queen of the Witches.) He claimed to have discovered this manuscript among the peasants of Italy. It contained the secrets of "la Vecchia Religione" or the Old Religion. Though Leland's "discovery" has since been discredited by scholars, Aradia made many contributions to the Wiccan revival, including emphasis on the goddess as its main deity. Most Wiccan paths use some form of the "Charge of the Goddess" found in *Aradia*: "Once a month, and when the Moon is full, Ye shall assemble."

Two works of folklore had special impact on the Wiccan revival. *The Golden Bough* (1922), by Sir James Frazer, explored the widespread existence in pre-Christian times of fertility cults based on the death and rebirth of a god, often seen as both consort and son of the goddess. In 1948, Robert Graves published *The White Goddess*, discussing the ancient and beautiful cult of the earth and moon goddess of many names.

Margaret Murray, folklorist, anthropologist, and Egyptologist, had an even greater influence on the development of modern witchcraft. In *The Witch Cult of Western Europe*, she traced witchcraft to a pre-Christian religion centered on a horned deity she identified as Dianus, or the Roman Janus, a two-faced god. As described by Murray, this was a fertility cult similar to the ones described by Frazer in *The Golden Bough*. The god's death and rebirth reflected the cycle of the seasons and crops. The high priestess of the coven of thirteen members typically took the name of Diana. This "Dianic" cult celebrated eight great **SAB-BATS** during the year, at the solstices and equinoxes, plus four "cross-quarter" days. Lesser **ESBAT** ceremonies were celebrated at each full moon. Murray believed that this religion originated in Britain, created by a race of "Small People" who later entered European folklore as fairies, elves, and pixies. Murray identified at least two of the cross-quarter festivals as preagricultural (May Eve and November Eve), having more to do with the fertility of animals than of crops.

Murray's views, though much criticized by modern anthropologists, especially for her uncritical acceptance of testimony given under torture during the witch trials, hugely influenced a generation of occultists. Gerald Gardner cited her theories as corroboration of his revival of witchcraft.

## Wiccan Beliefs

As practiced today, few generalizations can be made about modern Wiccan witchcraft. Unlike traditional ceremonial magic, witchcraft puts little emphasis on the "correct" recitation of incantations or exact pronunciation of names and spells. In fact, neo-pagan witches are encouraged to use their goddess-given creativity to create new spells, invocations, and rituals, which often take the form of poetry or songs. Many books of these rituals have been published, and more continue to be published every year, each giving birth to its own "path." A writer trying to create an authentic witchcraft ritual can feel confident as long as she stays within certain parameters.

---

Witches meet in covens, usually on the night of the full moon, and are led by a high priestess. Principal gods are the Triple Goddess, known by many names, and her consort, the Horned God of the forests. Their rites celebrate the cycle of the year through the ritual drama of the goddess and her consort, from their courtship and marriage through death and rebirth. Gardnerian and Alexandrian covens traditionally practice their rites "skyclad" (i.e., in the nude) but there are many "robed covens" as well.

The most central belief of all Wiccan groups is the Wiccan Creed (or Rede): "An' it harm none, do what ye will." Attributed to Gerald Gardner, it puts the Wiccan movement well within the definition of white magic. Gardner probably based it on Aleister Crowley's governing principle, derived from sexual magic: "Do what thou wilt shall be the whole of the Law. Love is the Law, love under will." Related to this is the general Wiccan belief of threefold return: If a spell is cast unjustly, the effects will rebound on the spell-caster in triple strength.

The most common form of spell used in Wicca is candle magic. A candle of an appropriate color—red for love, green for health and prosperity, blue for mental tranquility, and so on—is anointed with oil and then burned. The witch then meditates upon the flame, using visualization to imagine the desired outcome.

In recent years, the many groups of practicing Wiccans tried to come to some agreement on beliefs. The Pagan Federation identified three universal beliefs in Wicca: (1) adherence to the Wiccan Creed, (2) love of nature, and (3) a belief in reincarnation.

### Common Elements of Wiccan Ritual

1. A circle is cast and sacred space purified through the use of the elements, fire, earth, air, and water.

2. Powers are invoked to guard the circle and aid the rites. These powers of the four directions are variously referred to as Mighty Ones, Lords and Ladies of the Watchtowers, etc.

3. Music, dancing, chanting, and/or running in a circle around an altar are used to raise a "cone of power."

4. The coven partakes of a "feast," usually of crescent moon-shaped cakes and wine.

5. "Drawing down the moon" is the most typical ceremonial act, though methods of doing so differ considerably. The high priestess "draws down the moon" in some ceremonies. In others, the high priest "draws down the Horned God."

## Tools of the Craft

Aleister Crowley identified eight tools or "weapons" of magic. Though Wiccan covens differ in which ones they use, all use some, though meanings attributed to them may vary.

**athame:** black-handled, double-edged dagger used for sacred activities

**biolline:** white-handled dagger used for carving and other "mundane" activities

**cauldron or cup:** represents element of water, female principle, the womb, the Grail

**censer of incense:** used to create a purifying smoke, or smoke in which an apparition can take shape; may be a flat stone, shallow bowl of sand, or thurible of brass, ceramic or wood, set on a three-legged tripod or hung from chains

**pentacle:** round disk of metal inscribed with a pentagram; represents the element of the earth

**scourge:** a whip or cat-o'-nine-tails, used to purify but never to draw blood

**sword:** represents the element of fire

**wand or stang:** represents the element of air

## The Gardnerian Path

Gerald B. Gardner founded modern witchcraft or Wicca in the 1950s in England, where witchcraft was illegal until 1951. He based it on a combination of influences from traditional witchcraft, folklore literature, and his experiences with Aleister Crowley and various ceremonial magic traditions. Gardner, called the "Grand Old Man of Witchcraft," wrote *High Magic's Aid* (1949), a novel containing two initiation ceremonies, plus *Witchcraft Today* (1955) and *The Meaning of Witchcraft* (1959). Citing Margaret Murray, he claimed that Wicca is the surviving remnant of pagan rites from pre-Christian times.

Some Gardnerian covens today claim "apostolic" succession from Gardner's original coven on the Isle of Man. Others are neo-Gardnerians, basing their rites on published accounts of Gardnerian rituals.

---

Gardner composed "162 Laws of the Craft," contained in the secret *Book of Shadows*, the major text of Gardnerian witches. The main one of these, called the Witch's Law, limits the working of witches to so-called "white magic," as previously mentioned: "An' it harm none, do what you will." Gardner claimed the book was very ancient, inherited by him from his parent coven, but it contains much material authored by Aleister Crowley and sections from Leland's *Aradia*. Initiates swear to keep the book secret and copy their own versions in longhand from their high priestess's or high priest's copy. Though all give an oath never to reveal its contents, various versions and excerpts of the *Book of Shadows* have been published. The mistakes and misinterpretations became so divergent that Doreen Valiente, high priestess of Gardner's coven, cooperated with Janet and Stewart Farrar in publishing what she claims is the correct text in their 1984 book *The Witches' Way*. Valiente is credited with emphasizing the goddess in Wiccan rites, while downplaying much of the sexual magic derived from Crowley.

Gardnerian witches hold their rites in the nude or skyclad, based on the Celtic belief that nudity provides supernatural protection and, possibly, because of Gardner's own interest in nudism. Adornments traditionally include a girdle, sometimes made of a nine-foot-long braided red yarn used to measure the magic circle. The witches usually wear necklaces, and often other rings and jewels. The high priestess may wear a tiara.

The Horned God is called Cernunnos on the Gardnerian path. The Triple Goddess—Maiden, Mother, and Crone—is worshipped under many sacred names. Gardnerian witches avoid using these names in common speech, referring to her as "the Lady" or "Aradia."

A circle is cast using a ritual similar to one found in *The Key of Solomon*, followed by the Charge of the Goddess, often drawn from Leland's novel *Aradia*.

During rituals, the priestess incarnates the goddess and "draws down" the power of the moon into a nine-foot circle protected by candles and ritual, where the power is raised further through dancing and meditation before being used to work spells and other magic. According to *Harper's Encyclopedia of Mystical and Paranormal Experience,* Gardner identifies eight methods of raising magical power in his *Book of Shadows:* (1) meditation, (2) chants, spells and invocations, (3) trance and astral projection, (4) incense, wine and drugs, (5) dancing, (6) binding parts of the body with cords, (7) scourging, and (8) ritual sex.

Witches advance through three degrees of initiation: priest or witch; magus or witch queen; and high priest or priestess. After completing the third, called the Great Rite, they are qualified to "hive off" and become the high priest or priestess of their own coven. The Great Rite is widely believed to be a sacred act of sexual union, either symbolic or actual. Symbolic sexual images pervade Gardnerian ritual as, for instance, when the blade of the athame is dipped into a cup of water or wine.

## The Alexandrian Path

Alexander Sanders claimed to have been initiated into witchcraft by his grandmother at the age of seven. Later he began his own system of witchcraft, perhaps after having been refused initiation into a Gardnerian coven, though this rumor has never been documented. However, he took many, if not most, of the elements of his ceremonies from Gardner. The Alexandrian ritual can be found in Stewart Farrar's *What Witches Do.*

Alexandrian witches refer to the goddess and her consort as Aradia and Karnayan. They use a version of the Gardnerian *Book of Shadows.* Elements shared by the Gardnerian and Alexandrian paths include: skyclad ceremonies, ceremonial scourging, anointing with water and wine in the "five-fold kiss," and the use of a ritual password: "Perfect love and perfect trust." Alexandrian ritual adds a unique element to the initiation ceremony: pricking the finger of the initiate so that all pledges are sealed with blood. The Alexandrian path also uses herbal extracts to "condense" ectoplasm, and borrows John Dee's "angelic language" from enochian magic.

## The Dianic Path

Dianic covens worship the goddess in a more or less monotheistic way in her three aspects of Maiden-Creatrix, Mother, and Old Crone (although the Mother aspect does take a consort in most covens), or as a Triple Creatrix: Moon, Queen of Mysteries; Sunna, Queen of the Stars; and Mother Earth. Rituals emphasize the moon; the myths, lore, and mysteries associated with the thirteen lunar months; and the Beth-luis-Nion tree alphabet of ancient Britain. Robert Graves's *The White Goddess* is their basic reference. Dianic covens are very ecologically concerned and environmentally active.

One branch of the Dianic path is **FEMINIST WITCHCRAFT**. On this path, men are excluded from covens. Z. Budapest, who claims a family tradition of witchcraft, is credited with starting the first feminist coven in 1971—the Susan B. Anthony Coven. More recently, Starhawk's writings, especially *The Spiral Dance*, greatly influenced this path. Feminist covens worship both moon and sun goddesses, but more influence than usual is attributed to the sun, under names such as Sunna and Lucina. Matriarchal ideas and institutions predominate.

## The Church of Wicca

Though some witches argue that this is not a true Wiccan path, many covens are based on its teachings. Gavin and Yvonne Frost established the School of Wicca and began offering correspondence courses in witchcraft. The lessons combine certain ritual elements of Wicca with a monotheistic belief in an abstract, unknowable god. Students advance through ten levels of the astral plane, called "The Side." The aim is progressive reincarnation into higher levels. Kundalini sex practices, including introitus, are part of the course, but the system is considered antimatriarchal. The Egyptian ankh, symbol of regeneration, and the artificial phallus play important symbolic and ritualistic roles.

## Seax Wicca

Raymond Buckland wrote *The Tree*, subtitled *The Complete Book of Saxon Witchcraft*, in 1974. It outlines a ceremonial system based on Saxon mythology and Wiccan ritual. Cerridwen, the goddess of the cauldron, heads the list of deities. Se-ax is the Saxon name for the athame. Buckland outlines a complete guide on self-initiation and how to start a coven. He makes no claims of ancient origins for his rites, recommending them on the basis of their effectiveness.

## The Fairy Paths

First revived in the early 1970s by Victor Anderson and his student, Gwydion Pendderioen, the path of Fairy Wicca incorporates elements of European folk magic and material from the Gardnerian elements of European folk magic and material from the Gardnerian *Book of Shadows*. Pendderioen later founded Forever Forests, dedicated to the Green Man, aimed at reforestation of the Earth.

Another fairy path honors the Irish fairies, the Tuatha D'Danann. Kisma Stepanich, among others, has published several guides to Wiccan rites based on Gaelic fairy lore. Dana is their goddess. She receives offerings of warm milk and honey with a pat of butter melted into it. The Fairy Queen, who takes various other names as well, prefers violets, rides often at night, and lives beneath an enchanted mountain where a mortal year passes in a single evening.

Fairy shamans wear a cloak of invisibility made of bird feathers over simple hooded gowns and mantles. They carry staffs or magic wands, often tipped with crystal, a magic bag of tricks, and make music on a "musical branch," a rattle made from the branch of a tree and hazelnuts, the symbol of wisdom. Many smoke pipes.

Fairy Wiccans use the usual athame, cup, and pentacle in their ceremonies, held inside a fairy ring. Other objects used in spells include the four traditional Gaelic talismans: the Sword of Nuada; the Spear of Lugh, Undry; the Cauldron of Dagda; and the Great Fal, Stone of Destiny. Those on the fairy path study the Oghans of the alphabet of trees described in Graves's *The White Goddess.*

Spells, many using butter and milk, invoke various fairy spirits and much ritual use is made of herbs and teas. The tradition of "crossing with butter" to mark possessions survives folklore: People put butter on their cats' feet to keep them from wandering. Other spells are cast using white candles and quartz crystals.

Cows are considered sacred on the fairy path. They represent Dana in her aspect of the white cow. Cows are driven between two fires in a ceremony to insure the fertility of the earth.

### Eclectic Paths

The creative bias of Wicca encourages many seekers to combine different elements from other paths with their own individual vision to create new paths. Among them:

George Patterson of Bakersfield, California, began the **GEORGIAN PATH.**

Wiccans with Hebrew backgrounds explore their prepatriarchal roots on a path they call **JEWITCH**. Rites are held on Fridays, when they light white candles to invite Shekinah, the Sacred Bride, into their homes.

The **PAGAN WAY** is an open, nature-oriented path that demands no initiation or membership of participants. It sponsors large, public celebrations at the sabbats, and sometimes at the full moon, which incorporate many of the sacred rituals of Wicca without the vows of silence and secrecy imposed on initiates.

The **SOCIETY OF THE INNER LIGHT**, otherwise known as the Western Mysteries, was founded by Dion Fortune in the 1920s. At first it owed much to the rituals of the Golden Dawn, of which Fortune was an initiate. But after her death, it moved away from pagan influences. Today, it's a mixture of Alexander postural techniques, dianetics, and scientology.

**CHAOS MAGICK** is a product of the 1980s. It combines magical and occult traditions with quantum physics and computer technology. Its creed can be summarized as "Nothing is true. Everything is permitted." Ultimate responsibility is placed on the individual.

In addition, many "solitaires" practice witchcraft outside of a coven, choosing rituals that appeal to them from the immense literature on witchcraft, or designing rituals of their own.

### Traditional and Mystery Cult Revivals

A wide variety of traditional religions enjoy a modern revival as people seek to rebuild their links to Earth and its seasons. Based on the newly available folklore studies, various ethnic groups now recreate the religious rites of their forefathers (and mothers). Others feel more drawn to archaic religions examined in archeological works. A swarm of nature-oriented Earth religions, most based on the gods, goddesses, and mythology of old, attract adherents.

Rituals typically include the elements found to make effective psychodrama by the ancient masters of Greek tragedy: rhythmic chanting, songs, drums, flutes, pots of flame, and smoking torches. Garb invariably includes robes, often color-keyed to the cult member's level of initiation.

Mythology as well as religions provides exceptionally rich fields to mine story ideas. The drama of family strife among the Egyptian pantheon, for instance, has been successfully repeated many times. Osiris is killed by his brother Set, avenged by his son Horus. Shakespeare's *Hamlet* uses the same plot, as does Disney's *The Lion King*. The psychological theories of Carl Jung explain the attraction of these archetypes as stories that can be told again and again.

## Druidism

The Druids resumed their rites early, reestablishing the summer solstice festival at Stonehenge in the late 1880s. They follow as closely as possible the Druid practices recorded in literature, including the ritual cutting of mistletoe, and festivals at the solstices and equinoxes. Druid groups are particularly active in ecology projects, reforestation, and the protection of sacred sites. Ritual garb includes white robes, torques of precious metals, and crowns of oak or other leaves. The National Eisteddfod, the annual Welsh competition of music and poetry, is conducted as a ritual using Druidic symbols.

AR NDRAIOCHT FEIN, established by Isaac Bonewits, represents one path of neo-pagan Druid practice. Initiates are organized in groves named for various sacred trees, and they wear white berets and long white robes. Sacrifices of tree branches, fruits, flowers, and vegetables are offered. Symbols include a circle pierced by two parallel lines and a branch sprouting from an oak stump. It is an order of scholars and artists.

The ORDER OF BARDS, OVATES, AND DRUIDS was organized in 1717, eventually growing to become the largest Druidic order in the United Kingdom and Europe. Initiates achieve the three grades of scholarship by studying healing and divination, in addition to the Arthurian and Grail cycles of myths. Full Druids can form their own groves. The organization is especially active in replanting sacred groves.

The REFORMED DRUIDS OF NORTH AMERICA began in 1963 at Carleton College as a humorous protest against mandatory chapel services. A group of faculty and students declared themselves Druids, donned white robes, and began holding services in oak groves and on nearby beaches and hills. They recited ancient Welsh and Irish poems, passed the water-of-life (whiskey), and sang hymns to ancient Celtic and Gaulish gods: Danu, the Earth Mother; Be'al, the masculine spirit; and Dalon ap Landu, Lord of Groves. Other deities included Grannos of the Healing Springs; Braciaca, god of malt and brewing; Belenos, the sun god; Sirona, goddess of rivers; Taranus, god of thunder and lightning; and Llyr, god of the sea.

The organization named NEW REFORMED DRUIDS OF NORTH AMERICA recognizes many related groups including NORSE DRUIDS, WICCA DRUIDS, HASSIDIC DRUIDS, ZEN DRUIDS, IRISH DRUIDS (who conduct their rites in Gaelic), and various other eclectic orders of Druids. Arch-Druid

Issac Bonewits's work *The Druid Chronicles (Evolved)* provides history and liturgy for most of these groups.

## Celtic Traditions

The **PAN CELTIC** movement is one of the strongest in neo-paganism. Pipes, drums, and harps are used in rituals that aim to renew Celtic culture. *Inner Keltia*, the major journal of the Celtic revival, is published in Scotland. Neo-Celts participate in "dressing" sacred wells, believe in fairy folk, and celebrate great fire festivals at the cross-quarter days. The Celts named the Horned God Kernunnos or Hern the Hunter and identify him as Lord of the Animals and the Great Shaman. His image is found on the Gundestrop cauldron, one of the masterpieces of ancient Celtic art. The winter solstice is often celebrated with dancing in horned costumes.

The Celts begin their year at the feast of Samhain on the eve of November. At the feast of Beltane on May Eve, all fires are extinguished, then relit from Bel's Fire, sacred to the solar-fire god Bel (Balor or Belenus). On May Day, Celts dance around the maypole.

In the **IRISH** tradition, harps are considered essential to effective ritual and rituals are often performed in Gaelic. The fire goddess Bridget, goddess of fertility and healing, is honored. Her major festival coincides with Candlemas in early February. Magic is sometimes practiced through plaiting rushes, in which spells are woven into a basket or braid.

The **WELSH** and **CORNISH** traditions use the Mabinogeon myth cycle as a source of rituals, poetry, and deities. Merlin is a major mage.

The **BARDIC PATH** is an individual one within the Celtic and Druidic traditions. Devotees roam the Earth reciting mystical poetry, song and mythology.

## Neo-Viking Traditions

**ASATRU**, the Scandinavian "belief in the gods," recognizes two pantheons: the early agricultural gods, the Vanir, and the invading warrior gods, the Aesir. Gods include Frey, Odin, Thor, and Tir. Goddesses are Frig, Freya, and the Norns or Fates. The usual solstice and equinox days are celebrated with rituals, plus the annual festival of Althing and Ragnar's Day, March 28, celebrating the Viking sack of Paris in A.D. 875. The winter solstice was sacred to Odin; the spring equinox or "summer finding" when the color red appears in the ceremonies, was sacred to Thor; the Summer Solstice was sacred to Baldo and a time of great fairs and festivals.

**ODINISM** is a cult of Asatru that recognizes only the Aesir. In the Odinic Rite, established in 1973, an individual takes Odin as his person deity and undergoes a shamanic initiation based on Odin's sacrifice as described in the *Poetic Edda*. To gain knowledge, Odin hung on the world tree Yggdrasil for nine days and nights. You can see him today on the Hanged Man tarot card. The knowledge he gained was the ability to read the runes. Odinists base their conduct on the *Havamal*, Odin's sayings as a lawgiver, and seek to restore the rituals based on the eddas. They are organized in hearths and have a teaching order called the gothar. Larger assemblies, called witans, seek to make the knowledge of Odin more public. The Odinshof is an activist arm of Odinism organized to protect the remaining wild woods of the world through both ritual magic and political activism.

The **SKALKIC PATH** is the Norse equivalent of the Bardic tradition among the Celts.

### Mediterranean Traditions

The **FELLOWSHIP OF ISIS**, founded in 1976, seeks closer communion with the Egyptian goddess Isis. The organization, based in the incongruous confines of Clonegal Castle, Ireland, claims thousands of members worldwide, including a large following in Libya, the goddess's traditional homeland. Rituals draw on Egyptian sources and are held on the usual solstice and equinox dates. The Fellowship's values include love, beauty, truth, and abundance. It practices total religious tolerance, forbids sacrifice of any kind, and discourages asceticism.

The **CHURCH OF APHRODITE** also seeks love, beauty, and harmony with the goddess. Founded on Long Island in 1938 by Gleb Botkin, son of a doctor who served the last Russian czar, the church has three liturgies, which are performed in front of an altar bearing a reproduction of the Venus de Milo set against purple cloth. Frankincense and myrrh burn on the altar along with nine candles. The planetary sign of Venus stands in place of a cross.

The **CHURCH OF THE ETERNAL SOURCE** is a federation of revived Egyptian cults. In the 1960s, Harold Moss began to organize Egyptian costume parties for a club he belonged to in California, the Chesley Donovan Science Fantasy Foundation. Eventually these evolved into recreations of the rituals of the cult of Horus, the Egyptian god Moss felt most drawn to serve. Other people researched and reenacted the cults of Thoth, Osiris, Neith, Isis, and Bast. Adepts dress in the Egyptian manner, usually including beautiful jewelry. They study hieroglyphics and books about ancient Egypt, seeking out the best translations of the ancient texts. Dates are called by their Egyptian names. Although they have no holy book, they generally recommend Dr. Henri Frankfort's *Ancient Egyptian Religion* as a basic text. Each cult is autonomous and rituals are held separately, but all participate in a large Egyptian New Year's celebration held annually in mid-July at the first rising of Sirius.

## NEW AGE NEO-PAGANS

Recent years ushered in a phenomenal growth in neo-pagan paths. Many of them are combinations of elements from many traditional paths, combined with ideas drawn from astrology, Earth religion, and science fiction. In fact, science fiction and fantasy are fertile fields for developing religions. Margot Adler notes in *Drawing Down the Moon* that "science fiction and fantasy probably come closer than any other literature to systematically exploring the central concerns of Neo-Pagans and Witches." Persistent rumors in the science fiction community insist that L. Ron Hubbard began scientology on a bet with Isaac Asimov, another science fiction writer.

### The Church of All Worlds

Based on Robert Heinlein's *Stranger in a Strange Land*, the Church of All Worlds (CAW) was started by two students in Missouri in 1962. With a group of their friends, they recreated the ceremony of water brotherhood, Atl, from the novel, passing around a goblet of water, "grokking" each other's godhood, and repeating the mantra: "Thou art god. Thou art goddess."

Tim Zell proceeded to organize the group into "nests" of celebrants, who advance through nine circles of initiation named for the planets through study that includes long reading lists. They practice a new tribalism, based on the ability to grok a totally empathetic understanding of and merging of identity with each other and the earth. Serge King adopts grokking in his *Urban Shamanism*, saying Hawaiian kahunas develop an identical ability.

CAW members are into speed-reading, memory training, karate, yoga, autosuggestion, set theory, logic, survival training, snakes, and nudity. Besides Heinlein, Abraham Maslow's theories of self-actualization and the novels of Ayn Rand influenced the group. The CAW emblem is the tiki. CAW has no creed, but its goal is to achieve total telepathic union of all life on Earth.

Zell achieved a good deal of notoriety thanks to his winning performances at costume balls (complete with snakes), various DisCons, and the 1972 WorldCon. He withdrew from CAW and retired to California to establish a Bene Gesserit shaman training institute, based on Frank Herbert's novel *Dune*.

## Erisian Magic

Erisian magic or Discordianism worships Eris, goddess of chaos and confusion. It began in 1957 when two men in California claimed they were sprinkled with fairy dust in a bowling alley by Eris and inspired to form the Discordian Society, "a new religion disguised as a complicated put-on." The two, Robert Shea and Robert Anton Wilson (who took the name Mordecai the Foul), later wrote a science fiction trilogy about their new religion, the Illuminatus. Sacred symbols are the apple and pentagon. The group, called a cabal, follows the "Sacred Chou," exploring the polarities of humor and seriousness, order and chaos. The system has affinities with Taoism, anarchy, and clowning. Rituals are designed as nonviolent, absurdist, revolutionary, and surreal experiences, using paradox to expand the perception of reality. One Erisian ritual—the Ancient and Honorable Order of Bill the Cat, lord of the obnoxious and nasty, involving a crude caricature of the circle ritual—is sometimes used by other pagans as a check on egotism, pomposity, and taking themselves too seriously.

## Feraferia

This system of neo-paganism, begun by astrologer Frederick Adams, incorporates elements of the nudist, vegetarian, naturalist, and utopian movements. Its goal is a return to the peaceful existence that existed in a golden age before the beginning of animal husbandry, blood sacrifice, and the eating of meat. Adams believed paradises such as Eden, Avalon, and the Garden of Hesperides were distant memories of this utopian existence humans once lived among the trees.

FERAFERIANS worship Kore, the Young Maiden (also known as the Daughter of Demeter), Persephone, and the Nameless Bride of Eleusis. She manifests herself in the modern age as Alice in Wonderland, Peter Pan's Wendy, and, to some extent, Lolita and Barbarella.

Festivals use Greek ritual to retell the story of the maiden goddess and her lover in new terms. On May Day, the sun and moon become engaged. On the summer solstice, they marry. Lammas is their honeymoon. At the autumn equinox, they return home to harvest their crops. On Halloween, they prepare for sleep. At Yule, the goddess awakes to find herself alone and pregnant. At Candlemas, the new god moves in her womb, to be born at the spring solstice.

Devotees of Feraferia follow the Hesperian lifestyle, emphasizing organic gardening, tree crops, and reforestation projects. They eat a diet of fruit, nuts, berries, and leafy vegetables and keep no pets. Areas of interest include ecology, the wilderness, astronomy, astrology, and sacred building construction. They build temples in nature oriented to the four directions and positions of the stars and planets in the Henge, or mandala, design.

The **DANCERS OF THE SACRED CIRCLE** are an offshoot of Feraferia.

## The Sabean Religious Order

Frederic de Arechaga took the name Ordun and composed this cult from Basque, Yoruba, Sumerian, and Babylonian sources. The stars are worshipped in a temple of the moon, decorated with columns topped with white elephants. **Sabeans** believe that the past and the future are written in the stars. They study astrology, astronomy, herbalism, temple building, and the relationship of time and place.

Rituals celebrate the stars and planets in choreographed performances incorporating music, dance, and art, along with elements of mystery plays. Weddings among the Sabeans are called "eclipses" and divination determines the union's duration: A "solar eclipse" lasts for a period of years; a "lunar eclipse" only lasts for a period of months. Margot Adler, in *Drawing Down the Moon*, reports attending a feast at a solar eclipse celebration where a huge Caesar salad was mixed in a cauldron. All meat eaten is killed in a ritual manner, reminiscent of Kosher rites.

The major Sabean god is Am'n, the "hidden, numberless point," a source either single or plural, neither male nor female, representing total knowledge. Am'n is personified by several goddesses representing the seasons and races of mankind: the red goddess of autumn and the Native Americans, the white goddess of winter and Caucasians, the black goddess of spring and the African people, the yellow goddess of summer and the Orient, and the blue goddess, ruler of Leap Year and people living "beyond the earth." Women are represented by the sun and the metal gold; men by the moon and the color silver.

## THE LANGUAGE OF WITCHCRAFT

When writing about magic, archaic terms seem to sound right. Grammatically, thou and thee are singular, you and ye are plural.

Many paths of witchcraft use the greeting "Blessed Be." Spells are sealed with the phrase "So mote it be." The Wiccan passwords are "Perfect love and perfect trust." But, of course, as Gerald Gardner would be the first to tell you, nothing is written in stone. Thus, the following dictionary of terms can be used to help you create your own language for the rites and rituals in your work.

## DICTIONARY OF TERMS
## FROM WITCHCRAFT AND MAGIC

**Akasha:** All-pervading spirit ether.

**Ankh:** The mirror of Hathor and Venus, used in Egypt as a symbol of sexual union and the immortality of the gods. The yonic loop portion was painted red; the phallic cross, white. Known as the key of the Nile, a sign of the mystic union of Isis and Osiris, and said to release the annual Nile flood.

**apex:** A tall, conical hat, familiar to us as the headgear of Halloween witches; a brimless version served as the cap of Mithra and Frey; later worn by one of Rome's high priests, the Pontifex Maximus, and by various elves, gnomes and fairies, clowns, fools and dunces.

**athame:** Black-handled, double-bladed dagger used by witches to cast circles and other sacred activities. Magnetized at each new moon in certain paths. Name probably comes from "al-dhamme," the sacred knife of a Moorish Andalusian cult of moon worshipers known as the Double-Horned Ones.

**Autumn Equinox:** A sabbat celebrated on September 21–23; Celtic Mabon, Christian Michaelmass. Days and nights are of equal length. It is the time of the Elusian Mysteries of the goddess Demeter in ancient times.

Associated symbols: acorn, hazel branches, and brown and green candles. The witches' version of Thanksgiving.

**banishing:** This has three uses in witchcraft: the circle is banished at the end of a ritual; an individual may be banished from the coven or from The Craft; and an entity is banished in order to disable a harmful nonmaterial being.

**Beltane:** Celtic cross-quarter fire festival celebrated on May Eve, April 30–May 1; German Walpurgisnacht. Festival of the Fairy Queen. Marks the beginning of summer. Time of sexual license: "the lusty month May." Associated symbols: the maypole, flower garlands, wearing of the green. All fires relit from the Beltane fire made with nine kinds of wood.

**biolline:** White-handled knife used for carving; carried by a priestess.

**boomerang effect:** The belief of many witches that if you lay a harmful spell against an innocent person, it will return threefold.

**broom:** Associated with domestic magic, marriage, and midwives in ancient Rome; Gypsy marriages are still solemnized by "jumping the broomstick."

**Candlemas:** Sabbat cross-quarter celebrated on February 1–2; Celtic Imbolg or Imbolc ("the Womb"). A women's festival honoring Brigit or Brigantia, goddess of fertility, healing, and fire. Time of the Lesser Eleusian Mysteries. In Wicca, the most popular time to initiate new witches. Christianized as the purification of the Virgin Mary forty days after the birth of Christ. Associated symbols: red and white candles, plaiting of rushes, divination concerning the length of winter based on the weather (today popularized as Groundhog Day).

**candles:** Used extensively in spells; one of the easiest ways to cast spells in witchcraft. Usually anointed with oil. Spells may take three days, nine days, or one night to cast. Candles were sacred to Juno Lucina, Mother of Light, in Rome; her winter solstice festival of lights still survives in the Swedish tradition of St. Lucy's Day.

**cauldron:** Major female symbol of the old pagan world, symbolizing the womb of the goddess, able to assure rebirth or magic power to all who drank from it; frequently watched over by three goddesses, fates, or witches.

**chalice (aka cup):** Drinking from a cup of blood, and later, wine (blood of the earth) represents a major act of communion since earliest times; in pagan (and Jewish) marriage ceremonies, the couple drinks from the same cup to become "one blood." Symbol of water in the tarot deck; later replaced by hearts.

**circle:** A primary feminine sign, thought to be protective, drawn in a sacred manner at the beginning of every session of magic or witchcraft.

**cord:** Used in witchcraft to tie or bind a spell; often worn as a girdle during rites. Originally sacred to the Egyptian goddess Ma'at, keeper of the law; used in healing amulets in Babylon because of its connection to the umbilicus.

**corn dolly:** Harvest figure made of stalks of grain (called corn in Europe).

**coven:** Gathering of witches; originally supposed to contain twelve witches and a devil during the witch trials, mocking Christ and His apostles.

**covenstead:** Meeting place of a coven.

**The Craft:** Name used for the workings of both Freemasonry and Wicca.

**crossroads:** Said to be the site of witches' sabbats; sacred to Hecate and Hermes.

**deosil:** Clockwise motion.

**elemental:** Nonmaterial entities with the nature of one of the four elements: air, earth, fire, or water.

**esbat:** Celebration at one of the thirteen annual full moons.

**evoking:** Summoning entities of a lower order than mankind.

**familiar:** An animal or spirit kept to provide psychic support when working spells. The various "Small Peoples" were believed to be the familiars of witches during the witch trials. More frequently, the familiar took the form of an animal, usually a cat or dog, but sometimes a rabbit, goat, or other creature. In France, most familiars were frogs, sacred to Hecate; the fleur-de-lis is actually a symbol of three frogs.

**fetch:** A male witch who serves as messenger and assistant to the high priest and priestess of a coven; also called the summoner.

**gnome:** An earth elemental.

**The Grail:** Originally the Celtic caldron of regeneration, full of the holy blood of the goddess; later the goal of an immense Quest literature, containing much Celtic imagery mixed with Christian plot lines.

**The Great Rite:** A ritual merging the polarities of male and female, usually through symbolic or actual sexual activity.

**handfasting:** Wiccan or pagan marriage ceremony.

**herm:** Phallic pillar with a head of Hermes on top that once guarded nearly every crossroads in Europe; reworked into crosses during the Christian era. Originally a Greek tradition; oddly, the Aztecs had an identical practice in the New World. Travelers frequently made offerings to Hermes and Hecate, gods of the crossroads, and they were honored at festivals called Compitalia.

**hexagram:** Six-pointed star, now associated with the Jewish faith, but originally a Tantric symbol of the sexual union of male and female.

**hieros gamos:** Greek for "sacred marriage," the Great Rite (once widespread in the pagan world) by which a man became king through sexual union with the great goddess or her high priestess.

**hiving off:** Establishing a new coven.

**Host:** The Christian wafer representing the body of Christ in communion; its desecration was the charge in many witch trials.

**incantation:** The singing-in of a spell or charm.

**invoking:** Summoning an entity of a higher nature than human.

**Lammas:** Cross-quarter festival celebrated July 31–August 1; Celtic Lugnasad or Lughnassah. The Feast of Bread. "The Games of Lud," god of wisdom. Marks the beginning of the harvest season. First corn harvest and baking of first loaf from new crop. Traditionally the time of temporary "marriages" lasting a year and a day. Associated symbols: corn dollies, sheaves of wheat, grapes, green crowns, and candles.

**macrocosm/microcosm:** Principle that states the correspondence between large and small events—as above, so below.

**magus:** Male occult adept.

**maiden:** Assistant high priestess in a coven.

**maypole:** Center of the dance at Beltane when men and women celebrated the fertility of the new season. Origin of square dancing's grand right and left. The pole itself represents the May king's phallus.

**medicine wheel:** Circles, usually marked out with stones, in the American West. Thought to serve the same purpose as megalithic stone circles in Europe. Most have twenty-eight spokes, plus a center stone. Sun dance lodges are still built to the same pattern.

**pentacle:** A disk of metal, usually inscribed with a pentagram, placed on an altar to represent Earth.

**pentagram:** A five-pointed star, representing the earth and the fivefold path; variously called Solomon's Seal, the Star of Bethlehem, the Druid's Foot, and the Witches' Cross (witches "cross themselves" with the symbol). Ancient sign of "gateless" protection used in ritual magic and Wicca, since it's drawn with one continuous line; derived from the apple-core star of the earth. Sacred to Celtic death goddess, Morgan, whose devotees displayed it on a blood-red shield. Sign of the earth element in the tarot suit (today, diamonds).

**poppet:** Doll used by witches when casting spells, a very ancient practice dating back to pharonic Egypt.

**Prana:** Vital force of the cosmos operating on the etheric level.

**ring:** Traditional symbol of a bond between giver and wearer, as the peoples of Middle Earth discovered to their despair when they accepted Sauron's rings of power. Other magic rings in literature include those of the Niebelung, and Solomon's magic ring with which he enslaved the demon Asmodeus.

**runes:** Letters of an ancient Norse script, used for divination.

**sabbat:** Eight annual major festivals, falling at the solstices, equinoxes, and four cross-quarter days halfway between.

**salamander:** A fire elemental.

**Samhain:** Sabbat cross-quarter festival, October 31–November 1; All Hallows Eve, Feast of the Dead, Halloween. Marks the beginning of Mexico's Day of the Dead, when the gates between the worlds of the living and dead open, allowing the ghosts of dead ancestors to visit their descendants. The fairy hills in Ireland also opened on this date. Summerend, the beginning of winter. Associated symbols: black, red, white (the colors of Hecate), cauldron, black robes, masks.

**scourge:** Ritual whip, symbolic of firmness; cords sometimes made of silk.

**scrying:** Divination by gazing, usually into water, a mirror, or ink.

**scythe:** Curved blade derived from the crescent of the new moon; a symbol of the great goddess in her devouring aspect; later the tool of Father Time and the Grim Reaper.

**sigil:** A symbol used to embody a concept or aspect.

**sistrum:** Sacred rattle, originally used in the worship of Egyptian great goddesses, popular at pagan rites today.

**skyclad:** Ritual nudity.

**smudging:** Purification by smoke; a very ancient practice.

**spiral:** Sacred symbol dating to the Neolithic Age, connected with the ideas of death and rebirth. Spiral labyrinths and occuli (double twists resembling eyes) appear on many megalithic monuments, European cathedrals, and Native American rock paintings.

**star:** Believed in most ancient traditions to be the home of spirits, either of the yet unborn, the dead, angels, or gods. Composed of ether, the Greeks' fifth element, said to be lighter, finer, and more volatile than fire. The goddess is identified with the morning star (Venus) under many names: Astarte, Venus, Ishtar, Esther, Stella Maris. Lucifer (Son of Morning) and Christ both have associations with the morning star as well.

**Summer Solstice:** Midsummer Eve, Celtic Litha, celebrated June 21–23 on the night before the longest day of the year. Christianized as St. John's Day. Traditionally a festival of fire when bonfires burned on the hills all night. Associated symbol: wheel covered with flowers.

**swastika:** Ancient religious symbol of the four corners of the world. Arms pointing clockwise make it a masculine, solar symbol (used by the Nazis as their major symbol); arms that point counterclockwise indicate a feminine, lunar symbol.

**sword:** Symbol of fire, virility, and power. Most heroes of myth had magic swords forged in fairyland or by smiths of the underworld. At the hero's death, his sword was often a man's only possession; all else—the fields, flocks, and household—belonged to the woman. Sign of the Doom suit and the element fire in the tarot deck. (Later became spades, thanks to the Spanish word for sword, *espada*.)

**sylph:** An air elemental.

**talisman:** Like an amulet, but worn for a specific purpose.

**triangle:** Upright, symbolizes the male essence; reversed, the Yoni Yantra, symbolizing the genital area of the Threefold Goddess. Triangular cakes baked for sacred rituals by Egyptians, Jews (for Purim), and Scots (for Samhain).

**Undine:** A water elemental.

**Vernal or Spring Equinox:** A sabbat celebrated on March 21–23; Germaine Ostrara, became Christian Easter. Marks the beginning of spring, when days and nights are of equal length. The return of Persephone from the underworld. Associated sacred symbols: hare, egg, lily, the color white, doe, bow and arrow, silver and green candles.

**wand:** A magical rod of power representing the element of air, used in witches' rites; made of wood, bone, ivory, or amber, often tipped with crystals and decorated with ribbons and magic stones. Used in love magic. A symbol of mercy. Dionysus (Bacchus) carried a wand made of a fennel stalk topped with a pinecone. Fairy wands are tipped with stars. The sign of air in the tarot deck; later became clubs.

**Wiccaning:** The pagan equivalent of Christening.

**widdershins:** A counterclockwise direction.

**Winter Solstice:** Germanic Yule, December 21–23. Shortest day of the year. Odin honored at a great feast. Time of the Roman Saturnalia, celebrating the birth of the Unconquered Sun; a time of gaming, exchanging presents, sexual license, and reversed social roles. Associated symbols: red and green candles, holly, mistletoe, ivy, oak logs, pinecones.

**Wotan's Cross:** A cross inside a circle given various symbolic meanings in paganism: the earth and the four directions; the sun embraced by heaven; the union of the rose (feminine) with the cross (male) in cabalistic symbolism.

## HERBS, PLANTS, AND ESSENCES USED IN WITCHCRAFT

**acacia:** sacred to Diana; used to commune with spirits

**angelica:** sacred to Sophia; restores harmony

**cinnamon:** attracts lovers, health, and luck

**Irish moss:** place under your rug for the "luck of the Irish"

**laurel:** good luck; worn by vitors

**mandrake:** hold the root as you conjure to strengthen spells

**myrtle:** sacred to Artemis

**patchouli:** sacred to Pan

**rose:** sacred to Diana

**rosemary:** offers protections; worn by pagan warriors into battle

**vervain:** sacred to Venus; used to banish evil

**violet:** sacred to the Fairy Queen

**witches broom:** purifies water

# CHAPTER 5

# Commerce, Trade, and Law in Contemporary Fantasy

## by Sherrilyn Kenyon

It is a common misconception that the Middle Ages was broken into three factions: those who worked, those who fought, and those who prayed. As with any broad generalization, this doesn't even begin to scratch the surface of the complex infrastructure and relationships of peasant, lord, and priest, especially since these three often overlapped with such occupations as warrior-priests or peasant soldiers, or my personal favorites, the peasants who became lords and the lords who were forced to work.

In the fantasy genre, these relationships can be even more blurred or more rigid depending on the author. In R.R. Mallory's short story "Sword Song," warriors are literally one with their weapons. Anne Lesley Groell uses aristocratic ladies as guild assassins in her novels *Bridge of Valor* and *Anvil of the Sun*. In a brilliant blending of medieval feudalism with fantasy, Kinley MacGregor's *Pale Moon Rising* shows us a magic-based society where vassals swear allegiance to the Mage-Lord and his underlings.

Similarly, when it comes to law in fantasy, the author is High Judge. However, the laws and punishments should be consistent within that world, unless the capriciousness or injustice of the person in charge is something you wish to illustrate.

Even though you and your imagination are the only limitations in fantasy, it still helps to understand the basic classes and positions held by medieval men and women. The following list should aid you in creating a unique world tailored to your story.

## COMMERCE

Throughout most of the Middle Ages, a peasant wasn't tied to the land (serfs were, but even they could escape). In the early part of the period, a peasant could escape his status by either becoming a fighter or becoming an apprentice to a trade—and on a much smaller scale, even a member of the church. There were, of course, other members of the lower class—Gypsies, peddlers, vagabonds, prostitutes, and the like. What generally segregated these people from their middle-class counterparts was a lack of land and money.

In the Middle Ages, the possession of land was the only real value a person had. Serfs who were bound to the land were infinitely richer than those who were cast off their lands, even though those without land were able to travel about.

These vagabonds were seen as disease carriers or thieves. Unfortunately, destitution often caused them to become those very things. A woman without money usually turned to prostitution where she contracted numerous diseases, and both men and women who were denied jobs turned to theft.

With so many villages and even towns xenophobic, most people couldn't find work once they left their lands. The only way to circumvent this was to go somewhere they had family who could vouch for them, or to carry a letter of reference from their previous clergy member or lord.

The idea of the cutpurse or thief took on a noble air with some of the troubadours who were many times vagabonds themselves and who often tried to dignify the homeless wanderer. However, it must be noted that most minstrels were nobility who had dropped out, or were forced out of their traditional place in society.

### Lower Class

**acrobats/jugglers:** These performers traveled about the countryside in search of either an inn, tavern, fair, castle, or court where they could perform. Since they could go long periods of time without finding a place to perform, many of them turned to theft and other crimes to make ends meet.

**adamist:** A gardner or tiller of any field.

**adamite:** Term for a nudist, usually a poor pilgrim or hermit who was doing penance for something.

**alchemists:** Charged with turning common items into gold, alchemists had a tenuous place in society. Often the brunt of superstition and hostility, they were left alone and ridiculed, except in extreme times when they might be singled out as warlocks and punished by extreme measures.

**artists:** Commissioned to paint portraits of people, they had a reputation for seduction, thievery, and other crimes. Though looked down upon by most of society, they were left alone unless they committed punishable crimes.

**barber:** One who cut hair, but also let blood to cure infections.

**bard:** A musician or minstrel who usually sung only of heroic deeds. Like acrobats, they traveled in search of donations to live on. Many bards and minstrels were nobles who either dropped out or were forced out of their noble status.

**bear baiters:** Much like a modern rodeo clown or matador, these intrepid spirits would bait bears and run from them for the amusement of their patrons.

**beggar:** Usually a mentally or physically handicapped person who was unable to work. They either begged in the street or frequented alms houses and hospitals so they could eat. However, it was also a common occupation for those who didn't want to work; these people were seen as frauds and, if caught, could be severely punished.

**chamber maid:** Usually of the peasant class, these young women went to work in either a middle- or upper-class household as cleaning servants.

**chambrieres:** Women who tended cows.

**champion:** A man or knight who hired himself out as a stand-in for trials by combat. Some were permanently retained by nobles or towns, and in some cases, several were retained to participate for both the accuser and the accused. Of course, this profession was considered the lowest of the low, and the shame of a father being a champion was passed on to his children who were sometimes not allowed to own property. It was also a highly dangerous occupation, since most of the time the champion shared whatever punishment was dealt to the accused.

**churl (aka serf):** The lowest class of peasantry. As early as the ninth century, it was also used alternatively for husband. (Never say medieval folk didn't have a sense of humor.)

**comandarreses:** Women who hired out other women as servants or wet nurses.

**comedians:** Just like their modern counterparts, these individuals traveled around telling jokes for profit. They would sometimes be forced to commit crimes to survive, or they would tell a joke that didn't meet with the tastes of their hosts. In such cases, the punishment could be quite severe.

**dancers:** Male or female, they traveled in search of arenas in which to perform. They were often condemned by the Church, but the lay society enjoyed seeing them. The best engagements were found around festivals, holidays and celebrations.

**dwarves:** People short in stature who often hired themselves out as oddities, jesters, or fools.

**dyer:** One who dyed cloth. They were looked down upon by everyone and were easy to spot due to their dye-stained fingers. Most were male, but some females also plied this trade.

**fishmonger:** One who dealt in fish. Though profitable, for an obvious reason it wasn't a very prestigious trade.

**fishwife:** A woman who sold fish.

**fools:** Most were similar to comedians, the primary difference being that these were people who were permanent members of a nobleman's entourage. They often made scathing political commentaries masked with humor.

**footpad:** One who robbed on foot, usually on a road or highway.

**fortune-tellers:** Though they were often part of the Gypsy clan, there were others, some even born of noble households, who were able to read tarot cards, palms, bones, stones, runes, tea leaves, crystal balls, and mirrors. Their readings took up much time and were usually very detailed. The common form of payment was silver. The Church completely banned such practices and called for death as a punishment. Lay courts, however, held more to the old Roman laws and they made a determination between beneficial and malevolent diviners. Beneficial practitioners were often left alone or fined; those judged malevolent were put to death. In times of famine or pestilence, a local priest or friar could single out fortune-tellers and use them for scapegoats. They then would be hanged or stoned to death by the very people they had once helped.

**freebooter:** A thief or pirate, most often with a devil-may-care attitude.

**friar:** Often seen by the local priests as competition for local charity and giving, friars had a raunchy reputation as purveyors of sin. They preferred to frequent towns and most especially taverns, and were infamous for performing forbidden ceremonies such as secret weddings, last rites for those to whom it had been denied, and so forth.

**gypsies:** Though not part of the Middle Ages until the mid-fifteenth century, Gypsies are undeniably a part of fantasy. Medieval Gypsies were feared and often met with horrible deaths and punishments from both the Church and lay courts. Seen as purveyors of sin and sorcery, they were ranked with Jews and generally avoided.

**heretic:** This was a term applied to many different types of people. Heretics were witches, political enemies, or anyone who contradicted the Church. For those found guilty of it, the penalty was almost always death. However, it should be noted that there were large groups of heretics that were allowed to live in peace, even though the Church condemned them. It was only when these groups began to threaten local church or lay officials that they became objects of persecution.

**imp:** One who grafted feathers on hawks or falcons to aid them in flight. Also, a devil-child.

**jongleurs/minstrels:** Traveling musicians who essentially sang for their supper. Their songs could be heroic, religious, or bawdy depending on the needs or wants of their audience. They were often from noble families, but were either left to their own accord or were second-born sons with no inheritance. Though women were rare, there were a few who chose this career. Many of these ended up pursuing criminal activities to make ends meet.

**kidnapper:** A popular occupation in the high and late Middle Ages. These were often common-born thugs who grabbed travelers off the roads, or they were hired by someone to go into another person's home and kidnap them. The punishment for this crime was death.

**mercenary:** This term could be applied to low- or high-born men who rented out their military service for a fee. Many mercenaries banded together and sold their services as a group or traveling army. They also had reputations for turning on the very people who hired them, or of keeping the spoils of war for themselves.

**midwife:** A woman who was in charge of delivering babies (a task that was too tedious for a doctor to bother with). Midwives usually passed their craft down from mother to daughter and were most often of peasant stock. Many also attended to other female health issues and diseases. Their cures were often more humane than those of their so-called learned colleagues. When some of their cures proved more beneficial, some of their unscrupulous and jealous male counterparts would call them witches or heretics.

**mimes:** Actors and actresses. Condemned by the Church, mimes could be male or female if they were a traveling band who performed for taverns, inns, courts, castles, and fiars. If they were involved with the Church, however, they were exclusively male.

**oracles:** One through whom the gods speak. A mainstay of fantasy, these are revered religious figures who are often sanctified or at least tolerated by the Church. They are usually hermits or other people who have withdrawn from society and must be sought out by those in need of their help.

**pardoner:** Men licensed by the Church to sell indulgences, or absolution, for sins. Many of these men were so corrupt (and a large number unlicensed) that the pardoner was often considered a criminal. Thus the epithet "penny-preacher" was born, indicating that anyone could buy absolution for a penny.

**pawnbroker:** Worked the same way as the modern pawnbroker, although they could also be loan sharks. Although they could be fined if caught, they were most often viewed as a despicable but necessary part of society.

**peasant:** Simply means rural laborer. They could be free or tied to the land where they worked. Those who were free often sold themselves out for other types of labor or took a second job as a peddler or household servant. In the worst of times, they would also sell their children and even spouses. Once slavery was banned, they abandoned offspring in lean times. Most countries allowed them to regain their children later if they came upon them in good times and could repay the people who had kept the child during those years.

**peddlar:** A traveling vendor, usually male but at times female, who roamed the countryside. Though most were common born, they were often entrusted to carry messages and such during times of war. Despite such activities, they were tolerated by all nobles and royals as a necessary and vital part of the economy.

**penitent:** Someone (male or female) who was repenting their sins. They were often found as pilgrims or just rootless wanderers clothed in rags (or nothing at all), with ashes smeared on their bodies.

**pilgrims:** Men and women who were traveling to a holy shrine. Many of these people tended to fall to the wayside and used their pilgrimage as a cover for a variety of crimes. Also, some women would be robbed or would otherwise find themselves without enough money for the trip. Most of these women turned to prostitution. So many pilgrims were victims of crimes that they began traveling in large groups, such as the group of pilgrims in Chaucer's *Canterbury Tales*.

**poacher:** A man or woman who illegally killed game. Most of the time, poaching was an act of desperation. If caught, the punishment was blinding, amputation, or death.

**prostitutes:** Though usually a tolerated crime, when lawgivers decided to punish women who sold their bodies, they chose a variety of means. Punishments ranged from merely cropping the prostitute's hair or shaving her head to abysmal types of death.

**serf:** A man or woman who lived off a section of land and had to make a labor payment to the landowner for the privilege of living there. They could easily find themselves homeless if the land was sold or given over to the Church. With little or no money of their own, they often became vagabonds.

**shepher:** Tended sheep.

**skald:** A minstrel-poet similar to a bard and usually of Danish origin.

**slave:** A man or woman owned by another person. Many slaves in the Middle Ages were used as prostitutes or by artisans who needed many servants or laborers for their particular trade. Females tended to be used primarily for household tasks, and men for apprentice/journeyman type work or other heavy menial labor tasks.

**soothsayers:** For some reason in fantasy and classical literature, soothsayers tend to be blind in one or both eyes. They are usually elderly, bedraggled, and dirty. They can be meddlesome, and often put in their two cents without being asked. Though they can be punished by a nobleman who doesn't want to hear the truth they speak, they are often left alone and deemed addlepates. Those who appreciate their words pay them with either food or with copper coins.

**spinner (a.k.a. spinster):** Usually a position held by women, spinners spun fibers into threads and threads into textiles.

**stew-holder:** One who ran a brothel. Stew-holders were charged with having their prostitutes examined on a monthly basis to ensure their health. If they were found to be selling girls or boys who were disease carriers, their penalties could be harsh. Overall, they were left alone, but in times of censure, they could be run out of town, tarred, or killed.

**swineherd:** One who tended pigs and hogs.

**thieves:** A generic term for people who took what didn't belong to them. The punishment for theft depended on what was stolen and from whom. Thieves suffered amputation, branding, blinding or death.

**tinker:** One who repaired or made metal items. They were usually travelers, but some had shops.

**usurer:** One who loaned money for profit. Denounced by the Church and hated by everyone, usurers were often ostracized by society. It was tolerated as a necessity.

**wet nurse:** A woman who sold her breast milk. Usually, they were women whose own child had died, but there were a number of cases of them being new mothers who hired themselves out to motherless infants or to wealthy women who didn't have the time, inclination, or nutrient-rich milk to feed their own infant.

**wolf's head:** An outlaw. In Old English, it meant one who was to be hunted down like a wolf.

**woodcutter:** One who chopped wood for a living or to subsidize their income.

## Middle Class

**almoner:** One who collects and dispenses alms to the poor. He or she is usually employed by a wealthy or middle-class household, and it is his or her duty to gather table scraps and see them dispensed after every meal. The title can also be given to a member of the church who fulfills this position on a regular basis.

**apprentice:** These were either boys or girls who were indentured to a trade between the ages of five and seven. The actual time of their servitude was worked out when they were apprenticed, but the average length was seven years, at which time they became a journeyman or journeywoman and entered a guild.

**armorer:** One who made armor (steel, iron, or leather) or chain mail.

**arrow-smith:** One who made arrow heads.

**avener:** In charge of a stable.

**bailiff:** Overseer of the manor. Same as a steward or sheriff, he could be charged with managing household affairs, or with overseeing local laws and courts.

**beekeeper:** Usually a man who kept the bees and sold their honey and honeycomb.

**blacksmith:** One who worked with iron or black metal.

**brewer/brewster:** Brewed ale and the like.

**burgher:** A citizen of a town.

**capper:** One who made caps.

**chandler:** Maker of candles.

**clockmaker:** The first mechanical clock of the Middle Ages appears around 1271 and portable clocks appear in the early fourteenth century.

**clothier:** Maker of clothes.

**cobbler:** Repaired shoes.

**cooper:** Maker and repairer of wooden vessels such as barrels, baskets, tubs, pails, etc.

**constable:** Chief military officer of the household. In the absence of the lord or king, he would lead forces to protect the castle or country.

**confectioner:** Maker of sweets.

**cordwainer:** A shoemaker.

**cutler:** A knife maker.

**daserii/deiciers:** Dicemaker.

**draper:** Cloth dealer.

**fletcher:** One who made or dealt in bows and arrows, or an archer.

**fuller:** One who cleaned or thickened cloth.

**glassblower:** Maker of glass and glass products.

**glover:** Maker of gloves.

**goldsmith:** One who designed and made gold products.

**groom:** A stablehand.

**hayward:** In charge of maintaining fences and enclosures and, at times, for herding stray cattle.

**herald:** Heralds had a variety of roles. They were charged with assigning, designing, and identifying coats of arms. In their original and simplest forms, they were merely messengers sent to deliver letters and missives.

**housecarl:** Royal bodyguard.

**jewelers:** Makers and sellers of jewelry.

**knave:** A boy who served in the lowest capacity in a household. A lowly servant.

**knight:** In its pure form, a servant or boy. It didn't become synonymous with a military person until the twelfth century.

**leech:** A monk appointed to care or bleed the sick, so named after the animals they sometimes used.

**marshal:** A farrier, or one who was entrusted with the military affairs of a royal household.

**man-at-arms:** Soldier.

**mercer:** A man who dealt in silks and velvets. Merceress is the female counterpart.

**merchant:** One who bought or sold goods.

**miller:** One who ground corn. Corn in medieval England was a generic term for any kind of grain or seed.

**monk:** A member of a commune of other men sworn to poverty and celibacy. The practice of those two things varied greatly from individual to individual.

**physician:** A trained doctor who tended the sick. They attended and taught at the universities and were paid more than surgeons. Many of the better physicians were retained by the wealthy.

**poulterer:** One who dealt in poultry.

**prefect:** Governor or overseer in a variety of offices. Could govern a city, town, village, or manor.

**prelate:** A bishop or archbishop usually of noble birth, but sometimes rising from a wealthy middle-class family.

**priest:** One who performed public religious ceremonies.

**scribe:** Can mean a variety of things. One who interpreted the law. A clerk or secretary, or one who translated or copied manuscripts.

**scholar:** A university student. They were infamous for their licentiousness, purveyors of confidence scams, and as wastrels (good-for-nothings).

**seneschal:** Could be a steward, or a governor of a city, or a member of a high noble household who oversaw judicial matters.

**shepster:** Dressmaker.

**sheriff:** Oversaw the local court and was the chief administrator of the shire laws.

**spurrier:** One who made spurs.

**squire:** A servant or a youth of noble birth who assisted a knight.

**steward:** Overseer of the castle and demesne lands (land possessed by an individual, usually a lord).

**surgeon:** The practical doctor. The surgeon was responsible for bleeding, as well as for pulling teeth and other more grisly responsibilities that were too common for physicians to bother with.

**tailor:** One who cut cloth.

**tavern/innkeeper:** One who ran or owned a tavern or inn.

**vintner:** Maker of wine.

**weaving/weaver:** One who wove cloth; usually a woman, but there were also men in the industry.

## Upper Class

**abbot, abbat:** In charge of a monastery. Usually a man of noble birth.

**abbess, abbadise, abbas:** In charge of a nunnery or convent. Usually a woman of noble birth.

**archbishop:** Highest ranking bishop. Almost always a man of noble birth.

**baintighearnas:** Ladyship (Scottish Gaelic).

**banneret:** A military commander who led knights under his own emblem or banner.

**baron:** Tenant-in-chief who holds lands from the king or an overlord.

**baroness:** Wife or widow of a baron.

**baronet:** Nobles who don't have a title, but are members of the House of Lords.

**bishop:** Director of a diocese. Usually of noble birth.

**cardinal:** Member of the Pope's council. There are three ranks of cardinal: Cardinal Bishop, Cardinal Priest, and Cardinal Deacon.

**ceann-feadhna:** Chieftan (Scottish Gaelic).

**chieftan:** Ruler of a clan.

**countess:** Wife or widow of an earl.

**duchess:** Wife or widow of a duke.

**duke:** Title for relatives of the royal family.

**earl/eorl:** Highest of the nobility (not of the royalty).

**jarl:** A Norse or Danish chief or underking.

**jarless:** The wife of a jarl.

**kim:** Ruler of chief (Celtic term).

**king:** Ruler of a kingdom. Referred to as Your Grace or Sire.

**knight:** In the early part of the Middle Ages, they were seen as lowborn thugs (even if they came from a noble family). It wasn't until the eleventh century that they began to gain respectability. And by the twelfth, they were almost always of noble family with noble lineage (either real or fabricated). Supposedly held to a higher standard of conduct, most knights tended to forget their vows and held the view that might makes right. Knights were the cavalry of the army or, in more modern terms, they were tanks. A fully armed knight was virtually indestructible, at least in the early part of the period. As time went on, special weapons were designed to neutralize them such as canons, handguns, and estocs (thin knives designed to slip between the plates or rings of metal).

**knight-errant:** Wandering knight in search of adventure.

**lady:** A courtesy title given to any female of noble birth. If she was single and had no property of her own, her name was styled Lady *First Name*, for example, Lady Alice. If she was married or widowed, she could be called Lady Alice, or Lady *Her Lands/Castle* (Lady Nottingham or Lady of Nottingham).

**laird:** Scottish term for a leader or nobleman who held lands directly from the king. He was usually styled as *The Clan Name* (The MacDougal).

**lairdess:** Wife of a laird.

**lord:** A courtesy title given to any male of noble birth whether he had land or not. If he was without land, he was simple Lord *First Name*, for example Lord Stephen. If he had land, he could be Lord Stephen or Lord *His Land/Castle* (Lord Nottingham or Lord of Nottingham).

**miles:** Attached to the end of a knight's name as a designation of his status (French term).

**mother superior:** Title of an abbess.

**pope:** The head of the Catholic Church. Almost always came from noble families (or, at the very least, extremely wealthy middle class).

**prince:** Son of a king, or husband of a queen. In conversations, he was called Your Highness.

**princess:** Daughter of a king or wife of a prince. She was referred to as Your Highness.

**queen:** Wife of a king or a female ruler. She was referred to as Your Grace or Your Royal Grace. If she had children and/or if the king was dead, she would probably be called Queen-Mother. If the king were alive, she was properly called Queen-Consort. The basic title Queen meant a woman who ruled in her own right.

**sir:** Title attached to the name of a knight, clerk, or scribe.

**tighearnas:** Lordship (Scottish Gaelic).


## PUNISHMENTS

**amputation:** The removal of a body part, the exact one to be determined by the judge. Usually it was something that had to do with the crime, for example, a thief lost his hand, or a Peeping Tom lost an eye. However, this was not always the case, and any body part could be removed, for example, testicles, breasts, tongues, or ears. It is interesting to note that at one point in the Middle Ages, this was such a common punishment that people who had accidentally lost body parts such as eyes, ears, and/or limbs would carry certified notes that assured people that they were the victims of an unfortunate accident or battle rather than criminals.

**banishment:** This was used for treason or just about any crime when the judge or king didn't want a convicted person hanging around their territory. Banishment was most often used with noblemen and women, but could also be used for those in lesser positions. The duration of the banishment would depend on the crime and position of the convict. At one point, it became quite fashionable to force people to take pilgrimages to specific holy shrines, or to force them to walk from shrine to shrine until the saints forgave them for their crime. Just how did one know when the saints had forgiven them? The chains they were supposed to wear supposedly fell from their arms or legs. It was often reported as a type of advertisement for shrines just how many prisoners had gained their freedom while visiting such and such church or relic.

**beheading:** Reserved for capital crimes, it was accomplished by a variety of means, the most common of which was with the convicted person's head being placed on a stool or block and an axe being used to strike off their head. In other cases, a sword was used to whack off the head of the convicted felon while they knelt before their executioner. Some countries had laws that only allowed so many strokes to complete the deed. If the person survived, they were set free, but more often than not, it resulted in a long, painful death for the convicted while they slowly bled to death from their wounds. It was also customary for the head to be placed on a pike and publicly displayed for a designated amount of time.

**blinding:** Prescribed for various crimes, including robbery, rape, and so on. It involved having one or both eyes gouged out.

**boiling:** A person was placed inside a large cauldron and literally boiled alive.

**branding:** This involved having a red-hot iron placed against the naked skin. In some countries there were specific designs to designate what crime had caused the brand to be given.

**burning:** This is most often associated with heresy and witchcraft, though it should be noted that it wasn't the usual punishment in the Middle Ages for witchcraft. Hanging had that dubious honor. It was, however, used for various crimes such as treason, rape, and abduction.

**cucking stool or ducking stool:** A punishment chair used to confine a person for public humiliation where they were either set in the town square or led through town. Also used for dunking in water. Usually reserved for prostitutes, witches, heretics, scolds, disorderly women or fraudulent tradespeople.

**dungeon:** A room where the accused was kept in a near-naked or naked state and forced to live on three morsels of bread and three draughts of stagnant water. The accused was always denied light and some of them were kept inside with a board and weight placed on their chest.

**embowelling, disembowelling (most commonly referred to as drawn or drawing):** The removing of organs. This was usually performed on people who were awake and very conscious of what was being done to them.

**excommunication:** This was the trump card of the Church and was used for all manner of crimes, petty and large. It meant that the person couldn't attend mass or have any sort of benediction from the Church. In the later Middle Ages, one couldn't marry while under this, nor could one receive the last rites or confess their sins.

**fine:** Most punishments could be commuted to a fee penalty, which meant that the rich seldom paid physically for their crimes. Those who couldn't scrape together enough money, or those accused of the severe crimes that couldn't be commuted to fines, suffered the full torture of the court.

**flagellation:** Flogging. This was used for most any crime and as a way to induce confessions. The exact whip took on a variety of forms, from just a simple leather whip to one laced with shards of glass or steel spikes.

**garrotting:** This involved having the convicted person strangled with a cord by an executioner. It was the chosen means of Spanish execution, but can also be found in other countries.

**hamstringing:** This involved cutting the convicted person's hamstrings, thus crippling them. It was used commonly for robbery and prostitution, and as a means of compelling testimony.

**hanging:** One of the most common forms of execution. It was usually done at crossroads in order to gain the widest audience. Those executed were often left hanging until their bodies decomposed.

**hung, drawn, and quartered:** The convicted felon was hung until they were barely alive (in the event they passed out, they were revived), then they were disemboweled and what remained of their body was cut into four pieces and buried in four parts of the city, town, or village.

**impaling:** This was performed either with a red-hot poker or stake being driven through the rectum. In some cases, the convicted person was placed on a greased pole and they struggled to remain above the stake as long as they could. Invariably, they would lose their fight and be impaled. Again, it was customary to leave those impaled on public display.

**imprisonment:** Imprisonment wasn't used through much of the Middle Ages, but in time it did become more and more fashionable. It should be noted that many of those imprisoned were usually political hostages who were too valuable to kill, more than they were people who had actually committed crimes. Where a person was imprisoned would depend on who they were and why they were being detained. Many political hostages were kept in lush towers with servants and some of the lesser noble, rich, or middle class were kept half naked in dungeons. (This was also a method of keeping rich Jews until their relatives could pay ransom.)

**iron boot:** Fit to cover either the leg and foot, or just the foot, it allowed wood or wedges to be hammered into specific places of the feet of those being questioned. It was a favored device of the Inquisition.

**judicial duel or trial by combat:** Fought on foot or on horseback, it involved numerous weapons. The choice of weapon would depend on local custom, which would stipulate it was the accuser's choice or a predetermined choice decided by the accused's social status and/or alleged crime. Not only could the accuser or accused demand a trial by combat, but they could also challenge any witness who testified. Throughout most of the Middle Ages, women, physically infirmed people, children, and clerics were not banned from participating, and there are several cases of them having to take arms against trained men. Although it should be noted that most courts did allow them to choose a champion to fight in their stead. There were also champions for hire, but it was a dangerous occupation since, for most of the Middle Ages, the champion shared whatever punishment the accused was given, for example, death, amputation, or dismemberment.

**ordeal by boiling water:** The defendant was ordered to fast and pray for three days. When the day arrived, a mass was held and a priest oversaw the event. A single ordeal was used by those accused of minor offenses. In this, the accused had to plunge his hand up to the wrist and, in some cases, retrieve a stone or ring from a kettle of boiling water. In the event of a triple ordeal (used in more serious offenses), the accused had to plunge his arm up to the elbow. The wound was then bound and sealed with a judge's signet. After three days, the wound was examined and if it bore no sign of burns or scalding, the defendant was released. If the burn was evident, then the accused was convicted.

**ordeal by cold water:** The accused was bound by both hands and feet. A piece of rope with a knot was attached to her midsection, and the accused was lowered into the water. If the accused and the knot floated, then she was adjudged guilty. But if the accused and the knot sank, she was innocent.

**ordeal by fire:** The three-day preparation was identical to an ordeal by boiling water. After three days, a woman who was suspected of adultery was forced to place her naked foot against six, nine, or twelve red-hot ploughshares. In other cases, the accused was blindfolded and made to walk across the red-hot ploughshares. However, the most common form of punishment in an ordeal by fire was for the accused to walk nine feet while carrying a red-hot lump of iron. For minor offenses, the hot iron weighed a pound, but for treason, secret murder, counterfeiting, robbery, or any other felony, the weight was three pounds. Upon completion, the wounds were wrapped for three days and then examined. If the wound was still intact, he was guilty. If no wound was evident, he was innocent.

**oubliette:** A tight-fitting hole that allowed those imprisoned in it to neither sit nor stand, forcing them to endure an uncomfortable position of complete torture. There are two arguments for the name, which is obviously derived from the French verb *oublier*, meaning "to forget." One argument is that it was a place to put someone you wanted to forget; the other is that those put inside an oubliette would quickly forget their sanity.

**outlawry:** This was used to punish those who fled before they could be tried. What it meant was that the accused was no longer entitled to the benefits of the law, and anyone who came across that person should hunt her down like a wolf. A standard fee of five shillings would be paid to the outlaw's killer, and anyone could kill an outlaw with immunity. Any lands owned by the outlaw would be forfeited.

**pilgrimage:** Due to the high cost of imprisoning someone, this became a fashionable way to get rid of the undesirables. They were condemned for a certain time to walk from shrine to shrine. If the crime was severe, they would be forced to pilgrimage until they died. The only reprieve from this life sentence was if one of the saints took pity and the convict's chains miraculously fell from him. Since this didn't happen very often (to say the least), the propensity to hand out this type of sentence made the roads very dangerous for everyday people and other pilgrims. This is the reason that group pilgrimages and caravans became very popular.

**pillory:** This had two forms. One was simply stocks placed on a pillar for better display. The other consisted of manacles and an iron circle around the neck that held the person to a pillar. It was used for any number of crimes, including adultery, perjury, public drunkenness, spousal abuse, and others. It allowed the convict to be ridiculed, abused, and molested by anyone passing by. This made female convicts particularly susceptible to rape.

**pulled apart:** This was used for more severe crimes, including abduction (which was called raptus or rape regardless of whether the woman was physically violated), treason, murder, and other such larger crimes. It usually consisted of a person having each of his limbs tied to separate horses. The horses were then whipped into a run, resulting in the person being pulled apart limb from limb.

**pulley (a.k.a. squassation):** Another popular implement of the Inquistion. The victim of this torture had his hands tied above his head, and his feet were tied to the floor or the bottom of a frame. A set of weights was then attached to rope holding his hands and then dropped suddenly. This would disjoint the arms and/or legs of the victim.

**quartered:** The person was cut into four pieces and buried in four sections of the town. The thinking behind this practice was that on Judgment Day, the person wouldn't be whole and would therefore be denied entrance into Paradise.

**rack:** An iron or wooden frame where victims were placed for interrogation. Pulleys would allow the victim to be stretched to unbearable degrees. It was another favorite of the Inquisition.

**sanctuary:** Any criminal, regardless of his deed or sentence, was given sanctuary by the Church if he could make it to Holy Ground. Any person who violated this code by dragging the felon out was excommunicated.

**stocks:** Essentially, a thick board with a large hole in the center and two smaller holes on the left and right. A cut bisected the board lengthwise through the center of the holes, allowing the top to be raised and a convict's head and hands inserted. The top was then brought back down and locked into place, securing the convict. Sometimes holes for the feet were also included. This was commonly used for any crime, especially misdemeanors. Like the pillory, it placed the convict on public display for ridicule, abuse, and molestation by the citizenry.

**water torture:** The accused was either dunked into water repeatedly or had a large amount of water poured over his face.

**wergild (a.k.a. wergeld):** In England, the amount of money owed a victim's family by a murderer. The amount was on a fixed scale relative to the victim's social position. In tribes where money was scarce, the payment was made in cattle or other livestock.

## TRADE AND BARTER

Though it is a common belief that everyone in the Dark Ages bartered, this has been proven false. Archeologists have uncovered proof that a monetary system remained in place throughout the entire medieval period, even in the early centuries after the collapse of Rome. Those with enough coins were always able to buy luxury items and the collection of coins was quite prevalent. Wages continued to be paid.

---

However, those who were poor did barter. In fact, this helped found the whole feudal world, wherein one traded work for protection or some similar service. Of course, this is a gross oversimplification; even in the earliest times, those who had coins could pay instead of work.

Peasants were allowed to work their land as long as they either provided their landowner with a certain amount of work or a certain amount of their produce or, in some cases, both. Whatever was left over was either sold or traded for what they needed. Many peasants also took on side jobs as servants or peddlers to make ends meet. One common way to earn extra money was in rounding up hawks and falcons that had escaped mews or jesses and returning them to their lords, who often paid a tidy reward.

Some peasants were lucky enough to escape their poverty by becoming members of the Church (though most were banned from high office) or by entering apprenticeships. However, it should be noted that most apprenticeships went to those of the merchant class. Apprentices usually began their training between the ages of five and seven. Their parents negotiated a contract with their master for how long the apprentice would serve and be trained in a particular trade.

Most tradesman chose to have their children trained in the same profession, though there are some cases of them choosing complementary trades. For example, a dressmaker might have a daughter or son trained as a silk weaver or capper.

Many women were employed as sellers and laborers, but their pay was usually substantially lower than their male counterparts. Most women tended to work for family members, and those who were apprenticed seldom went to work for themselves.

Most women married another in their profession and went to work in his store. Though some women did attain high rank in the guilds, almost all women were banned from holding office or voting on guild matters. However, it should be noted that if a guild member died, his wife could continue to run his shop until the day she remarried.

Fairs and markets were important aspects of both guild life and medieval life in general. Some fairs were biannual or annual events, while others ran continuously. Merchants, entertainers, and the like would gather in a designated area and sell goods and services to their patrons. These fairs were also good places for thieves, prostitutes, and cutpurses to make money.

If the market was set in a town, where a person set up his shop was usually highly regulated. Tanners, butchers, fishmongers, and others who had smelly or distasteful jobs tended to be segregated out of the other districts and usually located downwind of the town. One area might be set up for clothiers and those selling textiles, while another area would be all the metalworking trades. And, of course, those of ill repute would be confined to their own district.

The key to fantasy world-building is that the layout of the story, the monetary system, the laws, et al are completely up to you, the writer. However, these elements must make sense, or the reader will become frustrated or confused by the gaps in your logic. For this reason, you may want to choose a real setting such as medieval England or ancient Rome and alter it to fit your needs and ideas.

# CHAPTER 6

# Fantasy Races

## by Andrew P. Miller and Daniel Clark

Any attempt to survey the multitude of races that exist in legend and imaginative literature is open to criticism of being incomplete in some areas and too inclusive in others. The obvious dilemma is the question of how one defines a "race" in fantastic literature and legend. In reference to humans, the term *race* is fraught with political and cultural implications; in general, it refers to similarities and differences in certain physical characteristics like skin color, facial form, or eye shape. Political and cultural affinity factor into the debate as well and are sometimes more important than an individual's particular genetic heritage. But humans as a group are far more similar in appearance than the groups that populate the landscape of the imagination. Bushmen and Celts are virtually indistinguishable in comparison to the differences between merfolk and trolls. But just as with defining human races, there are considerations beyond the physical that enter into the issue. It's not just a question of which arbitrary physical features to consider since the differences in these imaginative beings are long established; it's really a question of what distinguishes a fantastic *race* from a fantastic *creature*.

The terms *race* and *creature* suggest differences, and one difference is in total population in a group. It's easy to see that a unique being like the Hawaiian shark man is a creature and not a race. Or that rare beings like the rocs are creatures and do not constitute a race. But there is a qualitative difference between the way groups of beings, like elves and giant squids, are portrayed in fantastic stories that has to do with a metaphysical hierarchy. It's not merely a question of humanoid shape; elves are obviously patterned on humans—often they are more diminutive and more beautiful than the average human—and giant squids are patterned on their smaller counterparts in the real animal kingdom, but what about the Yahoos and Houyhnhnms of Jonathan Swift's *Gulliver's Travels?* The Houyhnhnms, outwardly equine in shape, have a complex society and appreciate art and intellectual pursuits, whereas the Yahoos, outwardly human in shape, have no language and live in packs in the forest like wild dogs. Obviously, similarity to human shape is not the most important factor in determining the difference in race and creature.

As *Gulliver's Travels* points out, we must not be too anthropomorphically bigoted when we determine where various groups rank on the Great Chain of Being in fantastic stories. Instead, we tend to be prejudiced by the nonphysical attributes and values of humans. For our purposes in this chapter—and this seems to hold generally true for the body of fantastic literature and legend—we define race using the following criteria:

- Physical Similarity: This one is pretty obvious. Elves look like elves, dwarves like dwarves.

- Population: It can't be a unique being and still be called a member of a race. Now there can be exceptions to this; Tolkien, at the end of *The Trilogy of the Ring,* suggests that the fantastic races are slowly dying out and humans replacing them. A writer could create a scenario in which a being is the last of her kind, but the implication is that there once were many more.

- Procreation: The ability to create offspring. This also implies gender, sexual relationships, children, and familial groups.

- Reason: Call it intellect, intelligence, thought, rationality, sentience, awareness. Members of a race, by virtue of not being creatures or animals, are capable of forethought, of being motivated by needs and desires that are not purely physical.

- Culture: Call it culture, call it society, call it politics. A culture is constituted of beings with common beliefs, values, traditions, art, and language—all things that involve needs separate from the purely physical and that arise from social and political relationships.

Of the five criteria, the latter two seem to be the most crucial in determining whether a fantastic being is a creature or a member of a race. To return to the example from *Gulliver's Travels*, the Houyhnhnms clearly qualify as a race—one that embodies what we would normally consider to be all the best virtues of humans. The Yahoos, however human in appearance, are merely animals to be controlled and used for their brute strength as draft animals.

The technique that Swift employs, that of elevation, is one way of doing something new or unusual in the fantasy genre. Stories of the fantastic are so old that it is often difficult for a writer to do something unique in such well-worn territory. By elevating horses and reducing humans, Swift makes a striking social statement about human society. Richard Adams employs elevation beautifully with rabbits in *Watership Down* and *Tales From Watership Down*. The rabbits have a complex social structure, politics, art, and even religion and myth. But both writers are using mundane creatures, not fantastic ones. The irony is that the fantastic races—elves, dwarves, giants, and the like—have become morbidly clichéd in fantastic literature. Many writers have dealt with this problem by using elevation as Swift and Adams did, or by employing humor or parody. In some cases, writers have adapted fantastic races to fit into contemporary or science fiction settings. Other times writers adapt an existing legendary race into a new race. In the rest of this chapter, we hope to help writers overcome this problem by offering some different perspectives on the "standard" races, suggesting some techniques for avoiding the cliché, and proposing new arenas from which to draw inspiration.

## DWARVES

In physical appearance, **DWARVES** are short in stature, much shorter than humans, and sometimes they are misshapen, with heads or shoulders disproportionally larger than a human's. They tend to be bearded, and are identified with the underworld, whether as their home or as a place they frequent (since dwarves are quite often miners). In Norse mythology, dwarves lived in the caves of Nidavellir. The dwarves in Norse mythology were also exquisite craftsmen, often making magical items. The dwarves Brokk and Eitri made such treasures as Mjollnir, the hammer of Thor that always returned to his hand; Gullinbursti, a boar with golden bristles that could travel over air, sea and earth; and Draupnir, the gold armband that on every ninth night, produced eight more rings just like it. This is similar to the fairy tale of Rumplestiltskin, who could spin straw into gold. Dwarves usually have reputations for being helpful, though they could wreak revenge on hapless mortals who wronged them.

Tolkien (with possible exception of Disney's seven dwarves) again provides the standard by which dwarves have been seen in fantasy literature. Tolkien's dwarves are drawn from the Norse legends as well. The dwarves of Middle-earth were workers of metals and stone. At the height of their glory, they crafted magical and mechanical wonders and lived in a mountain stronghold complete with secret doors that couldn't be distinguished from the side of the mountain. Physically, the dwarves were short, stocky, and had beards of different colors, including, at least in one case, blue! Middle-earth dwarves also had a tendency to sing; when Bilbo Baggins first meets dwarves in *The Hobbit*, they make up a song about him. Tolkien's dwarves could also be fierce warriors.

In his Discworld novels, Terry Pratchett uses parody to play on several clichés about dwarves, particularly those established by Tolkien. In their native lands, Pratchett's dwarves are miners and usually dwell in subterranean caverns. This goes along with many old ideas of dwarves. Pratchett's dwarves seem fairly typical, even to the description of the dwarves as being short humanoids with heavy beards. Of course, both sexes have heavy beards and sometimes even the dwarves can't tell each other apart. But Pratchett's dwarves also move into the city, particularly the unique city of Ankh-Morpork. In the city, the dwarves tend to adopt barbarian names and pretend to be sword-carrying warriors. They have dwarf restaurants specializing in various rat dishes. Like Tolkien's dwarves, Pratchett's dwarves have a penchant for song. In fact, they gather at night in low-ceilinged dwarf bars to sing their songs, all of which have the same words: "Gold, gold, gold, gold ... " Additionally, Pratchett's dwarves have also turned the culinary arts into a military art; a good loaf of dwarf bread can be used as a cudgel, shield, or projectile weapon.

## ELVES

One of the most common fantasy races in legend and literature is the race of **ELVES**. They appear in a variety of fairy tales such as "The Shoemaker and the Elves" and have different appearances according to different legends. Many elves are portrayed as tall and bewitchingly beautiful, but they are sometimes classed among the more general "little people" or fairies and are small in size. (This is the image of the pointy-eared elf, usually dressed in forest green.)

In whatever form, elves tend to have magical abilities. Some elves are considered to be benevolent spirits, such as "Light Elves," while others are considered malevolent, or "Dark Elves." In the Norse myths and stories told in the *Elder Edda* and other works, light elves lived in Alfheim, a realm near Asgard and Vanaheim, the lands where the Norse gods lived. Dark elves lived in Svartalfheim, a realm somewhere below Midgard, or Earth. Norse dark elves had little distinction from Norse dwarves. In fairy tales, many elves seem to be amoral. They like playing tricks and having fun and don't particularly care about the consequences.

In fantasy literature, J.R.R. Tolkien drew upon such legends, particularly the Norse legends, setting the standard (and the eventual cliché) for the depiction of noble light elves. Tolkien's elves were tall, elegant, with an unearthly beauty. When the elf-lord Glorfindel was first seen by the hobbit Frodo in *The Fellowship of the Ring*, "it appeared that a white light was shining through the form and raiment of [Glorfindel] as if through a veil." The elves of Middle-earth were artisans, scholars, and musicians, and had taught men language and other skills. They controlled power and magic and were a force for good; an elven blade was anathema to dark forces. Elven horses were faster than other horses and never let a rider fall. Most of the elves were magnificent and benevolent beings who looked out for the well-being of all in Middle-earth. However, in *The Hobbit*, Bilbo and company run into a group of elves that sang from the trees whom the dwarves considered foolish. In later books on Middle-earth, the elves were defined into specific subgroups, explaining the differences between them.

Andre Norton, in her classic Witch World series, adapts the legends of the elves differently. One of the countries of the Witch World is Escore, whose most powerful native is Dahuan, Lady of the Green Silences. The Lady has many magical abilities and her form constantly shifts. While she can leave the Valley of Green Silences, her power is definitely tied to the land and she is powerless when away from it. Norton adapted elves and fairies and threw in a dose of nymphs as well to create Dahuan. Perhaps, since Norton was well read in fairy tales, this Lady of the Green Silences was an adaptation of the Green Ladies, tree elves that could be found in certain trees (much like nymphs). Like the Green Ladies, Dahuan had power over trees as do her **GREEN PEOPLE OF THE VALLEY**. Unlike Dahuan, however, Green Ladies had dark purposes in many English folktales.

In *Stalking the Unicorn*, Mike Resnick does two things to make his elves noncliché. First, he puts the elves in a modern, urban setting, even if it isn't quite an urban setting we're used to. Resnick's elves live in an alternate Manhattan, one that exists out of the corner of the eye where they drive colored elephants though the streets in lieu of cabs. Resnick also uses parody to make fun of the elf cliché. In that book, John Justin Mallory, a Manhattan detective, is hired by Murgensturm, an elf, to find a unicorn. Murgensturm is indeed green with pointy ears but he has some other unusual characteristics, not the least of which is his almost insatiable sexual appetite. Mallory and Murgensturm square off against a demon and a treacherous leprechaun named Flypaper Gillespie. The whole book takes a humorous look at many fantasy races.

## FAIRIES

The term **FAIRY** (sometimes spelled faery) tends to be a general designation that applies to a wide variety of beings known alternately as the **LITTLE PEOPLE** or the **FAIR FOLK**. Fairies have different shapes and can appear to mortals in different forms, usually that of a beautiful male or female. Some fairies are small, winged, and female (like Tinkerbell), while others are closer to human stature. Fairies have a variety of abilities, one of the most powerful being that of the "glamour," which allows them to fool humans with illusions. Fairies have their own sense of what is proper and polite, and the smallest slight can result in a fairy punishment on a hapless mortal.

Fairies usually are found living in mounds or fairy hills, which are occasionally accessible to mortals. In most legends, time flows differently in fairy realm—one hour there may equal a year in our world! Mortals who partake of fairy food are usually stranded forever in the land of fairy, for mortal food will never again sustain them. Fairies do have some dealings with mortals, particularly in the custom of the changeling. Fairies will steal human children and leave one of their own or a doll in exchange for the child. Morgan le Fey, of Arthurian legend, was supposed to be part fairy.

Shakespeare's *A Midsummer Night's Dream* is an early literary use of the fairy. In Shakespeare's play, Oberon and Titania are king and queen of the fairies. They also meddle in mortal affairs. These ideas of Shakespeare's were recently updated by Neil Gaiman in the comic book *The Sandman*. In the comic book, Morpheus, the personification of Dream, makes a pact with Shakespeare. He will give Shakespeare ideas in exchange for two plays, one of which is *A Midsummer Night's Dream*. Dream commissions this play as entertainment for King Auberon and Queen Titania. The court of fairy arrives on earth to see Shakespeare's play, and members of fairy appear throughout the comic book series.

Gaiman also takes readers through the world of fairy in the comic book limited series *The Books of Magic*. In the first limited series, Tim Hunter is destined to become the world's greatest magician. As such, he is taken on journeys to be shown magic. One of these journeys is to the realm of fairy, where he goes to the fairy market and is offered his heart's desire for a year of his life. He also meets Queen Titania, who tries to trap the young boy into being her servant for the rest of his life.

*The Books of Magic* was continued as an ongoing series by John Ney Reiber. The fairies, especially Titania and Auberon, play major roles through-out the series. Tim Hunter has many interactions with the fairy, especially since Titania claims to be his mother and the authors keep developing this as a subplot. He also has an adventure in which he has to save Auberon from an enchantment after the fairy king journeys to earth. In a later story line, Tim's girlfriend Molly finds herself trapped in fairy and becomes the rival of a vengeful Titania. Molly eats a berry grown in fairy and ceases to be human. After their appearances in *The Books of Magic*, Titania and Auberon were featured in their own limited comic book series called *The Book of Faery*. That series detailed the mortal origins of the fairy queen and how she became both queen and mother.

Throughout these series, the authors take a look at the race of fairy and incorporate the legends into the story lines and mythos that they are creating.

By creating political and personal intrigues as well as giving individual fairies personalities, they breathe new life into the little people. It should also be noted that both authors use other myths and folklore in their writings, and blend them with contemporary themes and story lines.

Julian May's *Saga of Pliocene Exile* does something completely different with the fairy race; her series is a time travel story. In the future era of the Great Milieu, people who do not fit in with the galactic society can choose to be exiled back into Earth's Pliocene era by a one-way time machine. The story focuses on a group that chooses such a path. However, once they arrive in the past, they find Earth inhabited by the **TANU**, an extraterrestrial race that has been exiled to Earth from their own galaxy. The Tanu are beautiful, exceptionally tall humanoids who wear golden torques around their necks to amplify their latent psychic abilities. The Tanu possess such powers as telekinesis, telepathy, mental coercion, and illusion casting. Their illusions— **GLAMOURS**—can bewitch or bedevil the average human. In fact, the Tanu keep most of the humans as slaves or servants this way.

The descriptions of the Tanu match legends of the fairy found in many European mythologies. For example, May uses the notion of the fairy rade in her story. According to European legend, the fairy rade was an elegant procession of the best of fairy bedecked in their fineries and jewels. May's version is the flying hunt, during which the Tanu hunt Pliocene creatures, using their telekinetic powers to fly and their illusion-casting powers to make themselves beautiful. According to May's account, the Tanu *are* the origin of the legends of the fairy rade and all fairy legends.

## GIANTS

**GIANTS** have appeared in various forms and mythologies throughout the world. In Greek mythology, the **TITANS** were the children of Gaea, Mother Earth, and Uranus, the Heavenly Sky. They were of gigantic stature and each Titan governed a certain realm, such as Oceanus over the ocean. Cronus led them but was eventually dethroned by his children, led by the god Zeus. Gaea also gave birth to other giants such as the one-eyed **CYCLOPES** and giants that had one hundred arms and fifty heads. (The multiheaded giants had been imprisoned by their father and the Titans never released them after

Cronus came to power. Because of this, they helped Zeus and the gods defeat the Titans.) Another race of giants sprang from Uranus's blood when he was killed by Cronus. They were also defeated by the gods. Antaeus was a giant who was building a temple out of skulls. As long as he touched the earth, he was unbeatable. Hercules held him in the air and strangled him.

Norse mythology has even more stories about giants. The **ROCK** and **FROST GIANTS** lived in Jotunheim and often battled the gods; at Ragnarok, the giants were to rise up against the gods to aid in the destruction of the world. The thunder god Thor was the chief enemy of the giants. However, some gods, like Freyr, married giants. Loki, god of mischief, also wedded a giantess and produced three terrible offspring: the monstrous Fenris Wolf; Jorgumund the Midgard Serpent; and Hel, the goddess of the dead. Several individual giants held importance. Ymir was the first giant, the father of the frost giants, and was formed from fire and ice. Odin and his brothers killed Ymir and created the world from this body. Surt or (Surtur) was the giant who ruled over Muspel, the land of fire. At Ragnarok, he will set fire to the world. Utgard-Loki was a king of the frost giants. Skilled in magic and trickery, he beguiled Loki and Thor into degrading contests while they were in his realm.

Giants also appear briefly in the book of Genesis: "There were giants in the earth in those days ... " And, of course, Goliath was the giant slain by David. Fairy tales have their giants as well, with "Jack and the Beanstalk" being one of the best known. Giants, as they most often appear, are malevolent creatures who seldom bear goodwill toward humans. They may possess magical abilities and often hoard magical items and treasure.

Stephen Donaldson, in his *Chronicles of Thomas Covenant: The Unbeliever*, uses giants effectively as a race, through they are not the villains. They are denizens of the Land, the world that Donaldson creates. They help Thomas Covenant in his journeys, particularly when he sets off to find the One Tree. The giants are a seafaring race who travel in stone ships. They have names that reflect their occupations, such as Saltheart Foamfollower. These giants are a noble and majestic race who stand as allies with the forces of good against the evil Lord Foul.

## GOBLINS AND ORCS

**GOBLINS** appear in many folk and fairy tales as mischievous creatures, bewitching and tormenting men. Goblins in folk tales often wear caps and are depicted as misshapen and bowed little people. They are associated with the earth, live among tree roots and cracks in rocks, and are meddlesome but not usually dangerous.

Tolkien's goblins are more extreme than the mischief-making sprites of legend. His goblins infest the tunnels and mountains of Middle-earth. Like dwarves, they can make things and dig tunnels. Unlike dwarves, the things they make are seldom beautiful and are usually dangerous. The goblins and dwarves were ancient enemies, most likely because they inhabited the same areas. Tolkien's goblins are misshapen and quick, or at least quicker than dwarves, and can manipulate rock. When they attack Bilbo and the dwarves in *The Hobbit*, they appear out of a crack in the cave wall and then seal it behind them as they leave. Tolkien's goblins are also more dangerous to human, dwarf, and hobbit, perfectly willing to take their enemies' lives. Tolkien also used the goblin race as a basis for his orcs.

**ORCS** had been mentioned in folklore before Tolkien, but the term "orc" was usually given to sea beasts or sea serpents with sharp teeth that preyed on whales (the term becoming *orca*). Tolkien changed the orc into a type of goblin, keeping the sharp teeth and giving them broad faces and slanting eyes. Tolkien's orcs live underground, battling dwarves for caves, and can only come out at night or when the sun doesn't shine, for most of them cannot stand the sun's rays. They were the evil servants of Sauron, the Dark Lord in Tolkien's world.

Like she did with the fairy, Julian May adapts the goblin legend to fit her science fiction universe. The Tanu's enemies are the **FIRVULAG**, or the little people. The Firvulag come in many different shapes and sizes, and their different appearances are reminiscent of goblins, kobolds, trolls, and occasionally giants. The Firvulag also possess a wide variety of psychic abilities, though they usually don't possess the power of their Tanu cousins. Chief among their psychic abilities is the power to cast illusions. The Firvulag are often referred to as the shape-changers because they are adept at illusion. They engage the Tanu in ritualistic battles.

Actually, both groups are part of the same "bimorphic" race and had arrived on earth together in their spaceship. May even throws in the legendary fairy anathema to iron in her creation of her exotic races: Both the Tanu and the Firvulag are vulnerable to the metal. She gives this a genetic rationale instead of a magical one.

## HALF-LINGS AND HYBRIDS

**HOBBITS**, Tolkien's most famous creation, are adaptations. Tolkien calls them **HALF-LINGS**, and they resemble various little people from legend. They range from about two to four feet high, averaging about three feet. In Middle-earth, this is smaller than dwarves. They seldom wear shoes since they have tough soles like leather and curly hair covering the tops of their feet. The most common color for their hair is brown. When they wish, they can move almost silently through the forest. They wear brightly colored clothes and enjoy drinking tea and smoking pipes. They frequently live in comfortable holes tunneled into hills, although they eventually move into small cottages.

Half-lings started appearing in other works as well, sometimes resembling hobbits and sometimes as creatures that were half human and half some other creature, basically hybrids between the human race and a fantastic race. In Terry Brooks's *The Sword of Shannara*, for example, the hero Shea is a half elf.

## MERFOLK

Water-breathing races have appeared in a variety of legends. The Greeks had their sea nymphs, the Nereids. Triton, the son of Poseidon and the Nereid Amphitrite, had the tail of a fish. In fact, his name became a generic term to describe men with the body of a man and the tail of a fish. More commonly, these legends developed into the tales of **MERMAIDS** and **MERMEN**, whose chief characteristic as a race is their half-fish forms and their ability to live underwater but not on land. Mermaids sometimes had a reputation for mischief if not disaster. Though some mermaids gave up their tails to join men on land, there are also stories of mermaids dragging mortal men beneath the waves to join them. Other times, mermaids caused shipwrecks, especially if one had fallen in love with a sailor. Hans Christian Andersen's "The Little Mermaid" is probably the most famous tale of merfolk. In his classic story, the little mermaid trades her voice for legs and the chance to win a mortal husband. Of course, the original tale does not have the happy ending the Disney version put on it.

Andre Norton offers a different spin on water-breathing races. Living in the Witch World's Escore are the **KROGAN**, who dwell in the waters of their world. They are mostly human in appearance with some noticeable differences. The Krogan have webbed feet and hands, pale glistening skin, and gills in their necks. They possess their own type of magic as well. They may not have the tails of fishes, but their water-dwelling habitats suggest the legends of the merfolk and possibly those of river gods, naiads, and other water-dwelling spirits.

## TROLLS

Similar to giants, **TROLLS** are popular bad guys in legends. When Thor was not fighting giants, he was often off fighting trolls. Trolls are often large in size though not as large as giants. They are associated with rocks and being rocklike in both durability and intelligence. According to some legends, trolls turn to stone if they are struck by sunlight. Trolls usually live in caves or mountains, though sometimes they dwell under bridges and accost innocent goats.

J.R.R. Tolkien provides a variety of trolls. In *The Hobbit*, Bilbo and the dwarves encounter three trolls in the woods. These trolls have heavy faces, tree-trunk-sized legs, and vulgar mouths. They are named William, Bert, and Tom and plan on eating the dwarves, a race the trolls despise. Luckily, Tolkien's trolls have the legendary weakness to sunlight and the group tricks them into arguing until dawn, at which point they are turned to stone. In the later tales of Middle-earth, trolls are the servants of evil, scaled creatures with skin as hard as rock. Sauron, the Dark Lord, changed them for this purpose.

Robert Asprin, in his Myth Adventures series, updates the cliché through humor and parody. The series' hero is Skeeve, an apprentice magician. One of his companions is the beautiful Tananda. She has gold skin and green hair, and hails from the dimension of Trollia, where the men are trolls and the women are trollops. Besides working with the pun, Asprin also works with the stereotypes. Tananda may be built like a brick castle, but she is smart, witty, and a competent assassin. Her brother, Chumley, is first introduced as the gigantic, dull-witted "Big Crunch" with "scraggly hair, long-rubbery limbs, and a misshapen face." He picks up Skeeve and says, "Crunch likes little persons.

Crunch likes little persons better than Big Macs." But he soon drops the cliché troll persona to show an eloquent, thoughtful, shy, caring person beneath the troll's frightening outer appearance. Chumley is also a vegetarian.

Terry Pratchett also plays with the idea of trolls. Instead of turning to rock when exposed to sunlight, Pratchett's trolls are already made of rock. More specifically, they are silicon life-forms with rock bodies, diamond teeth, and an appetite for minerals (and only occasionally people). Pratchett's trolls are mostly slow-witted (since they have rocks for brains), but some manage to go beyond that, especially when they move to the city. There, Chryophase the Troll is one of the leaders of the Ankh-Morpork crime syndicate.

In Pratchett's world, like Tolkien's, dwarves and trolls are natural enemies. They often tussle when they come into contact with each other in the city. However, in *Men at Arms*, a satire of modern human times, he has members of both races join the Ankh-Morpork City Watch in an affirmative action campaign, which had been partially brought on by the Silicon Anti-Defamation League. The outcome is hilarious, touching, and fresh.

## MINOR RACES

Other races appear with less frequency in legends and literature. **GNOMES** are similar to dwarves, though are usually depicted as having more human proportions than often misshapen dwarves. Like dwarves, gnomes generally live underground.

Mike Resnick plays with this idea in *Stalking the Unicorn*. His gnomes also live underground in the subways. The Gnomes of the Subway congregate at subway stops and eat subway tokens.

In his three books *Truckers, Diggers, and Wings* (collected as the *Bromeliad* by the Science Fiction Book Club), Terry Pratchett uses science fiction to update the gnome legends. Pratchett's Nomes look exactly like humans but are only four inches tall (much like Lilliputians). They have very short life spans (usually not living past their teens) but live accelerated lives, at least to humans. One group of Nomes makes its way into the Arnold Brothers store in London and meets the store Nomes. The store Nomes had thought themselves unique in the universe and, of course, the universe is the store. The Nomes had built a culture around the store including kingdoms and fiefdoms based

------------------------------------------------------------------------

on departments such as the Duke de Haberdasheri, Lord Protector of the Up Escalator and Knight of the Counter, and the Abbot of Stationeri. Eventually, they discover that they are not native to Earth and find their lost spaceship.

In Greek mythology, **CENTAURS** were half horse and half man. They were human from the waist up and a horse from the waist down. They were usually shown to be barbaric and savage, though the centaur Chiron tutored many of the great heroes of Greek mythology. Centaurs seemed particularly vulnerable to excesses of wine and found human women attractive. At the wedding of the King of Lapithae, a centaur got drunk and tried to abduct the bride. The hero Theseus, best known for killing the Minotaur, saved the bride by slaying the centaur. The centaur Nessus was responsible for the death of Hercules; when his wife, Deianira, suspected the hero of being unfaithful to her, she poisoned him with the centaur's blood.

In contemporary fantasy, Piers Anthony uses the centaurs as a race in his humorous Xanth series. He plays on both the belligerent aspects of the race as well as Chiron's tutorial scholarly activities. When the magician Dor goes back in time, he has to convince the somewhat savage centaurs to continue building a castle for the king. Later in the series, the young Dor is tutored by the centaur Cherie. He also recruits a centaur magician and scholar named Arnolde to help him travel into the mundane world (i.e., the world as we know it). In the "present" time frame of the series, centaurs are the scholars and poets of Xanth.

## NON-WESTERN RACES

Most fantasy novels feature magical races from Western or European mythologies and folktales. But of course, Europe does not have a monopoly on legendary races. Such races can be found in the folktales, myths, and stories of other cultures as well.

For instance, Hawaii has its own race of little people called the **MENE-HUNE**, and these little people resemble many of the fairy folk of Europe. The menehune were small in size, described as dwarves. They had supernatural abilities such as the ability to shape and cut rock with greater skill than any human hands could ever achieve. Most of their work was accomplished overnight, and never done during the day, such as building a great irrigation ditch that stretched for miles. They could also vanish into thin air. The king of the menehune sounds much like a leprechaun. In one tale, he was described as being dressed head to foot in brilliant green with a crown of emeralds. The menehune made deals with humans and instead of being paid in cream or honey, they were paid off in fish. At one time, the number of menehune was so vast that a line of them stretched for miles.

Other types of fairylike creatures appear across the world. Hindus knew of a type of fairy called **ASPARAS**, whom they believed lived in fig trees. Also called sky dancers, their appearance to mortals at turning points in their lives (such as weddings) was a blessing. Appearing to dying men on battlefields, they conveyed hope in the afterlife instead of fear. On occasion, asparas would use their charms to distract scholars from learning things they shouldn't know.

Other fairylike beings appear in Eastern and Pacific myths as well. In Thailand, the **PHI** resemble fairies and inhabit natural places like trees and waterfalls. Like European fairies, they could demonstrate both good or ill will toward humans. Sometimes beautiful and sometimes bewitching, fairies appear throughout Pacific mythology. In Japan, they are the **TENNIN** and **YOSEI**; among the Maori, they are the **PATUPAIAREHE**; in Java, they are called **ASPARI**.

Other mischievous and dangerous little people are also known in these cultures. The **PONATURI** are wicked shape-changing sea fairies that battle Maori heroes. The **TIPUA** are other wicked shape-changing spirits known to the Maori. If the setting was right, a fantasy author could make these beings into a viable fantasy race instead of the more cliché fairies of Western culture.

Some Native American legends have their mythical races, too. In an Algonquian legend, the god-hero Glooskap encounters a giant named Winter. Winter casts a spell of cold over Glooskap and the god slumbers for six months before the spell wears off. When he awakens, he travels southward and eventually comes to a land blooming with flowers. There he spots beautiful little people dancing. These little people are called the Elves of Light. Glooskap snatches Summer, their queen, and takes her with him to once more encounter Winter. Summer's warmth and power eventually melt the coldhearted giant. Another Algonquian legend tells of the fairy wives, named Weasel, that were married to Marten.

The Iroquois also have stories of giants made of stone who planned to attack the Iroquois but were defeated by the god of the west wind. Little people, according to the Iroquois, made all the beautiful things on Earth and helped to protect humans from monsters.

## CREATED RACES

Many authors create their own races through the methods of adaptation and elevation. As previously mentioned, Andre Norton adapted elves and merfolk. She also adapted the legends of werefolk for two separate races, the Gray Ones and the Were Riders. The **GRAY ONES** are intelligent, fierce fighters that are half men and half wolves. They are also capable of magic, particularly as a group. The **WERE RIDERS** are native to the land of Arvon. These men have the ability to alter their shapes to look like specific beasts such as boars, horses, and snowcats. Each Were Rider has his own animal form, usually reflective of his personality. The Were Riders have their own codes, customs, and magic adapted from various folklores.

Norton also uses adaptation and elevation for a race of horselike creatures known as the **KEPLIANS**. When they first appear in the series, they are evil creatures. Beautiful black steeds, they trick innocents into climbing on their backs and then carry them away to their evil master. The Keplian is an adaptation of the kelpie, or water horse, a legendary creature that had similar abilities. Later, in *Key of the Keplian*, she elevates the Keplians into a race. The dark horses become creatures of light and allies to those who fight against evil. They even create their own haven and code of conduct.

Norton adapts/elevates other creatures into races as well: **FLANNANS** are bird/human hybrids; **RENTHANS** are intelligent creatures similar to antelope or deer; the **VRANG** have bird bodies and lizard heads. There are also intelligent **LIZARD FOLK**. All of these races communicate telepathically with each other and their human allies.

Mercedes Lackey does similar things in her Valdemar series. Valdemar is in many ways reflective of the Witch World. She has several races that are her versions of Norton's earlier creations: the lizardlike **HERTASI**; the antelopelike **DYHELI**; and the birdlike **TERVARDI**. The large wolfen **KYREE** fall into a similar category. These races, for the most part, play minor roles in the world of Valdemar. Of more importance, however, is the author's elevation of the **GRYPHON** into a race. (Norton has gryphons in the Witch World as well, but not as a race.) Lackey's gryphons were created by Urtho, a great mage. He used several types of birds as models, such as eagles and falcons. Lackey is very precise in talking about bird types, probably because she helps rehabilitate different types of raptors. For instance, gryphons, like many Earth raptors, must mate in flight and can only conceive when magic is added to the coupling. Lackey's gryphons co-exist with human and nonhuman species, and help with guard duty, politics, and city planning. The gryphons also have their own mages and are in every way the equals of their human colleagues.

David Weber in *Oath of Swords* creates the world of Norfressa, a land with five races of Man. Four of these are familiar to fantasy readers: humans, elves, dwarves, and half-lings. Weber's elves are immortal and withdrawn. His dwarves are rich, but the one we actually see in the book is a merchant and not a miner. The half-lings have curved horns erupting from their foreheads. Some of the half-lings, the Purple Lords, are arrogant aristocrats who enjoy having a stranglehold on the main water route, while others are rough-and-tough sailors.

But the fifth race is different. The **HRADANI** look like humans except for their ears, which are foxlike and tufted. Hradani are also larger in stature than most humans, some topping seven feet tall. But Weber creates more in the race than just pointy ears. The Hradani are tribalistic and tend to the savage and barbaric side. They trust few outside their own clan and are mistrusted if not despised by the other races of Man. Birthrates are low and Hradani women are considered precious; rape is the worst crime imaginable. But what really distinguishes the Hradani is the Rage, a state of mind that can engulf a Hradani and make him almost unstoppable. Pain and wounds don't matter, only killing. The Rage was inflicted upon the race by wizards hoping to use the Hradani as a weapon. Instead, the Rage shields the Hradani from most spells and magic, thus making them immune to the magicians. Weber adapted the stories of Berserkers in order to create an entire race of Man for his novel.

## INDIVIDUALIZATION AND CHARACTERIZATION

Although there are several ways of creating or adapting new races and new outlooks on races, one of the surest ways of bringing a race to life is by creating an individual from that race and making him a fully developed character.

---

For example, Asprin introduces trolls by presenting Chumley as a real person. Asprin demonstrates Chumley's intelligence and his big heart through his interaction with the other characters. Pratchett does the same for the troll Detritus. Though slow-witted, the troll develops a friendship with his co-worker, the dwarf Cuddy. Pratchett's dwarves also come alive through Carrot, the six-foot adopted dwarf, and Corporal Littlebottom, a female dwarf who also joins the Guard. Norton's Dahuan brings the Green People to full realization as Orsya of the Krogan does for that race. Gaiman and Reiber make Titania a complete character with wants, desires, and secrets. Lackey's gryphon Skandrannon's love of adventure, his vanity, and his devotion to his family make him as human as anyone. To be a successful dwarf, troll, fairy, elf, gryphon, or whatever, the character must come alive. That is one of the true keys of breathing new life into a clichéd race.

## CHAPTER 7
# Creatures of Myth and Legend

### by Andrew P. Miller and Daniel Clark

Writers of fantasy, horror, and science fiction are often looking for obstacles for their heroes. And what better obstacle than a nightmarish monster carved from the fears and imagination of the ages? Myths and legends from around the world provide us with a wealth of creatures to use in our stories. What you'll find here is a brief survey of fantastic creatures from around the world. Not all of these are monsters, but all are strange, wondrous, and fabulous creations and their stories are waiting to be continued in the hands of the skilled author.

## ALPHABETICAL LISTING OF CREATURES

**banshee:** In Irish legend, the banshee is a female spirit that voices her strange wail when a death is imminent. Banshees are usually attached to a specific family and wail when a member of that family is near death. Banshees have streaming hair and red eyes from weeping. Some accounts only give them one nostril. In Scottish legend, the equivalent is the **Little Washer of Sorrow**. In this case, the female spirit appears at the side of a stream washing the clothes of the soon to be departed.

**bunyips:** Making its home in the waterways of Australia, the bunyips are often described as having a crocodile's tail with the rest of its body resembling either a bandicoot, an emu, or a man. They can have manes or heads covered with weeds, and their feet are turned backwards. One constant in the tales of bunyips is the fact that the bunyip's cry can be heard as a terrifying booming noise coming from the swamps. Bunyips devour people, preferring women and children.

**Chimera:** A child of Typhon and Echidna, the Chimera had the head of a lion, a goat's body, and a snake's tail. Her breath was a deadly blast of fire. The hero Bellerophon killed the Chimera with arrows while flying above it on the back of Pegasus.

**Coyote:** In the mythology of the Plains, Southwestern, Great Basin, and central California North American Indian tribes, Coyote is primarily a trickster figure, and for many of these tribes, he is also the creator or culture hero. Coyote stories often involve other animal characters such as Badger or Raven or Wolf, and they are all presented as behaving and talking like men with animal heads. As the culture hero, Coyote is responsible for giving to humans the knowledge of fire, weapons, arts and crafts, or the sun. Sometimes Coyote is presented as a foolish character, easily duped by others. At times, he is also presented as lewd or mischievous.

**Cyclopes:** The Cyclopes are giants who have one eye in the center of their fore-heads. The first Cyclopes were said to be children of Gaea, Mother Earth, and Uranus, the Heavenly Sky. They helped the Greek god Hephaestus in his forge. Polyphemus, the cannibalistic Cyclops who menaced Odysseus in The Odyssey, herded sheep and was a son of the sea god, Poseidon.

**djinn (a.k.a. genie, jinni, djinni, djin):** In Arabian and Eastern legends, the djinn are spirits capable of great magical feats. They can be either benev-olent or malevolent to human beings. Magicians can conjure and control these spirits to do their bidding. Djinns are commonly bound into rings and jewelry, or in the most famous case, Aladdin's lamp. Related to djinns are peris and efrits. A **peri** is usually a much more benevolent spirit, often giving directions and help to humans. They opposed evil djinns. **Efrits** were almost always evil and dangerous spirits.

**dragons:** Dragons appear in various mythologies and legends. The Greek mon-ster **Echidna** was supposed to be half dragon. In Babylonian myth, **Tiamat** was the great she-dragon that battled the god Marduk. In Norse mythology, **Fafnir** kept guard over his hoard until killed by Sigurd. The hero Beowulf was eventually killed by a dragon. In English tales, St. George killed a dragon and rescued a young virgin.

The most familiar form of the western dragon is a great flying reptile. It has large batlike wings, a serpentine tail, sharp claws or talons, and lots of teeth. These dragons usually breathe fire and some have a penchant for virgins. Often, like Fafnir, they are known to hoard gold and jewels. Dragons are hard to kill but almost always have one vulnerable spot for the hero to find.

**oriental dragons:** These differ from their western counterparts. In China, dragons are more benevolent creatures of great power, often counted peers of the gods. They are usually associated with the elements, particularly water. Each river and stream has a dragon or dragon-king associated with it. Their features vary, often being an amalgam of various animals. They often have heads of camels, antlers of deer, eyes of a hare, scales of a fish, and talons of eagles. Although they are quite often wingless, they sometimes have bat wings. Chief of the Chinese dragons is **Lung**, who controls wind and rains, monsoons and hails. The **Great Chien-Tang** is another important Chinese dragon who commands all river dragons.

Japanese dragons are similar to Chinese dragons in appearance and function. There are dragons representing the four elements and a dragon rules each sea.

**fantastic horses:** In many myths, the sun is pulled through the sky by fiery horses. **Papillon** is the fiery steed of the faery queen Morgana. The Valkyrie rode great flying war horses onto battlefields to choose the heroically slain. Others include **Al Borak**, the horse that carried Mohammed up to heaven; the man-eating horses that belonged to King Diomedes in Greek mythology; and **Sleipnir**, the eight-legged horse of the Norse god Odin.

**feng huang:** The feng huang or "red birds" are the Chinese equivalent of the **phoenix**. They are rare and beautiful birds that are extraordinarily long-lived. With the unicorn, the tortoise, and the dragon, the feng huang is one of the four spiritual animals of Chinese lore. Legend says that the Chinese musical scale came from the song of the feng huang. "Feng" designates the male of the species and "huang" the female. The feng huang have bright coloring like peacocks and pheasants, but have curling tails and long claws. The rainbow plumage of the feng huang represents undying love—one of the five basic cardinal virtues—because of the devotion between the feng and the huang. Stories say that the chariot of the immortal Jade Emperor is pulled by feng huang and that they live in the Vermilion Hills, a borderland of sorts between worlds. The feng huang's appearances in legend are rare and coincide with times of prosperity. The feng huang's departure brings calamity and it is said that the feng huang will reappear again only when China is at peace.

**Goliath:** In the Old Testament of the Bible, Goliath was the Philistine warrior who challenged King Saul of Israel and his army to send forth a warrior to engage in man-to-man combat in order to decide the war between the Israelites and the Philistines. David, a boy who tended sheep for the army, was strong in his faith in God and took up the challenge, defeating the heavily armed Goliath with only his sling and some stones. David then killed Goliath and cut off his head with Goliath's own sword. David's success in battle was a testament to his faith in the Hebrew god and to his worthiness to be ruler of the people of Israel.

"Goliath" is often used as a term to refer to an individual or party that is so large and powerful that it seems impossible to defeat, but which may be brought down by a smaller, more clever, and more faithful challenger.

**golem:** The golem was created by a Jewish rabbi in the city of Prague. The Jews who lived in the ghettos of Prague were being persecuted. The golem was constructed as a means of protection. Made of clay, it was given life when the rabbi wrote the word *shem* ("name") on a piece of parchment and put it in its mouth. He also wrote *emet* ("truth") on its forehead. The golem was strong and defended the Jews. However, the city began to fear its own creation, so the rabbi destroyed the golem by changing the word *emet* to *met*, which means death.

**Gorgons:** Sisters to the Graeae, the Gorgons were three in number: the immortals **Stheno** and **Euryale**, and the more famous mortal **Medusa**. These women were said to have wings and sometimes claws, but their most outstanding feature was that they had snakes for hair. The Gorgons' looks could turn people into stone. The Greek hero Perseus slew Medusa with a magic sickle after watching her reflection in a shield. Pegasus is said to have sprung from her blood.

**The Graeae:** Sisters to the Gorgons, the Graeae were three gray women with one eye and one tooth, which they passed back and forth. According to some accounts, Perseus snatched the eye and tooth and wouldn't give them back until the Graeae told them the secrets of the Gorgons.

**Grendel:** The monster of *Beowulf* is described only as a gruesome creature that hunts the Danish moors. He is "descended from the race of Cain" and bears Cain's mark. He is humanoid in shape, nearly gigantic in stature, and incredibly strong and fierce. Only Beowulf's great strength is Grendel's undoing when he rips the monster's arm off. Grendel nearly bleeds to death in the marsh before Beowulf beheads him on his deathbed. Beowulf must also confront and slay Grendel's mother as she seeks revenge. (John Gardner's *Grendel* retells the story from the monster's perspective, making him an almost sympathetic, tragic character.)

**harpies:** Usually portrayed as creatures with the head and breasts of a woman and the body of a large bird, harpies are known for their foul smell that ruins anything they come near. Called the **Hounds of Zeus**, they were sent by Zeus to punish the prophet Phineas. Whenever Phineas went to eat, the harpies descended, fouling the food. Two of the Argonauts, sons of the North Wind, defeated the harpies.

**hell hounds:** Various myths speak of fearsome canines inhabiting the underworlds. Most famous is probably **Cerberus**, the three-headed, snake-tailed hound that guards the way to Hades. Cerberus was fierce but could be overcome by brute strength as when Hercules subdued him, or lulled by song as when Orpheus entered the underworld. **Garm** was the hound of Hel in Norse mythology.

**hippocampus:** A hippocampus is half horse and half fish; the name itself means "sea horse." They have the head and forelegs of a horse, but the legs end in powerful webbed fins and their mane is a fin. Their long, horselike bodies end in a fish-tail. In Greek mythology, the sea chariot of Poseidon is drawn by hippocampi. For merfolk, the hippocampi are steeds prized for their ability to travel swiftly through the seas.

**hippogriff (a.k.a. hippogriffin):** The hippogriff was the offspring of a gryphon—a half eagle/half lion—and a mare, and was considered by medieval writers to be a natural, nonmagical beast. It had the body of a horse and the forelegs, claws, wings, and beak of a gryphon, which were basically identical to those of an eagle. The hippogriff is often associated with the sun, the gryphons and horses of Apollo's chariot, and the **Pegasus**. The hippogriff's story is told in *Orlando Furioso* by Ariosto, most episodes of which are derived from Greek and other legends. The hippogriff was originally tamed by a magician named Atlantes who lived in a castle in the Pyrenees where Rogero, the magician's foster son, was kept prisoner. Eventually Rogero escaped and took the hippogriff as his mount. In one adventure, it was ridden by Rogero as he tried to save a damsel from sacrifice to a sea beast, an episode that greatly resembled one of Perseus's adventures.

The hippogriff eventually passed into the hands of one of Charlemagne's knights, who then learned from Saint John how to defeat the pagan Africans. In the end, the hippogriff was set free into the mountains and never seen again.

**hoop snake:** A creature of American folklore, the hoop snake puts the end of its own tail in its mouth and rolls across the ground. The hoop snake can move so rapidly that it cannot be outrun, and the only way to escape it is to jump through the hoop it makes, which so confuses the hoop snake that it just rolls on and on and cannot turn back.

The hoop snake may be related to the **uroboros**, a symbol of eternity and cosmic unity in Greek and Egyptian art. The uroboros depicted a snake with the end of its tail in its mouth, drawn in the shape of a circle. The **Midgard Serpent**, which in Norse mythology encircles the world by holding its tail in its mouth, is a type of uroboros.

**Hydra:** The Hydra was a child of Echidna and Typhon. Dwelling in the swamps of Lerna, this deadly poisonous, nine-headed creature had one head that was immortal. Whenever any head was struck off, two more took its place. Hercules killed the monster by using a torch to sear the necks so no new heads would spring up. He buried the immortal head under a rock.

**incubi and succubi:** These spirits or demons visit people in the night for sexual intercourse. **Incubi** are male spirits that visit women during their dreams. Incubi can impregnate mortal women; one child from such a union was Merlin. **Succubi** are hideous females that trick sleeping males into intercourse. The succubi seem to be related to **Lilith**, the first wife of Adam. Expelled from Eden, Lilith became the mother of demons. She is also said to visit men in the night, looking for semen so she can bring forth more of her brood.

**Jabberwock:** "The Jabberwock with eyes of flame" is a creation of Lewis Carroll and appears in the poem "Jabberwocky" in the book *Through the Looking Glass and What Alice Found There*. It also has "jaws that bite" and "claws that catch" and "burble[s]" when it walks. It apparently lives near the "jubjub bird" and the "frumious bandersnatch" (also Carroll's inventions). The young hero of the poem dispatches the Jabberwock with a "vorpal blade" that goes "snicker-snack."

**Jersey Devil:** Stories of the Jersey Devil come from the Pine Barrens of New Jersey, a surprisingly isolated and sparsely populated region. No one is quite sure when stories of the Jersey Devil originated; some believe they began only 150 years ago, while some say they precede colonial times.

The most popular version of the Jersey Devil's origin says that in about 1735, a woman named Leeds, who was the mother of twelve children, discovered she was to have a thirteenth child and cried out in frustration that she was sick of children and that this one could be the Devil—and, as it turns out, it was. Another story says that the Jersey Devil was born in 1850 as the result of a Gypsy's curse on a young girl. In both stories, the monster escaped into the woods shortly after its birth and still lives there.

The Jersey Devil is said to have a head like a horse or ram; large, bat-like wings; and a long, serpentine body. Occasionally, there are outbreaks of stories about the Jersey Devil, the largest during the week of January 16–23, 1909. Eyewitness accounts are documented in newspapers of the time, most of them reporting eerie sounds coming from the direction of the Delaware river and a strange glowing creature flying through the sky. The hoof prints of a strange animal were reported in odd locations, such as on the roofs of houses or near chicken coops.

**Kappa:** In Japanese legends, the Kappa is a type of water demon that likes to drown its human victims. The Kappa has a skinny body with a large, bowl-like head filled with water. It also has a tortoise shell on its back and smells of rotten fish. Besides drowning its victims, it eats them as well. However, it is not an intelligent demon and can be fooled quite easily. A person confronted by the Kappa needs only to bow politely from the waist. The Kappa will return the bow, spilling the dangerous water from the top of its head, and will be powerless to drown its victims until it has reclaimed the water. By that time, the person can escape.

The Kappa is also appeased by the gift of a cucumber. The cucumber has to have a person's name and age cut into it. If the person throws this cucumber into the water, the Kappa will remember the gift and the person will be safe from its clutches.

**kelpie (a.k.a. water horse):** This Scottish water spirit can either be mischievous or deadly. It has several forms, including that of a hairy man and a beautiful horse. As a horse, it lures men to ride it. Then the rider finds himself unable to get off and the kelpie returns to its watery home. Depending on the nature of the kelpie, the man either merely gets dunked or he is drowned. In some cases, he may be eaten. River kelpies usually only dunked their victims. The **Each-Uisge**, found in lochs, was the more dangerous and lethal. (In Ireland, the **aughisky** are water horses of saltwater streams and lochs. They are also man-eaters.) In horse form, a kelpie can be identified by its backward hoofprints. Kelpies can be controlled with the use of a bridle, but it is not a good idea to use one for long since it also has the power to inflict curses.

Kelpies can also take on the shape of handsome men to lure women into their domain. In this form, the kelpie can be identified by shells and seaweed in its hair.

**Kraken:** The Kraken is a sea monster so huge, according to legend, that it can be mistaken for an island. This enormous size accounts perhaps for the ambiguous description of it. Sometimes confused with the giant octopus, the Kraken is said to be tentacled, but little else can be said authoritatively. Sailors can easily be swept from ships, and the ships themselves crushed by the monster. In calm seas, sailors look for bubbling and boiling waters that indicate the Kraken is surfacing. Some legends have it that there are *two* kraken, created when the world was made and existing for as long as the world exists.

**Lamia:** The first Lamia was one of the many conquests of Zeus. Hera, Zeus's jealous wife, cursed Lamia and gave her a monstrous form: a woman's head, a snake's body, cloven hooves and a lion's tail. Hera also killed Lamia's children. Lamia then went about killing children in revenge. She eventually had other children known as lamiae. In some accounts, these daughters had monstrous forms similar to their mother's. In other accounts, they were beautiful young women. The accounts agree, though, that Lamia's children sucked the blood from their victims and are thus similar to **vampires**. Lamia is related to Lilith in that both are cursed women responsible for a demon brood.

**leprechauns:** Probably the most famous of Irish fairies, leprechauns are little people that are usually shoemakers. They can be identified by their hats, breeches, and big-buckled shoes. Leprechauns are also wealthy and known to hide pots of gold and other treasure, though they part with the secret of their stash only if tricked. Exceptionally clever and tricky, very few mortals ever get the best of the leprechaun.

**Leviathan:** In the generic sense, "leviathan" refers to any huge sea animal, but in the Old Testament it is used in several places to refer to a specific monster or monsters. In Job, the creature is depicted as a fierce monster with nearly impenetrable scales and terrible teeth. In Isaiah, the Leviathan is called the "coiling serpent" and the "gilding serpent." Psalm 74 refers to a "monster in the waters." But in Psalm 104, however, the leviathan is described as "frolicking" in the sea, apparently a different sort of creature. Some scholars have speculated the crocodile may be the basis of the Leviathan of Job and Psalm 74, and that Psalm 104 may be referring to a whale. In most uses, however, the Bible creates an image of a fierce mysterious creature that is an adversary of God.

**Lorelei:** A water spirit of German legends, the Lorelei is known for both her beautiful appearance and her beautiful song. In fact, like the Greek sirens, the Lorelei's song is nearly irresistible and lures men to their doom. The creature takes its name from the large rock of the same name in the Rhine river, upon which it sits and sings.

**manticore:** A creature associated with India, a manticore has the head of a man, the body of a lion, and a tail like a scorpion's (although some accounts describe the tail as a spiked ball). It has three rows of teeth and can shoot the spikes from its tail like arrows. A manticore is a savage beast with a voracious appetite and often preys on people.

**The Minotaur:** Unlike centaurs, the Minotaur was a unique monster, half man and half bull. He was the son of Queen Pasiphaë of Crete and a bull. The sea god Poseidon gave the bull to King Minos to use as a sacrifice, but Minos liked the bull and preferred to keep it for himself. Angered by this, Poseidon made Pasiphaë fall in love with the bull. She had Daedalus, the master inventor, build her a wooden cow with which she could court the bull. When the Minotaur was born, Minos had Daedalus build the labyrinth to hold him. Minos also had the city-state of Athens pay a tribute of seven maids and seven youths to him, to be sent to the Minotaur. Eventually, the Athenian prince and hero, Theseus, came to Crete. With the help of Ariadne, Minos's daughter, he killed the Minotaur while it slept.

The Minotaur has been depicted in several ways. The most common is a human with a bull's head. The second is closer to a centaur, with a human torso and horned head atop a bull's body.

**monstrous wolves:** Gigantic or monstrous wolves appear in a variety of folktales and myths. In Norse mythology, **Fenris** or **Fenrir** Wolf was the son of the god Loki and a giantess. His siblings were Hel and the Midgard Serpent. Besides being of gigantic form, **Fenris** was incredibly strong. The gods feared him and tried to chain him but he broke all of their chains. Finally, the gods had the dwarves forge a magic chain called Gleipnir that was exceptionally thin but exceptionally strong. Fenris would only agree to be bound by it if one of the gods placed his hand in the monster's mouth. The war god Tyr did. The chain would not break and Tyr lost his hand. At Ragnarok, the twilight of the gods, Fenris finally breaks his chain and kills Odin. Fenris is then killed by Odin's son, Vidar.

Also in Norse mythology, giant wolves chase the sun and the moon across the heavens. They occasionally catch them, causing eclipses. Odin also kept two wolves called **Geri the Ravenous** and **Freki the Greedy**.

**naga:** The naga originated in Indian myth, but can be found in legends throughout southeast Asia. It is a semidivine and semihuman creature in the form of a snake; both more powerful and wealthy than humankind, nagas dwell in lands under the earth or beneath the rivers and seas. But nagas are inferior to humankind because they have no soul and therefore can achieve no enlightenment. Nagas have seven heads, hooded like cobras, and resemble the Hydra. Like the Hydra, nagas are associated with water, particularly rainfall and all the good and bad connected with droughts and floods.

In early legends, nagas withhold water from the earth and must be slain to end droughts. In others, villains seeking to destroy or imprison nagas must be defeated in order to prevent drought. In Buddhist legend, Buddha's superior spiritual and moral power persuades the nagas to relinquish the rains during the proper season and in the proper quantity. In another Buddhist legend, the bodhisattva (the "Buddha-to-be") chooses to be reincarnated as a naga and discovers how terrible it is to live without a soul. This and other stories show a close relationship between Buddha and the nagas, and he is often depicted seated on and protected by a naga.

**Nemean Lion:** The Nemean Lion was gigantic and ferocious. His hide was so tough that swords and arrows bounced off him. Hercules eventually killed the beast by strangling it. Hercules then wore the lion's pelt as protection.

**nymphs:** Nymphs are spirits or personifications of natural objects such as trees, rivers, streams, and mountains. They are represented as beautiful maidens. In Greek mythology, **dryads** and **hamadryads** are spirits of trees. Dryads live in forests and hamadryads have connections to specific trees. Their lives were as long as the trees in which they lived. **Oreads** are the nymphs of the mountains. **Naiads** are water nymphs, inhabiting streams and rivers. The **Nereids**, fifty in number, were sea nymphs and the daughters of the sea god Nereus.

**phoenix:** The phoenix is closely associated with legends of the sun and appears often as a symbol of immortality, rebirth and power. According to legend, the phoenix lived in an eastern paradise of eternal springtime where there was no hunger and no night. The phoenix was larger and more graceful than the eagle; its head, breast, and back were scarlet, its eyes were sea-blue, its feet purple, and its iridescent wings were many colors. The phoenix did not eat grass or prey on other animals; it consumed the very air.

The phoenix lived there for exactly one thousand years; at the end of its lifetime, it left paradise and flew west until it reached Arabia. There it gathered perfumes and spices, which it took to the coasts of Phoenicia where it built a nest in the tallest of palm trees. It then began to sing its death song, a song so beautiful that even the sun god was said to stop in his tracks. Then the sun went on, and the phoenix's nest caught fire from the sparks of the sun, burning the bird and its nest to ashes from which the new phoenix rose.

The new bird then took the ashes of the old nest to Heliopolis, the City of the Sun, in Egypt and placed them on the altar of the sun temple. As the phoenix flew east, it was joined by all the other birds of the world—even predator and prey—which flew in peace as they accompanied the phoenix to the border of paradise.

Different legends give different life spans for the phoenix: some say 350 or 500 years, some 7,006, others 1,460, and still others but a day. The phoenix has been a powerful symbol in many cultures; it was used by Christians to represent Christ and the Resurrection; the Romans used it in the fourth century to represent the promise of the rebirth of the Roman Empire; and the phoenix was used in a symbol for Joan of Arc after her death. The phoenix appears in Chinese legend as the feng huang, a beautiful and musical bird more like a peacock than an eagle, and appears in Japanese legend as Ho-ho, which is often used to symbolize the royal family.

**puca (a.k.a. pooka, puck, pwca):** Puca are English woodland faeries with diminutive human forms, known for mischievousness and trickster-like qualities. Though the puca are often depicted as **satyr-like**, they are not known for lasciviousness. In Britain, puca became known as **puck,** and eventually **Robin Goodfellow** came to be known by that name. He was a shape-shifter and preferred the company of animals, though he liked humans who appreciated and acknowledged his existence and persecuted those who scorned their lovers.

In Wales, puca are called **pwca** and are considered to be ill-tempered and ugly, often quarrelling among themselves. In German and Scandinavian countries, the puca are goat-bodied creatures called **kornblockes**. They are said to help grow grain and corn, but will steal or spoil it if given a reason.

**satyrs and fauns:** Half goat and half man, satyrs bound through the woodlands of mythical Greece, usually in pursuit of nymphs. Mostly human in appearance, satyrs have goat legs and hooves and small horns on their heads. The Greek god **Pan** also had the same physical characteristics. Some accounts say that the fauns are the Roman version of satyrs, while other versions say that fauns are half deer and half man, and have much gentler natures than satyrs. They are named after the Roman god **Faunus** who later became identified with Pan.

**ruhk (a.k.a. roc):** The ruhk, giant birds known in the Middle and Far East, come from Arabic legend and are described in the Arabian Nights stories as being so large that they blot out the sun when they fly. One of their eggs is as large as 148 chicken eggs and they feed elephants to their young. When they fly, the beating of their wings creates wind storms and lightning. In some Arabic legends, the ruhk never land on earth except on Mount Qaf, which the Arabs considered to be the *axis mundi*. In other legends, the ruhk live on in certain islands in the Indian Ocean, but they often fly to India, Arabia, and Africa to find food.

In the Arabian Nights stories, Sinbad has more than one adventure involving a ruhk. In one story, Sinbad, marooned on an island, discovers a ruhk egg. He waits until the ruhk lands, then ties himself to the ruhk's enormous, tree-trunk-sized leg, thereby escaping the island when the ruhk goes in search of food. In another adventure, Sinbad and his sailors discover a young ruhk hatchling and kill and feast on it. When the parents of the bird return, the sailors flee to the sea and the two ruhk drop boulders on the ships, sinking them.

The ruhk appear to be similar to another giant bird of Arabic lore: the **anka**. Allah is said to have created the anka to kill and eat most of the wild animals of Palestine so the Israelites could move into the country. Allah forgot to remove the bird, however, and it went on ravaging the countryside, making large parts of that country barren and uninhabitable.

**Sasquatch:** "Sasquatch" is an Indian word made popular in the 1930s by the stories of J.W. Burns, a British Columbian writer. Burns used the name for one of his characters, a giant Indian who lived in the wilderness. The character was quite popular and the name was used by a hotel and an annual festival in Harrison, B.C. The local celebration drew the attention of others who reported having seen a large, furry, humanoid creature, which soon was given the name Sasquatch. Most accounts of the Sasquatch are of a single creature, glimpsed only for a few seconds as it moved through the woods. When a bulldozer operator named Jerry Crew found a large, human-shaped footprint in Northern California and made a plaster cast of it, the creature who made it was dubbed **Bigfoot**, and the names Sasquatch and Bigfoot have become synonymous. By almost all accounts, the creature is described as larger than a man, covered with dark fur, and very shy of human contact. One man reported being captured by a band of Sasquatch, and a group of miners near St. Helens claimed that their camp was attacked by "giant apes" throwing rocks after one of the miners shot an "ape" earlier in the day. Such stories of violent aggressive behavior by a Sasquatch are very rare.

**Scylla and Charybdis:** There are two main versions of the story of Scylla in Greek mythology and for each, the details vary widely. In one account, Scylla is a young woman whom the fisherman-turned-sea-god Glaucus spies and falls in love with. She refuses him because his mermanlike body is repellent to her. Gaucus seeks the help of Circe, asking for a love potion to turn Scylla's heart. As he tells his story, Circe falls in love with Glaucus, but he remains devoted to Scylla. In her anger, Circe prepares a poison for Scylla and pours it in the bay where she bathes. The poison turns her into a horrible creature that is rooted to the rocks on shore. In some accounts of this version, Scylla is a water sprite and she is the daughter of Phorcys and Crataeis, Typhon and Echidna, or Poseidon, and Glaucus is only a fisherman.

In the other main version of Scylla's story, she is seduced by her father Poseidon. When Amphitrite, Poseidon's wife, finds out, she goes to Circe for help in punishing Scylla, which Circe does with the potion that turns her into a monster. Some descriptions have Scylla-the-monster with both the heads of serpents and fierce dogs; in others she has twelve legs and dog heads on long serpentlike necks. All accounts consistently describe Scylla as turned into a hateful monster seeking to destroy anything that comes within her reach.

Today, Scylla is the name of a great rock that juts out of the sea between the tip of Italy and Sicily.

Charybdis is more mysterious in origin: in some accounts, she is a monster that lives under a rock on the Sicilian side of the strait. She traps sailors by creating a gigantic whirlpool, which sucks their ships under water. In other accounts, she is the whirlpool itself.

**sea lion:** The sea lion belongs to a class of part-lions like the Chimera and manticore, but is also associated with water- and merfolk. The sea lion has the front part of a lion—the forelimbs and claws, the maned head—and the hind parts of a large silvery fish. The sea lions live in packs along rocky seacoasts where they hunt for schools of fish or shipwrecked sailors. Their powerful jaws and claws make them very dangerous when angered, and their powerful tails and webbed forelimbs make them very fast in the water. Their bellowing roars can be heard even underwater. It was said that sailors could hear the packs of sea lions bellowing in hunger as the ships approached rocks and dangerous coastal areas.

**selkies and roanes:** Selkies are English sea fairies while roanes are Scottish. Normally, selkies and roanes have seal forms. Both can, however, shed their skins to reveal human bodies. They particularly like to become human to dance the night away. Humans can capture selkies, particularly female selkies, to be their wives if they can steal the selkie's or roane's skin away from her. The captured fairy may make a good wife but will always long for the sea and will return if she ever finds her skin. Selkies are also reported to be more hot-tempered than roanes and can cause storms if angered.

**shark man:** Similar to a werewolf, the Hawaiian shark man is capable of changing back and forth between man and shark. As a shark, he possesses all the attributes of the animal and usually preys upon members of his village. The most famous shark man was **Nanaue**. The son of a mortal woman and a shark god, Nanaue had a shark's mouth on his back. When he entered water, he changed into a shark, but he was vulnerable if he could not get to water. When he was found out, he fled to another village and was eventually trapped by fisherman, cut into small bits, and burned.

**sirens:** In some accounts, sirens are said to have the bodies of birds and the heads of women. Other sources say no description can be found since no one survives them. The chief characteristic of the sirens is their song, which no man can resist. Ancient sailors who heard the sirens were lured to their doom. The Greek hero Odysseus had his men stop up their ears, then had the crew tie him to the mast. Even so, their song nearly drove Odysseus mad. In another tale, Orpheus used his superior vocal skills to get the Argonauts past the rocks where the sirens lived.

**sphinx:** Creatures known as sphinxes appear in a variety of cultures, particularly Egypt, Greece, and Babylon. Sphinxes are generally known to have the bodies of lions, the wings of eagles, and the face and chest of humans. The monument of the Sphinx at Giza is supposed to represent Horus, the sun god. The Greek sphinx was a child of Typhon and Echidna and plagued the city of Thebes. She asked everyone her riddle, and those who could not answer, she devoured. Her riddle was, "What walks on four legs in the morning, two legs in the afternoon, and three legs in the evening?" Finally, Oedipus answered the riddle with the answer of a "man." A man crawls on all fours as a baby, walks upright as an adult, and uses a cane in old age. The sphinx supposedly killed herself in fury at having been thwarted.

**The Stymphalian Birds:** These birds lived along the shores of Lake Stymphalus in ancient Greece. They were about the size of cranes and had beaks and talons of bronze. Some accounts say they could shoot their bronze feathers like arrows. As one of his labors, Hercules had to rid the lake of the birds. With the help of the goddess Athena, he drove them into the air and shot them with arrows.

**tengu:** The tengu of the Japanese Shinto religion are strange half-man, half-bird creatures. In some accounts, they have the body of men and faces of birds, and carry large fans of feathers. In others, they look like men with wings, bird-claws for feet, and beaklike noses. They are mischievous creatures and are often credited, or blamed, for teaching humans how to use weapons of war. Sometimes, a tengu will possess a human, causing the victim to show great skill in battle. When the tengu spirit is driven out, the victim has no memory of what happened.

As creatures of the Shinto religion, tengu were fierce enemies of the Buddhists in the Middle Ages. They often tried to tempt, fool, or carry off Buddhist priests and set fire to Buddhist temples. The Buddhists forbade the worship of the tengu and even had a mythical place called the "tengu road," an area of the spirit world reserved for hypocritical priests who had forsaken their vows.

**Thunderbird:** Like many fabulous birds, the Thunderbird of North America was considered to be the source of high winds or storms. A sacred bird to Native American Indians, the Thunderbird represents a force against evil, a creature with highly acute senses that can never be surprised by evil. The Thunderbird can never be summoned or invoked in a battle against evil; it comes of its own will or not at all. Its attack is always signaled by the thunder of its great wings.

As a spiritual force, the Thunderbird is often referred to as a singular creature, but in legend and story, it is sometimes spoken of as more than one creature, suggesting it is a species of bird. Descriptions of the Thunderbird vary as well. Pacific Indians describe a bird so immense that it has a lake on its back, which is the source of rain. Mountain Indians conceive of the Thunderbird as a small red bird that shoots lightning from its wing tips and makes thunder with the beating of its wings.

**trickster:** The trickster figure appears in many mythologies around the world: in Greece as Hermes; as Coyote in the American Southwest; as Eshu-Elegba and Ananse in Africa; as Susa-no-o in Japan; and as Loki in Norse mythology. In many cultures, he is the culture hero, responsible for bringing the arts to his people. Stories about Trickster, particularly in Native American Indian and African lore, depict a character getting by on his wits against more powerful enemies.

**Typhon and Echidna:** Typhon was the last child of Gaea, Mother Earth. She bore him to fight against Zeus and the Olympian gods. He was gigantic with over a hundred flaming heads. Some accounts say these heads were serpents' heads that appeared beneath his waist. Other accounts say that he was human to the thighs. In any case, he was incredibly strong but ultimately defeated by Zeus and trapped under Mount Aetna. His mate was Echidna (a.k.a. *Echidne*). Echidna was a beautiful woman from the waist up. Below the waist she was dragon or serpent. She was also the mother of monsters, including the Hydra, Cerebrus, Chimera, and others.

Another half human, half dragon appears in Greek mythology as well but was not considered a monster. His name was **Cecrops** and was considered a king and hero and possibly the founder of the royal house of Athens.

**unicorns:** The unicorn originally had many different descriptions, but the most common image is that of the white horse with flowing mane and tail and the single spiral horn sprouting from its forehead. Unicorns can be both fierce and gentle. Its horn can pierce anything, though it has to be careful of ramming it into a tree and getting stuck. The unicorn's horn has magical properties, chief of which was the ability to either detect or nullify poisons. For this reason, the horn was much sought after. Unicorns can easily be trapped by using a virgin as bait. The pure maiden sits in the woods and the unicorn will approach and place his head in her lap. It is then easy prey for hunters. Besides humans, the other natural enemy of the unicorn is the lion.

**wendigo:** A North American Indian spirit, the wendigo inhabits the woods of Canada. It is a man-eating ghost that usually preys on hunters. Its tactics include whispering noises and making sounds that drive the hunter or woodsman into reckless terror. The victim then runs into the wendigo's ambush. It seems to also have had the power to possess people. Wendigo possession could be stopped in its early stages by a shaman.

**werewolves:** Stories of men turning into beasts are common in most cultures. In Roman myth, Jupiter turns **Lycaon** into a wolf as punishment for the man's savagery. In most cases, the werewolf or were creature gives up his or her human form completely to take on the shape of the animal. These transformations normally occur at night and the person returns to human form with daylight. One way to tell such a shape-changer is to see if wounds inflicted on the animal form appeared on the human the next day. The **wolfman** image, along with the legends of silver bullets and wolfsbane, are creations of Hollywood and have little to do with actual folklore.

While European tradition has the werewolf, other cultures have their version. South America has the **were-jaguar** while African folktales mention **hyena men**.

**vampire:** Stories of spirits or demons or undead creatures that require the blood of the living for sustenance are part of the mythology of many parts of the world. In *The Odyssey*, for example, Odysseus descends into the underworld but is unable to speak with the shades of the dead until he feeds them the blood of a sacrificed sheep.

Other stories of vampirism involve corpses, not just spirits or ghosts, that rise out of the grave and seek the blood of the living. A twelfth-century English chronicle by William of Newburgh tells of an evil man who died without confessing, but was given a Christian burial nevertheless. He would rise out the grave every night and walk the town's streets, his flesh rotting and infecting the air with a plague that killed many. Finally he was exhumed so the corpse could be burned, but it was found to be bloated and when struck with a spade, the man's body gushed with the warm blood of the people he had killed with the disease he had spread. The corpse was burned and the plague ended.

In Europe, stories of blood-sucking spirits and animated corpses merged, and "true" printed accounts of vampires began to appear in the sixteenth century. An account from Belgrade in 1732 describes a vampire being dispatched by driving a stake through its heart and burning the body.

In 1610, **Elizabeth Bathory**, the so-called vampire countess of Hungary, was suspected and convicted of using the blood of murdered peasants in her potions. She was actually convicted of sorcery, but was not described as a vampire until many years later.

Literary vampires became popular in English fiction in the nineteenth century, but Bram Stoker's *Dracula* in 1897 set the standard for all that followed. Our contemporary conception of the vampire as elegantly dressed, erotically attractive, and intriguingly foreign can be traced to Stoker's *Dracula* and its film adaptations.

A number of standard "rules" govern vampires and vampirism. For one, a vampire must spend the night searching for its victims, but at dawn must return to its grave. Anyone bitten by a vampire becomes a vampire upon death. One can tell a vampire by examining the corpse; if the corpse is not decayed or has some color, it is likely a vampire. Holy water will burn the flesh of a vampire, causing it to shriek in pain.

The legends built up around vampires give them a variety of powers including the ability to merge with shadows; shape-change, particularly into bats or wolves, though sometimes ticks and spiders; and the ability to mesmerize with their eyes. Vampires also have a variety of weaknesses. In some stories, vampires cannot enter a home without being invited in. They shun religious symbols. Garlic, mustard seed, and other herbs can keep them away. They can be killed with a stake through the heart, though this may not be a permanent solution. Permanently destroying a vampire requires not only the stake, but beheading the vampire, stuffing the mouth with garlic, and burning the body.

**yeti:** The word "yeti" is Tibetan, which originally referred to a mountain spirit or demon, but has come to describe a creature known also as the **Abominable Snowman**, which is something of a misnomer since it seems to be neither abominable nor live only in the snow. Conflicting accounts of sightings of the elusive creature and contradictory and questionable physical evidence make the yeti out to be either a bit smaller than an average-sized man or nearly ten feet tall. What is consistent is that the yeti lives in the Himalayan mountains, is human-shaped and covered with fur, and seems to be an herbivore. In Russia, it is known as the **alma**, and is more apelike in appearance with long arms and short legs. In China, legend tells of the **Wildman**, who is covered with grayish red fur and looks like plaster models of Peking man.

---

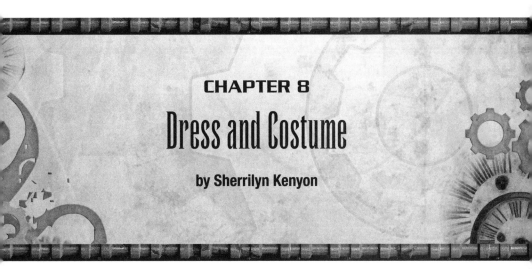

# CHAPTER 8
# Dress and Costume
### by Sherrilyn Kenyon

Costuming takes on a very important role in fantasy writing. It sets the tone for a story and can also tell the reader much about the character. Hooded robes or other voluminous garments appear any time the writer wants to add mystery to a character or conceal the character's identity. Clean, well-made silk dresses and capes imply wealth, while dirty, threadbare rags show poverty. An eye patch gives a character an evil air, but replace that patch with a belled cap and he becomes a jester. Just as in the theater, a costume can tell your audience volumes about a character in very few words.

Unlike historical writers, fantasy writers aren't bound by any set of rules. They are free to pick and choose whatever fashions and forms work best for their story. But in order to help keep the medieval pageantry so often associated with this genre, the following list should prove invaluable whether you are dressing kings or peasants.

## MATERIALS

**black-work:** A gorgeous Renaissance invention, black-work was simply embroidery done with black silk.

**brocade:** A tightly woven fabric with a raised pattern. Originally, the pattern was done with either gold or silver threads, but over time other threads were used. This was a material strictly reserved for only those who could afford it.

**canvas:** A coarse cloth made of flax or hemp. It was worn by all.

**calico:** A white cotton imported from India. Reserved for the rich.

**cambric:** A fine white linen.

**damask:** A silk fabric that was woven with various, often elaborate, patterns and designs. This was an expensive cloth reserved for royalty and nobility.

**embroidery:** Though not a fabric, embroidery was highly prized and often decorated even the poorest of fabrics. Peasant designs were simple, often nothing more than just geometric shapes. Noble clothing was much more elaborate and the stitches were often done with gold and silver thread.

**flannel:** A lightweight woolen fabric, flannel was often used as undergarments, bandages, and wash rags. It was available to all.

**freize:** A thick woolen cloth that was often used for outer garments. Worn by all classes.

**fustian:** A type of scarlet cloth, it was a lightweight silky material that also bore a resemblance to velvet. It was an expensive fabric worn by those who could afford it.

**gold and silver tissue:** A lightweight fabric that had gold or silver threads woven into it. For the most part, it was reserved for royalty. However, richer nobility and even a few enterprising wealthy merchants might also acquire a bolt every now and again.

**holland:** A very finely woven lawn material that was often used for shirts and undergarments. Usually reserved for the rich.

**lersey:** A woolen cloth, often ribbed, worn by the wealthy.

**lawn:** A finely woven linen reserved for the wealthy.

**linen:** Cloth made from flax and used by all.

**musterdevilliers:** A gray woolen cloth reserved for the middle and upper classes.

**russet (more commonly known as homespun):** A coarse woolen cloth that was most often reddish brown or gray colored. Russet was a favored material of the lower classes, but could also be found among the poorer nobility.

**samite:** A silken cloth that was often interwoven with gold. Reserved for the wealthy.

**satin:** Fabric made of silk that was shiny on one side. Reserved for the wealthy.

**scarlet:** Not to be confused with the color, scarlet cloth was most often red, but could also be a number of other colors. It was a softer cloth that draped in folds. Usually reserved for nobility, it could also be found in the possession of outlaws.

**serge:** A woolen fabric used for clothing and all types of other supplies; bedcovers, hangings, funeral drapes, shrouds, and so on. It was used by all.

**silk:** An expensive cloth woven from silk threads in the Orient. Originally reserved only for royalty, it gradually became used by the rich who could afford it.

**taffeta:** A plain-woven glossy silk reserved for the rich.

**tartan:** A twilled woolen fabric named for its tartan coloring and design.


## COLORS

**black:** First associated with the Vikings, black was worn by all and eventually became the color worn by mourners, the elderly, and scholars.

**blue:** Light blue was worn by all, but dark blue was worn by higher-ranking nobles and royalty until it became associated with scholars and apprentices.

**crimson:** A bright red worn by the wealthy.

**flame:** A bright red-orange reserved for the wealthy.

**gold cloth:** Reserved for royalty.

**green:** All shades. Worn by all.

**murrey:** Deep purple red. Worn by the rich.

**parti-colored:** Clothes that were often made up of several different colors like a Harlequin doll.

**purple:** Reserved for royalty and very high-ranking nobility.

**red:** Worn by all.

**red-browns:** Extremely popular and worn by all.

**scarlet:** A vibrant shade first reserved for royalty and then worn only by nobility.

**silver cloth:** Reserved for royalty.

**siskin:** Light greenish yellow worn by the wealthy.

**slate:** A gray blue. Worn by all.

**tan:** A light brown worn by the nobility.

**tartan:** A plaid pattern of Scottish origin, the unique colors and pattern of which denote the wearer's clan or family.

**tawny:** A brownish yellow color that was popular. Worn by all.

**watchet:** A light greenish blue worn by all.

**white:** Worn by all, but preferred by the nobility and royalty.

**yellow:** Worn by all.

## WOMEN'S CLOTHING

**aprons:** Used by middle- and lower-class women, they could be a variety of colors.

**barbe:** A pleated piece of linen similar to the barbette and widows, it was worn underneath the chin of widows and over the chin to denote a noblewoman.

**barbette:** A linen band that wrapped around the head, under the chin. It was usually pinned.

**butterfly headdress:** Worn at the back of the head, it was made of wire covered with fabric, and was draped with a fine gauzy veil that draped over the wearer's forehead and down her back. The almost right angle differentiated it from the hennin.

**caps:** Made of linen, these were often worn over frets or with barbettes or wimples.

**caul (aka fret or crispinette):** A coarse hair net made out of silk, gold, or silver. It was worn only by royalty and nobles.

**chaplet:** A padded roll that was worn on the head much like a hat. It was often bejeweled and embroidered. Variations of this could be horn-shaped or heart-shaped to where it dipped low around the forehead of the wearer. Some were extremely wide and high. It was most fashionably worn with the houppelande.

**cloak:** An outer garment worn to keep the wearer warm in cool weather. Often semicircular or square, its shape was dictated by whatever was currently fashionable. Most fastened with a chord or brooch. However, there were a few styles in the early Middle Ages that fit over the head. Wealthy and nobles often lined their cloaks with fur.

**cote-hardie:** A gown that was cut tight to the hips and then fell in folds to the ground. A row of buttons down the front were used to fasten it.

**crispinette:** *see* Caul.

**dagged or dagging:** Scallops cut into the fabric for decorative purposes.

**diadem:** In the Middle Ages, it was a crown or golden chaplet that denoted royalty. In fantasy, they can either be the former, or are more akin to chain mail in that they are made of finely riveted silver or gold. Oftentimes jewels are interwoven with the metal. These elaborate pieces drape over the forehead and down the back. They are worn by priestesses, enchantresses, demons, ladies, and thieves.

**fillet:** A stiffened piece of linen, it was molded into a wide headband that was worn like a hat. Often it was placed over the barbette or a veil.

**fitchets:** A hole cut into the cote-hardie that allowed the wearer access to her purse, which was hung on the girdle.

**fret:** *see* Caul.

**girdle:** A leather or metal belt worn about the hip. The style and length varied depending on the fashion of the day. Sometimes a purse was tied to it.

**gloves:** Made out of leather or fabric, they were worn during winter for travel. The wealthy and nobles had gloves lined with fur and some of these were scented with flower oils.

**headdress:** This name referred to the combination of a wimple and veil, or the fillet and barbette, or barbette and veil, or a cap and veil or barbette.

**hennin:** The high pointed headdress that most people associate with the Middle Ages. It often had a piece of sheer veil worn over it, or it could have a lirapipe attached to the point. It was constructed on a wire frame either left bare or covered with fabric.

**hose:** Either thick like a sock or thin like the modern-day counterpart, they were fastened about the knee with a garter.

**houppelande:** A long gown that fell loose from the shoulders. It was belted at the waist and the collar was often high and tight.

**kirtle:** Generic name for a dress. It could take a number of shapes and did so throughout the period. It was most often used to refer to the tight-fitting undergown or smock.

**lirapipe:** A long streamer that was attached to a chaplet, hennin, or heart-shaped headdress.

**mantle:** A cloak worn indoors for state functions. It was attached to the dress with brooches or was tied with cords.

**pelisse:** A jacket-type covering that was often worn over a dress and sometimes for outdoors.

**purse:** A sack made of leather or cloth, it was drawn closed with cord or leather straps that were usually long. The cords were then fastened to the girdle and the purse hung down to about midthigh.

**sideless surcoat:** This was an outer dress worn over a smock or kirtle. The sides were left open and cut to the hip. The neck could be square or round depending on the fashion. It was worn by the rich and often as court dress, or for state functions.

**sleeves:** Due to the rapidly changing fashions, these were often made to come off so the owner could update the sleeves without throwing out the costly yardage of the dress. Women were also known to give a sleeve as a token to a knight or lover.

**smock (aka undertunic):** The chemise or gown worn beneath a dress. In some styles, it was fully concealed and in others either the sleeves or skirt (or both) were visible.

**supertunic:** A strip of material with a hole cut out for the head. It could have the sides sewn shut, or were sometimes left unsewn. In the Middle Ages, it appeared around 1200 and was worn only by the lower classes. The sides were sewn up and the ends of it were tucked into the sides while they worked. Though similar, it should not be confused with the sideless surcoat worn by the rich and nobility.

**tippet:** A white piece of linen that was attached to the upper arm and worn to trail down to the floor. It was a purely decorative piece.

**undertunic:** Another name for the chemise or smock. It was worn beneath a gown and, depending on the cut of the gown, was hidden completely or seen.

**veil:** These could be long or short depending on fashion. Some were worn down the back while others were wrapped about the shoulders. Often a circlet or band was worn to help hold it in place. If not, it was pinned to the hair.

**widows:** A wimple worn over the chin with a series of pleats down the front.

**wimple:** This covered the throat and was often tucked into the neckline of the dress. Most often it was worn with a veil over it.


## MEN'S CLOTHING

**braies or breeches:** Pants. The lower classes tended to wear looser pants and the nobles or wealthy wore more form-fitting ones. Many of these either had feet made into them (some of which had leather sewn onto the bottom so they could be worn without shoes) or with loops to secure them on the foot when they were worn with boots. They were usually secured at the waist with a drawstring.

**cap:** Any of a variety of small, usually brimless hats.

**chaperon:** Similar to the woman's chaplet, it was made of material rolled up around the head. Extra material was placed up top and allowed to drape to one side. It was often worn with a coif.

**chaplet:** Same as that worn by the women.

**cloak:** Like the women, these took on a variety of shapes and styles and were worn to keep the wearer warm in the winter.

**codpiece:** When the hose were so long that they met and were tied together at the waist, a small triangular piece covered the joining. This codpiece could be made of a similar or contrasting color and was obviously seen with the shorter gypons and houppelandes.

**coif:** Similar to the barbette, they were made of white linen and covered the head and ears. Black coifs denoted scholars and elders.

**cote-hardie:** Worn over the gypon, it originally went to the knee, then was shortened to where it barely reached the hips. The front was fastened with buttons. Poorer men wore a cote-hardie of medium length.

**cowl (aka hood):** These covered the head of the wearer during inclement weather and often came to a point that draped down the wearer's back.

**dagging:** Scallops cut into the material to decorate the gorget, hem of the tunic, or sleeves.

**doublet:** A tailored tunic worn over the undertunic. The front of it was often stuffed to make the wearer appear more broad-shouldered. The length of it depended on fashion.

**folly-bells:** Worn by noblemen and jesters alike, these small bells were hung on little chains from the girdle.

**garnache:** A supertunic that was allowed to drape over the shoulder to below the elbow. Like the supertunic, it was either left open at the sides or sewn together.

**gorget:** The cape part of a hood or cowl that covered the shoulders.

**gloves:** Usually made of leather for the rich and linen for the poor, they were worn out-of-doors. Nobles and high officials would often wear them indoors as well.

**girdle:** A belt that wrapped around the waist, the style and length of which varied according to fashion.

**gypon:** Another name for a doublet.

**hose:** Made of linen or wool, these were pulled over the braies up to the knee and were gartered or cross-gartered to the shin. Wealthier men and noblemen often wore loose hose that reached all the way up their inseams.

**houppelande:** A loose gown that hung from the shoulders and was belted to the waist. The collar was high and tight. Richer men wore it long or short, and merchants and the poor wore it calf-length. A slit was made at either side or down the center to allow for greater mobility.

**jerkin:** Identical to the houppelande except that the collar was cut low into a circle or square.

**kilt:** A knee-length pleated skirt worn by Scottish men. Kilts were usually made of tartan to display the wearer's clan or family.

**lirapipe:** This was the name given for the hood when the point of it was extended and left to dangle down the back to the wearer's feet. Sometimes it was coiled around the head or neck.

**pallium:** A togalike garment, it was draped over the shoulders and hip.

**phyrgian cap:** A cone-shaped cap made of wool or linen, the brim of which was folded up.

**purse:** Men wore purses similar to the women's.

**supertunic:** A strip of material with a hole cut out for the head. Some of these also had a slit cut up the center to allow the wearer to ride a horse. The sides were often left open, but could be sewn shut. Supertunics generally hung down to midcalf.

**swords and daggers:** Neither of these were worn with civilian dress. However, both men and women often kept a small knife with them that they used for eating.

**tippet:** A long streamer that hung from the elbow, down the wearer's leg.

**tunic:** A typical shirt, the style and cut of which varied according to fashion.

**undertunic:** An undershirt. More pious laity would sometimes have this made out of horsehair or another coarse material (hence the term "hair shirt").

## SHOES

Poorer people wore sandals or ankle-length shoes that were little more than leather tied onto their feet. Boots were mostly worn by men and they took on a variety of styles from shin-length to thigh-length. Wealthy men often had them lined with fur and would turn down the tops to show off the lining. Women wore shoes made of leather and wealthy women would sometimes have them made of fabric.

## CHILDREN'S CLOTHING

Both boys and girls were dressed identically to their parents. Babies were swaddled in blankets or lightweight linen and their limbs tied, much as you see the character Eora Danan swaddled in the film *Willow*. The thought behind this was that infants, whose movements can be somewhat spastic, would hurt themselves with their flailing about.

## CLERGY

Nuns wore simple dresses, the style and color of which were determined by their order. Most wore veils and once the wimple came into fashion, they wore the two together. Crucifixes were often tied to their girdles and some wore wedding rings to symbolize their marriage to God and the Church. Although not sanctioned as part of their uniform, many sisters wore silk chemises beneath their coarse dresses. Some of these chemises were even dyed red! And on the opposite end of the spectrum, the extremely pious would sometimes wear horsehair shirts beneath their robes to chafe their skin and remind them of the suffering of Christ.

Monks and priests wore homespun robes, the color and style again dictated by their order. Most wore a wooden cross around their neck, and leather sandals or shoes on their feet. Bishops, archbishops, and popes wore silks, the style and color of which is virtually unchanged today.

Priestesses and sorceresses are seen in a variety of outfits. In Kinley MacGregor's story "Born on Fire," her priestesses wear golden robes similar to monk's robes. In Pamela McCutchinson's *Golden Prophecies*, we see priestesses dressed as Romans. And in *Wizard of Seattle*, by Kathy Hooper, sorcerers and sorceresses are dressed in everyday clothing.

Since wizards and sorcerers are often associated with religious figures (most likely due to the mystic legends of the Druids), they are often depicted in the same type of homespun robes, the colors of which tend to be black, white, brown, or navy. The somewhat cliché image of the wizards' robes are dark garments embroidered with stars or moons; leave this kind of garb for the Disney movies, not your novel. A much more realistic representation is that of Merlin in the film *Excalibur*. There, Merlin wears monk-like robes and a metal skull cap.

## CHASTITY BELTS

Although chastity belts have been used in a number of fantasy novels over the years, they were not a part of the European Middle Ages, although there is evidence to show that they were used in the Far East during that period. Chastity belts have a variety of forms, the most common of which is the belt made of a magical, nonrusting metal that either the heroine or her love must quest to find a way to open it. We see just such an example in David Vierling's *Armor Amore*.

Another type of chastity belt is that made of cloth and bound with a magical spell to keep all the men at bay, or one that has a magical knot that only a designated lover can undo. This latter is the type Marie de France uses in her novel *Guigemar*. In this epic, the lady begs for the hero's shirt and he wraps it around her in such a manner that no man can remove it without cutting it. The heroine swears only to love the man who can undo the knot without violence and, of course, that is only the hero.

# CHAPTER 9
# Arms, Armor, and Armies

## by Michael J. Varhola

Few fantasy stories would be complete without powerful warriors, skilled soldiers, and the armies they head (or fight against), not to mention the tools of their trade—weapons and armor.

This chapter is designed to provide writers with an overview of ancient and medieval arms, armor, and armies so that they can effectively include these things in their stories. Other aims are to give writers authentic terminology they can use in their stories, point them in the right direction for doing more research, and help them think about how and why arms and armor were used and developed.

## ARMS

When arming characters, there are several things that writers should take into account. Among these are what the people in question use their weapons for, what their level of technology is, and what their material resources are.

The sorts of weapons a culture uses says much about that culture and are determined by their chosen forms of combat. For example, long, slashing swords and javelins might be favored by warriors who fight from chariots or horseback. Missile weapons like bows and slings are likely to be preferred by warriors who make their living hunting when not waging war. Maces, picks, and other heavy, crushing weapons are the sort that will be used by soldiers who need to penetrate the defenses of heavily armored opponents. Long, sharpened paddles used for rowing canoes might be the primary weapons of a riverine jungle people. Steel-bladed swords, spears, and arrows might be issued to the professional soldiers of a wealthy city-state.

The technology level of the people in question and their available material resources will dictate the material form of the weapons to a very great extent. For example, are they operating at the level of a Stone Age, Copper Age, Bronze Age, Iron Age, or even some age unknown in our world? Warriors of a primitive people unable to work metal and living in an area devoid of appropriate rocks might utilize "Bone Age" technology, arming the edges of heavy wooden clubs with bone shards and making spear- and arrowheads from sharpened pieces of bone.

Writers should also consider the attitudes that people of their cultures have toward their weapons, for example, the warriors of the various Germanic peoples (Goths, Saxons, Vikings) had a spiritual reverence for fine weapons. The antithesis of this attitude was found in the Roman republic, where soldiers regarded weapons as necessary tools to be brought forth when needed and then put away until needed again.

## Weapons Terms

Most weapons can be divided into several broad types, that are explained below. For some, subgroups or various regional or variant names are also provided in parentheses. Not all are exactly synonymous, but are at the least in the same family of weapons. For example, a gaesum and a pilum are both types of javelins, but are not identical in form or function.

Weapons inflict three broad types of damage: crushing (clubs, maces), cutting (axes, broadswords), and piercing (arrows, spears, lances, longswords).

axe: Many shapes, sizes, and varieties of this weapon have been used throughout the world for about fifty thousand years. Stone Age peoples used flint-headed axes with wooden hafts; medieval men-at-arms used heavy, steel-headed two-handed axes like the **bardiche** to hack through plate armor; and warriors in India used axes with hafts and heads forged entirely out of steel, the weapons ornately decorated with koftgari etch work. Axes were used extensively by primitive or barbarian warriors because they could serve as both tools and weapons.

**bow:** Bows have been used by hunters, warriors, and soldiers the world over since prehistory. **Self-bows** consist of a single piece of flexible wood. **Composite bows** are made of one or more pieces of wood reinforced with layers of horn and sinew. In all cases, the string is markedly shorter than the bow itself in order to provide tension.

Short self-bows can have pulls ranging from forty or fifty pounds for the primitive hunting bows of forest peoples, who operate at short ranges, to seventy or eighty pounds for an English longbow with typical ranges of 230-250 yards, to about 110 pounds for some types of East African bows. Composite bows allow for much stronger pulls, the Turkish variety of this weapon having a pull of 150 or 160 pounds with typical ranges of 360–400 yards.

**club:** Basically an extension of the fist, simple wooden clubs were the first hand weapons and were used universally. Their descendants, **composite clubs**, were similarly widespread, and consist of wooden clubs with stone or metal heads, sometimes simply round but more often armed with metal flanges or spikes. Examples of these include **maces, morning stars,** and **flails.**

**crossbow:** Crossbows have advantages over bows in that they allow mechanical power to be substituted for muscle and can be kept readied to fire longer than can bows. Disadvantages include having a rate of fire much less than that of bows.

Crossbows probably appeared in Europe in the eleventh century and were developed into progressively more powerful weapons over the course of the next few centuries. The lightest had wooden bows and could be cocked by hand. The most powerful, called **arbalests,** had steel bows and could only be armed by use of a windlass, goat's foot lever, or similar device. Such weapons could pierce armor and constituted such a threat to armored knights that for a time the Church banned their usage against Christians (a ban about as effective as those being called for against handguns today).

Crossbows fire bolts, or quarrels, broad-fletched projectiles less than half the length of arrows.

**dagger:** Usually double-edged and used for both slashing and thrusting, the dagger is a universal weapon. Daggers were often used as secondary weapons to be resorted to after being deprived of a primary weapon (their concealability enhanced this usage), or used as an offhand weapon.

Daggers were also made for special purposes. For example, the Indian **peshkabz** had an acute point and reinforced spine, so it could be rammed through mail armor; and the French **misericorde** was long and narrow, so it could be thrust through openings in the armor of knights who had been knocked to the ground.

Amongst people with limited metalworking abilities, long copper, bronze, or iron daggers sometimes served as primary weapons.

**javelin:** Such light spears are designed for hurling, rather than melee, and generally have about twice the range of thrown close-combat spears. Some, notably the **pilum**, were forged with a soft metal neck that bent upon impact. This made it impossible to hurl back, hard to withdraw from a wound; and, if stuck in a shield, weighed it down and made it difficult or impossible to use. (Gaelic **gaesum**; Roman **pilum**)

**lance:** In its simplest form, a spear used by a mounted warrior whose horse is equipped with spurs. Used by such a soldier, a lance could be couched under his arm when charging in order to put the weight of the horse behind the impact of the weapon. During the Middle Ages, the lance developed several features, including hand grips and guards, and specialized heads. The term "lance" is often erroneously used to refer simply to a spear. No other melee weapon can inflict as much shock and damage as a lance wielded by a mounted warrior with stirrups, as the weight of the horse is behind the attack.

**polearm:** Any weapon consisting of a head mounted on a haft, the former usually of metal and the latter usually of wood. The spear, a dagger blade mounted on a pole, is the simplest form of polearm. Throughout the world, innumerable types have been used, ranging from the modified peasant tools to highly specialized arms designed to penetrate heavy armor. Examples include the **bill, guisarme,** and **fauchard,** weapons used by European peasants in time of war; the **bec de corbin, Lucerne hammer,** and **halberd,** all designed to help infantrymen stand up to or even overcome heavy cavalry; and the Japanese **naginta** and Indian **hoolurge,** both polearms with broad cleaving heads.

**sword:** No class of weapon has been so revered or romanticized as the sword. Swords represent a relatively high level of technology and economic development, in that they were made almost entirely of metal and were thus expensive and labor-intensive. Swords were produced in a great variety of shapes and sizes, and several general types are described below, loosely in the order of their technological development.

**bastard sword:** Also called a hand-and-a-half sword, this is a weapon that can be wielded with either one hand or two. Examples include the **khandar** of India and what was called a **sword of war** during the European Middle Ages.

**broadsword:** A sword three or more feet in length with a rounded or spatulate tip used for chopping or slashing. Examples include the iron swords of Dark Age barbarians and of Middle Eastern chariot peoples.

**khopesh:** A bronze sword of ancient Egypt about two feet long with a heavy, cleaverlike, D-shaped blade. What is most interesting about the khopesh is that its form was adopted throughout the ancient world and it became the grandfather of an extended family of cleaverlike shortswords that includes the **falcate** of Spain, the **kopis** of Greece, the **sax** of the Danes, and the **kukuri** of Nepal.

**longsword:** A double-edged, long-bladed sword with an acute point that could be used for slashing or thrusting. Most of the swords carried by the knights and men-at-arms of the Middle Ages were of this sort, although these can be divided into more than a dozen broad types. Representing a higher technology level than most broad- or shortswords, such weapons were deadlier and almost always made of steel. **Rapiers** are an example of an especially thin, long version of such a weapon.

**protosword:** A wooden club shaped like a sword and fashioned with acute, swordlike edges, or armed with chunks of stone, glass, or other sharp objects. Such weapons were made by peoples who recognized the superior form of the sword, but were unable to produce the true metal swords. Examples include the **macahuitl** of the Aztecs, and the shark-toothed **tebutje** of the Gilbert Islanders of Micronesia.

**scimitar:** A curved, single-edged slashing sword, typical of Middle Eastern and especially Arabic peoples. The **saber** is a type of scimitar designed for equestrian troops.

**shortsword:** Broad-bladed, usually double-edged swords about two feet in length were popular amongst many peoples. Roman soldiers carried the steel **gladius**; Celts wielded leaf-shaped bronze shortswords; West

Africans used broad-bladed iron shortswords. Shortswords were often made by people who had not achieved a high level of metalworking ability and used a relatively soft metal, such as copper or low-carbon iron. Broad, thick blades helped to make such weapons strong enough for use in battle.

**two-handed sword:** Heavy, two-handed weapons of this sort tended to be five or six feet in length, twenty-five or more pounds in weight, and used for hacking. The best examples of such weapons came into use from the fifteenth century onward. Specific examples include the **zweihaender** of the German landsknecht mercenaries and the **no-dachi** of Japan.

**stirrups:** Although not a weapon as such, stirrups caused one of the great revolutions in the history of warfare. They allowed mounted warriors to use high-impact weapons like lances and to more effectively fire bows from the saddle. Since the earliest days of European warfare, disciplined formations of heavily armored infantrymen, exemplified by Roman legionnaires, had dominated the battlefield and could withstand attacks from cavalry, which were largely relegated to the role of skirmishers. Stirrups were invented around 200 B.C. in China, during the early Imperial period. They were introduced in Europe one thousand years later by Muslim invaders. The first European warriors to adopt them were probably the mounted troops of Charlemagne, who heralded in a millennium of battlefield dominance by cavalry.

## ARMOR

Throughout history, various sorts of armor have been developed to protect combatants, and weapons have been improved upon and specialized for the purposes of penetrating that armor.

In fantasy art, movies, and literature, warriors are often depicted wearing little, if any, body armor. In reality, however, most historical warriors endeavored to equip themselves with as much protection as possible, and unarmored or lightly armored soldiers were generally hacked to bits by those who were better equipped. Armor stands between a soldier and the weapons that others are trying to kill him with, and its value cannot be underestimated. Armor can deflect or absorb weapons blows that would otherwise maim or kill their wearer.

The following section is an overview of the use of armor and provides authentic terminology. After all, anybody can write, "Duke William donned his helmet," and that might be good enough. If you have to, however, it is nice to be able to write, "Duke William donned his spangenhelm, then pulled his ventail up to cover his throat and jaw, tying off the corners of the mail flap to the sides of his coif."

Armor can be broadly divided into helmets, shields, and body armor.

**HELMETS** are often the most crucial and universally worn pieces of armor, even among nonwealthy troops. Head wounds are the most bloody, disabling, and lethal, and nothing is more important than preventing them. Broadly speaking, a helmet can include anything from a bronze skull cap, a thick cotton turban, an iron great helm, a conical steel helm, with a noseguard or a hood of mail.

**Shields** are devices held in the user's nonweapon hand and are actively used to block weapon blows or enemy missiles. Shields can be of any shape, size, or material. Shields must strike a balance sturdiness and maneuverability; a shield made of plate steel may stop any weapon, but would be impossible to lift; one made of paper might be easy to carry and move about, but obviously wouldn't stop weapon blows very well. Most have a wood core or frame, a covering of leather and metal fittings if available. Other materials have included wickerwork, turtle shell, and even reinforced cloth and silk.

**BODY ARMOR** in some form has been worn for thousands of years in every place that human beings have made war upon each other. The materials such armor was constructed of depended on what was available, the technology level of the society constructing it, and the needs of those wearing it. For example, the peoples of Mesoamerica made armor of quilted cotton because cotton was readily available, they did not have metalworking technology, and they really did not need anything considerably better against the Stone Age weapons they faced.

Throughout the ancient world, many sorts of body armor were used, including coats of mail, scales, rings, and plates. Armor ranged in complexity from leather cloaks studded with metal worn by Assyrian soldiers to the extremely complex panoply of the Samurai, which consisted of dozens of specialized pieces of finely crafted metal and silk armor. Padded clothing was always worn under armor to reduce chafing and help absorb blows.

For many centuries after the fall of Rome in the fifth century A.D., most European warriors wore leather armor, sometimes augmented by metal studs or rings; waist-length, short-sleeved coats of mail, and remnants of Roman armor.

---

By the eleventh century, the best-equipped warriors wore a **HAUBERK,** a knee-length coat of mail, and a **SPANGENHELM,** a conical helmet made of four sections of wood and leather set in a metal frame with a nasal, a metal bar protecting the nose and upper face. Shields during this period tended to either be a few feet wide and round, or about four-feet high and kite-shaped, the latter type favored by cavalrymen. Vikings, Normans, and many early crusaders were equipped this way.

Mail was gradually augmented with additional pieces. By the thirteenth century, it was being reinforced with **COATS OF PLATES,** typically cloth or leather vests with rows of metal plates sewn into them—pieces of plate metal to protect the elbows, knees, and shins. Cylinder-shaped **GREAT HELMS** were adopted by many warriors, and the kite shield was abbreviated into the **HEATER** shield.

European body armor reached its developmental peak in the fifteenth century. Armor was almost entirely made of plate metal components and was characterized as **FULL-PLATE.** Shields were either smaller or abandoned altogether because of the greater protective value of armor.

The progressive competition between weapon smiths and armors was abruptly settled in the sixteenth century with the spread of firearms. Armorers tried to conquer this by creating increasingly heavy breastplates, but eventually had to concede the contest. Complex, expensive, highly protective suits of armor were still made for a few centuries, but used only for tournaments and pageants. Battlefield armor was abandoned piece by piece until by the eighteenth century, even helmets were abandoned—for a time.

Since then, firearms have continued to evolve and become more deadly, while no effective defenses have been developed to counteract their effects. Even modern bulletproof vests are not completely protective against firearms. Such armor is really only effective against handgun ammunition or explosive fragments, and generally cannot withstand rifle fire; protects only the torso and its vital organs, not the limbs or head; and it is not provided to regular soldiers in any case. Bulletproof helmets do exist and are issued to U.S. military personnel, and some form of helmet is worn by the soldiers of most armies. If anything, this is a reminder of the importance of head protection, one of the first and most universal forms of personal defense.

## Armor Terms

Several specific sorts of helmets, shields, and armor, along with various armor terms, are described below. Pieces described as being plate armor are usually worn in conjunction with other pieces to form transitional-plate or full-plate armor.

**aventail:** A flap of mail that hangs down from the back of a helmet to protect the wearer's neck.

**bard:** Armor for a horse, which could be constructed of much the same materials as armor for human. Individual pieces included the **chanfron** or **champfrein**, a piece designed to protect the horse's head.

**bevor (a.k.a. beaver):** A piece of mail or plate armor that protected the chin and lower face, often attached to the bottom of a helmet with hinges if made of plate, or part of a coif if made of mail or padded cloth.

**breastplate:** A metal plate designed to protect the torso. In their simplest form, breastplates may be square or round pieces, a few hands across in width and worn strapped onto the chest. Those worn by ancient Greek and Italian warriors were of bronze and cast to look musculatured. Steel breastplates came into use in Europe during the 1200s to augment chain mail and by the 1500s were one of the many plate steel components of full-plate armor.

Backplates were a typical counterpart to the breastplate, but were notably absent among some armies. For example, many Greek soldiers had only breastplates, causing rout in battle to be thought of as tantamount to suicide as it left an unprotected back exposed.

**breaths:** Narrow slits or holes in the close helms and great helms of the Middle Ages used to breathe through.

**coif:** A hood of mail, often attached to a coat of mail. In India, mail with an attached coif was often referred to as **ghughuwa**.

**couter:** A piece of plate armor that protects the elbow, attached to the upper and lower arm guards by hinges.

**cuisse:** A broad piece of formed plate armor that protected the thighs. Such armor typically wrapped around the front and sides of the thighs but left their backs unprotected.

**fauld:** A mail skirt worn under plate armor to protect the groin.

**flutes:** Corrugations in some plate armor of the late Middle Ages that gave it additional strength but did not add to its weight. A characteristic of what is known as Maximilian Armor.

**gauntlet:** A heavy leather or metal glove. Those of the Middle Ages designed for use with plate armor often had articulated steel fingers.

**gorget:** A heavy piece of plate armor designed to protect the neck.

**greave:** A piece of armor, usually of metal but possibly of hardened leather, used to protect the shins. Greaves were used from the earliest times, from Bronze Age Greek warriors to sixteenth-century European knights.

**haute-piece:** A ridge of metal on plate shoulder armor designed to prevent horizontal cuts to the neck.

**helm, helmet:** A piece of armor designed to protect the head. There are innumerable names and variations, but a few notable ones follow.

> **arming cap:** A padded, lightweight cloth helm worn underneath a heavier metal helmet, or by itself by troops of modest means.

> **barbute:** A Renaissance helm with an opening for the face shaped like a rounded "t," the barbute is based on an ancient Greek helmet and was revived because of the Renaissance veneration for the classical world.

> **close helmet:** A plate-armor helmet of the late Middle Ages that fitted very closely around the head and was looked through by means of narrow sights or eye slits. Such helmets often consisted of two or more pieces that were bolted together around the head of the soldier. Examples include the **armet**.

> **great helm:** A heavy, round helm of the early Middle Ages that looked a bit like a bucket or can with eye slits. The great helms of knights often had their heraldic devices mounted on top of them.

> **khula-kud:** A Persian or Indian helmet, traditionally consisting of a round steel cap, a noseguard extending down from the brim, an aventail, and a pair of hollow metal pipes attached to either side of the front, used to hold plumes.

> **morion:** A broad-brimmed, high-crested helmet of the Renaissance, usually associated with the Spanish Conquistadors.

**lance rest:** A metal hook attached to the breastplate of plate armor and used to help keep a lance level during a charge.

**lorica segmentata:** This characteristic armor of the Roman legions consisted of horizontal bands of iron protecting the abdomen and torso, with smaller vertical pieces to protect the shoulders. A knee-length skirt of metal-studded leather strips protected the lower part of the body.

**mail:** A type of armor made up of interconnected links of metal. In most examples, each ring of metal is attached to four others, creating a tough, flexible mesh, which is called the "four-in-one pattern." Such armor was worn throughout Europe, Asia, and North Africa.

Mail is often referred to (somewhat redundantly) as **chain mail**.

**pauldron:** Pieces of plate armor designed to protect the shoulders.

**poleyn:** A piece of plate armor that protects the knee, which is attached to the thigh and shin armor by means of pins or hinges.

**sabaton (aka soleret):** A piece of plate armor used to protect the top of the feet.

**scale armor:** Armor consisting of scales of metal, horn, or leather on a coat of cloth or leather. Such armor was used by the Byzantine and later Roman armies, and was characteristic of the cataphractoi and clibinarus heavy cavalrymen.

**shield:** Shields are probably the earliest type of armor designed specifically for defense, and many sorts have been carried by troops through the ages. A few notable varieties are described below.

> **buckler:** A very small shield, usually a few hands wide and made entirely of metal. Such shields required great skill to use effectively.

> **heater:** A three-sided shield with a straight upper edge and two curving sides meeting at the bottom in a point, widely used during the Middle Ages.

> **hoplon:** The large, round shield of the ancient Greek heavy infantrymen.

> **scutum:** The large, semicylindrical rectangular body shield carried by Roman legionaries.

**side wing:** A piece of plate armor attached to knee guards to help defend against blows to the side of the leg.

**surcoat:** A loose tunic worn over armor during the Middle Ages that was usually emblazoned with a soldier's colors or heraldic markings.

**tasset:** A broad piece of plate armor used to protect the thigh.

**vambrance:** A piece of forearm armor.

**ventail:** A square of mail attached to the upper chest by two corners, the other two hanging loose across the chest when not in use. In battle, the wearer pulls the ventail up to protect his throat and jaw, tying off the loose corners to the sides of his coif.

--------------------------------------------------------------------------------

**visor:** A piece of a helmet covering the face, usually capable of being lifted on hinges or removed.

## ARMIES

Writers creating armies should understand the difference between warriors and soldiers. Warriors are the combatants of primitive or nonurbanized cultures and are judged largely on the basis of individual skill and ability. They tend to go into battle in loose mobs or grouped into warbands, and are led by warriors who lead by virtue of strong personality or heredity status.

Soldiers are the combatants of organized or urbanized societies and are trained to fight in units rather than as individuals. Soldiery draws its strength from numbers and cooperation at every level. Soldiers are organized into units, go into battle in formations, and are led by officers that have been appointed over them by the state or promoted based on merit and experience.

Troops can be formed on the battlefield in many ways, and different eras, places, and conditions have dictated various ways of doing so. In the classical world, units of troops tended to be drawn up in a straight line, with the strongest unit on the right flank. Infantry typically formed the core of such armies. Units of cavalry were deployed on the flanks to prevent an enemy from surrounding one end of the army. Units of cavalry might be deployed to the rear of the army and deployed as needed once a battle began.

In battle, commanders tried to force the enemy to retreat, rout, or surrender; completely annihilating an enemy was not always a desirable, necessary, or possible goal. Soldiers were deployed in order to maneuver around an enemy and attack its flank or rear, or break through its lines to do the same. Once this occurred, all or much of the breached army might break and run. At that point, cavalry was typically deployed to harry or eliminate the fleeing enemy.

Writers interested in describing battles should read about historic examples. Almost any detailed information about a battle will be useful, regardless of the period. The actions of the Second Punic War (218–202 B.C.), fought between Hannibal's Carthaginians and Rome's legions, are ideal reading for such purposes. Reading about the first defeat of Rome at the Battle of Lake Trasimene—Hannibal's quintessential victory with his double envelopment of the Roman army at Cannae, and his ultimate defeat before the gates of

Carthage at the Battle of Zama—will make writers infinitely more qualified to discuss the actions on a field of battle.

Writers should also be aware that the vast majority of combatants have no idea what is going on around them in a battle, and even commanders might have skewed ideas of what is happening. Tolstoy captures much of this battlefield confusion in episodes throughout *War and Peace*, his classic novel of the Napoleonic wars.

### Quality of Troops

Writers can mentally classify the soldiers of their armies according to their level of skill, training, and experience. These terms might be used to describe troops of certain types. For example, an experienced soldier might very well refer disdainfully to "green" soldiers, and a commander would certainly be cognizant of which of his troops were veterans.

Various units might have identifying names rather than generic descriptions: One company of green levies might be identified by their village of origin called "The Mill Village Militia"; a regiment of veteran mounted lancers might be named for their commander and called "Arikon's Winged Lightning"; and a king's elite palace bodyguards might be named for his mystical guardian and called "Blue Dragons."

**REGULAR TROOPS** will make up the bulk of most professional armies. They are soldiers with training in arms and maneuvers, many of whom will have seen some limited action, such as border skirmishes or putting down urban riots. Such troops will stand their ground in the face of all normal battlefield threats and, with proficient leadership, can be very reliable.

**GREEN TROOPS** may have little or no training, or be relatively well trained but have no experience. Thus, they may be as good with their weapons as regulars on the training field, or may even be able to march better. However, such troops have not been exposed to real action, and without strong leadership and steady units on their flanks, they are liable to break under any sort of duress; for example, during the War of 1812, Maryland militia troops at the Battle of Bladensburg broke and ran when rockets were fired over their heads.

**VETERAN TROOPS** have had extensive training and considerable experience. Units of such soldiers will invariably have a history and will practice rituals or pageants that recall their glories. Such troops might also be entitled to special honors, such as wearing a special device on their uniforms, carrying silver-plated weapons or being awarded extra pay. Most legionaries of the Roman Empire were veteran troops, and legions displayed their histories with standards that they carried into battle. The officers in charge of a unit of regulars will usually be a group of veterans.

**ELITE TROOPS** are the best soldiers, which will be formed into units. Some armies may have no elite troops at all, such as those with little experience at warfare, and they will be a prized component of those that do. Elite units in history include the **SACRED BAND OF THEBES**, a two-hundred-man unit that helped make the Greek city-state of Thebes formidable. They died to a man defending their city against the armies of Alexander the Great, who afterward wept for their valor. Elite soldiers are usually the leaders of veteran soldiers.

**HEROES** are unique soldiers with extensive training, experience, and special abilities, like magic weapons, great strength, or supernatural companions. They will lead units of veteran or elite soldiers or entire armies, or even operate independently. Beyond them are superheroes, demigods, demons, deities ... The possibilities in a fantasy milieu are unlimited.

The above notes are useful guidelines but can be bent as needed. Historically, even elite units have broken inexplicably, and green troops have stood their ground under harrowing circumstances. Some very dramatic scenes can be created by considering these facts.

### Types of Troops

Troops can be divided into several types based on their role in battle. Many of these troop types had specific names as well, usually based on the sort of equipment they used. For example, many classical world infantrymen were named for the type of shield they carried (Greek **HOPLITES** were named for their hoplon, a large, round shield).

**INFANTRY.** The most versatile arm of a military force are foot soldiers. They can operate under the greatest variety of conditions and with the least expense and equipment. Such troops also tend to be the least glamorous or rewarded of any sorts of soldiers.

**HEAVY INFTANTRY** are as heavily armored as possible (which may not be very heavy in some cultures) with close-combat weapons and perhaps secondary

--------------------------------------------------------------------------------

hurled weapons, and trained to fight toe-to-toe with the enemy in close formations. Examples include the Roman **LEGIONARY**, armed with javelins, shortswords, and daggers; the Greek **HOPLITE**, armed with twelve to eighteen-foot-long pikes; and medieval **MEN-AT-ARMS**, armed with armor-crushing weapons like battle axes, maces, and flails.

**LIGHT INFANTRY** wore light or no armor, or perhaps only shields and helmets. Typically, they served as skirmishers, launching missiles at the front ranks of an enemy force before close combat, dispatching wounded soldiers on the battlefield or chasing down retreating foes. Examples include the **VELITES** of Rome, armed with javelins; the **PELTASTS** of Greece, also armed with javelins; and the **PINDARIS** of India, armed with pikes and miscellaneous weapons.

**MISSILE TROOPS** typically wore no armor and could not engage the enemy in close combat. Such troops were often among the most highly trained of an army. Examples include the Balearic **SLINGERS** of the ancient world and the English **LONGBOWMEN** of the Middle Ages.

**CAVALRY.** The first sort of effective cavalry was **CHARIOTRY.** Forces of chariot troops conquered much of Asia and India in the second millennium B.C. Chariots are even more limited than horses in the kinds of terrain they can operate on, however, and once horses were bred strong enough to carry an armored man, more maneuverable individual cavalrymen eclipsed the chariotry, beginning around 500 B.C.

**HEAVY CAVALRY** used hand weapons like swords, spears, and axes; wore heavy armor; and fought in close formation, often stirrup to stirrup. The horses of such units were often as heavily armored as the men, equipped with bard of quilted cloth, scales, mail, or plate. Examples include the Byzantine **CATAPHRACTOI**; the armored **KNIGHTS** of the Middle Ages; and the **MAMLUK SLAVE SOLDIERS** of medieval Egypt.

**LIGHT CAVALRY** wore little armor and were used to skirmish against, harry, or pursue the enemy, usually using missile weapons, such as javelins or bows. Prior to the introduction of stirrups, most cavalry were of this sort. The best example of such troops were the **MONGOL MOUNTED ARCHERS**, who could fire accurately from the saddle while moving at a full gallop.

## Soldier Terms

Many of the following terms are selected to help writers think about how to organize their armies, for example, the names of various types or units or ranks. In addition to general troop types, there are also listings for various ranks, types of units, and specific troop types to help writers think about the special kinds of soldiers they can include in their armies.

Many of the following terms apply to the Roman and Macedonian armies, both excellent models for the armies of a fantasy world.

**acies:** A single Roman battle line. As would follow, **triplex acies** designates a three-line battle formation.

**agema:** A Greek term for an army in the field, and in the Macedonian army, an elite unit.

**alae:** The "wings" of a Roman battle line, usually formed by cavalry.

**Amazon:** A female warrior, this term originally referred to a tribe of woman warriors believed by the Greeks to live along the shores of the Black Sea. The term has subsequently come to be used in reference to any groups of female combatants.

**antesignani:** Roman soldiers who fought in front of the battlefield standards (i.e., usually first-rate troops) as opposed to the **postsignani**, troops who fought behind the standards.

**aquila:** The eagle battlefield standard of the Roman legions.

**arquebusier:** A soldier of the late Middle Ages or Renaissance who was armed with an arquebus, or handgun, a type of matchlock firearm.

**artillerymen:** In ancient and medieval times, the soldiers who crewed ballistae, catapults, and bombards, who were often considered mere laborers rather than true soldiers.

**auxilia:** Auxiliary foreign troops attached to Roman armies. Most of Rome's cavalry, archers, and slingers were auxiliaries, such troops typically being drawn from Gaul, Syria, and Spain, respectively.

**battalion:** A unit of about one thousand men, or ten companies. From the Swiss *battaile*, units of axemen and halberdiers raised during the Burgundian-Swill War (1474–1477) against the French.

**berserkers:** Warriors able to work themselves up into a frenzy before going into battle so as to fight more effectively in hand-to-hand combat. Such warriors might imbibe hallucinogenic or other drugs, such as the **Hashashim of Syria**, who ambushed and assassinated European knights on Crusade.

**blunderbuss woman:** A member of an elite female corps under the command of the king of Dahomey, Africa. Blunderbuss women and their counterparts, the **razor women**, were equal in status to men and were actually considered to be better troops. At their peak, they numbered some 2,400 and were used not just as bodyguards, but on the battlefield.

**captain:** In the ancient world and Middle Ages, a general term for the commander of a force of one hundred or more men; a company commander.

**cataphractoi:** Heavily armored cavalrymen, cataphractoi were armored from head to foot in mail reinforced with plate; even their horses were completely covered in scale armor. A sixth-century Persian document lists the arms and armor required of each individual cataphractus: lance, sword, mace, battle-axe, two bows and a bowcase, a quiver with thirty arrows, two extra bowstrings, mail, breastplate, helmet, greaves, arm guards, buckler, and bard.

Similar troops included the **clibinari** of the late Roman Empire. Because the extensive arms and equipment required by such troops was so expensive, each clibinarus tended to be of aristocratic background.

**centurion:** In the Roman army, a high-ranking, noncommissioned officer in charge of a century. Such veteran soldiers were the backbone of the Roman army.

**century:** A unit of the ancient Roman army numbering eighty to one hundred men at full strength.

**cohort:** A unit of the Roman army, numbering 480 to 800 men at full strength and composed of six to eight centuries.

**company:** A basic unit of troops, usually consisting of about one hundred or more troops and led by a midrank officer or senior noncommissioned officer. Specific examples include the Roman **century** (c. 80–100 men), the Macedonian **syntagma** (c. 256 men) and the Greek **pentekostos** (c. 128 men).

**conquistador:** Spanish adventurer-soldiers who conquered much of the New World in the sixteenth century. Firearms, horses, modern tactics, ruthlessness, and treachery allowed them to overcome Aztec, Mixtec, and Mayan forces that were vastly superior in numbers.

**cuahchic:** Shock troops of the Aztecs. Such troops were all elite veterans who opted to serve in the elite assault units rather than assume command as captains. Cuahchics were distinguished by Mohawk-style haircuts and typically armed with obsidian-edged clubs (**macahuitls**), padded body suits, and shields.

**colonel:** Literally, the leader of a column. In Western armies, a typical command for a colonel is a brigade, or about two thousand men.

**crossbowman (aka arbalestier):** A soldier armed with a crossbow. Such fighters began to come into use near the end of the twelfth century.

**Crusader:** European knights and soldiers who participated in the various religious Crusades that began in 1096, usually with the Holy Land as a goal.

**engineer:** Soldiers assigned the duties of constructing fortifications, field works, and obstacles, or the removal of the same. Prior to the rise of modern armies, the engineer was considered a civilian rather than a soldier. The word is derived from Latin and means ingenious, and points to the high regard in which expert engineers were held.

**escrimador:** Filipino warriors trained in the use of a straight fighting stick who are reputed to have defeated Magellan's swordsmen in combat.

**federati:** Gothic warriors and aristocracy who were given military training by the Roman army in the third century A.D. This double-edged program meant trained Goths formed a buffer between the Romans and more fearsome enemies, but also that the Goths acquired skills (both military and administrative) that would later be used against Rome.

**general:** The leader of a body of at least several thousand men, a group usually characterized as an army. In armies with complex structures, a great variety of officers might serve under a general, including colonels, majors, captains, and lieutenants. In simpler armies, all the main officers under the general might simply be referred to as his captains.

**handgunner:** A soldier armed with a handgun or hand cannon, early forms of firearms.

**hastati:** The heavy spearmen of the Roman army who occupied the first line in a three-line battle formation (*see* Acies). Literally, someone who used a hasta, or spear.

**hoplite:** Heavy infantry of classical Greece, named for the large body shields they carried called hoplon.

**horns of the bull:** An enveloping tactic used by Zulu armies. The army would attack in a half-moon formation, fixing the enemy with the central section of the army, allowing the flanking units to encircle the enemy and closing inward like a huge pair of horns.

**Huscarl:** Danish mercenaries in the pay of the Saxon kings of England. The main weapon of these staunch warriors was the two-handed Danish axe, which they swung in huge arc. Huscarls wore the Saxon **byrnie** for protection and used the Norman-style kite shield, as well as an older round shield. Despite their skill and fortitude, they were defeated at the battle of Hastings in 1066 by Norman cavalrymen.

**ile:** A cavalry unit in Greek and Macedonian armies.

**Immortal:** A class of ancient Persian infantryman.

**Jannisary:** Christian child raised to be a soldier by the Ottoman empire. Jannisaries were fierce, dedicated soldiers and often used as shock troops.

**knight:** This was the name applied to mounted warriors of aristocracy in western Europe from the ninth century onward. The **paladins of Charlemagne** were among the first knights of the European ages.

**legion, Roman:** The basic strategic division of the Roman army differed in size and composition over the centuries, but at full strength tended to range from 4,200 to 5,200 men. In the first century B.C. when Julius Caesar was battling the Gauls, a 4,800-man legion consisted of ten **cohorts**, each composed of three **maniples**, one each of **principles, hastati,** and **triarii.** Each maniple was composed of two centuries of eighty men, so sixty centuries made up a legion.

A legion might also have attached to it cohorts of auxiliary cavalry and infantry, many of them specialists, such as Gallic cavalrymen, Syrian archers, or Spanish slingers. Some 1,200 auxiliaries per legion was typical.

A Roman field army typically consisted of four or more legions.

**levy:** A commoner, usually a peasant, called up for military service.

**line units:** The regular units that made up the line of battle as opposed to guard or elite units.

**men-at-arms:** Typically, well-equipped and armed warriors of the Middle Ages of non-noble birth. Such men-at-arms were trump cards in close combat. So heavily armored and equipped were they, however, that they often could not fight very long, and the victor was often the man who could outlast his opponent.

**marines:** Troops trained to fight on shipboard or attack from a ship. They were distinct from sailors in that marines were stationed on vessels but did not actually operate them. In some military systems, marines are employed on shipboard to prevent sailor mutinies or to protect the ship's officers.

**militia:** Municipal citizen armies began to rapidly form in Europe around the eleventh and twelfth centuries. These armies not only defended their cities, but often furthered the ends of the city abroad. Some of them were quite puissant. The **militia of Ghent**, Belgium, for example, were not only an exceptional field force armed with bows, pikes, and swords, they were also widely considered specialists in siege.

**mounted infantryman (aka dragoon, hobilar):** A soldier who moved about on horseback or other means other than his own feet, but fought on foot as an infantryman rather than mounted as a cavalryman.

**musician:** Military musicians conveyed signals or made field calls, such as signal to attack or retreat. In armies where soldiers were trained to march, musicians used percussion instruments to beat a cadence by which a pace was set.

**oarsmen:** Rowers aboard oar-driven ships were most common in the Mediterranean Sea during the classical age of Greece and the dominion of Rome. Contrary to common belief, oarsmen were more often freemen than slaves and received decent pay for their services. Outside of the Mediterranean, oarsmen were usually also warriors, for example, the Viking raiders of the ninth century onward.

**orbis:** A ring-shaped tactical formation used by Roman troops, especially during an emergency, such as surprise attack by a numerically superior foe.

**peltast:** In ancient Greece, a light infantryman, named for his lightweight shield, or pelte, and armed with javelins.

**petardier:** A soldier who hurled pots of pitch or other combustibles onto the enemy from the walls of a castle. During the English Civil War, such troops were referred to as **grenadiers**. Eventually, this latter term took on a different meaning for an elite sort of soldier.

**phalanx:** Classic ancient Greek and Macedonian formation in which highly trained heavy pikemen, formed in blocks of eight- to sixteen-men deep, locked their shields into a wall and pointed their pikes straight forward. The first four or five pikes extended beyond the front of the formation, presenting a steel hedgehog to an enemy. When phalangists charged, the phalanx hit an enemy formation like a freight train.

The phalanx could be deployed in a variety of shapes, including a straight line, diagonal line, square, crescent, or wedge. Disadvantages were that it could only move in a forward direction, could not be used on the same breadth of rough terrain as other infantry formations, and was especially vulnerable on its flanks and rear. More fluid Roman formations were used to overcome and defeat the formidable phalanx.

**priest:** Holy men have fought alongside their flocks throughout the world. Mesoamerican priests served as elite troops or commanders; Hindu **brahmins** who were unable to find posts as priests took up arms as mercenary soldiers; and Buddhist **warrior monks** fought alongside the samurai of Japan.

Priests also fought with other soldiers during the Middle Ages. For example, during the A.D. 1066 Norman conquest of England, a **warrior bishop** accompanied the invasion force, wearing a chain mail hauberk and armed with a heavy spiked club. Christian holy men were forbidden by their religion to shed blood, so the club and mace were popular weapons with them.

**principe:** The soldiers in the middle rank of a Roman three-line military formation.

**rank and file:** Companies of soldiers parade, or maneuver, in ranks and files. Ranks go from left to right, and files go from front to rear. In European armies, junior soldiers were called **rankers** as opposed to their officers, who took up their posts outside of the mass of soldiers lined up in ranks and files.

**razor women:** An elite force of female soldiers employed by the king of Dahomey, Africa, most notably in the nineteenth century. At times, this force may have been utilized as a special bodyguard, but at one point it was 2,400 strong and apparently battle-ready. Their main weapons were long, two-handed razors, called **nyek-ple-nen-toh**, which could fold into their hafts like giant straight razors. *See* blunderbuss woman.

**regiment:** A grouping of several companies under a staff of additional officers (typically a major, lieutenant colonel, and colonel). In the sixteenth century when companies or bands of soldiers were so grouped and placed under a staff, they were said to be regimented.

**scout:** Soldiers deployed ahead of or to the sides of any army to detect the presence of the enemy. Examples include the Greek **prodromoi** and the Roman **exploratores**.

**sergeant:** An enlisted soldier who has achieved leadership through experience and time in service, rather than holding rank by virtue of a commission from the government. Often called noncommissioned officers (NCOs). In the Middle Ages, sergeant was the term given to the leaders of bodies of men-at-arms. (Roman **optio**, assistant to a centurion, and **centurion**, a company sergeant; Indian **nayak**, a corporal, and **subadar** and **havildar**, grades of sergeant.)

**shield wall:** A tactic in which combatants armed with large shields stood side to side, creating an unbroken defensive wall. The Vikings were famous for this maneuver, and are even said to have charged, swords pointed straight forward, while employing it.

**shock troops:** Soldiers used to force a breach in an enemy line by means of rapid, concentrated assault. Such troops usually had at least veteran status, and were as well or better armed and equipped than regular soldiers. Examples include the **cuahchics** of the Aztecs and the **janissaries** of the Ottoman Empire of Turkey.

**slinger:** A soldier armed with a sling. Men used these most primitive of missile weapons en masse through the thirteenth century. A trained slinger could accurately fire a projectile more than 225 yards.

**squad:** A small unit, usually the smallest battlefield division, comprised of around ten men. Examples include the Roman **contubernium** of eight infantrymen and **decuria** of ten cavalrymen, and the Macedonian **lochoi**, a file of sixteen men.

**syntagma:** A 256-man square of sixteen men in sixteen files, or lochoi, constituting the basic unit of the Macedonian phalanx.

**testudo:** A formation used in the Roman army in which shields guarded each side of a unit, including the top. Such a "tortoise" formation was used, among other things, to withstand massed sling or arrow fire.

**Trabanter Guard:** A ceremonial guard of troops composed of the henchmen and lackeys that surrounded a great man. A member of such a guard was called a trabant. From the German for "satellite."

**triarii:** Roman soldiers used as the final rank in the legion's three-line battle formation. By the time of the battle of Cannae in 216 B.C., the triarii were so rarely used in battle that it was customary to detail them to guard the Roman camp or to fall upon the enemy camp.

**turmae:** A unit of sixty-four Roman cavalrymen. During the second century, four turmae were attached to each legion of Roman soldiers, for a total of 128 troopers. In the third century, however, increased cavalry needs led to an increase to twenty turmae per legion, for a total of 640 troopers, or five times as many.

**Vandal:** One of a tribe of Germanic peoples probably originating in Denmark who conquered Roman-held Spain and North Africa in the fifth century A.D.

**velites:** Lightly armed Roman legionaries deployed at the front of a battle formation to skirmish with the enemy. When the enemy came within closing range of the velites, they retreated through gaps in the hastate, the next troops in the Roman line.

**Viking:** Viking warriors were among the most feared people of the Dark Ages, raiding coasts from Ireland to North Africa mainly in the ninth to eleventh centuries. Known for their skill and fierceness, Viking warriors went into battle wielding swords, battle axes, and spears. (They also used bows, but these were held in the lowest regard.) Common warriors wore little or no armor, while leaders often wore chain mail, sometimes reinforced with additional pieces of metal. Round shields and conical helmets were also commonly used.

## BEASTS OF WAR

From the earliest times, people have fought against animals, first as both hunted and hunter, and later upon the field of battle. Horses usually come to mind when people think of animals on the battlefield, but many other sorts of animals have fought alongside men as well. This variety in the real world hints at the possibilities for a fantasy world, where war beasts might be magically controlled or augmented, possess supernatural qualities, or be of a mythological nature.

**HORSES** allow for speed and mobility in battle unparalleled by foot soldiers. Nonetheless, they have their limitations and require proper care and lots of water and grain. Grass is not sufficient for horses expected to cover great distances, carry heavy burdens, and fight. Horses also cannot operate on the same breadth of terrain as infantry, and fare badly in rough terrain, marshlands, and mountains.

Before about 500 B.C., horses did not have the strength to support the weight of an armored man and were thus yoked to chariots. Chariot-mounted forces represented a revolution in warfare and swept over less well-equipped forces, reshaping the political face of the ancient world. The Aryan hordes that swept into India in the sixteenth century B.C. and crushed the Harrappan culture were charioteers, as were the Hyksos armies that overran and dominated Egypt for one hundred years.

Eventually, horses were bred to the point where they could support the weight of a combatant. Nonetheless, for many centuries, the value of cavalry was limited and could not stand up to heavy infantry. The invention of stirrups allowed cavalry to truly come into its own, as they allowed warriors to use couched lances and effectively fire weapons from the saddle.

Stirrups came into wide usage in Europe around 500 A.D., and issued in an age of equestrian dominance that lasted for one thousand years.

**DOGS**, man's oldest friend, were used in combat from the earliest times, guarding the hearths of primitive men and accompanying them on the hunt. As armies developed throughout the ages, dogs were a part of them, from the first-known usage of large mastiffs in combat in Tibet during the Stone Age.

Assyrians, Babylonians, Greeks, and Persians all subsequently used war dogs in great numbers, typically as sentries or as forward elements on the battlefield, where they could harry enemy scouts and help alert an army to the presence of the enemy. The Corinthians even treated war dogs as heroes and honored them with monuments. The classical historians Pliny the Elder and Plutarch discussed the role of dogs in warfare several times and described how they were equipped with armor and spiked collars, and used as shock troops to break up formations of enemy soldiers. The Huns, too, employed war dogs; mounted warriors carried their dogs perched on their saddles until they were sent into the fray. North American Indians also used dogs, both as sentries and in combat.

**ELEPHANTS** are the biggest and most intrinsically deadly of all creatures marched onto the battlefield. Alexander the Great witnessed such creatures in battle while campaigning in India and was so impressed with them that he added them to his own armies around 325 B.C.

Elephants were an important component of ancient armies for many centuries and were so widely used that one species, the African Forest elephant, became completely extinct. Such elephants were smaller than their Asian and African cousins, measuring less than eight feet at the shoulder. (The Asian elephant is about ten feet at the shoulder and the African elephant is some eleven to twelve feet at the shoulder.)

Elephants were used in much the same way that armored vehicles are used today. Elephants could be equipped with **HOWDAHS** to transport infantry or used as mobile firing platforms for archers or javelin men; they could have catapults or other weapons mounted on them (such as rockets in India) and be used to mount assaults on enemy positions; and they could be armed with iron headplates and used to batter down fortified gates or sections of wall. Elephants were particularly effective against cavalry, causing horses to panic. Some elephants are even purported to have been trained to wield huge swords with their trunks.

Other sorts of animals were also used for every sort of purpose. **BIRDS** carried messages from one part of an army to another, or from the defenders of besieged castles. **MONITOR LIZARDS** were used in ancient and medieval India to carry scaling ropes into besieged places. And **LIONS** and other great cats were used by Egyptians as combatants on the battlefield.

A clever fantasy writer could incorporate many such beasts into his stories. Possibilities include, but are obviously not limited to, fierce predators like wolves, tigers, or bears cut from their leads to tear into the fray; huge creatures like elephants or dinosaurs equipped with fighting platforms for whole crews of soldiers; or squadrons of warriors mounted on winged horses, giant bats, or huge pterodactyls.

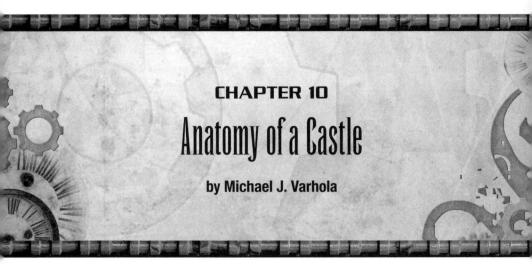

# CHAPTER 10
# Anatomy of a Castle
## by Michael J. Varhola

Castle is a word that brings to mind images of stout battlements, drawbridges over slime-filled moats, and dank dungeons. But for one thousand years of European history, castles were more than a source of colorful imagery; they were a critical bastion of security for the inhabitants of a chaotic, dangerous world.

Castles are some of the most interesting, evocative settings for fantasy stories and can be used in innumerable ways. Indeed, unique, well-described castles are virtually characters themselves. Thus, it is important for fantasy writers to understand what constitutes a castle, why castles have the parts they do, and how these elements function as part of the whole. In short, to write about such structures intelligently, writers need to have a working knowledge of the anatomy of a castle. Writers should also understand the differences between castles and other sorts of defense works, such as fortresses or walled cities.

Castles will not be part of all fantasy milieux, but some sort of fortifications will be a part of most of them. For example, in an empire with strong borders and safe and secure internal areas, there will be no need for functional castles but there may be border fortifications, possibly including large barracks to house soldiery, watchtowers, or long curtain walls (like **HADRIAN'S WALL** in Scotland or the **GREAT WALL** in China).

Except as noted, the emphasis of the following information is upon the castles of Europe and the Middle East during the period of A.D. 500–1500. However, much of it can be applied to fortifications in general, and notable facts about other sorts of fortifications are also mentioned. Information in this chapter is divided into three sections: the defensive components of a castle, castle life, and sieges. Attached to each section is a detailed listing of important terms, some of which are technical or even a bit esoteric. These glossaries are intended not just to define useful terms, but also to provide writers with terms they can use to convincingly include castles, their inhabitants, and sieges in their stories.

Historical notes appear throughout the sections and may not apply to fantasy writers who are not concerned with the precise time lines along which castles developed. Still, it is important to realize that military architecture evolved over many centuries and represented a long tradition of experience.

## CASTLES AND OTHER FORTIFICATIONS

Castles were fortified dwellings deliberately built for the security of a local lord and his followers in areas subject to little or no central political control. The primary purpose of true castles is defense, and any other uses are incidental or auxiliary.

Symptomatic of anarchic, fragmented societies, castles were not built casually or for their aesthetic value and were rarely constructed inside strong national states. Rather, they were built for protection against raiders, foreign invaders, or aggressive neighbors. From modest fortifications that sheltered a dozen warriors and their dependents, castles evolved through the Middle Ages into complex, durable citadels that housed hundreds. Some of the most well-situated, well-constructed and well-stocked castles never succumbed to their enemies whether by assault or siege.

From at least 2000 B.C., and perhaps much earlier, until the first century A.D., fortified cities were the major sort of defense in use. In the ancient world, city -states like those of Greece and republics like Rome fortified their urban areas, guarding their walls with citizen armies. Such states also built fortresses— fortified military bases—to guard mountain passes, rivers, and other strategic sites, and manned them with professional soldiers, usually far from home. Examples include the **GREAT WALL** of China and the **LIMES** in Germany.

During the Dark Ages and early Middle Ages, urban centers persisted as little more than fortified communities. Such towns, along with fortified dwellings,

---

cannibalized Roman forts, and other structures, were not true castles. Many fortified cities from the Middle Ages exist to this day, and some have even had their defenses reconstructed. These include Nuremburg and Rothenburg in Germany, Avignon and Carcassonne in France, and York in England.

True castles were built in Europe starting in the ninth century. Castle evolution coincided with the rise of feudalism, a hierarchical social system described in chapter one. Castles were usually built or controlled by the ruler of an area and used to defend its frontiers from invasion. Such castles would be given to leaders who had sworn fealty to the noble.

The lord of a castle usually had military control over the area immediately around the castle and maybe within a few hours' travel from it. He lived in the castle with his family, his soldiers and their families, and a variety of craftsmen, servants, and serfs. Frequently, the latter did not actually live in the castle but on its lands and near enough that they could quickly repair it in times of crisis.

Castles were the rocks upon which the tiny states of feudal lords existed, and a suitably built, stocked, and manned castle could allow a lord to wield great power within his realm and possible political importance outside of it. Historically, lords were able to tax people passing through their realms; imprison their enemies or shelter other people's; practice heretical, anachronistic, or illegal religions; and engage in mass murder or torture of undesirable inhabitants (as did Vlad Tepes, the inspiration for Dracula, and a disturbing number of other nobles in the Carpathian Mountains and surrounding region). These activities, whether sanctioned by a greater outside power or not, were possible in large part because of the security afforded by a strong castle.

In their simplest forms, castles were little more than fortified towers, or **KEEPS**. The Norman **MOTTE-AND-BAILEY** castles of the eleventh century, built by the vassals of William the Conquerer in England after he defeated the Saxons at Hastings in 1066, are among the simplest of all and constructed of an earthen hillock (motte) surmounted by a stone or wooden tower at one end of a palisaded yard (bailey). The knight commanding the castle lived in the tower and his household and serfs dwelt in buildings in the bailey.

Some of the largest and most complex castles have at their heart massive keeps, often centuries older than the rest of the castle. Such a keep might have originally been the entire fortification, and then been augmented throughout the ages as conditions required and resources allowed. One or several concentric curtain walls might surround the keep, surmounted by **BATTLEMENTS** and reinforced with large towers at their corners and smaller ones in between.

Effective castles made the most of local geography, such as rivers, coasts and heights, using man-made defenses to augment natural barriers. Indeed, building upon high ground is one of the most fundamental canons of castle architecture, making a staunch ally of gravity. Being situated upon a hill allowed a castle's approaches to be protected by several or even a dozen successive gates, or interlocked smaller forts, called **WARDS**. Defenses on heights also forced enemy soldiers to charge uphill laden with weapons and armor, to fire their missile weapons further upward, and to have critical walls and structures situated out of reach of their siege engines. Likewise, high above their opponents, defenders could see attackers from afar and dump rocks, hot oil and other weapons onto their assailants. Good castles also needed a reliable source of potable water, as thirsty defenders could quickly be brought to heel. Thus, the presence of deep wells or unhampered access to rivers or, in their absence, constructions like cisterns were common.

Castles were often built by invaders to dominate and control conquered country. (Niccolo Machiavelli discusses these uses of castles in *Art of War* and *The Prince*. Both of these books are must-reads for anyone interested in warfare and politics during the Renaissance.) For example, take a moment to consider the hundreds of castles built by William the Conqueror to control England after his victory at Hastings. Most of these were hastily built, economical motte-and-bailey castles, but they also built huge, square-towered affairs that came to represent a school of castle architecture. Indeed, the lack of Saxon defensive castles is one of the reasons William so quickly conquered England. It is completely inaccurate in *Robin Hood* and similar movies when the Saxons gaze upon Norman castles and claim that these massive stone structures were seized from their grandfathers. Most of their grandfathers would have actually lived in wattle-and-daub lodges.

Castles could not be safely ignored by an invading army. If ignored and left in the rear of even a strong army, mounted raiding parties could harass the invading force, cutting its supply lines or burning its camps. If the castles were attacked, months might be lost trying to take them, adding time and expense to a campaign and even stalling it altogether. And if an army was not strong enough, it might not even have been able to successfully capture or besiege a castle, especially if a relief force arrived from an allied castle. Thus, castles had both deterrent and defensive functions.

Fortification construction was a critical art and science, and often represented a major portion of a state's budget. Construction of simple fortifications, like motte-and-bailey castles, could be accomplished in a matter of weeks. More complex structures, like the walls of towns and cities, took years or even decades to complete, and might be refined and improved upon over the centuries. Ken Follett's *Pillars of the Earth* is a historical novel that traces the building of a medieval English cathedral over a period of decades, a story concept that could readily be applied to the construction of a major castle.

In fact, many castles evolved over a period of centuries. A good example of this is one of the most impressive castles ever built, the **KRAK DES CHEVALIERS** in Syria, which began in the eleventh century as a small Arab fortress. Acquired by the Crusader knights of St. John in 1142, it was enlarged into a rectangular castle. In the thirteenth century, a curtain wall was added, turning it into the massive concentric fortress that remains today.

Castle architecture evolved over the centuries, and the needs of the various ages can often be seen today in castles that were built over hundreds of years. For every sort of defensive construction, some siege weapon or technique was devised to overcome it. And for every siege technique, some countermeasure was developed to neutralize or lessen its effect. For example, some castles built in the twelfth and later centuries made use of shorter, thicker walls, sometimes reinforced with stone plinths at the bases of their towers, in order to better resist the latest form of siege weapon, the **TREBUCHET**.

The thirteenth century—a period of warfare, especially in the Middle East and southern and eastern Europe—represented a period of advancement in castle architecture. Developments included cross-shaped arrow slits; wooden shutters to provide greater protection for soldiers standing between merlons; and increased construction of round, rather than square, towers. On the other hand, while castle architecture did not develop much militarily in the fourteenth century, effort was put into making living areas more comfortable for the nobility. During this period, the nobility often lived in manors or buildings that looked like castles but were not militarily functional.

In areas where stability increased and national boundaries began to develop, castles became less important. In less secure areas, however, especially border regions, castles remained crucial. In Scotland, for example, where highland brigands posed a threat, fortified tower houses, with their characteristic L- or Z-shaped floor plans, were typical of the sixteenth century.

## Castle Construction

While most surviving castles are of stone, castles were, however, built with whatever was expedient. Some materials do not lend themselves to lasting hundreds of years, which is why castles made from them no longer exist. Examples of these range from simple motte-and-bailey castles to massive, complex timber fortresses built by the Russians and Vikings. In the former case, however, earthworks still exist and can be explored. This is also the case with the much earlier Bronze and Iron Age earthworks.

Castles might have been made of timber where no other materials were available in sufficient quantity. Timber was also cheaper and easier to work with, allowing for much quicker construction (perhaps half as long, all other factors being the same). The main disadvantages, however, included wood's vulnerability to fire and the fact that it would eventually rot. In other areas, stone was simply not available and other materials had to be used. For example, in the Low Countries (Belgium, Holland, and Luxembourg), brick was often used as a medium of construction.

Similarly, high ground was not always available and other measures had to be resorted to. When it was not possible to build on hills and ridges, other sorts of terrain could be exploited. In the Low Countries, castles often had large, wet moats, or were built in the midst of coastal marshes, their brick foundations rising directly from the muddy waters. Such fortifications were called **WASSERBURGS**.

Windows were never built at ground level, as this would have provided vulnerable entry points. Windows above ground level were often barred or shuttered, and shutters were sometimes provided with arrow slits or loopholes.

Square towers were the easiest to build and, with many notable exceptions, predominated until about the fourteenth century. However, the introduction of gunpowder artillery had the most profound effect on the development of fortifications, and quickly rendered useless many that had been powerful redoubts for centuries. Round towers, as a function of their shape, were able to absorb more damage from artillery fire, and also deflected projectiles more effectively than a flat surface. As gunpowder artillery came into use and spread (from their first likely use in Europe in 1326), so did the need for thicker, stronger, and more curved defenses. Eventually, gunpowder siege weapons became too powerful for traditional defenses to withstand, and castle architecture became decorative rather than functional. After this, defenses were designed to absorb damage rather than deflect it, with a return to earthworks (or walls with an earthen core sheathed in stone) and walls that became lower and thicker. This sort of architecture was exemplified by the work of the seventeenth-century French military architect Marquis de Vauban, whose legacy can be seen in polygonal, star-shaped forts built through the nineteenth century.

Castle architecture evolved throughout the world in response to the changing modes of warfare. Europe is by no means the only home to great castles; it is just one of the most familiar to us. In India, military engineers built castles that used a system of concentric walls with the outermost wall the lowest and each successive inner one taller—exactly the opposite of the trend of European fortifications.

Japanese castle architecture is noteworthy and interesting, and was the product of a science all its own. The most incredible example represents the synthesis of artistic sensibility and functionalism that is not seen anywhere else in the world; castles are usually utilitarian or beautiful, but those of Japan tend to be both, making use of complex systems of curtain walls and moats. A good example is the **HIMEJI CASTLE** near Kobe. Because effective gunpowder weapons were introduced earlier in Japan than in Europe, castles were effective well into the seventeenth century.

In a fantasy milieu like that of medieval Europe, most castles will be of small or medium size and controlled by minor nobility, like barons. However, in this setting, and certainly in a less traditional fantasy setting, castles might be the strongholds of many other sorts of inhabitants. These could include martial orders of priests in a fortified temple; a company of skeletal mercenaries led by an undead lord in a ruinous castle deep in a tangled wood; or a castle guarding a trading center that is maintained and manned at the expense of a major mercantile guild. Each castle that a writer describes or his characters visit can be made into a unique, memorable, significant subject.

Writers should consider factors like technology or magic when determining the properties of castles and other fortifications in their worlds. If cannons or other very powerful weapons are available, then high, square-towered castles will be an anachronism, and lower, earthen fortifications may be the norm. Similarly, if wizards or other spell-casters who can easily reduce or bypass the sturdiest walls are common, then traditional castles will be rather moot. There is no sense spending time and resources to build something that is really of no use. Other aspects of castle architecture might be affected by the presence of magic, even subtly. For example, illusory magics might be used to cloak the presence of sally ports, or elemental magics might be used to call up rainstorms, to provide water for the besieged, and mudslides for attackers camped in areas denuded of trees used for building siege engines.

Well-conceived, strategically placed castles can serve as ideal centers of action in a great many fantasy stories, and can be used to say much about those who dwell in them. Writers can include frontier forts of wooden towers and timber palisades manned by fur-clad hillmen; massive curtain walls of cut-and-fitted stone surrounding mercantile cities, their walls lined with the volunteer men and women of a republic state; or ancient citadels perched on mountainous peaks, the redoubts of xenophobic warlords and their minions.

To the peoples of medieval Europe, castles were homes, fortifications, and bastions of security in a chaotic world. They remained so for a full millennium until, beginning around the fifteenth century, gunpowder artillery made castles inviable and the rise of national states and their armies made castles unnecessary.

## Castle Terms

Where multiple terms exist for a given structure, the term closest to English is given with other terms provided parenthetically.

arrow slit: A narrow opening in a wall or **merlon** through which bows or crossbows could be fired. The inside surfaces were often angled, both to reduce the size of the hole from the point of view of an attacker and to allow a defending soldier to direct his fire in an arc (of up to about 60 degrees). Arrow slits were often crossletted (in the form of a cross) to more easily accommodate crossbows.

**barbican:** A stone building buttressed with towers almost always used as a gatehouse but sometimes as simply an **outwork**, and equipped with a drawbridge if situated on a moat.

**bartizan:** A small, round tower mounted on a wall or larger tower, and typically pierced with arrow slits or murder holes, or could even be a garderobe (latrine).

**bastion:** A structure bulging out from a curtain wall, looking a bit like a tower the same height as the rest of the wall. Its primary function was to allow flanking fire along the face of a wall.

**battlement:** The fighting area at the top of a wall, generally consisting of an area for soldiers to stand (either upon the top of a thick wall or on a catwalk), a parapet to protect soldiers up to torso level, and alternating embrasures and merlons.

**buttress:** A pillar of stone mounted against a wall or tower to reinforce it. Flying buttresses, characteristic of cathedral architecture, are attached to the building with a stone bridge rather than being up against it.

**catwalk:** A wooden platform that was mounted on a walk otherwise too narrow to fight upon, and used as a fighting surface, often in conjunction with permanent stone battlements, or as part of hoardings.

**crenellations:** Rows of alternating merlons and embrasures upon a battlement.

**curtain wall:** A straight section of defensive wall, generally at least twenty feet tall and five feet thick. Walls were usually somewhat thicker at their bases than their tops. For simplicity, writers can assume that a wall's base will be about 10 percent thicker than its top for every ten feet of height. Thus, a wall thirty feet tall and ten feet thick near the top will be 30 percent thicker, or thirteen feet wide, at its base. Tall walls were also reinforced with plinths and buttresses.

**drawbridge:** A gate that could be lowered or raised (rather than opened or closed like a door) using chains in conjunction with winches and counterweights. Contrary to popular conceptions about castles, only those with moats were likely to be equipped with a drawbridge. Timber planks at least a half-foot thick were needed for a drawbridge, which must be strong enough to support armored horsemen.

**earthworks:** A basic form of fortification, consisting of a ditch with compacted sides surmounted on one side by a rampart, built from the excavated earth. If means allowed, the ramparts were often equipped with a timber palisade. Simple castles might consist of nothing more than earthworks (e.g., a motte-and-bailey castle was made up of earthworks, augmented by a hillock and wooden or stone tower); during the Dark Ages, most fortifications would have been of this sort.

**embrasure:** The open space in a battlement between a pair of merlons. From about the thirteenth century, these were often reinforced with a set of shutters, often a single piece that could be angled to protect a man from frontal attack but allow him to fire downward.

**gatehouse:** The gate is perhaps the most vulnerable spot on a castle, and a strong structure was needed to keep it from becoming an Achilles' heel. A typical gatehouse consisted of a large square tower some two or three levels tall, often flanked with a pair of taller towers. Anyone entering the castle this way had to enter the gatehouse via the outer gate, pass through it, and then enter the castle through an inner gate. During an attack, anyone within the gate would likely have been subject to attack through murder holes in the ceiling.

Gatehouse roofs could be equipped with battlements and armed with catapults, ballistae, cauldrons, and braziers, or they could be manned by archers or arbalestiers. Typically, the outer gateway would be set with an iron-reinforced single or double door and/or drawbridge, the inner gate with a reinforced door, and either with a portcullis.

**hoardings:** A superstructure mounted on and projecting in front of a curtain wall, consisting of a sturdy wooden catwalk, a wooden wall set with embrasures or arrow slits, a peaked roof connected to the battlements, and murder holes in the floor to allow attacks against opponents at the base of the wall.

**keep:** A tall, heavily fortified structure that is the defensive heart of a castle. The keep typically served as the residence of the castle's lord, and the site of an assaulted castle's final defense. Early castles might have consisted entirely of a keep. Many of those of the late Middle Ages did away with the keep altogether, and concentrated on the strength of other defensive structures, such as curtain walls, towers, and gatehouses. (French *donjon*; German *bergfried*)

**loophole:** A hole in a wall designed for shooting a firearm through.

**machiolations:** A construction that projected the floor of the battlements over the front of a wall, and was often set with murder holes to allow attacks against enemies against the wall below; essentially like permanent stone hoardings.

**merlon:** The raised section of a battlement, set on a parapet and flanking embrasures, usually three or four feet wide and four feet tall; thus a four-foot-tall merlon set upon a three-foot-high parapet would create a seven-foot-high obstacle upon the rampart. Merlons may have arrow slits.

**moat:** A ditch surrounding a fortified area, which could have been either dry or wet (full of water). Wet moats could have been stone-lined channels full of rainwater, or connected with a stream or river; indeed, such a body of water could even border one or more sides of a castle.

**motte-and-bailey:** A style of castle typical of eleventh-century Europe. Most of these were simple fortifications consisting of a tower built on top of a motte (hillock), which dominated a palisaded bailey (yard) containing the domestic buildings of the lord's household. Such castles were typically built entirely on earth and timber.

**murder hole:** A hole, trapdoor, or slit in a floor that allowed attacks against a passageway or area below, often located in the gatehouse of a castle. (French *meurtrieres*)

**outwork:** A fortified structure that projected from or was completely outside of the walls of a castle, for example, a gatehouse on the far side of a moat that served as a first line of defense.

**palisade:** A wall made of wooden stakes or timber beams, and often used in conjunction with some other sort of defense, such as earthworks. Palisades could comprise the primary curtain walls of simple castles, be used for temporary field fortifications, or be raised to block breaches in stone walls.

**parapet:** A low wall, usually about three feet tall, built upon a rampart to provide cover for soldiers. Cover provided by parapets was augmented by merlons.

**pilaster:** A pillarlike construction used to reinforce walls.

**plinth:** Also called **batters** or **splays**, these were sloping supports that strengthened the bases of walls or towers and hindered attacks against them.

**portcullis:** A grill of metal or reinforced timber that could be lowered into a gateway and lifted by means of a winch and counterweights.

**sally port:** A small, heavily defended gate that could be used to launch surprise attacks against a besieging army. Such gates could also be used, if necessary or possible, as routes of escape or passages for secret messengers or emissaries.

## CASTLE LIFE

Even as the physical parts of a castle had certain characteristics, so did the homes and work areas of the people who lived within it and in its environs. The common people—peasants—lived predominantly in agricultural villages. Most of the peasants were serfs, the lowest level in the feudal system. They were tied to the land where they were born and which they worked, their rights and responsibilities determined by custom and the lord of the region. Most peasants lived in modest dwellings: wood-framed, thatch-roofed, and walled with wattle and daub (lattice walls covered with a muddy mortar) with one or two common rooms, which were also shared with livestock. For security reasons, their hamlets were almost always within a short distance of the castle or fortified town, so that they would have a place to take refuge in time of danger.

The lord of the castle had broad powers over the area he controlled. These included taxing the local populace a portion of the food they produced; calling upon them to provide labor or other services; rights to all wood and timber on the surrounding lands; and hunting rights to all game. (Robin Hood is traditionally considered to have been outlawed because he poached a local lord's deer.)

Lords did not always treat their serfs well, but they needed them since they were the economic base upon which the castle existed. Thus, the lord offered them protection and allocated various resources to them such as wood for construction and fuel. Hunting, on the other hand, was a jealously guarded privilege that was rarely relinquished by the nobility.

Within the castle, space tended to be limited and was utilized to its fullest extent, integrating defense and daily life. Attics of towers were used as rookeries for pigeons, which were raised for food. The lower levels of towers, when they were not solid bulwarks of stone, were used for storage areas, wellhouses, and dungeons. Small courtyards were used for herb and vegetable gardens, while larger courtyards were used for stables, the huts of castle staff, and workshops of craftsmen like blacksmiths.

In small, early castles, the great hall was used not just for communal meals, but as a common area where most of the inhabitants of the castle slept at night and where much of the work and social activity took place during the day. (This descends from the Germanic/Viking tradition of using great timber lodges in the same way.) In larger castles, living and work areas became as specialized as space allowed and the needs of the inhabitants required. The lord and his family had their own apartments. Soldiery were housed either in barracks or in small groups within furnished tower rooms. Servitors like cooks, gardeners, and craftsmen lived in huts along the inside walls of the castle.

Often, men and women were virtually segregated from each other, with each sex having their own activities and responsibilities. Commoners pursued their assigned tasks; knights, men-at-arms, and the lord and his sons trained for warfare or performed daily administrative duties; and women performed various vital crafts, such as tapestry weaving, and answered to the lady of the castle, who often oversaw the day-to-day functions of the castle.

The role of women in the life of a castle should not be dismissed. Historically, when a lord and his men were away at war or on hunting expeditions, or if they were killed, a lady was often responsible for ensuring that business continued as usual. Many ladies were necessarily excellent administrators and could run a castle as well as their husbands could, even to the extent of defending it in time of siege. And sometimes, when the regional social order allowed it or was not strong enough to oppose it, women might rule in their own right following the death of a husband or father (and in fantasy milieux, of course, this can become even more likely).

Castle walls were thick but, being built for defense rather than comfort, they were of uninsulated stone. Thus, castles tended to be chilly, damp, drafty, and musty. Their subterranean areas would be even danker, the walls encrusted with feather white niter. Because of these conditions, tapestries were hung on walls, cutting down on drafts and providing a form of insulation.

Furniture tended to be sturdy and made of wood. Benches were used at all levels of society throughout the Middle Ages, as were stools. Actual chairs were much less common and were used by lords, judges, or merchants, but not necessarily by anyone else around them. Castles did not have closets, so various sorts of chests and wardrobes were used to store clothing and other possessions. Beds tended to be short, not because people were that much smaller, but because many well-born people slept sitting upright. This was a result of a diet consisting almost exclusively of meat, which led to all sorts of digestive problems that caused less discomfort when sitting up than when lying prone.

Castles built in settings unlike the European Middle Ages may have characteristics different than those described above, and when writers are designing and describing their castles, they must take into consideration the individual cultures of the inhabitants of each castle. In a fantasy world, such considerations might extend to other races or species as well. For example, Muslim emirs would have areas dedicated to their **seraglio**, or harem; most medieval Indian rajas would have some sort of torture chamber; Christian lords would certainly have a chapel or maybe even a cloister for monks (indeed, a templar castle is essentially a combination cloister/barracks for religious soldiers); and stables would be of great importance in many traditions, for the horses of mounted European warriors or the elephants of Indian ones. The needs of nonhuman peoples might be even more specialized or elaborate.

## Castle Life Terms

The following list describes some of the people that lived in the castles and the various rooms, sections, or areas within a castle that might be relevant to a story. Writers should be able to envision how such areas might be modified for use in a fantasy environment. For example, in some worlds, an aviary might take up all of the largest tower in a castle and be home to the giant raptors ridden by the castles' knights.

**armory:** A room where arms and armor were stored, usually guarded by a stout, iron-bound door to which the castellan and perhaps one or two other people would have access.

**aviary:** A chamber, often in a tower, where the birds of prey used for hunting were kept, usually under the supervision of a falconer, a commoner trained in handling such creatures.

**barracks:** Areas full of bunks or pallets that served as living quarters for the men-at-arms dwelling there. Higher-ranking soldiers like sergeants might have shared a tower room together, and single knights might have had their own rooms.

**castellan:** An officer in charge of all the affairs of a castle who answered directly to the lord. Duties of castellan included keeping the castle in good repair and ensuring it was well stocked for any eventuality. In some cases, able castellans served as guardians for lords who had been orphaned but had not yet reached their majority. (French *chatellan*)

**chapel:** An area within the castle dedicated to worship. The word "shrine" might more properly apply to the small temples of non-Christian religions.

**cisterns:** Large containers used for holding water, especially in areas where a well could not provide enough water for all the needs of a castle or where a water supply could be denied in time of siege. Such containers could be several stories deep and were typically cut out of solid rock; similarly, small, natural caverns could also form the basis for cisterns. Historically, many besieged areas were able to hold out against attackers because of water stored in this fashion. Likewise, defenders of otherwise virtually impregnable fortifications sometimes had to surrender when overcome by thirst.

**crypt:** A room that was often built beneath the chapel, the crypt could contain the remains of the former lords of the castle and their families. An excellent place for morbid trysts, secret meetings, or forbidden rituals.

**dungeon:** An area used for imprisonment and torture. Such areas were common in the castles of most cultures. (French *oubliette*)

**garderobe:** Situated on an outside wall or in a small overhang tower, this area was a latrine with a hole that overlooked an area outside the castle onto which defecation could drop.

**great hall:** The central social area of a castle, a great hall usually had one or more long banquet tables, and walls lined with weapons, banners and other trophies won in tournaments and battles. It was in this area that communal meals were eaten, guests entertained, and strategy discussed with a lord's vassals. The great hall would have been the central area of the keep, or a less military building in the main courtyard of the castle. It was frequently the sleeping area for many of the castle's inhabitants.

**harem:** An area set aside by non-Christian, particularly Muslim lords, to house their wives or concubines. Such areas were often guarded by eunuchs (castrated men) or female warriors.

**kennel:** An area used for housing the dogs of a castle. In some castles, dogs were simply allowed to roam freely and allowed to feed on the refuse in eating areas. Dogs often had important roles in castles, with hounds being used in hunting and mastiffs used as guards or in war.

**kitchen:** In small or simple castles, food for the lord and his retainers could be cooked in the hearth of the great hall itself. Larger castles, particularly those set up to cater to nobility, would have separate, more elaborate areas.

**library:** In regions where literacy was not the norm, castle libraries were not common or extensive, or could have represented the legacy of former inhabitants. In the castle of a cultured lord or an order of monks, however, not to mention a wizard, sage, or alchemist in a fantasy milieu, a library would be of prime importance.

**smithy:** Blacksmiths, or farriers, worked iron into implements like horseshoes, nails, and tools, but did not fashion weapons or armor. A smithy would likely face onto the courtyard of a castle.

**stable:** An area for housing horses and storing the equipment used with them. The stables of large castles in cultures where horses or other mounts were important often had special officers in charge of them. Ideally, stables were not underneath or too near to living areas.

**storage:** Cool, dry areas were needed to store all the supplies necessary for running a castle and sustaining it through long winters and sieges. Basements beneath the keep and the lower level of towers were the primary storage areas.

**well:** Wells were often dug deep into the basement of a castle's keep or within another large tower.

**workshops:** Areas used to produce goods necessary for a castle that might not otherwise be available. Castles and their attached villages were often isolated from other communities and had to be self-sufficient. Thus, coarse cloth, furniture, barrels, and other goods would be manufactured in the castle or adjacent village, often in the homes of skilled peasants.

## SIEGE

Sieges can make for exciting reading, even though historically they tended to be dreary, protracted affairs, punctuated by episodes of violence and culminating in either withdrawal or a bloody assault.

Literally, the word "siege" comes from French and means "to wait," and most sieges were lengthy, tedious battles of attrition, often as ruinous to the besiegers as to the besieged. This section describes both the process of siege and other methods used to capture castles and fortified areas.

Castles were generally taken either by assault or by siege. A quick assault and overrun of a castle was most desirable, especially if this could be achieved by surprise. A successful siege, on the other hand, could take weeks, months, even years, and stood to decimate even the besiegers through disease, attrition, attack from relieving forces, or surprise attacks from the castle called **SALLIES**, which were made through small gates called sally ports.

The actual means of capturing fortified positions changed little from the earliest sieges right up through the fifteenth century, with the exception that siege weapons gradually became more powerful and destructive. This power culminated in the development of gunpowder weapons, which led to the decline of traditional fortifications.

Sieges were actually conducted very early in human history. Jericho, founded some eight thousand years ago and perhaps the oldest city in the world, fell to siege many times in its history, several times even before Joshua marched around its walls and brought them crashing down. The first protracted, complex sieges date from at least 1500 B.C., when the Assyrians were attacking neighboring Mesopotamian city-states, and when Aryan steppe dwellers were sweeping into northern India and overrunning the mud-brick citadels of the Harrappans.

Some peoples had a knack for **POLIORCETICS**, as the science of siege was known, and others did not. For example, the Romans excelled at siege and were able to take positions considered impregnable, like Herod's palace-fortress at Masada in what is now Israel, overlooking the Dead Sea (at considerable cost and time, nonetheless). Even peoples who were proficient at siege often had to pay a heavy price for their success.

Traditionally, defenders of a besieged castle were allowed to surrender unconditionally. If they did not surrender and their stronghold was subsequently taken, they were usually subjected unhesitatingly to slaughter, rape, and enslavement.

The familiar assault upon the walls resulting in the taking of the castle was usually the culmination of months or even years of preparation and activity. Such assaults were costly in terms of men and equipment, and less glamorous but more effective techniques were tried first.

The first step in a siege was to surround and completely cut off the castle, preventing the besieged from escaping or from being relieved by outside forces. Thus, the besiegers themselves were often in a precarious position with opponents to their fronts and backs. There is no more famous example of this phenomenon than Julius Caesar's first century B.C. siege of the Gallic fortified town of Alesia in France. Just as Caesar was compelled to do, besiegers often built earthworks to protect themselves from missile fire or attacks from the castle or their flanks.

Attackers usually had considerably more men at their disposal than the besieged. Otherwise, the besieged would not likely subject themselves to the perils of being holed up in their strongholds. Writers can assume at least twice as many men in the besieging army outside as there are within the besieged castle.

Wooden fortifications were more vulnerable to attack than stone structures. Fire could be used to burn down the walls, axemen could hack them down, and weapons like catapults and rams were considerably more effective against such structures than against stone. Many other specialized methods were also developed for reducing a castle's defenses. **SAPPING** could be very effectively employed against stone castles. **SAPPERS** would burrow into a wall, supporting the excavated area with timbers. When sufficient material had been removed from the wall or tower, the sappers packed the area with combustibles (from the fifteenth century onward, gunpowder was also used) and set fire to them. When the timbers burned away, the wall section collapsed, leaving a breach that could then be assaulted by troops.

Sappers and axemen were vulnerable to attack from boulders, boiling oil, and missiles dropped on them from above. Therefore, whenever possible, they approached the castle and labored under wheeled galleries, or moved up through covered trenches that were gradually being dug toward the fortification. Troops also worked at the base of a castle with no cover if the means of providing it for them were not available, but horrible casualties often resulted from this.

**HOARDINGS, BASTIONS**, and **MACHIOLATIONS**, defensive structures that projected out over a wall, were developed largely to help defenders prevent mischief by attackers like sappers. Through holes in floors of such projections, defenders could monitor the base of their walls, areas that would otherwise be blind spots to someone positioned on top of a straight wall.

MINING was another way to undermine castle walls. Out of sight of the castle, usually behind MANTLETS or even from within a nearby building, a shaft was dug downward and then gradually up toward the castle walls (shafts were angled in this way to help prevent defenders from flooding them).

Deep or steep-walled moats made close approach to a castle difficult, especially if they were filled with water. Even a dry moat that had to be crossed was an area devoid of cover that could easily become a deadly killing ground for attacking troops. Before troops could assault walls or employ engines like siege towers, rams, or sows, moats had to be negotiated. A common way to make moats passable to engines was to fill them will rocks or bundles of sticks (FASCINES); the filled area would then be covered with planks to ensure smoother crossing for the wheeled engines. Portable boats and pontoon or folding bridges could be deployed to allow passage by troops.

ESCALADE, or attack by use of ladders, was an often final and very hazardous method for capturing a castle. While archers, arbalestiers, and artillery engines attached the defenders manning the walls, foot soldiers ran forward with tall ladders and clambered up toward the battlements, fighting desperately to get on them. Defenders would launch missile fire, drop large rocks, and pour boiling oil or molten lead upon the climbers. They would also use polearms to push away ladders before assaulting soldiers could make it to the top.

SIEGE TOWERS, if available, could also be used to attack battlements. They were maneuvered up to the walls, and upon reaching them, the attackers dropped their attack ramps onto the battlements, allowing troops to pour out onto the defenders.

Most castles were not constantly subjected to attack and gradually fell into disrepair. Wooden structures like hoardings or catwalks rotted away over the years, and often were not maintained until a time of crisis, when they could be replaced relatively quickly. Whereas a large stone castle might take several years to build, the wooden superstructures could be added or replaced in a matter of weeks.

In addition to the replacement of wooden structures, castles often had to be prepared for siege in other ways. These included clearing the moat of debris; diverting a waterway so as to fill it, if appropriate; and repairing any crumbling masonry. Clearing all trees and vegetation within the largest possible radius of the site was also done to deny the enemy cover from missile fire, deny them wood for campfires or field quarters, and to prevent construction of siege engines.

SIEGE ENGINES were large, cumbersome, often expensive pieces of equipment and were rarely transported by an attacking army, especially as it was not always known at what point in a campaign a siege might occur (after all, any given lord might capitulate, become an ally, conclude a treaty, etc.). Rather, the tools and knowledge needed to build siege engines were brought and the weapons were constructed at the site of the siege.

Ironically, many of the biggest, most impressive, and most expensive weapons did not turn out to be the war-winners that they were expected to be, often exhibiting lackluster performance. A good example is the **Helepolis**, the "City-Taker," a siege tower built for the 304 B.C. siege of Rhodes. It was 140 feet tall with a dozen levels for troops and equipment, covered with iron plates, armed with thirty catapults and ballistae of varying sizes, and propelled forward by a crew of two hundred men operating a massive capstan mounted in its lower level. Several hundred more men pushed and pulled the machine as well. Despite its imposing appearance and size, the Rhodians managed to damage the Helepolis and the besiegers withdrew it from the fray, fearing for the fate of the expensive weapon.

Writers should be certain to take the special nature of a magical world into consideration when describing scenes of siege warfare. For example, a priest dedicated to elemental gods might cast his blessings upon a catapult boulder prior to its being fired; people native to subterranean regions might sap or mine more quickly or efficiently than normal humans; and large, winged creatures might be used to transport attackers over walls.

### Siege Terms

Many terms are marked with a (d), indicating an item that was used primarily by the defenders of a fortified area, or an (o), indicating an item used primarily by attackers. This represents the way various devices were typically used, however, and should not act as a restriction upon writers.

ballista: An engine like a large crossbow used to fire heavy javelins, employing twisting skeins of sinew for power. Ballistae were so powerful that a single bolt fired from one could skewer several men and penetrate almost any armor. Such weapons tended to be used as defensive weapons rather than by besiegers because they were not very effective against stone and required less space to operate than catapults. Along with catapults, ballistae were used in virtually every major siege for at least three thousand years. (Greek *oxybeles*; Latin *ballista, scorpio, cheiroballistra*)

**battering ram (o):** A heavy beam used to batter down doors or, more slowly, walls. In its simplest form, it was a big log carried by a dozen soldiers and used to stave in the door of a small castle. In its more complex form, a ram was shod with a wedge-shaped metal head, mounted on a carriage so it could be swung rhythmically, and either protected by a wheeled shed or mounted within a siege tower. Rams are among the oldest, and the most rudimentary, of siege engines. (Latin *testudo*)

**cat:** A wheeled shed used to protect troops while they moved toward a fortified position. Cats were often used to house battering rams or **screws**, and were sometimes attached to the rear of a siege tower, allowing additional troops to follow behind it.

**catapult:** A siege engine using an arm powered by great twisted skeins of cords to hurl rocks. Missiles of this sort had to be fired in great concentration and over a long period of time if they were to break through strong curtain walls or demolish towers, but could more easily clear walls of defenders, damage battlements, or crush wooden structures like hoardings. Like ballistae, catapults were used in almost every siege from around 1500 B.C. until about A.D. 1500. (Greek *lithobolos*; Latin *onager*)

**cauldron (d):** A large, cast-iron pot mounted over a brazier, which was used to boil oil or melt lead that could then be poured over walls or through murder holes onto attackers (causing horrible, lethal wounds against which armor was of little defense).

**crow (d):** A device consisting of a long, counterweighted pole and line that could be lowered over a wall by defenders and used to hook onto a besieging soldier, jerk him off the ground, and swing him into the castle.

**fascines:** Large bundles of sticks (usually five to six feet high and three to four feet across) with a variety of uses including reinforcing field fortifications and filling moats.

**gallery (o):** A covered wooden passageway constructed for the protection of besiegers, often made resistant to fire by being covered with green hides. Galleries were used to allow attackers to approach walls, dig siege ditches, and so on, and were often constructed in stages, gradually getting longer and closer to the castle.

**gastrophetes:** Meaning "belly bow," this was an early form of crossbow developed around 400 B.C. and apparently used as a siege weapon in classical Greece. Also called **Heron's gastraphete.**

**hoist (o):** A heavy frame mounted with a large counterweight and a lever, one end of which was equipped with a basket large enough to hold several attackers who could then be lifted up to the top of a wall.

**ladder, siege (o):** A tall ladder that was flung against the wall of a castle and used to scale it by besiegers. Such ladders frequently consisted of a single long timber set with crosspieces. (Greek *sambuca*; Mughal *narduban, zeenah pae* [a broad ladder])

**mantlet (o):** A large, wooden shield, propped up by supports or on wheels, which was used to shelter at least two besieging troops, typically those needing cover while loading slow weapons like crossbows. Mantlets could gradually be moved forward toward the walls of a castle. (Mughal *turah*)

**petard (o):** A crude explosive device employed by means of a hoist and used to blow breaches in walls.

**ram catcher (d):** A device consisting of a hook or fork on a long beam, which was lowered by defenders to catch a battering ram or screw being used against a wall, and then was rapidly lifted, breaking or dislodging the attacking engine. Grappling hooks on ropes might be used in this same manner.

**redoubt:** A small field fortification, often built on a natural or built-up piece of high ground, and typically consisting of earthworks reinforced with a palisade or fascines. Besiegers often built such structures. (French *bastille*)

**screw (o):** Sometimes called a **pick** or **sow**, this device was placed against a wall and used to bore a hole into it. Attackers using such a device typically needed the protection of a gallery. (Latin *musculus*)

**siege engine:** Any machine specially designed to assist in sieges. Many types exist, but they can be broadly classified into missile weapons and non-missile weapons. Engineers specially skilled in the construction of such weapons were very important members of ancient and medieval armies. On the other hand, the troops that operated such engines were generally the most lowly regarded, and were often considered little better than laborers. Such engines used enormous amounts of timber and were so massive in size and weight that they were usually built on-site (or, less frequently, prefabricated and transported to the site of the siege).

Missile weapons can be divided into four main categories: **ballistae, catapults, springnals,** and **trebuchets** (all discussed separately). A wide variety of terms were used for such weapons throughout the Middle Ages, although these can often be applied to more than one of the four classes of weapons and are not technical nomenclatures. These names can be put to good use by writers, and include **beugle, blida, scorpion, onager, bricole, calabra, fronda, engine, espringale, fundibulu, manganum, martinet, matafunda, mategrifon, petrary, robinet, springald, tormentum,** and **tripantum.**

Proper names were often applied to large or powerful weapons (for example, "Wolf of War," "God's Hammer"), and such names might be emblazoned on the engine itself.

Nonmissile siege engines included **towers, rams, screws,** and **mantlets** (also discussed separately).

**springnal:** A siege engine using the tension of a flexible arm to fire rocks and javelins. The arm would typically be made from laminated layers of planks and bent into firing position with a windlass. Of the four main classes of siege weapons, this springnal is the simplest and quite possibly the oldest. Those designed to fire rocks would have tended to be less powerful than catapults (not to mention trebuchets) and those configured for javelins would have been less accurate than ballistae. Nonetheless, it was doubtless a formidable weapon. Also referred to as a "spring engine."

**tower, siege (o):** Towers had to be taller than the walls they were being used to attack or dominate. Thus, they might be as small as thirty feet tall, but much larger ones are known to have been used. For example, at the siege of Lisbon in 1147, two towers eighty-three and ninety-five feet tall were used.

Because they were used to help clear walls of defenders, towers were sometimes called **bad neighbors**; they were also known as **belfries**.

Ropes and pulleys, powered by teams of oxen, were used to drag towers toward enemy walls. They were set up so that the oxen moved away from the walls, dragging the tower forward via the pulleys mounted in front of the tower. Another slower method was to have men inside the tower ratchet the wheels forward using crowbars. (French *beffroi, malvoisin*; Mughal *seeba*)

trebuchet: A huge, powerful siege engine that used a massive counterweight to hurl large rocks, or even dead cattle and horses; a typical trebuchet could hurl a three-hundred-pound rock about three hundred yards. The trebuchet came into use in the twelfth century and was the only major siege engine of the Middle Ages that did not have its origins in antiquity. Of all non-gunpowder missile engines, these were the biggest, slowest, most destructive, and most expensive. Writers should not underestimate the size of these monsters. They could be well over sixty feet tall, have an arm sixty feet long, be equipped with a counterweight that weighed twenty or even thirty thousand pounds, and required crews of dozens or even hundreds of men.

# Index